Vietnam on Trial

Westmoreland vs. CBS

Vietnam on Trial

Westmoreland vs. CBS

Bob Brewin *and* Sydney Shaw

NEW YORK Atheneum 1987

Library of Congress Cataloging-in-Publication Data

Brewin, Bob.
　　Vietnam on trial.

　　Includes index.
　　1. Westmoreland, William C. (William Childs), 1914–
Trials, litigation, etc.　2. CBS Television Network—
Trials, litigation, etc.　3. Trials (Libel)—New York
(N.Y.)　4. Vietnamese Conflict, 1961–1975—United
States.　I. Shaw, Sydney.　II. Title.
KF228.W42B74　1987　　　345.73'0256　　　85–47595
ISBN 0–689–11610–1　　　347.305256

FOR NORMAN J. SHAW (1922–1985)

AND FOR

2/9/3–3/3/3 UNITED STATES MARINE CORPS

REPUBLIC OF SOUTH VIETNAM

(1965–66)

Introduction

O N the last day of the Westmoreland vs. CBS libel trial, Judge
Pierre N. Leval told the jury, "We have watched the creation
in this courtroom of an extraordinary, unique and rich record for
historians to study. I suggest that the value of this proceeding may
have more to do with the record it has created for history than with
the verdict it could have produced."

This book taps that record in several ways. The 10,000-plus-page
transcript of the trial is a unique record of a uniquely democratic
process: much of the U.S. high command during the Vietnam War
testifying about that war before a jury of twelve ordinary men and
women. The scope of the issue in dispute—whether or not General
William Westmoreland engaged in a "conspiracy" to underestimate
the size of the enemy force he battled in Vietnam—narrowed the
range of the testimony on the war. Nonetheless, the trial showed the
capability of the American legal system to call all citizens, no matter
how elevated their station, to account.

Vietnam-era Secretary of Defense Robert McNamara had to
break his almost twenty-year silence on the war when he took the
witness stand. Even the super-secret National Security Agency put
some of its mysteries on the record.

The trial record also examines the inner workings of the most
powerful non-governmental institution in our society: television news,
particularly CBS News. Like the high command that ran the Vietnam
War, the high command—and the grunts—of CBS News had to answer for their actions.

Finally, the libel suit produced a record that the jury and the
public barely glimpsed. Thanks to the discovery process, attorneys
for both sides in the case had the rare opportunity to plumb the still-
classified secrets of America's most divisive war. This record, a mother

lode of more than a half-million pages of highly classified government documents, is the true legacy of the Westmoreland-CBS case. Because the two teams of lawyers, armed with the Freedom of Information Act, were seeking to determine the "truth" about a certain aspect of the war, the doors on government vaults were forced open.

Notes of Cabinet meetings in the Johnson administration were pried loose from the LBJ Library in Austin, Texas. The State Department gave up all of the weekly cablegrams U.S. Ambassador to Vietnam Ellsworth Bunker sent two Presidents (Johnson and Nixon) from 1966 through 1968. The Department of Defense as well as the Departments of the Army, Navy, and Air Force furnished documents by the boxload. The Central Intelligence Agency relinquished thousands of pages of TOP SECRET material, including two reports prepared for McNamara in 1966 and 1967 that told him the Vietnam War was unwinnable—no matter how great the force of arms the U.S. amassed, no matter how many Americans died.

Both sides in this case gave us carte blanche with these documents. For months before the trial and afterward, we sorted through this treasure trove, seeking as best as we could the material which would offer a new perspective on the Vietnam War. The second section of the book reveals what we discovered.

But the paper doesn't tell the whole story of the Westmoreland-CBS libel suit. The documents, trial transcripts, and depositions lack an essential quality: the personalities involved. Above all, this is a story about people. Although the major characters in this story still disagree with each other about the issues of the case, none would deny that a remarkably interesting group of people was involved.

We decided, for the most part, to let them tell their own stories in their own words. If there is criticism of any character in this story, it is generally from one of the other players. We do not care to sit in judgment, except for making the judgment that the story would be told best by its participants. We did this by covering the trial itself, not just referring to the voluminous paper record of the case. We also interviewed extensively the major characters, including General Westmoreland, CBS producer George Crile, Mike Wallace, Sam Adams, and the two chief attorneys, David Boies of Cravath, Swaine & Moore and Dan Burt of Capital Legal Foundation. We interviewed these people several times, before the trial, during the trial, and afterward.

After completing the manuscript, we decided that we had an obligation to offer these people, who had unstintingly given of their time, a chance to respond. This sense of obligation arose, in part, from our understanding of the mutual intractability that forced CBS and General Westmoreland onto a collision course that led to a trial.

We wanted this book to reflect a dialogue, so in June 1986 we sent a draft version to all the major participants in the trial.

We asked General Westmoreland, George Crile, Mike Wallace, the CBS legal staff, David Boies, and Dan Burt to read the draft and then submit their corrections, comments, and amplifications. (Sam Adams said he didn't need to read it. "Say anything you want about me.")

What did we learn? That we're not perfect. For example, some of the biographical data on General Westmoreland in the draft, which we obtained from standard reference works, was just plain wrong. Sometimes, the comments convinced us we were evenhanded. For example, Westmoreland complained that one section of a chapter was too favorable to CBS. Crile, after looking at the same section, complained it was too favorable to Westmoreland! Did we change anything after this dialogue? Yes, but not in a way that alters the tone or the thrust. In fact, once we began the exercise, we discovered that the players often gave us insights we would not have gleaned otherwise. The end result, we hope, is a richer and more accurate record.

Mike Wallace called this a "compassionate" book. That's fine with us. To paraphrase songwriter Woody Guthrie, we would rather write compassionate books than mean ones.

The reader is entitled to know of any possible conflicts of interest or close connections between the authors and any of the people in this book. Brewin writes a column for the *Village Voice*, a weekly newspaper published in New York. Victor A. Kovner, of the *Voice's* libel firm, Lankenau, Kovner & Bickford, represented George Crile of CBS during the libel trial. Harriette Dorsen, one of Kovner's partners, worked closely with Crile on the case. Her brother-in-law, David Dorsen, was one of Westmoreland's attorneys. Susan Lyne, Crile's wife, was the managing editor of the *Voice* from 1979 to 1981.

The publisher of this book is Atheneum, which is a subsidiary of the Scribner Book Companies, which, in turn, is a subsidiary of the Macmillan Publishing Company, publisher of a book that figured prominently in this case, *A Matter of Honor*, by Don Kowet.

Finally, Brewin served as a field radio operator with United States Marine Corps infantry battalions in 1965 and 1966, the same time Westmoreland was the commander of all U.S. troops in South Vietnam. Shaw was an anti-war activist.

We had a lot of assistance in getting this book from idea to finished manuscript and want to thank those who helped, especially

David Wiessler, Washington bureau chief of United Press International, Arnold Sawislak, assistant bureau chief, and Ronald Cohen, managing editor, for their gifts of time, understanding, and encouragement. Thanks also to David Schneiderman, editor-in-chief and publisher of the *Village Voice*, for his support. Our employers gave us the time and space to write news stories about the case as it unfolded.

We also want to thank two inspirational Texans, author Niel Hancock and our agent, Oscar Collier; our editor, Tom Stewart, who had the faith early and kept it; and the foot soldiers at both Capital Legal and Cravath, without whom we would never have been able to locate, let alone sort through, the documents. Especially warm thanks to Mike Peyton of Cravath and Laura Bandirali of Capital Legal. Most important, we are indebted to Kay McKee and Bob Deacy for helping us smooth over the rough spots that arise when two people try to do one book together.

SYDNEY SHAW
BOB BREWIN

New York/Washington/Lubbock, Texas
1984–1986

Contents

Illustrations

Part One

The Documentary

1.

One Man's Obsession

ON a cold, gray day in November 1969, Samuel Alexander Adams, descendant of the second President of the United States, stood in the attic of his Virginia farmhouse, stuffing hundreds of pages of classified CIA documents into a jumbo plastic leaf bag. As an analyst for the spy agency, Adams wanted to approach the task with meticulous logic and order, but this time he could not be overly concerned with neatness. He wrapped a second plastic bag around the bundle, then another, and hastily jammed the resulting mass into a wooden case that previously had housed twelve bottles of cheap Spanish wine. Adams nailed the box shut and wrestled it downstairs and outdoors. He had planned to lug it farther, but decided instead to risk the noise of an automobile and heaved the contraband into his jeep for the quarter-mile trip down the driveway, past groves of trees he had planted himself, and onto an unsuspecting neighbor's property.

Despite the chill, Adams' brow was glistening as he unloaded the crate, dragged it to a tiny clearing in the woods, and started digging. "The spot I picked was sheer rock and tree roots," Adams recalled. "It took four hours with a pickax, shovel, and crowbar to dig the hole. I felt very furtive and was sweating like hell. It was hard work and I felt guilty."

Halfway through the job, Adams heard a noise. Three figures were tramping toward him. He could just make out their guns and started to panic, thinking, almost in admiration, that the CIA had been on to him all along and now was closing in. But as the men came closer, Adams wiped his forehead with his shirt sleeve and trembled in relief. Only hunters.

With the box at last safely underground, he rearranged leaves, branches, and rocks, not even considering marking the cache. The Agency could spot something like that in an instant. Instead, he "triangulated" it, sticking a red thumbtack into each of three trees surrounding the hiding place, and hurried away without looking back.

He was scared. This was the dawn of the Nixon years, days of the Weather Underground, bloody protests against the Vietnam War, and heightened public suspicion of government activities. Just a year before, Robert Kennedy and Martin Luther King had been gunned down by assassins. Now hardhats fought hippies on New York City streets and the country was being torn apart by cries of police brutality from one side and demands for law and order from the other. Proponents of "Love it or leave it" squared off against draft-resisters shouting, "Hell, no, we won't go!" Although Adams was at the very heart of the Establishment, he had become convinced that America's military leaders were deliberately lying about the true size and nature of the enemy the nation was facing in Vietnam. His efforts to warn two Presidents had failed. Now, he believed, the CIA would fire him, and the documents that bore out his case would vanish. His life might even be in danger. Despite the secrecy agreement he had signed when he went to work for the CIA, he decided extreme action was warranted. He systematically photocopied the pertinent papers, smuggled them out of the Agency's Langley, Virginia, headquarters in his briefcase, and, later, stashed them in the crate.

Sam Adams hadn't set out to make waves at the CIA. In fact, the mild-mannered aristocrat had never intended to end up there at all. The son of Pierpont Adams, a broker with a seat on the New York Stock Exchange, he appeared headed for more gentlemanly pursuits, dutifully attending upper-class schools, including St. Mark's in Southboro, Massachusetts, and Harvard. After graduating with a degree in history in 1955, the same year as Edward Kennedy, he served in the Navy, briefly tried the life of a ski bum, then returned to Harvard law school, but tired of it after two years. He tried, and failed at, several other genteel professions, and by the time he decided to marry in 1962 he had drifted into banking. One day after the ceremony, however, he hung up his pinstripes. When he looked for work again the next year, the Central Intelligence Agency managed to lure him into its junior officer training program and he signed on more or less on a whim, never guessing he would be good at the work, never dreaming he would love it.

After learning the nuts and bolts of espionage, Adams landed on the Agency's Congo desk, where he began sorting through masses of raw data, absorbing everything he could, and soon astonished his bosses by accurately predicting that Uganda would invade the Congo in 1964. "It was one of the high points of my life," he recalled, saying it had taught him the importance of good files and "the sanctity of evidence," even seemingly unrelated bits of information, in making extrapolations. As a reward, he was assigned in late 1965 to study the enemy that U.S. forces were facing in the jungles of South Vietnam.

Although 200,000 American troops were in the Southeast Asian country, Adams was the Agency's only analyst devoting full time to researching the Vietcong. He worked on the task at his Langley desk for a while, learning what he could from weekly reports and statistics on VC defectors, but soon headed for Vietnam to investigate firsthand.

In Saigon, he spent a few days going through documents at the CIA station, then—on the advice of the station chief, who dismissed existing statistics as "not worth a damn"—traveled to the countryside to find out who the VC defectors really were. It was while looking through dossiers at the defector center in the dusty market town of Tan An in Long An province that Adams struck what seemed to be pay dirt. With the help of an interpreter, he counted some 150 communists defecting to the South Vietnamese side during a five-month period, including about 120 actual fighters—some of them North Vietnamese "regulars" but the vast majority guerrillas, or "irregulars," either Vietcong or members of "self-defense militias" within various villages. A glance at the official U.S. tally showed there were supposed to be only 160 Vietcong and militiamen in the area. If the official numbers had been true, only 40 enemy would have been left in the field. In his travels through the province, however, Adams had seen "bullets flying around all over the place"—the Vietcong controlled the countryside in Long An. His driver often floored the accelerator, barreling over bumpy roads at speeds up to sixty mph to outrun the guerrillas.

"I began to have this feeling that there was something funny going on," he said. "The statistics didn't make any sense." Confused, Adams went to the province headquarters and asked Colonel Anh, the South Vietnamese leader in charge, how many Vietcong there really were in Long An. The colonel told him there were at least 2,000, twenty times more than the official U.S. estimate. The seed of skepticism that would grow into an obsession was planted.

Back in Washington, Adams began to build a file of hundreds of captured documents, most of which appeared in bulletins published as often as three times a day by the U.S. military headquarters in Vietnam—known as MACV, for Military Assistance Command, Vietnam—to see if the estimates were accurate in other provinces. On August 18, 1966, one MACV bulletin caught his eye. It contained a report from Vietcong headquarters in Binh Dinh, a province in upper central Vietnam, that showed 50,000 guerrillas and militia in the area although the U.S. military's order of battle listed only 4,500.

Adams "did a double take." He realized that the numbers were probably wrong in other provinces as well, and since MACV estimated only 285,000 Vietcong in all of South Vietnam, the potential importance of his discovery sent him into a frenzy. The entire order of battle was worthless! "I started galloping around the CIA headquarters like Paul Revere," Adams said.

Adams knew that the order of battle, or OB, is a critical component of military strategy. When a general mounts a campaign, he must know the number of enemy troops he faces and their location, capability, weapons, and reserve pool. Knowledge of enemy strength dictates tactics. In World War II, as General Dwight D. Eisenhower contemplated the invasion of France, he faced a formidable German force. His first objective was to whittle down the number of enemy at the Normandy beachhead by ordering a counter-intelligence blitz to fool the Germans into thinking the attack would come at a different point. The trick worked. Hitler drew many of his troops away from Normandy, and when Eisenhower's OB showed a relatively weak force behind the beaches, the American general attacked.

Adams discovered the apparent gap on a Thursday and he scarcely left his office during the weekend, tediously comparing the numbers in other captured documents from the country's forty-four provinces to the numbers on the current order of battle. Examining evidence from Phu Yen, the province directly below Binh Dinh, he concluded that the official U.S. estimate reflected only one eighth of the actual enemy forces. The numbers in Phuoc Tuy province looked about right, but virtually all the other provinces showed apparent shortfalls. Adams was convinced he had stumbled onto the biggest intelligence find of the war.

On Monday afternoon, the analyst fired off the first in what became a series of memoranda, suggesting that the overall estimate of 270,000 enemy troops on the order of battle might be 200,000 men too low. The most optimistic military experts were saying that to win the guerrilla war, the United States must outnumber the Vietcong three to one. "The addition of 200,000 men to the enemy order of battle meant that somebody had to find an extra 600,000 troops for our side," he later wrote. Adams nervously awaited the response from the director's office on the seventh floor, imagining emergency briefings and meetings with President Lyndon Johnson. When days passed with no word from upstairs, Adams was puzzled. When the memo was returned to him on Friday, with no comment other than a notation that the CIA hierarchy had read it, he was aghast. Memos from his office were usually distributed to the Pentagon and the White House.

He wrote another memo with even more supporting details. A week later, when no word had come, Adams went to the seventh floor in person to investigate. He found his research stored in a safe in a manila folder stamped INDEFINITE HOLD.

After a third memo, the CIA finally allowed a version of Adams' study out of the building, but specified that it lacked official status. A copy did, however, eventually end up in Vietnam, at the Order of Battle Section of General William Westmoreland, commander of all U.S. forces in the country. Scores of analysts were working at MACV headquarters to keep tabs on the VC.

In the meantime, Sam Adams dug deeper, taking a closer look at MACV's monthly reports on enemy strength for the past two years. Although the number of regular, uniformed North Vietnamese soldiers had consistently increased, there had been no change in three other categories: the political infrastructure, which included Communist Party members and armed police; support troops such as medics and other specialists; and the irregulars, including the Vietcong guerrillas and the local self-defense militia—"guys in black pajamas" who planted the mines and booby traps responsible for thousands of American casualties. "Here we are in the middle of a guerrilla war, and we haven't even bothered to count the number of guerrillas," Adams later wrote.

With an escalating fervor, Adams expanded his document search and even began to pick up support from some Agency higher-ups. Adams said George Carver, assistant to new CIA director Richard Helms, told him at the time that he was "on the right track." He soon found the U.S. count of support troops was based on two-year-old data that appeared to be five times too low, and in the process stumbled across a whole new category of soldiers—"assault youths"—that wasn't even listed on the order of battle. In addition, he discovered the U.S. military was failing to count the Vietcong's political cohorts in the countryside. In late 1966, Adams concluded there were 600,000 Vietcong in South Vietnam, not 270,000.

As Adams churned out memos, irked but undaunted by the silence from above, a controversy over numbers was indeed beginning to stir at the top levels of the military command. It was not a good time for surprises. President Lyndon Johnson in early 1966 had launched the "war of attrition," giving Westmoreland the objective of killing and wounding enemy forces faster than Hanoi could replace them. At the same time, the President was hungry for "good news" to soothe a public that was haunted by the nightly TV images from the tiny Asian country and beginning to raise questions about the wisdom of intervening in a conflict that had been going on since 1945. An anti-war movement, begun the year before with a nationwide protest weekend, was picking up steam on college campuses. Pacifist David Dellinger visited Hanoi; Berkeley, California, student organizer Jerry Rubin was summoned to testify before the House Un-American Activities Committee; and Stanford University student vice president David Harris was jailed for draft evasion. More and more American troops were in South Vietnam—350,000 by 1966—and still more were approved for the next year, but Westmoreland was pushing to expand the war even further, saying it would hasten the end of the conflict.

Arguments over the various estimates of enemy strength escalated as fast as the war. General Earle Wheeler, chairman of the Joint Chiefs of Staff, called a conference in Honolulu to resolve the quarrel among the military, the Defense Intelligence Agency (DIA)—the Pentagon's intelligence group—and the CIA. Adams attended as a member of the CIA delegation. He was much heartened when Colonel Gains Hawkins, the head of Westmoreland's Order of Battle Section, told an early session of the February 1967 meeting, "You know, there's a lot more of those little bastards out there than we thought there were." Hawkins estimated an enemy force of about half a million. The conference eventually concluded that the numbers had indeed been too low and laid on MACV the responsibility for overhauling the order of battle.

But the controversy was far from over. The Honolulu meeting had no immediate impact on the official tally. In fact, that spring MACV began suggesting that the entire "self-defense militia" category be dropped from the totals, a plan the CIA opposed, pointing out that these fighters were responsible for many American deaths and that when they were slain, they were included in the body count.

In April, President Johnson called Westmoreland to Washington to report on the war and address a joint session of Congress. During this trip, at a White House meeting, the general said what his commander-in-chief had been waiting to hear: the United States had finally reached the cross-over point—that critical juncture when the enemy was dying faster than it could be replaced. (Ironically, Westmoreland based this statement on data prepared by men who became his chief accusers years later.)

That June, the National Intelligence Estimates Board—some forty representatives of the CIA, DIA, Army, Navy, Air Force, and State Department—convened its annual meeting in Washington, D.C., to gauge the progress of the war. Usually, this gathering of the intelligence community took about a week to reach a consensus. This time it would take almost six months. Almost immediately, the DIA did what appeared to be a sudden about-face, announcing it would back MACV's existing numbers. Then, at an August session of the same meeting at CIA headquarters, with the super-clandestine National Security Agency (NSA) joining the group at a massive U-shaped table, the military revealed its revised breakdown of enemy strength, with Gains Hawkins presiding over the slide-show presentation.

"I was just taken aback, amazed, made suspicious, because the old estimate, the previous estimate came out to basically 298 [thousand] and the new estimate was also 298 [thousand]," Adams later testified. ". . . In the second one they dropped all these self-defense types and they came up with the same number, and [after it was over] I went up to Gains. 'What the hell is going on here, Gains?' I asked. 'How do you come up [with] the same number?' And he sort of smiled and said nothing. He shrugged."

Adams soon learned at least part of the impetus for Hawkins' new figures. On August 21, the CIA received copies of two cables to General Wheeler sent the day before by Westmoreland and his deputy, General Creighton Abrams, Jr. The messages made clear the new "command position" on enemy strength: the self-defense troops (SD) and a sub-category, the secret self-defense forces (SSD), were to be marched out of the order of battle, primarily to deflect unfavorable news reports.

"If SD and SSD strength figures are included in the overall enemy strength, the figure will total 420,000–431,000. . . . This is in sharp contrast to the current overall strength figure of about 299,000 given to the press here," Abrams wrote, adding that the forces included many women and elderly, were poorly armed, and had "almost no military capability."

"We have been projecting an image of success over the recent months, and properly so," he wrote. "Now, when we release the figure of 420–431,000, the newsmen will immediately seize on the point that the enemy force has increased about 120–130,000. All available caveats and explanations will not prevent the press from drawing an erroneous and gloomy conclusion as to the meaning of the increase. All those who have an incorrect view of the war will be reinforced and the task will become more difficult." Westmoreland agreed, saying in his cable, "No possible explanations could prevent the erroneous conclusions that would result."

The Langley meeting ended in discord and, a month later, yet another order-of-battle conference was convened, this one on Westmoreland's turf, at MACV headquarters in Saigon, with the CIA facing off against Westmoreland's top intelligence experts: MACV's new chief of intelligence, General Phillip Davidson, and his aide, Colonel Morris; then-Col. Daniel O. Graham, who was chief of MACV estimates; and Hawkins. The soldiers explained they had "scaled down the evidence" in a way they felt most accurately reflected the enemy. Adams, who was arguing the CIA's position, became more and more convinced that the cuts were arbitrary. If MACV agreed to raise one category, it insisted on lowering another. Adams felt his suspicions had been confirmed when an Army officer told him and Carver, "You know, our basic problem is that we've been told to keep our numbers under 300,000."

Carver fired off a cable to CIA director Helms, saying that the talks were going nowhere and MACV was "stonewalling":

> Variety of circumstantial indicators—MACV juggling of figures its own analysts presented during the August discussions in Washington, MACV behavior, and tacit or oblique lunchtime and corridor admissions by MACV officers, including Davidson—all point to inescapable conclusion that General Westmoreland (with Komer's encouragement) has given instruction tantamount to direct order that VC strength total will not exceed 300,000 ceiling. Rationale seems to be that any higher figure would not be sufficiently optimistic and would generate unacceptable level of criticism from the press.

After meeting privately with Westmoreland and Robert Komer, the general's civilian deputy and a former CIA analyst who reported personally to President Johnson on the war, Carver apparently gave up. The conference ended September 13 with the CIA going along with MACV's position.

Carver, who had written his Oxford dissertation on Thomas Hobbes, began his final conference message to Helms with an enigmatic quote from an essay by the English philosopher. "Circle now squared," he wrote, indicating that he had done the impossible.

Sam Adams stayed on to discuss the "political cadre" category with the military's analysts. But, essentially, it was over. The bottom-line number of enemy troops to emerge on the National Intelligence Estimate after almost a year of bitter wrangling was 248,000 enemy fighting troops—some 22,000 fewer than the board started with.

At a post-conference party, Adams got drunk and railed at the military establishment. Then he returned to Washington, where George Allen, Carver's second in command and a longtime expert on Vietnam, angrily accused the CIA delegation of caving in.

"I was in a daze," Adams said. But he did not give up. For the seventh time that year, he appeared before the Board of National Estimates to try to get the numbers changed. He told the panel how MACV had "scaled down" the numbers, apparently arbitrarily; how Hawkins had confided to him during the Langley meeting that the number of guerrillas should be twice what he was arguing for.

The board showed great concern, he recalled. One member, Ludlow Montague, told him, "Sam, it makes my blood boil to see the military cooking the books." Another, Sherman Kent, the head of the group, asked, "Sam, have we gone beyond the bounds of reasonable dishonesty?"

"Sir, we went beyond the bounds of reasonable dishonesty last August," Adams told him.

The board, however, concluded there was no choice but to accept the numbers. An infuriated Adams composed yet another memo, accusing the military of lying, and blasting the Agency as cowardly and dishonest for going along. He sent copies to everyone. Nonetheless, two days later, CIA director Helms signed the estimate, along with Vice Admiral Rufus Taylor, deputy director of the Agency; Thomas Hughes, director of Intelligence and Research at the State Department; Lt. Gen. Joseph Carroll, director of the DIA; and Lt. Gen. Marshall Carter, director of the NSA.

Adams, disgusted with what he considered a "sellout," marched into Carver's office and resigned from the Vietnam Affairs staff, effective February 1.

The new numbers, meanwhile, had prompted military and government leaders to declare publicly that Vietcong strength was eroding. In November, Westmoreland told the National Press Club that the enemy's "guerrilla force is declining at a steady rate. Morale problems are developing within his ranks." Helms paraded the numbers in his New Year's briefing to Congress.

The glowing projections were short-lived.

On January 31, 1968, one day before moving to a new job at the Agency's newly formed Vietcong branch, Adams earned grisly vindication for his thesis as the North Vietnamese launched the massive Tet surprise attack. The night before, on the Vietnamese Lunar New Year holiday, 70,000 communist soldiers had stormed more than 100 South Vietnamese cities and towns, including Saigon, where a band of guerrilla sappers briefly overran the American Embassy, killing five GIs. In the ancient imperial capital of Hue, where enemy commandos slaughtered as many as 5,800 civilians and reduced much of the historic city to rubble, it took an entire U.S. Marine battalion to regain control. By the end of the month-long thrust, at least 2,000 Americans and 4,000 South Vietnamese soldiers had died. Although the U.S. military insisted the campaign was a tactical failure, saying that some 40,000 enemy had been killed, the Tet Offensive became North Vietnam's most important psychological victory and the turning point of the war. Sitting in the CIA situation room that day, Adams, like the long-unheeded apostle of the One True Faith, believed that the guerrilla forces inundating South Vietnam's major cities were proof positive that his numbers were right. It appeared many of the units involved in the assault were not listed in the order of battle.

The CIA immediately reopened the numbers controversy, and

Adams was thrust into the limelight. Bosses who had rejected his earlier memos were now accepting his updated analysis. Colleagues trooped through his office, slapping him on the back and congratulating him for being right. But Adams said any satisfaction was erased by the realization that thousands of American soldiers were killed at Tet. He was beginning to be less concerned with the figures than with his growing certainty that top military officials had purposely suppressed the truth.

Several weeks before the bold offensive, Adams had had a troubling conversation with Gains Hawkins, who had recently been transferred from MACV headquarters to Fort Holabird, Maryland. Hawkins had called, saying he wanted to meet unofficially to talk about the order of battle, and three days later he showed up at Langley, apologizing for the outcome of the Saigon conference and saying the summer of 1967 had been "the worst three months of his entire life."

The men, who shared an almost religious zeal for military statistics, pulled out their ever present calculations and spent a while discussing the various components of the order of battle. Then Hawkins turned suddenly to Adams and said, "Sam, there is something you ought to know."

Hawkins told Adams about a meeting with Westmoreland in May 1967, during which he had presented the general with much higher enemy-strength estimates. As he was explaining the new breakdown, using a "flip chart," Hawkins said, Westmoreland's famous square jaw went slack, the general looked shocked and "almost fell out of his chair."

He said Westmoreland responded, "What am I going to tell the press? What am I going to tell the Congress? What am I going to tell the President? I want you to take another look at those numbers."

Adams, growing more and more excited as Hawkins talked, furiously scribbed notes, trying to get down everything he said. In a second meeting after Tet, Hawkins repeated his charge that Westmoreland had wanted the numbers kept low to show "the light at the end of the tunnel."

Ironically, the first order of battle MACV released after the Tet Offensive reduced the enemy even further—to 204,126 men.

The crusading analyst, infused with renewed patriotic vigor after concluding that massive U.S. casualties at Tet could have been reduced or prevented, filed a complaint with Gordon Stewart, the CIA inspector general, against the Agency hierarchy, charging it with mismanaging research efforts. The action prompted Helms to authorize an internal investigation, but Adams still was not satisfied. He decided President Johnson's announcement that he would not seek re-election made it unnecessary to determine if the White House might have ordered a falsification, but Adams now turned his considerable energies on urging his bosses to let the new President know "the sorry state of American intelligence so that he could do something about it."

Helms asked General Maxwell Taylor, head of Johnson's Foreign Intelligence Advisory Board, to see Adams, and in late November the group took up the case. Notes of the session reveal the board talked to witnesses including Helms, Stewart, and Admiral Taylor, who told the panel that "at the time Adams was making his charges neither Adams nor anyone else had enough evidence to prove or disprove them."

Admiral Taylor also disputed Adams' claim that top U.S. officials had not been aware of possibly much higher guerrilla strengths. He said that President Johnson's special assistant in Vietnam, Walt Whitman Rostow, "knew and that General Abrams and others have been fully aware of the possible gross error all along."

Adams was not asked to testify, but the next week J. Patrick Coyne, executive secretary of the panel, met with him and urged him to prepare a full report and make recommendations. "I gave no indication to Mr. Adams as to what would be done with his recommendations and he made no inquiry in that regard," Coyne wrote in his notes of the meeting. When the thirty-five-page report was complete, however, Helms refused to forward it to the Foreign Intelligence Advisory Board.

Adams, unaware that the White House and the CIA had agreed to do nothing further with the report, protested and asked for permission to deliver it to Coyne himself, at which point the deputy director strongly suggested he resign if he chose to go outside official channels. Despite the warning, Adams passed the document along to an incoming member of Nixon's National Security Council staff. The White House, however, showed no interest.

Dejected, Adams gave up. Temporarily. Fearing retribution, he gathered up copies he had made of his precious documents and, stashing them in his briefcase, ferried them home a few at a time and hid them in his attic. But he couldn't bring himself to leave the Agency he loved. Instead, he threw himself into new projects.

His once promising career was in shambles. Although White House representatives described him as a "thoroughly amiable" and "a very bright and able employee," and Gains Hawkins calls him "probably the most honest man I ever met," Adams had, not surprisingly, become something of a pariah, particularly within the CIA. Carver questioned his judgment, calling him "half-cocked," "very prone to jump to conclusions, and very intolerant of the people who did not share the conclusions to which he jumped." Even friends who admired his integrity and tenacity agreed Adams' one-man crusade had sabotaged his future in the intelligence community. *The New York Times*, in a 1973 article, quoted one of his colleagues as saying, "The trouble with Sam is that he has always been right. He always told the truth and never cared whose toes he stepped on." Danny Graham and some other military intelligence officers were convinced Adams was crazy.

Knowing he had little to lose, Adams was soon locked in new and unsuccessful numbers games, urging the military to recognize a much larger Vietcong spy network—"the biggest espionage network in the history of mankind." Next, he tackled the Cambodian order of battle, fighting for a higher estimate of rebel troops.

Then, in 1972, with U.S. participation in Vietnam nearing the end, he decided to hoist the original order-of-battle banner one more time. "It was my patriotic duty," he said.

"One of the problems with this thing is, besides being quixotic, it was also an awful lot of fun," Adams recalled. "There was a lot of laughing going on. What can I do today, you know? And it wasn't the sort of elfish fun of a mischief maker. It was with the calm confidence of a Christian with four aces. Because I knew I was right. It became sort of fun to see what would happen to the next memo. Stir the ant heap."

But it was during this period that his marriage, which later broke up, began to show strain. He compared himself to the obsessed Captain Ahab in *Moby-Dick*, "bringing home another White Whale story." (Interestingly, Westmoreland's private plane was dubbed the *White Whale*.) His wife and son shared his fears of tapped phones, surveillance, and possible retribution. Adams said he "nailed the gold coin to the mast" when he began to collect the second batch of what would become known as "the purloined documents" and started trying to get Westmoreland court-martialed and Helms fired.

He wrote a memo to the U.S. Army inspector general, suggesting Westmoreland's participation in the order-of-battle dispute implicated him in three violations of the Uniform Code of Military Justice, including false official statements and conspiracy. He asked the CIA inspector general to investigate Helms, its director. He asked various congressional committees to take up his charges. All these efforts were rejected.

Then, in 1973, the government brought Daniel Ellsberg and Anthony Russo, former Rand Corporation employees who became two of Defense Secretary Robert S. McNamara's "whiz kids," to trial on charges of violating national security by leaking the Pentagon Papers to the press. The compilation and analysis of secret documents on the war, which had been commissioned by McNamara, contained, among other things, estimates of the enemy force in Vietnam—the same numbers Adams had been arguing against for seven years.

"Imagine! Hanging a man for leaking faked numbers!" Adams said. Although he still worked for the CIA, he traveled to Los Angeles to testify for Ellsberg.

The trial held an unsettling surprise, however. Gains Hawkins, who had also been asked to testify, steadfastly refused to corroborate Adams' theory of fixed numbers. He later wrote in the *Washington Post* that he was "committing, or at the very least flirting with, perjury" because he "despised Ellsberg and his partner and considered the publication of the *Pentagon Papers* of enormous psychological benefit to the Vietnamese Communists."

Upon Adams' return to Washington, many of his colleagues congratulated him for his spunk, but his bosses once again threatened him with firing. Although he managed to avoid immediate dismissal, he knew his days at the Agency were numbered. He began smuggling his latest collection of documents out of the building. He hid one batch in the attic of his farmhouse and took another stack, three inches thick, to Rep. Paul McCloskey, a California Republican who had also testified at the Ellsberg trial. When Adams asked McCloskey to keep them in his safe, he told the Congressman that he was afraid he might be executed.

Adams soon resigned. He kept himself busy mending fences on the 250-acre farm and toyed with the idea of writing his memoirs. But in late 1974, Adams' friend novelist John Gardner drew him out of obscurity, introducing him to a young editor at *Harper's* magazine named George Crile. Crile had learned some of Adams' story from Gardner and, always fascinated by tales of government intrigue and duplicity, convinced the gentleman farmer to write an article about his experiences. The *Harper's* piece, published in May 1975, just after the fall of Saigon, led Adams back to The Quest. He got a book contract and was asked to testify before New York Congressman Otis Pike's House Select Committee on Intelligence, which eventually agreed with Adams' theory in concluding that the Tet Offensive was unanticipated chiefly due to the military's "degraded image of the enemy." The dispute between CIA and MACV over enemy strength was a primary cause, the committee found, and "pressure from policy-making officials to produce positive intelligence indicators reinforced erroneous assessment of allied progress and enemy capabilities."

Publicity from the investigation led John Barrie Williams, an Army colonel who, as a major, had been one of the Defense Intelligence Agency's negotiators during the 1967 order-of-battle dispute, to call Adams and congratulate him, saying, "Right on." When Adams told his editor about the conversation, he was urged to change the focus of the book from an autobiography into an investigative report of what really had happened at that crossroads of history.

The *Harper's* article had been written from memory, but now Adams decided it was time to take another look at the documents that buttressed his charges. He retrieved the bundle he had given Mc-Closkey and set out to unearth the box he had buried in a panic on that chilly morning six years before.

This time, Adams experienced a different kind of fear.

"I made a discovery," he recalled. "Over a period of years, red thumbtacks get brown." He couldn't find the markers anywhere and even the woods looked unfamiliar. Frantic, he paced among the trees, searching.

"Finally, I got a crowbar and went to the area where I thought I buried it and started banging away, prodding the soil." A brief eternity later, one of his thrusts yielded a faint thud. He scrutinized the surrounding trees. Thumbtacks still protruded from the bark of two of the sentries.

Back at the house, in the attic where the box had originally been stuffed with documents, Adams got another shock. As he pried off the lid, he found that the plastic leaf bags had sprung a leak. "I discovered a wad of black scum and my heart more or less sank."

Not knowing what else to do, Adams left the decomposing mass of secrets to dry for several months and then decided to see what, if anything, could be salvaged. "I went up with a blunt-end kitchen knife, stuck it in the middle of the pile and the stack popped open. The edges had been eaten away, but the middle was preserved."

During the next five years, Adams would track down and interview 200 people for his book, half of whom were connected with the order-of-battle dispute. If he had been meticulous in his days at the CIA, he neared fanaticism in the new fact-finding mission, filling ream after ream of paper with intricate notes, biographies, and charts showing where each person fit into the larger puzzle. He went back repeatedly to ask more questions, contacting some of his subjects more than twenty times. His files would mushroom to encyclopedic proportions.

Sam Adams, analyst, took on an added dimension: Sam Adams, sleuth and interrogator. It was a CIA man's dream.

First, he compiled a list of principals, breaking them down into organization charts reminiscent of the ones he had used to keep tabs on the Vietcong. "You see who reports to whom," he said. "What you do is find out who worked where, everywhere. And then the next most important thing is what days they were in Vietnam—when they showed up and when they left—because that indicates what they know."

List in hand, he was ready to start, but finding the men was a project in itself. After all, the Pentagon does not give out names and addresses.

"The best single way of finding them was the Christmas-card list," Adams said. "All these guys were working together and they all wrote each other Christmas cards for the first four years after they quit."

A student of POW-interrogation techniques, Adams was a fastidious interviewer. Like the British Admiralty during World War II, he would first find out everything he could about his subjects, everything they *should* know, then, with strategy that would dazzle a chess champion, guide them into revealing information they might have preferred to keep to themselves. He asked bewilderingly intricate questions, pinpointing such things as where various officers sat in meetings, how they traveled there and with whom.

"You come in and let drop that you know this, that, and the other thing. And they think you know a lot more than you really do. Or a lot of times these guys forget things and you remind them of things they should know and very often they do know them."

Adams had to fit his interviews into his schedule at the farm ("reaping and sowing and all that"), but by the late 1970s he had managed to uncover startling information that helped explain the mysterious events from the previous decade, particularly the military's "scaled down" numbers.

Interviewing Barrie Williams and Colonel George Hamscher, both of whom had been with the Defense Intelligence Agency, he learned of a secret August 1967 meeting at the Pentagon, in the narrow room next to the offices of the Joint Chiefs of Staff. At this gathering prior to a session of the National Intelligence Estimate meeting at Langley, chief military negotiator Danny Graham arbitrarily slashed the military's own estimates of Vietcong units to keep the enemy total under 300,000, they said.

Hamscher, the representative of CINCPAC—Admiral Ulysses Grant Sharp, Jr., Commander in Chief, Pacific—later testified, "I remember clearly saying, 'look, Danny, we can't do this. This is wrong.' And he looked at me and said, 'Hamscher, if you've got a better way of doing it, let's have it.' "

Many of the men spoke of Graham with open hostility.

"He cut the numbers," Adams said. "This was entirely out of character in intelligence terms. The worst thing you can do is jack around with evidence. This sent people shooting up through the walls."

Gains Hawkins, who was living in West Point, Mississippi, running a home for the elderly, backed off his Pentagon Papers stance and confirmed he had been operating under a ceiling in 1967.

General George Godding, who had headed the MACV delegation to the OB meetings, denied there had been any deception. But he backed up part of Hawkins' story, saying he also had met with Westmoreland before the fateful slide show that convinced Adams MACV was tinkering with the numbers. Godding said Westmoreland told him to "stay within the parameters of the May OB," a number which was under 300,000.

General Joseph McChristian, who served as Westmoreland's intelligence chief until June 1967, revealed that he had tried in May 1967 to send a cable to CINCPAC and the Joint Chiefs of Staff alerting them to substantially higher guerrilla forces than were carried in the existing order of battle. But when he took the message to Westmoreland for approval, his commander said, "If I send that cable to Washington, it will create a political bombshell." The cable was never forwarded.

Some of the interviews turned up secrets Adams had not even suspected. Two officers who had analyzed enemy infiltration for MACV told him that not only had the numbers been slashed in the order of battle, but the true number of enemy infiltrating from the North was also being suppressed. During 1967, Westmoreland's official reports showed that about 8,000 Vietcong per month were sifting into South Vietnam from various points along the Ho Chi Minh Trail, but Lieutenant Michael Hankins and Lieutenant Bernard ("Bernie") Gattozzi told Adams they had been reporting much higher figures—more than 25,000 per month—in the five months preceding the Tet Offensive. But the higher numbers, which should have alerted America to the fact that the Vietcong were massing for the biggest surprise attack of the war, were consistently rejected by the brass. Danny Graham, Westmoreland's chief of estimates, had put a stranglehold on the politically unfavorable numbers, they said.

Gattozzi told Adams that one officer, Lieutenant Colonel Everette Parkins, a well-respected West Point graduate who had intended to make a career in the military, was fired in October 1967 for angrily challenging a superior after MACV refused to release his reports of the higher infiltration.

Lieutenant Richard McArthur, who had been MACV's analyst in charge of Vietcong guerrillas, told Adams that shortly after Tet he returned from R&R to find that some 35,000 soldiers had been slashed from his province-by-province estimate chart. McArthur said when he asked his commander, Lieutenant Colonel Paul Weiler, what had happened, Weiler responded, "We had to do it" and urged him to "Lie a little, Mac, lie a little."

Others from the Combined Intelligence Center, Vietnam, (CICV), including Colonel Russell Cooley, Gattozzi, and former Commander James Meacham, eventually expanded on McArthur's tale.

Adams found Meacham, the officer in charge of putting out MACV's first official post-Tet enemy-strength estimate, by writing BUPERS, the Bureau of Personnel of the Navy. The letter was forwarded to London, where Meacham was chief military correspondent for the *Economist*, and Meacham wrote back, agreeing to an interview. While in London, Adams persuaded Meacham to turn over the letters he had written to his wife during that period, confessing that MACV was faking the numbers.

"We started with the answer, and plugged in all sorts of figures until we found the combination which the machine could digest," Meacham said in one letter. "And then we wrote all sorts of estimates showing why the figures were right which we had to use, and we continue to win the war."

Cooley, who was working at the Fairchild Data Center in Mountain View, California, referred to this process as "reverse engineering." He said Danny Graham had ordered the procedure, ultimately demanding that CICV's computer data base be altered to "make the transition into this post-Tet period look a little more smoother and rational."

Meacham said Graham, who denied having engineered any such falsification, wanted the changes in the computer to go back as far as six months.

As the story expanded, dislodging an orchestra of whistle-blowers, Sam Adams was totally consumed by the narrow slice of history. He was toiling away on his manuscript in 1980 when he got a call from George Crile, the *Harper's* editor who had gotten his story across in 1975. Crile was now a producer at CBS News, but his call had nothing to do with business.

"My three-year-old daughter had never seen a farm," Crile recalled. "The only trees and grass she had ever seen were in Central Park." Since Crile knew a man who lived on a farm, he called Adams and asked if they could come down to Virginia.

During the visit, Adams eagerly explained what he had learned in his interviews—that the order-of-battle controversy had been much bigger than a mere inter-agency catfight. He showed Crile his bulging files, one for each actor in the numbers drama, and as the two men pored over the hefty "chronologies" that outlined Adams' chain of deceit, the idea for a television documentary was born.

2.

One Man's Work

F O R George Crile III, the handsome son of a prominent Cleveland family, the chance to bring Sam Adams' Vietnam conspiracy theory to a wider audience was an irresistible challenge. As he sat in the book-lined study of Adams' Loudoun County farmhouse, listening to his host embellish layer upon layer of apparent collusion, his reporter's mind raced far ahead of the conversation at hand. He was thinking television. Granted, a program about the subject would have to be made up of interviews—"talking heads," in television jargon—rather than action, and he would have to find a way to make the show look exciting. Some of the heads might refuse to talk when the cameras started rolling. But it could be done. A major scandal, Crile concluded. It had all the elements that set his imagination in motion: power, moral issues, and historical impact. His feeling of indignation grew as Adams droned on. Someone had to get this story out.

It was not the first difficult project Crile had felt compelled to tackle. Easy stories bored him. But many colleagues suspected it was unbridled ambition rather than moral conviction that led him from one sensational report to another. His favorite topics—the Third World and political corruption—suggested a reformer's passion, but his demeanor—reserve bordering on aloofness—seemed anything but passionate. They surmised that Crile's level gaze, rarely revealing emotion, must be focused squarely on The Top. He wanted to be a star like ace correspondent Mike Wallace or news anchor Dan Rather.

Others, however, including several CBS luminaries, saw Crile as the journalist's journalist, treading ground few others would risk. They accepted his cool manner as an outward manifestation of enviable self-discipline. If Crile sometimes seemed arrogant, so be it. It was because his work was all-important. If he was driven by ambition, it was the ambition of a would-be Lincoln Steffens.

"I think it has something to do with moral arrogance," Crile said, readily acknowledging that he puts some people off. "I can't tell you what it is, exactly, but too many people felt it not to take it seriously. Most of my stories that I pursued dealt with arrogance of power or things going a little bit out of control."

Crile's moral fervor was grown in Cleveland, where, as president of his class at the University School, an exclusive country day school, he pushed unsuccessfully to install the honor system. The biography in his senior yearbook boldly predicted that he would "top every crisis in honor."

The best clues to his motives, however, lay in his family legacy.

In a childhood filled with power, intellect, excitement, energy, and ambition, where dinner conversations often turned into highly charged cerebral parrying, Crile and his three siblings quickly learned from their exceptional parents to scrutinize authority and question traditional thought.

His paternal grandfather, George Washington Crile, pioneered surgical techniques including the first successful blood transfusion, founded the world-famous Cleveland Clinic, and wrote books on topics ranging from surgery to the effects of war on the physical and mental health of nations. When the Crile family patriarch reached his seventies, however, he refused to put down his scalpel, continuing to operate although his eyesight was failing. Several times, he endangered patients by accidentally slicing into their arteries, and Crile's father, Dr. George (Barney) Crile, Jr., a young resident at the time, often was called upon to patch up the blunders.

"He would try to get my grandfather to stop operating," Crile said. "But he was accused of being ungrateful and all the rest. I think it had a long-term impact on him in terms of rebelling against the arrogance of surgeons at that point, against surgery in general."

Barney Crile made his reputation by challenging the surgical establishment. In the 1950s, when the prevailing cancer treatment was not only surgery but "getting rid of as much as you can," he told women that radical mastectomy was not their only choice.

Crile calls his father, who drew the ire of the local medical association for the revolutionary theory that was more than a decade ahead of its time, the "savior of the American breast."

If Crile inherited the crusader's bent from his father, it was his mother who inspired him to communicate. Jane Halle, the half-Jewish and half-Irish Catholic daughter of the founder of Halle Bros. department store—the Saks Fifth Avenue of Cleveland—was the driving force behind a series of adventure vacations that led to the couple's 1950s best-seller, *Treasure Island Holidays*. The entire Crile clan, with faces painted on their bottoms to repel sharks, dived for sunken treasure on these pre-aqualung jaunts while Mom and Dad cranked away with an underwater camera. Crile said the films, which his parents showed at meetings of the National Geographic Society, were "pretty good travel documentaries. As a family, we were a little like a documentary unit."

Childhood joy was marred, however, by his mother's cancer, which began in her breast and ultimately spread to her brain. She was treated by the same methods her husband favored, and although massive radiation brought a reprieve from the cancer's steady progression, she eventually died from the disease Barney Crile was dedicating his life to contain. Before her death, the couple wrote another book, *More Than Booty*, describing their life together.

The young George Crile had often helped his father in the laboratory and, frustrated by what he felt was the ineffectiveness of cancer research, rejected the family profession. Cancer became, instead, a metaphor for him. Working as a cub reporter in Gary, Indiana, he would equate the "evil of this dreaded cancer" with corruption in government. Later, when his father stumbled across what for a brief time looked like a cancer breakthrough—shrinking tumors by applying heat—he refined the symbolism.

"One of the things you learn in life, and with wisdom in reporting, is that casting a light on something does illuminate it but it may not do anything more than let you know how bad it is," he said.

On the road to this wisdom, however, Crile managed to irritate a number of people, beginning with newspaper publisher Walter Ridder, who gave him a job on the *Gary Post-Tribune*.

Crile met Ridder while living with his aunt in Washington, D.C., and attending Georgetown University's Foreign Service School between years at Trinity College in Connecticut, where he graduated with a degree in history. Kay Halle, an "authentic character," substantially expanded her nephew's already wide horizons. "George Gershwin had written 'Summertime' on her piano and Buckminster Fuller had hung out at her house," Crile related admiringly. "She cooked scrambled eggs for FDR on the night he was elected President and was responsible for getting Winston Churchill his honorary citizenship." Under his aunt's patronage, Crile met Ted Yates, an NBC documentary producer who was later killed in the 1967 six-day Arab-Israeli war; landed a job with investigative columnists Drew Pearson and Jack Anderson; and decided to become a journalist himself. He also made plans to marry Anne Patten, and eighteen-year-old descendant of John Jay. Her stepfather, columnist Joseph Alsop, was a leading advocate of the Vietnam War.

As Crile's future took shape, a CIA analyst only a few miles away was embroiled in the statistics fight with America's intelligence community that would one day shake up both men's lives. Sam Adams dragged his argument higher and higher through the layers of the government, threatening to hand-deliver his formal complaint about CIA management to the White House, while Crile was socializing with Johnson administration officials who would one day testify against him in court. Among the guests at Crile's September 1968 wedding were former Defense Secretary Robert S. McNamara, Deputy Defense Secretary Paul Nitze, and National Security Adviser Walt Whitman Rostow.

After the wedding, Crile served a brief stint in the Marine Corps reserve, then boldly headed to the *Washington Post* to ask for a job. Editor Benjamin Bradlee diplomatically recommended that the young man follow his example and learn the ropes in the nation's heartland, so Crile asked Walter Ridder if he could work on his newspaper group's latest acquisition, in Gary.

"Gary was where I came alive. Where I first learned about the world," Crile said. "I met mayors, reform politicians, crooked politicians and truck drivers and steelworkers and housewives and Olinsky organizers and Nader lawyers and government do-gooders. I encountered violence for the first time, and voter fraud. I discovered corruption. I had seen an incredible amount of the world through travels, but I hadn't seen what it's like at the foundations of an industrial American city."

As George Crile earned his street education, his bride, whose stepfather had once written, "The problem of the cities . . . is the most urgent, the most difficult, and the most frightening American domestic problem . . . since the Civil War," became assistant press secretary to Gary's first black mayor.

"I loved it," Crile recalled. "I could have lived in Gary forever."

Walter Ridder came to feel differently. He said Crile took advantage of his relationship with the publisher and disrupted the newsroom. "If you didn't believe him or agree with him, he got angry." Ridder said he routinely checked and rechecked the facts on Crile's stories because he didn't trust the brash young reporter's accuracy.

The turning point was a story about a rampant "malignancy": the "out-of-control corruption and thuggery" at the city tax assessor's office. Crile, in a fiery eleven-part series, told of the assessor "blackjacking" local citizens, building private businesses with kickbacks, and forcing city workers to spend their hours lining his pockets. He said he had IRS files to back up his charges and tape-recorded interviews with local businessmen.

Ridder claimed the tax-assessor epic couldn't be checked out. He refused to print it. Soon afterward, Crile was "promoted" to cover the Pentagon in Washington, D.C. "It was probably their means of getting me out of Gary so they wouldn't have to run the story," he said. "But I couldn't sleep at night. I had to get the story out to save Gary, Indiana."

The story, apparently leaked by a lawyer working with consumer advocate Ralph Nader, eventually wound up in a community-action newspaper run by Saul Olinsky, under the headline, "Articles the *Post-Tribune* Would Not Print." Crile was promptly fired.

Although Crile came to believe that his zealousness had been more than a little naïve, his interest in the tax-assessor story did not go away. When he moved on to *Harper's Weekly*, a short-lived spinoff of *Harper's* magazine, his Sam Adams-like tenacity led to a 1972 reprise of the entire tale, complete with the charge that the *Post-Tribune* had not run the story because the Ridders were getting tax breaks (a charge Walter Ridder flatly denied, saying the advantages Crile referred to were directly related to changes in tax laws). The episode also introduced Crile to libel actions. The tax assessor, who went to jail after the *Harper's* article was published and another *Post-Tribune* reporter found sources willing to back up Crile's original charges, sued *Harper's* for $5 million. The case was dropped five years later, but it cost the magazine half a million dollars to defend itself.

Harper's editor Robert Shnayerson later told the *Washington Post* that although there may have been some errors in the story, "we were not malicious" and "I felt good about defending George to the hilt because he had picked his enemies so well."

But Shnayerson also observed what he called a "martyr inclination" in Crile. "He is determined that he is so abstractly right and everyone else is wrong. It's a very religious kind of zealotry . . . a puritan mentality—which I mean in the original sense, the quest to purify, to be pure."

Adams' saga of a military cancer crippling the nation and its top leaders during wartime by choking off critical intelligence filled Crile with moral outrage. "When I met Sam, I heard someone who was telling me exactly the same kind of thing in a bigger arena than I had thought about in Gary. Which is, you can see the problem, but no one will let you report it." He urged Adams to reveal the story in *Harper's* and personally wrote much of the 1975 article, "Vietnam Cover-Up: Playing War with Numbers," which appeared under Adams' byline.

That same year, Crile again investigated the rich and their taxes, this time in a free-lance story for *Washington Monthly*. He accused big businesses and wealthy individuals, including hard-line conservative publisher Richard Mellon Scaife, of getting substantial tax breaks on their property holdings in Pennsylvania due to a crooked assessment firm.

While at *Harper's*, Crile "invented a chapter of American history," as he tells it, by exposing a secret CIA project—Operation Mongoose —in the Florida Keys that was launched following the Bay of Pigs invasion. His story about American agents training a clandestine army of Cubans led to a Senate investigation. It also attracted the attention of CBS, which hired Crile as a consultant/reporter and set him to work with producer Judy Crichton on a documentary, "CIA: The Secret Army." Richard Salant, who was president of CBS News at the time, called the show "one of the all-time great documentaries." Crile still refers to it as his finest work.

The CIA program, which aired in 1977, won a blue ribbon at the American Film Festival, and a 1978 co-production, "The Battle for South Africa," won a George Foster Peabody Award and an Emmy. Crile's star was rising quickly at the network.

But the glimmer faded somewhat with an April 1980 documentary, "Gay Power, Gay Politics," which Crile co-produced with Grace Diekhaus. The show, which displayed the promiscuity of San Francisco's homosexual community and accused it of pressuring politicians for its special interests, infuriated gay groups. The organizations protested to the now-defunct National News Council, which agreed two of the complaints were warranted. One, it turned out, was a violation of the network's guidelines. A segment of the documentary had been edited in such a way as to make it appear an applause sequence came at an earlier point than it really had.

Crile's critics, including some of his CBS co-workers, later pointed to the gay complaint and the *Harper's* suit as evidence of chronic carelessness. His quick success as a producer was unwarranted, they said. He cut corners to make his points.

But Crile and other of his colleagues said such criticism, particularly from within CBS, may have been due in part to the fact that he was a loner, totally immersed in his work. He had little patience for co-workers whose efforts fell short of his own. At the same time, he had little contact with the network hierarchy because CBS Reports, the documentary unit, was removed from the mainstream of CBS News.

When the criticisms eventually surfaced as public charges, Crile challenged his detractors to examine his work. The documentaries were not contrived to elevate him to star status, he insisted. He pursued them for highly personal—yes, moral—reasons.

"They were all difficult to do. Particularly for television. 'The Battle for South Africa' was a story nobody wanted to do. I almost became a joke trying to sell it. And it was something I wanted to do for my own reasons. And the gay show was a crazy show to do. It's a disastrous show to do, which I was warned about before."

The Vietnam story, an even more difficult challenge, would also lead to disaster.

But on that day in the spring of 1980, sitting in the stone farmhouse nestled in the Virginia hills and talking with Sam Adams about the former CIA man's new evidence against the military, Crile saw not problems ahead but the makings of a fine documentary.

There were, of course, hurdles. Crile would have to convince network officials to approve the project. And before they would give the final go-ahead, he knew he would probably have to serve up filmed interviews with at least some of the men who could corroborate Adams' story. Back in New York City, he tried the idea out on his boss, Howard Stringer, who at the time was executive producer of CBS Reports.

Stringer, a hearty newsman in the best *Front Page* tradition and a British citizen, had been drafted into the U.S. Army two months after he arrived in the country to work for CBS. He served in Vietnam as a sergeant in 1966 and 1967. The Oxford graduate could have resisted induction, but did not. He was a staunch believer in the draft, calling the non-volunteer Army "the only place Americans get to meet their country."

An accomplished documentary producer himself, Stringer was interested in Crile's idea, but he had serious doubts. Would these military men—some of whom were still on active duty—risk their status by going on national television?

Crile kept in contact with Adams, checking and rechecking the new evidence. By November, he was ready to write a "blue sheet"— the proposal a producer submits to get a documentary approved. Thanks to Adams' substantial research, this blue sheet packed more detail than most. Its sixteen pages not only outlined the main points of the drama in chronological order, but also excerpted damning tidbits from the stack of TOP SECRET documents and letters Adams had collected over the past fifteen years.

On November 24, Crile submitted the plan, proposing he be allowed to produce his first solo documentary—the "story of how the U.S. Military command in Vietnam entered into an elaborate conspiracy to deceive Washington and the American public as to the nature and size of the enemy we were fighting," noting, "This is, of course, the most serious of accusations, suggesting that a number of very high officials—General Westmoreland included—participated in a conspiracy that robbed this country of the ability to make critical judgments about its most vital security interests during a time of war."

The proposal repeated the words "conspiracy" or "conspirator" twenty-four times, naming Colonel Danny Graham as the "key conspirator" but concluding, "It is for us to go beyond—to find out whether Westmoreland was acting on his own authority or whether, as it seems more likely to me, he was receiving direct authorization or at least encouragement from above. The task will be to follow the trail of the conspiracy, to see how far up the chain of command it goes—first to the Pentagon, to the Joint Chiefs of Staff. Then to the Secretary of Defense, Robert McNamara, and finally to see what the White House knew about it."

Stringer later explained the multiple references to conspiracy this way: "That was George trying to sell an extremely reluctant executive producer. The length of the blue sheet reflected a massive amount of skepticism on my part." But Stringer pointed out that he never doubted the premise of the show, just Crile's ability to line up the interviews.

While Stringer deliberated over the proposal, along with CBS News vice president Bob Chandler and CBS News president Bill Leonard, Crile headed to the row of airy, river-view offices on West 57th Street in New York that housed the correspondents on television's top-rated show, "60 Minutes." He was looking for Mike Wallace. Crile, who had known Wallace for several years, wanted the veteran newsman to join the project as its chief correspondent. Wallace's participation would improve the chances of getting the show approved and, more important, he was the best person at CBS to handle a demanding project built around one difficult interview after another. Wallace had another virtue as well. He had gotten to know Westmoreland on a reporting tour in Vietnam in 1967, the exact time frame the documentary would cover. After spending a day traveling around the countryside with Westmoreland, he had come away saying Westy was "a good troop general." Westmoreland had since written to Wallace, expressing admiration for his reports on "60 Minutes."

Wallace was a busy man, obligated to complete some twenty-five segments a year for "60 Minutes," but he was definitely interested. "It was a hell of a story and I knew it," Wallace said. "I wanted to be part of it."

Stringer, who had known Crile for four years as "a thorough, industrious, energetic" producer with "an ability to do difficult, complex projects," soon decided that the show should get at least tentative approval. He urged his own bosses to say yes, meeting more than five times with Chandler, who later testified he had some reservations about Crile's experience and readiness to work alone. Chandler also said he expressed concern over the accusations that had grown from the gay show. But the brass eventually agreed that Crile should proceed alone. "George's work in accumulating that evidence [on the blue sheet] was proof of his skills," Stringer said.

Sam Adams, they said, could be hired as a consultant on the project (he would eventually get $25,000), but if a documentary resulted and Adams appeared on screen, he would have to be identified as a CBS employee. Chandler and Leonard also approved Mike Wallace as the chief correspondent on the show, although Crile would have to do most of the on-camera interviews himself.

Crile had a green light to go out and try to buttress Adams' charges with filmed interviews.

By this time, Crile already had taken at least one step he would later regret, lining up a thirty-year-old free-lance film editor to join the project when the time came. Ira Klein had done a lot of work at "30 Minutes"—the daytime "60 Minutes"—combining snippets of film for mostly "soft" features, and was, at the time, working on segments for the network's "Magazine" show. He came well recommended by Crile's former co-producer and close friend Grace Diekhaus and seemed eager to work on the long-form project. He appeared to be a good choice for the job.

"He seemed very nice and agreeable," Crile said. "I wanted somebody, at the time, who would not mind doing this kind of 'talking head' show which had very little opportunity for a film editor to do interesting things. It was not a film editor's dream. I thought Ira would appreciate the shot at having an hour and would not mind going through it."

Stringer raised questions about Klein's inexperience, but Crile prevailed, arguing that the Vietnam documentary would not require great technical expertise. "I expressed concerns, but agreed that [editing] the broadcast was not likely to be . . . a very complicated job," Stringer said.

Joe Zigman, a longtime associate producer, joined the project soon afterward, and by early February the burgeoning documentary unit had acquired a researcher, Alex Alben, who had previously worked on the network's election coverage. Klein hired Phyllis Hurwitz, an assistant film editor, away from ABC.

For a while, however, it looked doubtful that any of these assistants would ever be needed. Shortly after Crile started the interviews in January 1981, working from a list Adams had compiled of eighty former officials with knowledge of the events in question, he began to fear that Stringer and the other CBS executives might be right. Virtually no one was willing to talk before CBS's cameras.

Crile and Adams had decided that the best place to start was in California with Lieutenant Colonel David Morgan, who had served as deputy chief of Westmoreland's Order of Battle Section in 1967.

Morgan would be able to confirm a dramatic event that Adams had unearthed during his book research and Crile had described on the blue sheet. Crile had written that, after the final Saigon order-of-battle conference where the enemy was cut to 299,000, "In a scene out of *Catch-22* [Morgan and his boss, Colonel Gains Hawkins] move from desk to desk in the large building housing the 100-odd Vietcong analysts and order their junior officers to march tens of thousands of soldiers out of their columns."

It was because Morgan and Hawkins removed so many troops that the final strength figure would be lowered to 242,000. Hawkins had already agreed to be interviewed, but Crile also wanted to ask Morgan about the alleged slashing of enemy-infiltration figures in the months leading up to the Tet Offensive. Adams believed the colonel could finger Danny Graham as a prime architect of the deception.

Morgan had already told Adams of his part in the "*Catch-22*" episode: "We cut lots of units . . . it was terribly wrong. We had no criteria for dropping people. It was guesswork. There was nothing to back it up. Why did we do it? To make ourselves look good, to make Danny Graham look correct, so we could prove we were winning the war."

The former MACV intelligence expert, Adams projected, would be an easy interview.

He and Crile arranged to meet with Morgan and then flew to California, eager to capture the confession on film. Morgan, however, had other ideas. He might choose to tell all to Adams, or even to Crile, but not to a nationwide TV audience. The men spent hours trying to sway Morgan, who later said, "I waffled between the idea of doing it and the idea of not doing it, ended up by saying I would not do it, at that particular time, anyway."

Morgan did agree to call another former officer whom he had helped Sam Adams get in touch with before: Lieutenant Colonel Everette Parkins, the West Pointer who apparently had been fired for challenging a superior over the faked numbers. But Parkins also refused to play any part in the CBS project.

The first person who agreed to be filmed was Adams' good friend Joe Hovey, a former CIA analyst who had worked in Saigon in the late 1960s. In November 1967, Hovey had prepared a report predicting the Tet Offensive. Adams, who had been assigned to review the report, said Hovey's warnings were largely disregarded because, according to the military's numbers, the Vietcong did not have enough men to pull off such a massive maneuver. (Adams had edited in a comment saying that enemy strength could be twice as much as believed, but Agency higher-ups promptly deleted it before passing Hovey's study along to the White House.)

"All hell was going to break loose . . . ," Hovey told CBS. "Up until now, the war had been going along at a—at a steady pace. Very violent, but still at a steady, relatively low-keyed, long-term pace. Now suddenly what you're talking about is Armageddon, you know. The walls are going to come crashing in. They're coming at us with everything they've got."

Crile asked him, "Did it make sense to you what the VC were about to do?"

"Actually, it did not," Hovey replied. "Because I was still—again, I had no knowledge of these large reinforcements pouring down the Ho Chi Minh Trail. And from what I knew of enemy strength estimates, and compared with the kind of power that the American Army had in the country, it just seemed to me insane."

It was a start, but not enough.

Next, Mike Wallace interviewed Marshall Lynn, one of the junior military-intelligence officers whose figures apparently had been cut by Morgan. But Lynn, now an advertising executive in New York City, did not add as much to the story as Crile had hoped, and the film was never used.

The project really began to take shape several days later, when Crile interviewed Colonel George Hamscher on camera. Hamscher had told Adams about the August 1967 meeting in the narrow Pentagon room adjacent to the offices of the Joint Chiefs of Staff where the MACV delegation met and, under the direction of Colonel Graham, cut the enemy-strength figures enough to keep them below Westmoreland's alleged "ceiling." Asked about the ceiling, Hamscher said "the message we got" is that MACV couldn't "live with a figure higher than" 300,000.

"I was uneasy because of the bargaining characteristics," the colonel said. "This is not the way you ought to do it. You don't—you know, you don't start at an end figure and work back. But we did."

Hamscher described the Pentagon meeting as "a group grope," prompting Crile to ask, "To fake intelligence estimates?"

"That's your characterization, and that's too strong for me," Hamscher replied, but conceded, "My misgiving was that we were faking it. There was manipulation, yeah."

Hamscher also confirmed that the cuts of various enemy units were done "arbitrarily."

Next, the CBS cameras captured on film Lieutenant Richard McArthur's tale of the altering of MACV statistics post-Tet, when, he said, his commanding officer told him to "lie a little."

By this time, Alex Alben was working his way down Sam Adams' list of eighty names, collecting facts and arranging for interviews, and Phyllis Hurwitz started assembling portions of the completed interviews into a presentation reel that Crile could use to persuade his bosses to let him continue. Bob Chandler had just been moved to another job at the network and Roger Colloff, previously CBS News president Bill Leonard's deputy, replaced him. The screening for Colloff, who would now make the decision on Crile's project, was targeted for late March.

Adams became a well-known figure in the CBS Reports offices, often bringing flowers from his farm to the secretaries and leading detailed "chronology sessions" with Crile and his assistants, reading at length from his meticulous notes on the yellow legal paper.

As they traveled around to document Adams' charges, the producer and consultant were somewhat of an odd couple—Crile with his Ivy League outfits and restrained manner, and the ebullient, eccentric Adams, full of rural mannerisms despite his own Ivy League heritage, often clad in a parka and lugging a duffel bag stuffed with his "traveling chronology." (The mobile version was smaller than the whole but still a formidable companion.)

But the men also had a great deal in common, sharing a personal determination to make public what they believed to be a dark chapter in American history. They became friends.

The participants in the order-of-battle controversy would never have stepped forward if it hadn't been for Adams, Crile said. The men trusted Adams because he, like them, had been part of the intelligence fraternity. They were glad to plug in the holes for Adams' "scholarly after-action report" and often had no idea how important their remarks were.

Also, with Adams involved in the documentary, "people knew you had the information on them. They knew I knew what they knew."

"But Sam was not always the most helpful person," Crile said. "His interest was somewhat indiscriminate. His dedication to the story was so intense . . ." that he sometimes caused witnesses to withdraw. Before the first interview attempt, when the men tried to persuade Morgan to go before the cameras, Crile told Adams that he would start the questioning and if Adams wanted to "hop in," he could. "When Sam hopped, however, he overstated the case," Crile recalled.

Before the screening for Colloff, Crile completed three more filmed interviews, all with former officers who could back up Adams' contentions.

In London, James Meacham, looking much more like an English aristocrat than a former Navy commander, repeated the anguished story he had confessed first in letters to his wife and then to Adams. Colonel Graham, he said, had instructed him and Colonel Weiler to alter data in MACV's computer after Tet.

"We didn't say no," he told Crile in the interview, which would later become part of the documentary. "I mean, this thing wasn't our private property. It belonged to the intelliigence directorate. We were the custodians of it. We didn't like what Danny Graham proposed to do. We didn't want him to do it. At the end of the day, we lost the fight, and he did it.

"Up to that tiime, even though some of the current estimates and the current figures had been juggled around with, we had not really tinkered with our data base. . . ."

Gains Hawkins described on camera how he had briefed Westmoreland on the higher enemy-strength figures in May 1967 and told of Westmoreland's shocked response. He confirmed his absolute agreement with Adams that the official troop estimates had been too low, saying, "There was never any reluctance on my part to tell Sam or anybody else who had a need to know that these figures were crap, they were history, they weren't . . . worth anything."

As the CBS cameras moved in tight on the balding former colonel's face, Hawkins said, "I am a staff officer, and I defended the command position. I did it in full knowledge, and if there's any—if it was immoral or illegal or reprehensible, the fault is here. It doesn't go anywhere else. I defended the—the command position on the figures."

Crile already had Hamscher saying the orders had come from Westmoreland, and the next interview subject, MACV's top intelligence officer, General Joseph McChristian, also laid the responsibility for any statistical deception squarely on the commander of U.S. forces in Vietnam.

McChristian, who had been Hawkins' boss in 1967 and, like Westmoreland, was a product of West Point's Long Gray Line, said he, too, had briefed Westmoreland. "When General Westmoreland saw the large increase in figures that we had developed, he was quite disturbed by it. And by [the] time I left his office, I had the definite impression that he felt if he sent those figures back to Washington at that time, it would create a political bombshell."

McChristian told Crile that Westmoreland had refused to accept his analysis and held up the cable due to "political considerations."

After a discussion of the maximum figure Westmoreland allegedly had ordered his officers to stay below, Crile asked the steely general, "To put a ceiling on enemy strength estimates . . . what does that constitute, sir?"

"From my point of view, that is falsification of the facts," McChristian replied.

George Crile persisted with this line of questioning, asking, "Are there statutes in the Uniform Code of Military Justice that would speak to that situation?"

McChristian's answer was the ultimate jab at a former cadet.

"Not that I'm aware of," he said in measured tones. "But there's something on a ring that I wear from West Point that the motto is: 'Duty, Honor, Country.' It's dishonorable."

The excerpts from the collection of often emotional interviews came across as raw and powerful when Colloff, Stringer, and Wallace screened the presentation reel in the last week of March 1981.

So far, Crile had delivered what he promised. He had produced some of the whistle-blowers on camera. The network brass gave him final approval for "The Uncounted Enemy: A Vietnam Deception" with a possible air date in September.

As Crile, Adams, and Wallace set out to interview the remaining accusers, in addition to the military and government leaders who disagreed there had been any deception, film editor Ira Klein searched through thousands of feet of TV footage from the 1960s. He would eventually create a collage of helicopter shots, student demonstrations, war scenes, and political speeches to intersperse with the interviews, illustrating the mood of the times.

The mood of the documentary unit, meanwhile, was upbeat. Colonel Russell Cooley, who had been reluctant to go on camera, finally relented and delivered a compelling performance. After telephone conversations with Mike Wallace and Crile, Westmoreland agreed to an interview on Saturday, May 16. And Sam Adams, despite a penchant for lengthy explanations, told his story with brevity and force in his May 12 session with Wallace.

Crile, in his excitement, wrote Wallace a memo, saying, "The Adams interview was not only a terrific interview. It looks beautiful. Now all you have to do is break General Westmoreland and we have the whole thing aced." Crile went on to enumerate "the areas where Westy seems to be guilty as hell and where you should direct your energies." But the producer cautioned Wallace against immediately confronting the general with Adams' charges. "I think that we should avoid at all costs casting the interview as a Westmoreland vs. Sam Adams affair."

Wallace essentially followed a pre-set battle plan, firing off question after question that Crile had outlined for him. The cameras closed in so tightly on Westmoreland that his eyes, nose, and mouth often filled the entire frame. The general faltered with his answers. His face reddened and his tongue darted nervously over his lips as Wallace framed yet another question. He was clearly rattled.

(In a 1985 interview, Crile defended the camera style, saying: "Every interview was done the same way. Every interview had the same closeness. Every interview had the same lighting. Not the exact same lighting but the same intended lighting. And probably the largest reason why the documentary was so harsh on Westmoreland is because of the way he looked. You see, the kind of intensity you get that makes you feel good about a person up close, like Gains Hawkins, can do the opposite if the person is looking uncomfortable. No one will ever shoot with less-tight closeups. It doesn't make sense. . . . If you're talking to someone who is talking about something that is important to them—an artist, a composer, describing the moment when 'Summertime' came to him, how he sat at the piano—if your cameraman did not have that shot tight, you would kill him. Because you would deny not just the emotion, you would deny the creative message he was giving you.")

Westmoreland explained that he had doubted Hawkins' estimate because it included villagers that might not be capable of combat, saying, ". . . in my opinion it was specious." Asked why he had refused to forward McChristian's May 1967 report of a larger foe, he conceded, "I didn't accept it because of political reasons. . . ." Pressured to explain other officers' charges that the official estimate had been arbitrarily slashed, he said, ". . . who actually did the cutting, I don't know. It could have been my—my chief of staff. I don't know. But I didn't get involved in this personally."

Whatever Westmoreland said, he looked guilty. Crile, who had never expected the interview to proceed so dramatically, said later that "it changed the course of the show."

"The interview was a classic," Crile wrote Wallace in a memo following the encounter. "It keeps growing in my mind. I don't think you could have possibly done a better job; I certainly know no one else could have. It was wonderful having you as our champion." He suggested that they book an interview right away with Danny Graham and try to get former Defense Secretary Robert McNamara to talk as well.

Graham, as expected, flatly denied the charges.

"I never blocked any reports," he said. "Nobody that I know of blocked any reports. If anybody had blocked information going forward, it would have been me. But I never blocked any information going forward. I'm not that dumb."

Asked about Meacham's accusation that Graham had ordered his men to tinker with the MACV data base, he said, "Oh, for crying out loud. I never asked anybody [to] wipe out the . . . computer's memory. . . ."

By this time, Crile said, the project had gained enough momentum that Sam Adams was no longer a major factor in convincing anyone to appear. With some potential witnesses, in fact, Adams was the problem that had to be overcome. His interrogation methods sometimes backfired—particularly when the two men visited Cooley to try to get him on film.

"Sam likes to know where somebody sat in the room, what kind of haircut they had, who got travel orders at the same time," Crile said. "Each question had the same importance. Cooley announced something innocuous and I heard a loud thump. It was Sam as he reached for his chest, pulled out his pen, and started to ask questions, quite out of control, rapid-fire."

Crile said he won Cooley's confidence and participation only after Adams turned in for the night.

Retired CIA Vietnam expert George Allen, who had refused to cooperate with Adams' *Harper's* article, told Crile, "I'll end up looking like a whistle-blower. I'm not." He did not want to do anything to hurt the CIA. But, like the others before him, Allen eventually felt "the burden of his public responsibility," Crile said. "All of them had a weight on their shoulders."

Thus, Allen agreed to be interviewed, saying on camera that the guerrilla-militia forces Westmoreland and Graham had dismissed as "women, children and old men" were "an integral part of the military potential of the Communist forces in South Vietnam. . . . They were the ones that ambushed our forces when they would enter VC-controlled areas. They were the ones who booby-trapped. They were the ones who helped the populace in general build the pungy stakes and other devices that inflicted losses on our forces. . . . They did have military potential. . . ."

The documentary, from Crile's perspective, was proceeding smoothly, perhaps even better than expected. But, at some point in the process, there began to be problems with Ira Klein.

"When we got going, I didn't think he was very good, for my way of working, at least," Crile recalled. "I do a lot of trial and error and I like a person who has opinions. . . . Ira was not responsive. He was introverted, didn't talk. He just didn't have much confidence, he wasn't used to this sort of thing. And very, very slow. Deathly slow."

At the beginning of August, Crile took off to Miami to do reports on the CIA and the drug trade for the "Evening News," leaving Klein to work alone with Zigman, looking for historical footage for "The Uncounted Enemy." "He panicked," Crile said. "He sat there, not doing anything other than getting paid. He wanted to do a good job and he felt time was running out."

Klein, however, thought the problem was Crile.

The film editor was convinced that Sam Adams was totally obsessed, a man who had lost all perspective. And he was beginning to believe that George Crile, in his drive to prove a conspiracy, had lost his journalistic balance. Klein later charged that Crile had coached Adams before Adams' session with Wallace. He complained Crile allowed George Allen—a reluctant witness—to come into the editing room to view film of other interviews, then questioned him a second time, in violation of CBS policy.

Wallace interviewed former National Security Adviser Walt Rostow, who said President Johnson had been well aware of the North Vietnamese troop buildup preceding Tet (although not in the magnitude discussed by Gattozzi, Cooley, and Hawkins), but none of the session would be included in the documentary. Klein later contended that Rostow and other officials were excluded because their testimony contradicted what Crile had set out to prove. He also blamed Crile's absence from the office for his own slow progress in melding the elements of the broadcast.

Crile said he eventually stopped trying to talk with Klein, and when the film editor insisted he needed help to finish the project, Crile agreed with relief. Another editor, Joe Fackovek, whom Crile described as a thorough professional, was brought in to assist in guiding the documentary to completion.

Network officials who screened the show in October and November were "overwhelmed" by what they saw. Crile's first solo documentary would air January 23, 1982.

At 9:30 p.m. that Saturday night, a burst of gunfire shattered the jungle quiet and Vietnam battle scenes flickered across the monitors at CBS affiliate stations. Mike Wallace faced his television audience and launched into the brief introduction designed to hook viewers before the first commercial break: "The only war America has ever lost. The war in Vietnam reached a dramatic turning point fourteen years ago this month . . . ," he said, going on to describe the Tet Offensive as a puzzle to Americans who were being told the enemy was running out of men.

The seasoned correspondent then spoke the sentence that would haunt CBS for the next three years:

"The fact is that we Americans were misinformed about the nature and the size of the enemy we were facing, and tonight we're going to present evidence of what we have come to believe was a conscious effort—indeed, a *conspiracy* at the highest levels of American military intelligence—to suppress and alter critical intelligence on the enemy in the year leading up to the Tet Offensive. . . ."

3.

One Man's Honor

ON the Thursday before the broadcast, retired General William Childs Westmoreland was sitting in the living room of his Charleston, South Carolina, home, eating breakfast and paying only scant attention to a nearby television set tuned to the CBS news show "Morning with Charles Kuralt and Diane Sawyer." The first light of day was filtering in through the double French doors that led to the backyard garden. From his seat, he could see the salmon-hued stucco carriage house that served as his office, a marvelous clutter of current paperwork and memorabilia from a forty-year military career. The top of the baby grand piano behind him was crowded with assorted photographs from a four-star Army family: brides and ancestors next to shots full of flags and former Presidents. Around the corner, in the entrance hall, stood the bronze bust of Westmoreland as *Time* magazine's 1965 "Man of the Year." The entire room—a comfortable mélange of various furniture styles, floral fabrics, and Asian accessories—held bits of the history of the man who led U.S. forces in the first half of the Vietnam War.

But as he sat ramrod straight in his cane armchair, Westmoreland wasn't thinking about Vietnam. He had virtually forgotten the irritating interview with Mike Wallace. His mind was on a more immediate maneuver: scooping a banana slice from his bowl of cereal and preparing to drink his coffee and orange juice.

When Sawyer began talking about a documentary the network planned to air on Saturday, however, he quickly lost his appetite. Mike Wallace and George Crile were on hand, she said, to discuss "The Uncounted Enemy: A Vietnam Deception," which showed that "the American government in Washington was deceived about the enemy in Vietnam. Specifically, in 1966 and 1967, deceived about how vast their numbers were." The U.S. military command, she said, had been behind the deception.

Suddenly, Westmoreland's own face filled the TV screen in an excerpt from the upcoming program. He saw himself—eyes full of confusion and nervously licking his lips—explain to a relentless Wallace that he had refused to accept General McChristian's higher troop-strength estimates "because of political reasons . . . because the people in Washington were not sophisticated enough to understand and evaluate this thing. And neither was the media."

The interview-advertisement went on for almost fifteen minutes. Sawyer asked questions of the producer and chief correspondent and they replied, using film clips to make their point, that Westmoreland had ordered strength estimates kept below a ceiling of 300,000. The promotion ended with Wallace saying, "Prior to Tet, according to Westmoreland, there were 224,000 men available to the enemy. He claimed 50,000 had been killed, of that 224,000, during the first four weeks of Tet. Three-to-one wounded to killed is the ordinary ratio. Question: If that is so, who were we fighting after Tet? Everybody was gone. And yet he asked for 206,000 more troops to fight a phantom enemy."

Sawyer thanked Wallace and Crile, saying, "We're going to be watching Saturday night." The segment ended, but Westmoreland continued to stare in disbelief, frozen by what he had heard and seen.

"I was absolutely shocked," he recalled. "I just about fell off my chair. I couldn't believe it. Diane Sawyer had venom in her voice. I started thinking at that time in terms of a press conference."

Westmoreland immediately called his good friend Dave Henderson, a Washington, D.C., public-relations executive with whom he had been planning to go goose hunting on Maryland's Eastern Shore the following Monday.

"He said that he had just seen the morning broadcast on CBS news and it appeared that the documentary was going to attempt to make him look like a criminal," Henderson later testified. "He was quite disturbed and upset, somewhat at a loss as to what to do about it."

Henderson said he dismissed one of Westmoreland's ideas— writing an article to "set the record straight"—as "too little, too late." Instead, he recommended holding a press conference as soon after the broadcast as possible, although the general confided that he "didn't have the means to do it."

"I did," Henderson said. "I said, 'I do, and I will—pro bono.' " Henderson, a tall, soft-spoken gentleman with the slightest trace of a drawl from his Kentucky boyhood, also recommended that they put off the goose hunt until the next season.

Later that day, Westmoreland agreed to let Henderson, a partner in the firm Alcalde, Henderson & O'Bannon, handle the counterattack. But he insisted on paying out-of-pocket expenses. By Friday, Henderson had reserved a room at the Army-Navy Club, hired a video company to tape the documentary, and sought advice from a friend, retired General Harold Johnson, who had preceded Westmoreland as chief of staff of the United States Army.

Before the program aired, there was another promotion on the CBS news. TV sections in newspapers across the country carried a bold ad showing a faceless coven of military men seated at a table imprinted with the large black letters: CONSPIRACY.

"CBS Reports reveals the shocking decisions made at the highest level of military intelligence to suppress and alter critical information on the number and placement of enemy troops in Vietnam," the ad said. "A deliberate plot to fool the American public, the Congress, and perhaps even the White House into believing we were winning a war that in fact we were losing. Who lied to us? Why did they do it? What did they hope to gain? How did they succeed so long? And what were the tragic consequences of their deception?"

Westmoreland, although well warned that the documentary had "lynched" him, elected not to watch it on TV. Instead, he attended a long-scheduled social event, the Alfalfa Club's annual black-tie dinner in Washington. But during the next two days he became intimately familiar with CBS's charges against him as he read through the transcript of the show to select sections to replay and rebut at the news conference.

His anger grew as he compared what he came to call "the Saturday-night massacre" with his memory of the interview with Wallace. He knew he had come across poorly on camera, but "I thought that I answered Wallace's questions," he said. "I shut out any [conspiracy] thesis that they might have. . . . The full transcript of my remarks was far different than the thrust of what they showed on the broadcast."

But the editing was only part of the story. The documentary also quoted former officers from his command, some of them from Westmoreland's alma mater, the United States Military Academy. They were accusing him of being *dishonorable*, delivering a direct hit to the center of his being. Westmoreland took the inscription on his 1936 West Point ring—"Duty, Honor, Country"—quite seriously.

His father, James Ripley Westmoreland, whose small bank in the cotton-mill town of Pacolet, South Carolina, was the only one in the county to survive the Great Depression, had often counseled him that duty is "the sublimest word in our language." The quote, from a letter Confederate General Robert E. Lee wrote to his son Custis, a West Point cadet, was no coincidence. Westmoreland came from a grand

Southern tradition and was "born to be a general," his historians say, although his father was not a soldier. The family had fought in the Civil War and some members had never quite accepted the outcome. Westmoreland, who jokingly refers to the conflict as "the first war of Northern aggression," recalled in his memoirs feeling some trepidation about telling his great-uncle, a former Confederate soldier, that he planned to attend West Point, alma mater of Northern Generals Grant and Sherman. "That's all right, son," his uncle said after a long silence. "Robert E. Lee and Stonewall Jackson went there too."

"Westy"—as his friends and troops call him—loved the military, loved West Point, idolized the World War I commander General John J. Pershing, and admired General Douglas MacArthur (the Army's chief of staff when Westy was a cadet), who referred to the academy as "the soul of the Army." MacArthur, who later distinguished himself even further in World War II and Korea, told the graduating class during Westmoreland's first year that the military code taught at West Point "has come down to us from even before the age of knighthood and chivalry. It will stand the test of any code of ethics or philosophy."

Westy took MacArthur's words to heart.

"An officer corps, my West Point education emphasized, must have a code of ethics that tolerates no lying, no cheating, no stealing, no immorality . . . ," Westmoreland later wrote in *A Soldier Reports*. ". . . If an officer corps is to serve the nation as it should, firm dedication to a high moral code must always be the goal."

He learned that the veracity of an officer's word was without question. He considered other officers absolutely trustworthy until proven otherwise. And his trust in the loyalty and judgment of other West Point-trained officers was unswerving.

First captain (the senior cadet officer) of his graduating class, Westy finished 112th out of 276 in academics at West Point, but ranked eighth in tactics—a natural leader. Flying grabbed his passion, but a slight vision defect led him to develop his battle expertise in artillery, and by the time the United States entered World War II in 1941, he had advanced to captain. He started out commanding an artillery battalion that fought Rommel in North Africa and Sicily, headed for France via Utah Beach in Normandy in 1944, and by the end of the war rose to the rank of full colonel, chief of staff of the 9th Infantry Division in Germany. He met the Russians on the Elbe and sent patrols into Potsdam.

Back in the states in 1946, he finally got airborne, commanding parachute troops at Fort Bragg, North Carolina, and by the Korean War he was commanding the 187th Airborne Combat Team. Westy was known for always picking up his chute from the same pile as the enlisted men, and his fame among his troops spread further several years later when, during a training maneuver with the 101st Airborne at Fort Campbell, Kentucky, sudden wind gusts killed seven men on a parachute jump. Westmoreland, by this time a major general, was dragged in the mishap and thereafter jumped first to test wind conditions personally.

Westmoreland's career was almost as flawless as his belief in the military code. He had rows of battle ribbons; had known the most famous American generals—Eisenhower, Patton, Pershing, MacArthur; taught at the Command and General Staff College and the Army War College; became a brigadier general at thirty-eight and the Army's youngest two-star general at forty-two; was secretary of the General Staff; as part of his Pentagon assignment took management courses at Harvard Business School (at the same time Sam Adams was toiling away as an undergraduate); and in 1960 returned to West Point as superintendent, overseeing the cherished academy that had given him the credo that had carried him through two wars.

He was disciplined only twice in forty years—once, as a second lieutenant at Fort Sill, Oklahoma, in the 1930s, for failing to pay his commissary bill on time, and in Hawaii several years later for going twenty miles an hour in a ten-mph zone. "I was caught three consecutive times speeding, if you can call it that, by the Military Police," he recalled. "My regimental commander called me into his office and he dressed me down and said he was going to ground me or take my car away from me for a month, which he did."

When Westmoreland assumed command of all U.S. forces in South Vietnam in July 1964, he transplanted his textbook code of ethics to the jungles. He directed his men always to carry written rules of conduct toward civilians. His officers were given fifteen additional directives, printed on a card he distributed in July 1966. Topping the list was this command: "Make the welfare of your men your primary concern, with special attention to mess, mail and medical care."

Despite Westmoreland's best efforts, of course, Vietnam turned into a disorderly and disappointing war, unlike any other ever fought by the United States. Besides the unusual tenacity of a foe, a daunting 900-mile hostile front, and tactical limitations imposed by politicians, diplomats, and previous treaties, it was the first war without press censorship and the first to be covered by television news. It was fought in the living rooms of America. "Considerations were given to press censorship and they were ruled out," Westy said. "I did not approve at the time of the initiation of press censorship." He later wrote that it was "my duty, in view of the controversy surrounding the war and the critical nature of news reporting, to explain to the press and on television how and why we did things the way we did."

Eventually, however, he had some second thoughts. Westmoreland loved his troops and was proud of them, calling them "magnificent" and saying "a commander could have had or expected no more than they gave." Likewise, most of the men greatly admired their leader, in part because he constantly traveled throughout the country to be with them, despite the danger. On those trips, Westmoreland became disturbed by what many of them told him. Despite the mighty effort the military and the White House eventually put into trying to manipulate press coverage, he said, "They never thought—and I got this everywhere I went—they were getting a fair shake from the media."

Westmoreland also was convinced that his command was not getting a fair shake. His disgust with television news in general and CBS in particular peaked on February 27, 1968, when anchorman Walter Cronkite, after a trip to Vietnam, delivered his personal appraisal of the Tet Offensive and the expected battle at Khe Sanh.

" . . . It seems now more certain than ever that the bloody experience of Vietnam is to end in a stalemate," Cronkite said. " . . . To say that we are closer to victory today is to believe, in the face of the evidence, the optimists who have been wrong in the past. To suggest we are on the edge of defeat is to yield to unreasonable pessimism. To say that we are mired in stalemate seems the only realistic, yet unsatisfactory, conclusion."

Cronkite concluded his commentary by saying, " . . . the only rational way out then will be to negotiate, not as victors but an honorable people who lived up to their pledge to defend democracy, and did the best they could."

The report was a shock to Westmoreland, who considered Tet a decisive U.S. victory. In the general's view, Cronkite was not demonstrating great insight and vision. Rather, he was so powerful that his words became self-fulfilling prophecy. Westmoreland wrote in his memoirs, " . . . Press and television would transform what was undeniably a catastrophic military defeat for the enemy into a presumed debacle for Americans and South Vietnamese, an attitude that still lingers in the minds of many."

Westmoreland retired in 1972, but his uneasiness about the media persisted. By the time the U.S. involvement in Vietnam ended, he was horrified by America's perception of the war and the plight of returning veterans. The general set out on a one-man public-relations mission. He appointed himself spokesman for the war.

"I said to myself, who has had more experience in this arena than I? [General] Abrams maybe, but Abrams was dead. . . . Who can speak out on behalf of those who gave the Vietnam War their best, particularly the enlisted men? Who is in a better position to try to straighten out the record? Me. Who else? McNamara could have done it but McNamara chose not to.

"So, I said, 'I'm going to be the champion and I'm going to talk.' I don't think I ever turned down an invitation to speak on Vietnam."

Westmoreland delivered some of the speeches before conservative groups and sympathetic audiences. But he also traveled unflinchingly into hostile camps, speaking on college campuses and addressing liberal organizations. "I was booed, I was hissed and everywhere I went there were placards telling what a bad person I was. But I took it. It was a price I had to pay."

Many criticized his mission, saying Westmoreland was either naïve or merely eager to improve his historical status, but his former troops seemed to appreciate the tireless effort to explain a war like none other ever fought—with soldiers averaging nineteen years old, one-year tours of duty, no fixed front lines, and the ever present specter of television. On the November 1982 weekend the Vietnam Veterans Memorial was dedicated in Washington, D.C., the architects and engineers of the unpopular war stayed well out of sight. Westmoreland, however, spent hours visiting the hotels mobbed with thousands of his former soldiers. They pressed forward solemnly to shake Westy's hand. Clad in mufti but every inch a general, he offered words of encouragement and praised the disabled. (By this time he had filed his lawsuit, and many of the men shouted, "Get CBS!")

Westmoreland arrived two hours early for a parade before the dedication and spoke with almost all the units assembled in the marshaling area. "Most of them wanted me to march with them," he recalled. "I said, hell, I'm not going to march with you guys. And they said, general, why in the hell aren't you marching with us? Well, I said, I'm going to march with Alabama. Why by damned do you want to march with Alabama? And I said, they're leading the parade and I'm going to lead them." The men cheered.

The dedication of a statue at the Vietnam Memorial in November 1984 was a more organized affair. President Reagan spoke and the participating politicians and military officials were segregated from the masses by double fences, metal-detectors, and police patrols. Westy, however, wandered deep into the crowd, greeting former grunts on his way to visit the polished black wall bearing the names of almost 58,000 fallen soldiers, including his brother-in-law.

Westmoreland's devotion to his educational mission impressed the equally "obsessive" CBS consultant Sam Adams. "We're really quite a lot alike," Adams said.

The general later admitted, somewhat ruefully, that it was probably his willingness to speak out on Vietnam that encouraged George Crile to pursue his documentary, which would have taken a much different shape without Westmoreland's participation.

It was Mike Wallace who first contacted Westmoreland about the show.

"He said that CBS was doing a special program on Vietnam and to give it authenticity, he would be very grateful to me if I would help them with the program," Westmoreland later said in court. "I asked him a few questions. I said, is this going to be a '60 Minutes' type program? And he said, oh, no, this is going to be an educational and objective program."

Westmoreland liked Mike Wallace, who he believed was an honest reporter. The correspondent had traveled with him briefly in Vietnam and at one point during the war had checked out a rumor involving the general's wife. In Hong Kong, a Chinese businessman of dubious reputation apparently had told Wallace he had entertained Westmoreland's wife at a dinner party aboard his yacht. When Westmoreland said there was no truth in the rumor, Wallace abandoned his story. "There are reporters who wouldn't have bothered to check that out," Westmoreland said admiringly. "I didn't think that Mike would double-cross me."

The general said George Crile called somewhat later and essentially repeated what Wallace had said, never mentioning Sam Adams, Russell Cooley, Gains Hawkins, George Hamscher, General Joseph McChristian, or the order-of-battle controversy.

"I had no forewarning that they were going to talk about that. I was misled as to the thrust of the program. [Crile] told me he was going to write me a letter that would outline the areas [to be covered in the interview], and time went by and I never received a letter."

The letter, which Crile said he read to the general during the forty-five-minute telephone conversation, was waiting for Westmoreland at the Plaza Hotel when he arrived in New York City on Friday, May 15, the night before the interview.

"Using the Tet Offensive as a jumping off point," Crile wrote,

we plan to explore the role of American intelligence in the Vietnam War: how well did we identify and report the intentions and capability of the enemy we were facing.

Among the questions we will be considering:

1. Did American intelligence adequately predict the Tet Offensive and the nature of the attack? Were those with the need to know adequately alerted? Were we surprised by the scope and timing of the attacks?

2. Was the Tet Offensive an American victory or defeat? Why did so many Americans consider it a defeat when most military men claimed it was a major victory? How should we think about this critical event?

3. Did the press present a reliable picture of the enemy we faced and the state of war?

4. What about the controversy between CIA and the military over enemy strength estimates?

5. What are the differing views of the enemy and progress in the war as seen by Lyndon Johnson, Dean Rusk, Robert McNamara, [CIA Director] Richard Helms, Walt Rostow and of course, Gen. William C. Westmoreland?

We will, of course, want to discuss other areas as well, such as the anti-war movement and the pressures that anti-war sentiment placed on those responsible for making decisions about the war. But the focus will be on the performance of American intelligence during the war. . . .

Earlier in the week, following the phone conversation with Westmoreland, Crile had written Wallace a memo about the upcoming interview, hinting that the general might not be fully prepared for what CBS was planning.

" . . . He didn't complain about any of our proposed areas of interest," Crile wrote. "He puzzles me—seems not to be all that bright. I spoke further with him about the strength estimate controversy. . . . He goes so far as to claim that Tet demonstrated to him that MACV itself had been exaggerating enemy strength estimates. . . . We have certainly covered our asses, technically at least. But I am a bit worried that he just doesn't understand that we are going to be talking to him about American intelligence, military intelligence during the Vietnam War."

Westmoreland indeed did not understand, for whatever reason. He readied himself for the interview by rereading his autobiography and stopping by the Army history office in Washington, D.C., to review the cables he had sent before the Tet Offensive. He did no research on the dispute over enemy troop strength.

Arriving for the session the next morning, Westmoreland began to sense what was ahead when he said hello to Mike Wallace. "He was rather cool . . . toward me, which was contrary to the way he had acted when I had met him in Vietnam."

Besides Wallace, assembled in the hotel room CBS had rented for the occasion were two cameramen, a sound technician, Crile, associate producer Joe Zigman, and Crile's friend and former co-producer

Grace Diekhaus. Sam Adams, who had attended the other on-camera interviews, was absent. Westmoreland did not learn of Adams' involvement in the project until sometime later.

Westmoreland said he also was unaware of the camera techniques being used. Many TV interviews are shot with only one camera, with the reporter's questions and reactions—if needed—filmed later and inserted at the appropriate point. For "The Uncounted Enemy," however, the CBS crew was using two cameras: one trained on the interviewer and the other on the interview subject. Westmoreland thought this arrangement was designed to switch back and forth to whoever was talking. In reality, every reaction of both men from start to finish was recorded.

The lights were very bright and the general felt his lips getting drier and drier.

"When Mr. Wallace was talking I didn't know I was on camera," he said. "And with my lips being very parched, they tended to dry out very rapidly, I was wetting my lips, preparing to answer Mr. Wallace's next question. I didn't know I was on camera in the process, but when Mr. Wallace was talking, the camera was always on me. . . . I didn't realize that until I saw the show."

Later, in court, Westmoreland joked that at least some good had come from the lip-licking debacle, saying, "My wife acquainted me with this wax stuff you put on your lips, which I have used ever since."

He did not joke about the way the interview unfolded.

The first question was about Tet, and Westmoreland agreed that the campaign was "a major turning point" because it led President Johnson to seek a negotiated settlement, primarily due to the press and the "false perceptions" it imparted to the American people.

Then Wallace zeroed in on the main topic: enemy troop strength. He asked Westmoreland about the killed-to-wounded ratio at Tet. If 30,000 or 40,000 Vietcong were killed, how many were wounded?

Westmoreland answered that the ratio was about three enemy wounded to every enemy killed, but later modified his answer, saying that "the three-to-one ratio is a very specious ratio" and "not an official ratio."

In March 1968, Westmoreland had said that some 50,000 enemy were killed during Tet. Wallace was using the three-to-one ratio to show that as many as 200,000 Vietcong could have been put out of commission in the campaign. If MACV's enemy-strength estimates just before Tet were correct, that would leave fewer than 25,000 enemy in the field although the war would continue another five years.

Westmoreland was getting nervous. Wallace seemed to have the wrong idea about the casualty ratio, and his subsequent questions about the strength estimates Westmoreland had refused to accept from Hawkins and McChristian in August 1967 were even more disturbing. The general began to feel that he was under attack.

"My first thought was to get up and walk out," he said. "But then I remembered those '60 Minutes' programs, where they'd show pictures of people walking out and that was always put in the context of guilt."

As the three-hour interview ground on, Crile was sitting behind Westmoreland, taking notes as Wallace reeled off the questions the producer had prepared for him. "On one occasion I saw him flashing a board on which he had something written . . . his advice to Mr. Wallace," Westmoreland recalled.

Eventually, the general got mad. "I realized that I was not participating in a rational interview, that this was an inquisition. And I also realized that I was participating in my own lynching," he said. "The problem was that I didn't know what I was being lynched about."

The questions about numbers continued. Wallace confronted Westmoreland with the charges from Hawkins and McChristian, grilling him about the alleged command decision to hold the order of battle below a ceiling of 300,000. Westmoreland tried—futilely, he felt—to interject that, in his opinion, after the Tet Offensive ended, it became clear MACV had in fact *overestimated* the size of the enemy.

Crile had not warned Westmoreland that his former officers had spoken out against him. During a break to change film, the general turned to the producer and spat, "You rattlesnaked me."

Westmoreland said he remembered complaints from a young CIA analyst named Adams, although, as he later explained, "Sam Adams was not a household word with me." He dismissed the CIA's analysis as that of "fairly low-ranking people 12,000 miles from the battlefield." He told Wallace that MACV's intelligence was superior. We "dealt with every village, every hamlet, every province as—as a— as a separate item. We didn't use extrapolation in order to come up with the figures." Then he repeated a familiar argument, insisting that many of the troops Adams and the others were concerned about were really civilians—old men, women, and young boys with no military capability. These protests would be included in the broadcast.

But the general's memory on exact figures was fuzzy. He volunteered to do more research and talk with Wallace again when his recollection was clearer. He gave Crile and Wallace the names of other officers who might know more about the numbers dispute, urging them especially to talk to General Phillip Davidson, who had served as his chief of intelligence after McChristian. But Wallace replied, "General Davidson is a very, very sick man." Sam Adams had told CBS that Davidson was a cancer patient, presumably terminal.

"I told Mr. Wallace time and time again an answer to the same questions, and of course my answers were ignored, and it was like a

broken record," Westmoreland said. "Time and again we would come
back to the same thing, and I realized that he and Mr. Crile had
orchestrated a scenario so that they would go for the kill. They wanted
to go to my jugular. It became very evident. I realized that I was
ambushed."

Back in the stucco office in Charleston's historic riverfront district, Westmoreland tore into action. He called Danny Graham and
rehashed the disastrous interview, warning him that Wallace was
likely to be calling to ask him also to go before the CBS cameras. He
dug up the cables, notes, and transcripts he had been unable to recall
in New York City. On June 6, he wrote a letter to Wallace and Crile.

"The session with you in New York City on Saturday, May 16,
was interesting . . . ," he said, but went on to add, " . . . It seems to
me that your researchers perceive intelligence as a much more precise
matter than it is in fact.

"If it is your purpose to be fair and objective during your quest,
which I must assume you intend to be, I suggest that you interview:
Ambassador Ellsworth Bunker, Mr. Robert Komer, Lt. Gen. Daniel
Graham, Gen. Walter Kerwin, Jr., Mr. George Carver (former) CIA
[the Agency director's special assistant on Vietnam] and Mr. William
Colby.

"Another individual is a colonel who was associated with Colonel
Hawkins whose name I believe was Morris. General Graham may be
of help in identifying him."

Among the documents Westmoreland included with the letter was
an official infiltration report from April 1968 and part of a transcript
from a November 1967 "Meet the Press" program. During the interview, Mike Wallace had asked about the level of infiltration in the
months preceding Tet and the general had responded, " . . . I would
say it was in the magnitude of about 20,000 a month. That's actually
—and this tempo started in the—in the fall and continued."

Wallace then had reminded Westmoreland that when he had
appeared with Ambassador Ellsworth Bunker on "Meet the Press" in
1967, he had told moderator Lawrence Spivak that the infiltration
rate was between 5,500 and 6,000 a month. Wallace had pressed the
general to explain the contradiction and Westmoreland had stam-
mered, "Sounds to me like a misstatement. I—I don't remember making it. But certainly I could not retain all these detailed figures in my
mind. . . . And—And—and if I—if I said that, I was wrong. I was
wrong."

In a note attached to the enclosures in the letter, Westmoreland
pointed out that his entire statement to Spivak was: "I would *estimate*
between 5,500 and 6,000 per month, but they do have the capability
of stepping this up." He also wrote that "there was always a time lag

of several months between actual infiltration and that confirmed by the MACV intelligence office. . . . As of November 1967, infiltration was carried on the running tabulation as 5,900. Hence my estimate given to Larry Spivak was generally correct. You will note in the tabulation that infiltration did not reach the 20,000 mark until January 1968."

When he wrote the letter, Westmoreland wanted CBS to correct his statements, but this time it was Crile who didn't understand. In a memo to Wallace, he wrote, "Westmoreland doesn't bring anything to our attention that is particularly relevant. Certainly nothing that causes concern and requires a new look at anything we have been asserting." The general had not specifically *asked* for a correction. Wallace had gone over the infiltration question six times during the interview and each time Westmoreland had repeated the 20,000 figure. As for the documents, Crile had already seen them all.

The producer answered the letter, thanking Westmoreland for his suggestions. But, except for Danny Graham, none of the people the former commander recommended were included in the finished show. Crile did interview Colonel Morris by telephone and traveled to Washington to talk to Carver just twelve days before the broadcast, but he and his colleagues never talked to General Davidson, who was far from being on his deathbed. Davidson had been seriously ill eight years earlier, but had survived and even remarried. Davidson later said he never received a telephone call or letter from CBS requesting an interview.

It was too late to include Carver in the documentary, but Crile's notes from the interview show that the CIA man who had "squared the circle," presumably caving in to MACV's alleged ceiling after meeting with Westmoreland in September 1967, thought both Danny Graham and Sam Adams were off the mark with their accounting. Carver told Crile that after Tet, "Graham was proven wrong because if his estimates were right, the enemy couldn't have mounted such an offensive. But if Sam were right, the enemy should have been able to mount a second offensive."

Another interview, conducted much earlier, could have buttressed part of Westmoreland's contention that no one withheld information from President Johnson. Walt Whitman Rostow, Johnson's national-security adviser, had told Wallace, "[Johnson] knew that starting in the autumn of 1967 that . . . the North Vietnamese regulars were infiltrating at a higher rate."

Asked about the guerrilla militia and political cadre, Rostow said Johnson had been well aware of the military debate "essentially about whether they had underestimated in the past the scale of that category." But he said neither he nor Johnson had been aware of any

MACV deception or any charge that there was an attempt to put a lid on estimates of enemy troop strength.

The documentary—already packed with other fragments of a complicated story told by many people—was getting too long, however. The Rostow interview was scrapped, with Crile informing the former Cabinet officer of the decision in a letter shortly before the program was aired.

Westmoreland was stunned after hearing Diane Sawyer's promotion for "The Uncounted Enemy," but he was furious as he worked on his rebuttal following the broadcast. Reading the transcript at Dave Henderson's Arlington, Virginia, office, he saw that the infiltration figure of 20,000 had been included in the show, without explanation. The quote from his long-ago interview on "Meet the Press" was also reprised, but the end of his sentence—"they do have the capability of stepping this up"—was missing. Reading on, he found that the program had included his statement about the three-to-one wounded-to-killed ratio, but omitted his later remark that the ratio was "specious."

As he prepared his presentation in the makeshift war room, Westmoreland was also on the telephone, talking to his former officers, asking them to stand up once again for their onetime commander. It would be a reunion of the Old Guard.

Danny Graham, the 1946 West Point graduate fingered by CBS as a "key conspirator," assisted in the hasty strategy sessions. So did General Walter "Dutch" Kerwin, who had been Westmoreland's chief of staff in Vietnam and had served as a deputy when Westmoreland was the Army chief of staff.

In a nearby office, Charles McDonald, a retired Army historian and friend of Westmoreland's who had helped him write his memoirs, worked to put together a press kit, assembling relevant documents from 1967 and 1968.

Gains Hawkins and General McChristian refused to attend Westmoreland's news conference, saying that CBS had accurately represented their viewpoints. But four former high officials besides Graham did join the emotion-packed, two-hour event: Vietnam Ambassador Ellsworth Bunker, Dr. George Carver, General Phillip Davidson, and his former assistant, Colonel Charles Morris.

Addressing the reporters assembled in the Army-Navy Club, Westmoreland accused the network of orchestrating "a vicious, scurrilous, and premeditated attack" on his character. The interview with Wallace, he said, was "a star-chamber procedure with distorted, false, and specious information, plain lies, derived by sinister deception—an attempt to execute me on the guillotine of public opinion."

Westmoreland's defenders followed his lead, one by one decrying the documentary. Danny Graham introduced the taped segments particularly disputed. Carver said it was he, not Westmoreland, who had decided that the troops in question be dropped from the order of battle.

Graham and Westmoreland demanded an apology.

The news conference went very well, in Westmoreland's opinion. Virtually every major paper in the country carried a story about it. There was no apology, but on the CBS "Evening News" that night, anchorman Dan Rather said the network's news operation planned to "give further study to the specific allegations made at the news conference." The next day, unknown to Westmoreland, network vice president Roger Colloff told George Crile to prepare a written response to the charges.

The silver-haired general was prepared to wait and see what the network would do. Shortly after the news conference, however, he got a phone call from Sally Bedell, who at that time was a reporter for *TV Guide*. At first, the general thought the magazine might want him to write an article detailing his side of the "Uncounted Enemy" story. Almost, but not quite, Bedell explained. She and a colleague had been commissioned to investigate the making of the documentary and prepare a major piece for the nationwide weekly.

Once again, Westmoreland chose to talk to the press.

4.

Attacks and Investigations

In the days following the broadcast and Westmoreland's counter-attack, as the general waited in vain for an apology from CBS, the Vietnam War monopolized the nation's editorial pages for the first time in a decade. Although America's TV viewers scarcely noticed "The Uncounted Enemy" (the show ranked seventy-ninth among seventy-nine prime-time programs that week), it kindled an instant emotional reaction within the press, which for years had been variously blamed for or credited with influencing the outcome of the conflict. *The New York Times*, well known for its reluctance to take television seriously, fired the first volley at Westmoreland. On the Sunday morning after the show aired, under the headline "War, Intelligence, and Truth," the newspaper of record said in an editorial:

> A CBS documentary on Vietnam last spring has surprising present pertinence. 'The Uncounted Enemy: A Vietnam Deception' showed that Lyndon Johnson was victimized by mendacious intelligence.
>
> Withheld from him was the fact that the Vietcong had twice the 285,000 troops he was told they had just before the 1968 Tet Offensive. Those 'captured documents' of which he boasted were in truth packed with accurate information—but the summaries he received were doctored. . . .
>
> What makes this report more than a matter of history is America's continuing preoccupation with guerilla war elsewhere, notably in Central America. El Salvador is not Vietnam and fortunately the United States' involvement is much more modest. But as policy is pitched to the strength

of rival forces there, the reliability of intelligence estimates is as important now as before Tet. . . .

. . . President Reagan would be well advised to protect himself by finding out how much Lyndon Johnson knew— and when he knew it—about the last war in its most crucial period.

William F. Buckley, Jr., hardly a liberal, said in a February 2 column published in the *Washington Post* that the program "absolutely establishes that General Westmoreland, for political reasons, withheld from the president . . . information about the enemy."

Robert Healy, in the *Boston Globe*, wrote that "Washington, Congress and the American people were misled" because General Westmoreland "could not deliver the bad news to a President who would not listen until it was too late."

Newsweek praised CBS for "trying to set the record straight," and Hodding Carter, Carter-administration State Department spokesman-turned-columnist, wrote in the *Wall Street Journal* of the military's "appalling lies" and warned against a similar situation in El Salvador.

A February 7 *Washington Post* article by Philip Geyelin praised CBS and painted even more comparisons with current intelligence issues in Central America.

The same day, however, *The New York Times* printed a reaction from the other side. The letter, from Walt Rostow, accused the newspaper of blindly swallowing CBS' version of the truth.

"The conclusion is false; and those who produced the documentary know it is false," he wrote. "President Johnson received directly and read voraciously the captured documents to which you refer—not summaries—as well as reports of CIA, State Department and AID [Agency for International Development] officers in the provinces; prisoner-of-war interrogations; intercepts; and all manner of other basic information. . . ."

Rostow went on to say Tet had been no surprise and that "President Johnson was fully aware of the Vietcong Order of Battle debate, at the center of the CBS documentary. . . . It was precisely because Order of Battle estimates were so inherently difficult that we relied on the widest possible range of intelligence, never on the Order of Battle numbers alone."

Rostow pointed out that when he was notified in writing on January 15, 1982, that his interview would not be used in the CBS documentary, Crile included these words: "We did not suggest that the enemy's attack at Tet came as a surprise to the White House or to the American military command."

"Whatever Mr. Crile's intention, your editorial writer and every other viewer of the documentary had the right to draw a contrary impression . . . ," Rostow said.

George Carver told the *Christian Science Monitor* that LBJ had been aware of the OB debates, and the *Washington Post* printed a similar rebuttal from General Maxwell Taylor.

In a February 5, 1982, article titled "The Hatchet Job on West-moreland," Taylor referred to the numbers argument as "relatively trivial" and expressed amazement "at how readily a man of Buckley's background accepted the substance of the hatchet job on Gen. William Westmoreland by Mike Wallace. . . .

"The fact is that I was quite aware at the time of the nature of the issue that has stirred up this rumpus, as were most of the officials in Washington watching over the situation in Vietnam," Taylor wrote.

Two days after the Rostow letter appeared in the *Times*, the paper printed a response from George Crile, who demanded that the former national-security adviser explain the lack of any official record of increased North Vietnamese infiltration in the months preceding Tet if, as Rostow had written, "Everyone concerned, including President Johnson, knew this."

As the letters attempting to shape public opinion flew, an opinion that would ultimately have a towering impact on those involved in the controversial documentary took form far from public scrutiny. Within the confines of CBS itself, at least one person began to believe Westmoreland. Ira Klein, the young film editor on "The Uncounted Enemy" who had clashed constantly with Crile near the end of the project, had done a little research. Convinced the show was riddled with major flaws, he started making noise.

Klein, an attractive, athletically built man from a middle-class Queens family, was technically a free-lancer who started working for CBS in 1978 as an assistant film editor. His career moved forward steadily and his colleagues praised him as sensitive, creative, and imaginative, but the chance to work on Crile's program was unde-niably a big break. Klein wanted to take a major role in shaping the show. A film editor, to Klein, was more than just a technician. He was an equal collaborator, a sort of co-producer. In shorter films for "30 Minutes," Klein worked as a partner with the producer. Any idea of being an equal with Crile, however, soon was dashed. Crile seemed to make most decisions unilaterally, often rejecting suggestions Klein considered important.

Recalling the months he had spent on the "Uncounted Enemy" team, the film editor said the relationship with Crile was strained almost from the first. In one of the early conflicts, while assembling the first act of the show, Klein urged Crile to include a quote from Westmoreland that explained why the general had doubted the estimates of enemy troops proposed by Colonel Gains Hawkins and General McChristian. During the interview with Mike Wallace, Westmoreland said he remembered the briefings, but had suspected the new numbers because they involved "a shade of gray. You get down at the hamlet level, and you've got teenagers and you've got old men who can be armed and can be useful to the enemy, and who are, technically, Vietcong." Crile told Klein to include only the general's confirmation that the meetings took place. (Klein stitched the full quote back in after Howard Stringer, the executive producer, screened the show and insisted on the change.)

The rift widened in July 1981, Klein said, after he read the full transcript of Crile's interview with Hawkins, a star CBS whistle-blower. Hawkins said Ambassador Robert Komer—President Johnson's "four-star civilian" in Vietnam—had appeared at some of the intelligence briefings. LBJ must have known about the numbers dispute, Hawkins said, because his special representative "was acutely aware of every figure that was being presented, every figure that was being accepted, every figure that was being rejected or not approved. Thoroughly, completely aware. And you must assume that he was reporting . . . to the White House. Else why was he there?"

Klein remembered that CBS News vice president Roger Colloff, in approving the documentary, had urged Crile to try to extend his investigation into the White House. This seemed proof positive. Klein said he strongly urged Crile to interview Komer, then asked him again and again if he had done it. "But he just ignored me" and "said he was talking to Komer's assistant."

Klein was disturbed, but not overly so, because Crile had told him that Colloff and Stringer were reading all the interview transcripts. The editor assumed the higher-ups were playing a major role in shaping the film and taking care of any problems.

When it became clear Crile had no intention of including any of the interview with Walt Rostow, who also seemed to be saying President Johnson had known all, Klein's uneasinesss turned to disbelief and near-panic. He shared his doubts with associate producer Joe Zigman, who, he said, urged him not to get involved. Months before, he had complained to "Ziggy" because Crile allowed George Allen to come into the editing room. Nothing came of that conversation, either.

Besides worrying about the premise of the show, Klein was concerned that the documentary was behind schedule. In September

1981, the program was only slightly more than half assembled. The CBS brass at one time had hoped to get it on the air in September. Klein started to wish he could just walk out on the project.

Crile, on the other hand, appeared anything but concerned. In August, he began spending much of his time down the hall from Klein's editing room, helping another CBS Reports producer, Maurice Murad, on a story about the Miami drug trade. Klein felt Crile was neglecting his duties as producer for a chance to appear in Murad's show as a correspondent. Often when Crile worked on "The Uncounted Enemy," his girlfriend and soon-to-be wife, Susan Lyne— also a producer but not a CBS employee—joined him in the editing room, occasionally offering suggestions. Klein came to consider Lyne's presence an intrusion and, ultimately, improper. He barred her from his editing room.

The situation worsened when Crile ordered Klein to trim away most of the opening sequence, which Klein had labored over for many hours, piecing together bits of stock footage from the CBS archives to create an artistic effect.

But the differences became irreconcilable when Howard Stringer put a difficult deadline on the project, saying he wanted to screen it in October. Klein recommended hiring another editor to help out and Joe Fackovek was brought in, but still Crile neglected his work. A few days later, Klein said, he confronted the producer, imploring him to concentrate on the documentary so the project could be finished.

By this time, Klein was vexed by more than Crile's work habits. He had read many of the interview transcripts and begun to seriously doubt the premise of the broadcast. "They contained no substantial evidence that Westmoreland was responsible for, or even a participant in, a conspiracy."

Klein believed Crile had ignored masses of critical evidence in molding the show. Events that had troubled the film editor earlier now took on larger significance. He remembered that while reviewing the sequence about the Hawkins and McChristian briefings, Crile had seemed transfixed by Westmoreland's image frozen on the TV monitor. Staring at the screen in the half-light, Klein said, the producer had repeated over and over, "I got you! I got you!" Crile's reluctance to interview Komer and other top officials who opposed Sam Adams' theory began to seem almost sinister.

But Klein said he was pleased Crile was teaming with Fackovek on the final acts. He credited himself with manipulating the situation to force Crile to get some work done. He did not report his concerns to the network hierarchy.

The event that shattered the documentary team's uneasy peace came on January 13, 1982, two days before transferring the finished show from film to videotape. Klein by this time was concentrating most of his efforts on a new project for another CBS producer, Kent Garrett. Crile was in Washington, D.C., and Sam Adams was reading the transcript of the program to check for errors. Adams uncovered two mistakes—misinformation in questions Mike Wallace asked in the last act—that made it unclear whether Westmoreland's responses were usable. Reading aloud from Commander Meacham's letters, Wallace inadvertently had included margin notes made by Crile and Adams. The consultant wanted to write a letter disclaiming responsibility if the errors were not fixed. Carolyne McDaniel, the production secretary who filled in as a researcher after Alex Alben left CBS in September 1981, was near hysteria, saying she also wanted to make such a statement.

Klein told her to wait until Crile returned. Later that day, however, he found McDaniel in an editing room, screening the errors for production manager Terry Robinson, Grace Diekhaus, and Phyllis Hurwitz. Angry, Klein insisted that the mistakes be pointed out first to Crile. Crile could decide how to correct them.

The film editor also wanted to discuss another matter with Crile. While complaining about the misquotes, Adams had dropped a real bomb. He said General Davidson, Westmoreland's intelligence chief who had replaced General McChristian in 1967 and was supposedly dying of cancer, was instead alive and well in Texas, "healthy as a clam." Adams had picked up this alarming tidbit a month before but apparently kept it to himself. Klein knew Westmoreland had urged Crile to interview Davidson. So had other officials. Davidson was a key figure in the numbers dispute.

Klein said that when he told Crile about Davidson, the producer had no comment. When he brought it up again, several days later, Crile again ignored him.

Crile had plenty to say, however, about how to fix the misquotes. He directed Klein to remove one sequence, but asked the editor to deal with the other problem by splicing in a "cutaway" shot while Wallace continued to read. The soundtrack would remain the same, but the quote would become a paraphrase. Viewers would be unable to tell Wallace was still reading from the letter.

Klein at first refused to make the second edit, calling it a "purely cosmetic change," a distraction instead of a correction and therefore dishonest. He said he was ready to complain to Andy Lack, who recently had been promoted to executive producer of CBS Reports, but backed down when Crile told him that Colloff agreed on how to handle the gaffe. After all, Colloff was the big boss. But two days later, when Klein prepared to insert the cutaway, his orders were changed again. Lack had found out about the problem and called a meeting with Colloff and Crile. Following the conference, Colloff decided the erroneous remark should indeed be removed. As Klein snipped away the offending sentence, what little confidence he had in Crile's judgment also vanished.

After the broadcast, Klein braced for the backlash. He was not surprised by Westmoreland's fiery rebuttal nor by Dan Rather's promise that the network would study the general's charges. But he was totally shocked when he viewed the videotapes CBS News made of Westmoreland's news conference.

Crile, under orders from Roger Colloff to prepare a written response to Westmoreland and the former officials, screened the tapes in Grace Diekhaus' office in early February. As Crile and Adams took notes, Klein and Carolyne McDaniel watched, with Klein growing more and more agitated.

George Carver's statement that he, rather than General Westmoreland, had initiated a compromise dropping the self-defense forces from the order of battle, was devastating, Klein felt. When Carver said this, Adams "slumped in his chair."

Klein was also surprised to hear Westmoreland say, "I wrote a letter to Mr. Wallace and Mr. Crile in which I enclosed several contemporary documents to correct my imprecisions. . . ."

"I had not seen or heard about any such letter," Klein later said under oath. "I asked Crile what General Westmoreland was talking about, but he ignored me."

After the screening, McDaniel showed Klein the letters and documents from Westmoreland. Later that afternoon, Mike Wallace called from Central America. "Crile came back after the call and said, 'Mike is really depressed,' " Klein said.

The developments disturbed the editor, but he didn't decide to act until the next day, when Adams blustered into the cutting room where Klein was working with Phyllis Hurwitz and announced, "We have to come clean, we have to make a statement that the premise of the show is inaccurate. LBJ had to know."

At that point, Klein said, Hurwitz rolled her eyes and left the room. "I replied to Adams, 'Sam, isn't it a little late? Why weren't you telling George about this all along?' Sam said that he had been trying to tell Crile all along."

Now Klein was convinced that Westmoreland had been unfairly accused. Someone must alert the network, he decided. Just like Adams, Crile, and Westmoreland, the film editor was sure that what he planned to do was right.

"I made a conscious decision, considered the negative aspects," he said. "Really, it was a moral choice. There was nothing to be gained on my part. I thought that through very clearly, prior to walking into

Andy Lack's office. I think nobody will understand unless they're placed in that position. [You have] to do something about something you perceive as a terrible injustice to another human."

Klein knew his future at CBS was on the line, but he didn't care. He gathered up his courage and his documentation and went in to talk to Lack, replacing Howard Stringer, now executive producer of the "Evening News." Klein told Lack about Westmoreland's letter, about Carver's statement at the news conference, and about Adams' conversation in the editing room. He suggested that someone outside CBS be brought in to investigate. The two talked for an hour, with Lack asking many questions but declining to examine any evidence. First, he said, he wanted Klein to discuss the problems with Crile.

Crile insisted that he and Klein talk to Colloff, but the film editor refused. Instead, he returned to Lack's office. This time, Lack read the Westmoreland letter. He also called in Judy Reemtsma, who had replaced him as senior producer of CBS Reports, and Mike Wallace joined the discussion, asking a few questions of his own. Wallace was particularly interested in knowing why Klein had not come forward earlier if he felt there were problems.

Klein recalled that as Wallace left the room he said, "Don't worry, at '60 Minutes' this kind of thing happens all the time," a scenario Wallace flatly denies.

Lack called Adams, who dismissed Klein's version of events, but he did not order an investigation. Despite what Carver said at the news conference, Westmoreland had already gone on record as being the one who cut enemy troop-strength estimates by refusing to include the guerrilla militia. In the documentary, the general had said to Wallace, "It's a non-issue. I made the decision. It was my responsibility. I don't regret making it. I stand by it. And the facts prove that I was right. Now let's stop it." And whether or not the letter from Westmoreland constituted a request for a correction was largely a matter of personal interpretation, Lack decided.

When Klein returned from vacation two weeks later, he was astonished. No investigation was under way. He returned to Lack's office with more complaints. He told Lack that Crile had taken George Allen into the editing room to screen interviews with other whistle-blowers: a clear violation of CBS policy. Lack seemed shaken by the news, but ordered no inquiry. The investigation Dan Rather mentioned on the night of Westmoreland's news conference likewise had not materialized.

After the third meeting with Lack, Klein gave up his crusade within the network. The hoopla over the broadcast seemed to be dying down. Crile's eleven-page report to Colloff, submitted while Klein was on vacation, was reviewed and filed away. It caused no stir.

If Klein had read the report, he would have found that it addressed such issues as the omission of the Rostow interview, one of his alleged complaints. Klein did not know, however, that Colloff had already reviewed the entire Rostow transcript and agreed the segment should be cut. This was not the only instance in which Klein had just part of the picture, Crile said. Much of what Klein said had happened at CBS in 1981 and 1982 bore only slight resemblance to events other members of the documentary unit remembered.

As a film editor, Crile said, Klein was not, as he imagined, a co-producer, and did not have access to enough information to judge whether the show was fair. He said Klein saw only five interviews, did not read entire interview transcripts, and had no knowledge of the many interviews that were not filmed. Klein never mentioned that Davidson was healthy. He sat in on only one Adams "chronology session." He was not involved in assembling the portion of the film that included Rostow. He did not urge Crile to interview Komer. He did not bar Susan Lyne from his editing room; she decided to stay away because Klein was so hostile. He made up the story about the producer saying "I got you" to Westmoreland's televised image. And he never verbalized his complaints about the project, at least not to Crile.

Crile said it was he who decided, on Stringer's recommendation, to bring in Joe Fackovek to edit the final acts.

"When I suggested it to Ira, it was a disaster," Crile said. "He was telling people all over that everyone in the industry was going to think it was because he couldn't do it. He took it as a slight, and he went into a funk. I should have fired him. He just simply went underground. Never said anything."

Crile said that after Fackovek was hired "I confronted Ira. I said, what is it? Come out with it. What's wrong? Obviously you're furious, but say it. . . ." Crile said Klein refused to talk, so he dealt with the problem by turning more and more of the work over to Fackovek.

"Obviously I did not handle Ira right. I think he felt attacked somehow at the core of himself when I decided to bring on a second editor to meet our deadline. He just flipped. He felt it was disrespectful and humiliating somehow. Ira developed an obsessive hatred for me, that's indisputable. But the cause had nothing to do with General Westmoreland."

Zigman did not think Klein saw Fackovek as a "reflection on his competence," but remembered that the film editor was "getting nervous, getting upset, becoming irritable" during this time. At one point he even urged Klein to resign out of concern for his health.

Klein never complained about the Allen interviews, Zigman said. "Ira wasn't upset about it. No one else seemed to be upset about it. It wasn't a secret. I never heard any complaints about the way the show was being produced or how the project was going along. I knew [Crile] was trustworthy, honest, a good reporter."

Joe Fackovek said he "was never once aware of George Crile being devious, secretive or unfair," although he was at times a formidable boss. The veteran of seventy-five one-hour documentaries, including more than twenty-five award winners, described the producer as "a digger, and at times difficult to work for. . . ."

As a result, Carolyne McDaniel said, Klein "lost his balance"—the same charge Klein repeatedly leveled at Crile—and developed "an overwhelming and obsessive hatred for George Crile."

"Indeed, Klein has told me personally of his desire to undermine Crile's career," she later revealed in an affidavit. She said Klein seemed to resent the producer's personality, his privileged background, and his hard-driving style of work.

"By the final weeks of the documentary's production, Klein's anger at George Crile had become more important to Klein than the final product on which we were working . . . ," she said. The film editor's behavior became "erratic" and "he almost seemed to be trying to sabotage the documentary."

She said that when she told Klein of the minor mistakes Adams had discovered in the show, the editor criticized her, saying "it was 'George's responsibility to find errors' and that I should keep the information to myself and let Crile take the blame for any errors."

For his part, Adams denied ever saying they had to "come clean" after the broadcast, pointing out that such a remark would be "completely out of character." Klein, it seems, had prepared a 16mm version of the documentary for Adams to show at Concord Academy, where he had been named Father of the Year.

"My prime purpose going into the room was to get this 16mm version of the film so I could show it at my son's school. . . . Why would I show a movie of the TV show if I thought it was so lousy? On the other hand I can't imagine Ira just making that end of the thing all up. What I imagine I was saying was what I was saying all the time . . . that it seemed to me there might have been higher-ups involved. . . . He probably extrapolated from that."

Adams admits, however, that he may have mentioned President Johnson. "I might have said it seemed to me that LBJ might have been involved too," although "now it doesn't look as if he knew a hell of a lot."

As for Davidson, Adams said he did not recall mentioning his whereabouts to Klein and noted he would never say "healthy as a clam" because the correct expression is "happy as a clam."

Although he had given up trying to persuade CBS to see things his way, Klein said he did ask Crile once again why he never interviewed Robert Komer (Crile eventually talked to Komer in late March 1982). During the conversation, Klein said, Crile asked if Klein planned to talk to the two reporters from *TV Guide* who by this time were frequent visitors to the eighth-floor offices as they interviewed more and more people associated with making "The Uncounted Enemy."

Klein said he asked Crile, "Are you afraid I'm going to talk?"

*   *   *

Sally Bedell and Don Kowet, the other *TV Guide* reporter, had already interviewed Crile in two grueling sessions. The producer was in Honduras on assignment for the "Evening News" when CBS called him back to New York to talk to the reporters. The network had ordered everyone to cooperate with Bedell and Kowet.

The reporters struck Crile as "kind of crazy . . . like a good-cop, bad-cop team." They were not interested in the substance of the broadcast or even its accuracy. They wanted to steer clear of the numbers debate. In their proposal to *TV Guide*, the two said they intended only to examine how the show was made and "was it fair?"

This made Crile nervous. Even if the focus was fairness, they should try to find out what kind of research backed up the show, he thought. "We invited them to go into our files if they would, which they didn't. To go through the stuff with Sam, which they didn't."

As the reporters worked on their story, CBS Reports began to return to normal. Letters praising and condemning "The Uncounted Enemy" slacked off and Colloff, who had been in charge of fielding complaints about the show, was able to concentrate on other duties. Crile continued his work on the Miami drug-trade report.

It was not until April that the network got a glimpse of what lay ahead. Bedell and Kowet were examining more materials than Crile suspected. And someone at CBS was cooperating with *TV Guide* more fully than the network ever planned. Bedell and Kowet knew about George Allen's two interviews. When the reporters contacted Allen, they asked him about the interviews he had screened. They asked Joe Zigman if Sam Adams had been rehearsed. And, unknown to Wallace and Crile, the *TV Guide* team had also managed to obtain transcripts of complete interviews for "The Uncounted Enemy."

The magazine reporters, as it turned out, had a mole inside the network who handed over a good deal of privileged material and would be identified in the resulting article only as an "unnamed source." But CBS officials were sure it was Ira Klein, the disgruntled film editor, who betrayed the network.

Klein readily admitted he was a primary source of information for a book Don Kowet later wrote, but said he never agreed to be interviewed for the magazine story.

"I had at least two [sources] for the *TV Guide* article," Kowet said. "That place [CBS] leaked like a sieve and it still does. There are a number of people that are discontented."

Phyllis Hurwitz, Klein's assistant, was one of Kowet's chief sources. Howard Stringer, in a supposedly off-the-record conversation which Kowet was secretly tape-recording, also gave the magazine quite a bit of ammunition.

Stringer, who had been working on a five-part documentary series, "The Defense of the United States," while "The Uncounted Enemy" was being made, stood by the conclusions of the program, but admitted to Kowet, " . . . I did not give this broadcast the attention I should have. . . . I didn't vet it enough." (He later testified that "under the circumstances I was able to monitor it closely.")

Even more important, Stringer revealed that the network had "suspicions" about Crile, saying their doubts had "been my nemesis for some time." But the veteran producer was ready to take all the blame. "Ultimately, if I agree with your piece, as tough as it is, it does devolve on me, because I should have known I wouldn't get fair journalism off him," he said.

Stringer added, " . . . I must say I don't feel desperately sorry, and this is an awful thing to say, because I think Westmoreland should have been fired years [ago]." (Kowet, who later championed Westmoreland in his book, *A Matter of Honor*, responded, surprisingly, "So do I.")

In another tape-recorded phone conversation, Alex Alben, the documentary unit's researcher, told Kowet, "This wasn't a conspiracy directed by Westmoreland up . . . it was a conspiracy directed by Rostow and the National Security Council staff with heavy pressure from Johnson to show progress down. . . .

"By just showing one side, our documentary was . . . headed out of focus. . . . Yes, some suppression took place, but no, it wasn't generated by Westmoreland. . . . He was merely maybe the major tool of it in, you know—in Southeast Asia."

The CBS employees and ex-officials were helpful, but the unedited interviews for "The Uncounted Enemy" were a bonanza for Bedell and Kowet. After reading the transcripts, the reporters pinpointed several segments of the documentary where they felt statements were misrepresented to make a stronger case for the conspiracy theory.

In the first act, there was a reference to May 1967, when Gains Hawkins and General McChristian presented higher enemy-strength figures to Westmoreland. From Mike Wallace's commentary and the

presentation of quotes from Hawkins and McChristian, it appeared
that both men were present at the briefing and that only one meeting
occurred. In his full interview, however, Hawkins said he met with
Westmoreland at least twice. McChristian, on the other hand, only
confirmed that he left a cable with the higher numbers on Westmoreland's desk. There could have been three separate encounters, the
TV Guide reporters surmised. By mixing the events together, CBS
seemed to imply that McChristian, as well as Hawkins, got "the
message" to keep the numbers below a specified ceiling.

In another segment, Colonel George Hamscher was wrongly
identified as head of the military delegation to the series of order-of-
battle conferences convened at the CIA's Langley, Virginia, headquarters in the summer and fall of 1967. General George Godding
was in fact the leader of the MACV contingent—the same group
Hawkins represented—arguing for lower numbers while secretly
agreeing with Sam Adams' higher estimate. Hamscher worked for the
Defense Intelligence Agency. The foul-up, *TV Guide* concluded, im-
peached CBS's proof that Westmoreland gave specific instructions to
suppress the numbers:

> WALLACE: CBS Reports has learned that Colonel
> Hawkins was in fact carrying out orders that originated
> from General Westmoreland. Westmoreland says he doesn't
> recall those orders. But the head of MACV's delegation told
> us that General Westmoreland had, in fact, personally in-
> structed him not to allow the total to go over three hundred
> thousand.
> CRILE: Wasn't there a ceiling put on the estimates by
> General Westmoreland? Weren't your colleagues instructed,
> ordered, not to let those estimates exceed a certain amount?
> HAMSCHER: "We can't live with a figure higher than so
> and so—"
> CRILE: Three hundred thousand . . .
> HAMSCHER: —is the message we got.

In another instance, a quote from Westmoreland apparently
chosen by Crile to bolster the conspiracy theory seemed, to the magazine reporters, out of context in the show. The general had said
" . . . who actually did the cutting, I don't know. It could have been
my chief of staff. I don't know. But I didn't get involved in this personally." The quote was included in a sequence about the August 1967
meeting at the narrow room of the Pentagon where the numbers were
arbitrarily slashed. After reading the complete Westmoreland inter-

view, however, *TV Guide* determined the general had been referring to a meeting in Saigon several months later.

Kowet and Bedell even uncovered information suggesting that the meeting in the narrow room of the Pentagon might have occurred in 1968—after the Tet Offensive—rather than in 1967, as the documentary said.

Interviews with Everette Parkins and other officers cast doubt on CBS's assertion in the documentary that the former lieutenant colonel was fired for losing his temper and shouting at his superior over MACV's refusal to send on reports of higher enemy infiltration. According to the book Kowet later wrote, when the *TV Guide* reporters talked to Parkins about the firing, he told them, "I didn't hear the story until I heard it from you."

In the documentary, Mike Wallace had said Parkins' Army career was destroyed by the incident. Parkins, however, remained in the same job for almost two more months and in the service for five years after the incident, which he told Kowet and Bedell was due to a "personality conflict" with his superior, Colonel Charles Morris. It was Morris, he said, who did the shouting.

Morris said Parkins had indeed been fired, but remembered the argument as being over ratios of killed-in-action to wounded-in-action rather than infiltration. Morris' deputy, Colonel Lew Ponder, had witnessed the incident and agreed with Morris' version.

After Kowet and Bedell interviewed Crile, they concluded that he had got his wires crossed in reporting the Parkins episode. "Morris had insisted, said Crile, 'that he fired Parkins for not agreeing to carry through a methodology that he wanted to be done,' " Kowet related in *A Matter of Honor*, offering the transcript of the interview to show what may have gone wrong:

> TV GUIDE: You didn't ask him what kind of "methodology," what he meant by that?
>
> CRILE: I told him that the explanation as offered by the other people was that it was in connection with infiltration.
>
> TV GUIDE: Did he tell you what the argument was over?
>
> CRILE: It wasn't exactly clear to me what he was talking about. He was talking about a methodology. He said, "I had given him orders to observe a certain procedure which he would not do, and anybody who doesn't observe an order gets fired."

The *TV Guide* reporters were building what they believed to be a mighty case against CBS.

"Originally we thought it was an either-or story (presenting both points of view, but letting the reader make a choice)," Kowet said. But "there seemed to be an enormous diversion" in the facts. The reporters decided to take a stand against the network. This was no small story, they concluded.

The magazine's editors agreed. They approved an eleven-and-a-half-page spread for the article, the longest in the publication's history. Although the piece was massive by *TV Guide* standards, it was too brief to use all the material Kowet and Bedell had accumulated. They decided to omit evidence related to the Parkins firing and several other episodes. The finished story, however, contained more than enough charges to worry CBS. Titled "Anatomy of a Smear: How CBS Broke the Rules and 'Got' Gen. Westmoreland," it was scheduled as the cover story for the week of May 29, 1982.

The magazine, as usual, hit the newsstands a week before its cover date and the timing could not have been more embarrassing for CBS. On May 23 in San Francisco the network convened its annual affiliates conference, where CBS big shots showed up to wow local station managers in an effort to rally support for network programming. The riveting headline on *TV Guide*'s cover, decrying CBS in inch-tall letters at every hotel newsstand, did not make the network's mission any easier.

Van Gordon Sauter, who only months earlier had taken over as president of CBS News, denied that the article created a significant stir at the gathering. "It was not a compelling issue," he said. Roger Colloff, however, acknowledged there were some shock waves, telling *American Lawyer*, "I wouldn't want to ascribe it a number on the Richter scale, but there was certainly a tremor. . . . "

The story made some twenty charges, concluding, among other things, that internal CBS News guidelines had been violated. It alleged that CBS set out to make the show already convinced there had been a conspiracy and ignored evidence that contradicted the theory. It said CBS agreed to pay Adams $25,000 without thoroughly checking out his story and rehearsed him before interviewing him on camera. It said Crile screened interviews for Allen, a sympathetic witness, and interviewed him again, but didn't offer the same advantage to hostile witnesses, most notably Westmoreland. Nine witnesses appeared on camera to back up Sam Adams' story and there were only two to defend Westmoreland.

The story said CBS "pulled quotes out of context" and "misrepresented the accounts of events provided by some witnesses while ignoring altogether other witnesses who might have been able to challenge CBS's assertions."

The *TV Guide* reporters had managed to contact Davidson and learned from his physician that the general had been in good health for some time. Davidson told them, "If the figures on enemy strength were going to be manipulated, I had to do it. . . . Westmoreland gave no orders about intelligence matters that didn't go through me."

Bedell and Kowet, digging into the 112-page transcript of the unused Rostow interview, pulled out the quotes about what LBJ had known before Tet. They also said Sam Adams "now doubts the documentary's premise of a Westmoreland-led conspiracy."

The story's concluding paragraph seemed to be aimed squarely at Sauter:

"The network's lapses in the making of this documentary also raise larger questions. Are the network news divisions, with their immense power to influence the public's ideas about politics and recent history, doing enough to keep their own houses in order? If this documentary is any evidence, then the answer may be no. The inaccuracies, distortions and violations of journalistic standards in 'The Uncounted Enemy' suggest that television news' 'safeguards' for fairness and accuracy need tightening, if not wholesale revision."

Despite Sauter's professed nonchalance, his reaction showed concern, if not alarm. He knew by this point that Westmoreland was at least considered filing a libel suit and that the magazine article could encourage him. Sauter immediately called a meeting with Gene Mater of CBS Broadcast Group, Ralph Goldberg, an associate corporate lawyer, and news-division vice presidents Colloff and Robert Chandler to discuss a possible in-house inquiry into the *TV Guide* charges. Despite Sauter's sensitivity to libel problems, he apparently failed to recognize that a sudden CBS investigation could lend more credibility to *TV Guide*'s charges. And any report generated by such an inquiry might even end up in a court of law as evidence against CBS. Nonetheless, Sauter determined that the investigation should be a purely journalistic one, unsullied by legal considerations. Burton "Bud" Benjamin, a respected senior executive producer of CBS News, would lead the effort with no lawyers participating. ("I fundamentally abhor lawyers," Sauter admitted.)

"As president of CBS News, I felt it imperative to determine if CBS News standards had been violated," he later testified. "CBS News places great emphasis on adherence to its procedural standards."

On the third day of the affiliates meeting, the new president, whose only involvement with "The Uncounted Enemy" had been screening it before it was aired, made a speech to the assembled station executives. He did not say CBS supported the documentary or its conclusions. He only announced that CBS would probe all the charges, point by point, and issue a report.

Some at CBS have since characterized the move as a novice

president's too hasty attempt to placate affiliates that may not have needed placating, but Sauter still stands by the decision to investigate.

"We had no alternative but to do the Benjamin Report," he said in a 1985 interview. "When such detailed criticism is brought forth, we have a moral responsibility to examine [and then] make those conclusions known to the public. . . . Our accountability is significant." Silence from CBS would have cast real doubt on the network's credibility—its stock in trade, he said.

Sauter considered doing the investigation himself. Then he considered naming Roger Colloff for the task. But in the end he appointed Benjamin, a journalist for forty years, partly because of his reputation and partly because of the time needed to do the investigation.

"Bud said it would be a difficult task, but he would do it, because it was important to CBS News that it be done," Sauter recalled.

In retrospect, however, Benjamin may not have been the best choice. He was honest. Of that there was no doubt. His reputation was absolutely impeccable. He had worked at CBS since 1957, guiding Walter Cronkite's "Evening News" broadcasts through the 1970s. But his experience with documentaries was limited to straight history, not the kind of investigative report Crile and Wallace had constructed. Howard Stringer and others said although they totally respected Benjamin's opinions, they often disagreed with them. Benjamin's single-minded devotion to CBS and its traditions could be likened to religious fundamentalism.

*   *   *

On July 3, Benjamin began his investigation, making the same rounds as Sally Bedell and Don Kowet. He started with Ira Klein, who immediately confirmed that Sam Adams had been prepared for his interview with Mike Wallace.

"I also told Benjamin about the Allen screening between his two interviews, and about the two errors Adams discovered in the show in January and how they were dealt with," Klein later said in an affidavit. "I explained . . . that I had attended what was clearly a rehearsal prior to Adams' taped interview.

"We talked about Alben not being replaced, about Susan Lyne being in the cutting room, about my telling Crile we needed to hire an additional editor and about Adams' statement to Garrett and myself after Westmoreland's press conference that the premise was inaccurate. I told Benjamin how difficult Crile was to work with and about the times I had complained to Crile with no result."

One issue Benjamin zoomed in on was the use of the word "conspiracy" in the broadcast. Although the word was uttered only once in the show, he seemed concerned that Crile had used it twenty-four times in his "blue sheet" and that newspaper ads and on-air promotions for the documentary contained the word.

In the *TV Guide* story, George Crile had been quoted as saying, "It was absolutely proper to use the word conspiracy. We went through everybody before we used the word. It was the only word that worked for me to explain the pattern of events."

Roger Colloff told Benjamin the word had been selected only after considerable discussion. "We talked about it [conspiracy] at my and Bill's [Leonard] screening. Is the use of the word justified? We concluded that it was. It wasn't done haphazardly. . . . "

Robert Chandler agreed, saying, "I wasn't terribly upset by the word. . . . If people said what Crile said they would, it fit the definition."

Sam Adams told Benjamin he had no doubt MACV's efforts to juggle the numbers had been a "legal conspiracy," but added, "I thought early on that conspiracy was too strong a word. . . . The ad was overblown. . . . I'm not knocking George's judgment. . . . To me it's a much more tragic story."

Benjamin discovered that the pro-Adams witness George Hamscher, in his interviews with Crile, had disagreed with the word "conspiracy." So had Joe Hovey, at least when it was used to describe his own part in the drama. And so had former CIA director William Colby and Danny Graham. At Westmoreland's news conference, George Carver had called it a "mistake to interpret differences of opinion as necessarily being any evidence of conspiracy. . . . "

Mike Wallace told Benjamin that the opening to "The Uncounted Enemy" hadn't always contained the red-flag word. Wallace himself wrote the original opening. It began, "This is a mystery story . . . about duty, honor and country. . . . " Crile supported Wallace's opening, but it was scrapped because it wasn't hard-hitting enough.

Next, Benjamin called General Davidson, reaching him with little trouble although Carolyne McDaniel had told the investigator she had tried repeatedly, to no avail, to contact him during 1981. (Davidson sent Van Gordon Sauter a letter later that month, saying, "Mr. Crile totally ignored the one official, myself, who had to have been pivotal within the conspiracy he alleges.")

As Benjamin plowed along, reviewing transcripts, notes, and correspondence, screening tapes, and interviewing thirty-two people, including twelve CBS employees, Crile began work on a "white paper" countering the *TV Guide* item by item. At the same time, the producer orchestrated a massive letter-writing campaign, urging Vietnam experts and principals in the show to write Sauter and voice support for the documentary. He hoped the letters would improve his chance of surviving Benjamin's one-man inquisition.

Soon Sauter was deep in mail.

Gains Hawkins, who *TV Guide* claimed was quoted out of context, said he was "perfectly satisfied" that all his remarks were presented in context:

"Indeed, I was amazed at the skill of the documentary editors in preserving the text and flavor of my remarks. . . . " Hawkins went on to confirm that there had indeed been a ceiling of 300,000 on total enemy-troop-strength estimates during the 1967 OB conferences, adding that Colonel Morris at one point had passed him a piece of paper putting the figure in writing.

George Hamscher wrote:

"As a professional intelligence officer and a responsible player in that MACV numbers game, it hasn't been easy to acknowledge and describe my role. It's even more difficult to fix blame on others who might have acted as they did because they also thought they were doing what was best at the time. In more recent circumstances it seemed best to tell what happened in the hope that for once history won't be repeated. This is what CBS News tried to do, and as far as I'm concerned the documentary was produced as well as the events and people under examination would or will allow. I have no complaint about George Crile's conduct, or his product, which is more than I can say for Don Cowet [sic]. The CBS documentary did expose briefly some guilty personalities, which is what such productions do, but it wasn't a 'smear.' In my view, CBS owes no apology to anyone."

Pierre Sprey, who had served as special assistant to the Assistant Secretary of Defense, Systems Analyst, from 1966 to 1971, agreed, saying, "*TV Guide*'s distortions and omissions make it clear that 'The Anatomy of a Smear' is in itself a smear. . . . "

George Allen, in a letter to Sauter, said the show was "a reasonably fair and accurate depiction of the 1967 controversy over the 'order of battle' in Vietnam, that the thrust of the story was basically sound, that it was presented in a legitimate fashion."

Richard McArthur, who had told Adams about the altering of the military's data base following Tet, said "all statements made by me in the telecast were absolutely true. Mr. Sauter, the CBS Special was the most accurate portrayal of Vietnam Intelligence deception that I have seen to date. . . . As I see it, your staff broke no rules but only displayed examplary behavior."

Richard Moose, who had served as Walt Rostow's special assistant from 1966 to 1968, told Sauter, "There were so many games going on with numbers during that period in question that I don't wonder General Westmoreland, Dr. Rostow and General Graham can't remember what they said from one time to the next. I doubt if any one of them can keep straight what he said and wrote at various times or reconcile any of it with the facts as they became clear afterwards."

Thomas Powers, the Pulitzer Prize-winning author who wrote *The Man Who Kept the Secrets: Richard Helms and the CIA*, had high praise for the show. "I myself thought the program a model of journalistic technique—tight, scrupulous, lucid and convincing. I am sure Westmoreland and Rostow would not trouble themselves with CBS's reporting technique if they had a persuasive case to make against the substance of the story."

Gregory Rushford, who had led the House of Representatives' 1975 investigation of the OB controversy, told Sauter that Sam Adams "was the best intelligence analyst I ran across. His research was brilliant. . . . And he was correct."

Rushford pointed out that the CIA had never been able to tear down Adams' story in *Harper's*. "What a tragedy it will be for journalism if your internal investigation—like the shallow ones the CIA ran against Sam Adams—forces the George Criles out of the business," he wrote.

Crile was indeed having doubts about his future. After the *TV Guide* article appeared, few at work even wanted to talk to him.

"I was not brought into the president's office and asked, 'Well, what about this story, what about that, George? Do we have an answer or don't we? What's the story?' All you want in any normal circumstance like that is the right to defend your work. . . . The frustrating thing is there was no place to go. I wrote my white paper, but there was no one to talk to."

When the rebuttal was completed, all sixty-one pages of it backed up with classified documents and excerpts from interviews, Crile's outlook brightened briefly.

"Mike [Wallace] and Roger Colloff read the white paper and they said basically, we've got them," Crile said. "We've got answers everywhere. Hold your fire and don't talk to anybody, let CBS come back and, institutionally, respond for you. It'll be much more effective. So I held my fire and waited and waited and waited. . . . "

About five weeks later, on June 15, Benjamin interviewed Crile. He talked to him again on June 22. After the meetings, Crile's worries returned. The senior producer had not asked the right questions. He hadn't even seemed to appreciate how difficult it had been to get the CIA and military men to go on camera and confess their sins. " . . . He didn't ask me who I'd interviewed; he didn't ask me what the documentation was."

Crile was particularly upset by Benjamin's apparent fixation on the *TV Guide* charges. He asked Crile if Adams had been rehearsed, as Ira Klein had alleged. He wanted to know why sympathetic witnesses seemed to be treated more gently than "unfriendly witnesses." ("Why do you want to go adversarial if a person is confessing?" Crile asked at this point.) He spent a great deal of time asking Crile about the George Allen matter.

Crile told the investigator, "There was nothing basically wrong with the first interview. This was a personal thing with me. Allen was particularly concerned about ratting on the CIA. He looked like hell, looked guilty, on those questions about the CIA. . . . I felt very badly for what it would do to Allen. No, I didn't tell Andy Lack or Howard Stringer that I did the interview twice. I don't know if they knew. No, I didn't know this was a violation of the CBS Guidelines. Why was it?"

Benjamin replied, "How could it be spontaneous and unrehearsed if you interviewed him twice?"

"I honestly was not aware of it being a violation of the Guidelines," Crile repeated.

Later in the interview, Benjamin asked, "Why did Allen see the other interviews?"

"For the same reason as the second interview," Crile answered. "I know it's against the sensibilities of everyone here. . . . I don't think what I did there was right. Allen was caught in stage paralysis. He felt badly about doing the interview . . . he felt isolated as if he were a whistle blower. I wanted to show him he wasn't alone out there."

Benjamin's finished report included excerpts from the Allen interviews to demonstrate how Crile prompted his witness. At one point, Crile urged Allen to "come to the defense of your old protégé, Sam Adams." Later, he said, "We're going to keep at this until we get it right . . . until we feel comfortable." Crile told Allen, "George . . . keep your enthusiasm. You're on the right side."

Benjamin's questioning often turned to lecturing. When Crile said he hadn't felt it necessary to have more witnesses defend Westmoreland on the show because "Westmoreland was not the show," Benjamin told him, "He came out as the heavy, George." In another exchange, Benjamin asked, "Couldn't you have let Carver tell his story and let the audience decide—which we often do around here, George?"

The investigator was taking the hard, literal line. He seemed to be elevating the sixty-four-page CBS guidelines to absolute laws, when in fact many reporters at the network had never read them in full. In this meticulous application of form over content, it seemed to make little difference whether or not the truth had been served.

Frightened for his career, Crile wrote Mike Wallace a long, desperate memo, saying Benjamin appeared to be "accepting *TV Guide's* ground rules"—investigating only the process of the documentary, not its substance.

"Our silence is viewed as an admission of guilt. There are charges of a coverup and the impression that we are worried that the thrust of the show is indeed untrue." He said, "I think we should move heaven and earth" to get CBS to issue an interim statement saying it stands by the documentary. "I really think it's worth talking to Dan [Rather] about this."

Crile also criticized Stringer and Lack for not scrutinizing the documentary more carefully, but said Benjamin hadn't asked him questions about their role.

" . . . For Bud to suggest that we should have treated Adams in the same manner as we did Westmoreland seems to be totally absurd. Adams was in my office, wandering around the 8th floor for weeks. . . . One of the reasons I went through the so-called coaching session (which I think is a stupid charge) was simply to try to keep Adams from straying off into the role of the accuser. . . ."

Crile was "horrified" by Benjamin's apparent misperception of the show. The senior producer, he felt, saw it as a "grudge match" between Westmoreland and Sam Adams.

" . . . If my impressions are correct, and if this is in fact Bud's point of departure for considering this story, then I think we are in trouble—and if so, I want to have certain facts understood," Crile wrote to Wallace. "I believe they are equally important for both of us.

"So what am I saying? I'm saying I don't want to be the bureaucracy's fall guy here. And I know full well that your reputation has also become tied up in the outcome of this investigation in a very fundamental way. And I don't want you to indirectly became a fall guy either. This is a show that the news division commissioned with its eyes wide open—It was given exactly what it was promised. . . . "

"If there were failings here—in this explosive documentary which we all understood was going to be controversial—the man who was supposed to protect all of us and watch out for the reputation of the news division was Howard Stringer. And he is bad mouthing the show and apparently refuses to even read my White Paper."

Benjamin had read Crile's white paper. He had read virtually everything connected to the documentary, including all the unedited interview transcripts. But Crile was correct in presuming that Benjamin's conclusions would do little to restore his tarnished reputation.

One of the first things Benjamin noted in his fifty-nine-page report, which he handed over to Sauter and CBS officials on July 8, was that it appeared Crile had backed off from what he had written in the white paper, where he described the theme of the show this way:

" . . . In 1967, American military and civilian intelligence discovered evidence indicating the existence of a dramatically larger enemy than previously reported . . . that instead of alerting the country, U.S. military intelligence under General Westmoreland commenced to suppress and alter its intelligence reports, in order to conceal this discovery from the American public, the Congress, and perhaps even the President."

Benjamin said he had confronted Crile with *TV Guide*'s version of the show's thesis:

"The evidence amassed by CBS seemed to prove the U.S. military's intelligence operation in Vietnam, led by General Westmoreland, conspired to deceive president Lyndon Johnson, the Congress and the American public. Beginning in 1967, the documentary charges, Westmoreland had systematically underreported to his superiors, the size and strength of the enemy, in order to make it appear that he was indeed winning the 'war of attrition.' "

After comparing the two, Crile agreed that it was unclear who exactly was deceived by the manipulation of numbers. "Now that I look at it I would put a period after the words 'intelligence reports' and eliminate the rest of the sentence," he told Benjamin.

In this first section, however, the CBS investigator agreed strongly with Crile's observation, "Nowhere in the article do the [*TV Guide*] authors challenge the central premise of the broadcast. . . ."

The report continued along this line, addressing each of the charges. At one point, Benjamin scrutinized Wallace's small part in the show, concluding he was "hardly involved in the Vietnam broadcast. He attended some screenings, adjudicated some creative disputes and conducted four interviews for the broadcast."

Following the lengthy parade of charges and evidence, Benjamin's study ended abruptly with this terse summary of flaws the investigator had discovered in "The Uncounted Enemy":

   —The premise was obviously and historically controversial. There was an imbalance in presenting the two sides of the issue. For every McChristian, there was a Davidson; for every Hawkins, a Morris; for every Allen, a Carver.
   —A "conspiracy," given the accepted definition of the word, was not proved.
   —The double interview of George Allen.
   —The screening of interviews for Allen.
   —Sam Adams not being properly identified as a *paid* consultant.
   —Journalistic oversight which permitted two McChristian-Hawkins meetings to appear to be one meeting.
   —Journalistic oversight which permitted General Westmoreland to discuss one meeting which was then cut into a sequence about another meeting.
   —Other violations of CBS News Guidelines.

—The coddling of sympathetic witnesses.

—The lack of journalistic enterprise in trying to find General Davidson or in checking out his "illness."

—Imprecisions in the handling of the Hamscher introduction and in the "Meet the Press" matter involving Westmoreland's "correction letter."

Benjamin found it significant that the *TV Guide* reporters emphasized that the purpose of their attack "was not to confirm or deny the existence of the 'conspiracy' that CBS's journalists say existed."

"The reason for that may be," Benjamin wrote, "that even today military historians cannot tell you whether or not MACV 'cooked the books' as the broadcast states. The flow of definitive information is painfully slow and may never be conclusive."

But, he added, "To get a group of high-ranking military men and former Central Intelligence Agents to say that this is what happened was an achievement of no small dimension. These were not fringe people but rather prototypical Americans."

Benjamin ended his summary with a quote from Howard Stringer, who had told him, "If all the standards of fairness had been followed, it would not have changed the outcome of the broadcast."

If the report were stripped to its essentials, without Benjamin's interpretations, it might appear the only action everyone agreed was really wrong was letting Allen screen some of the interviews. Most of the other points *TV Guide* raised and Benjamin examined were judgment calls. Another producer might have done things differently. The same producer might have done them differently at another time, but Crile wasn't necessarily wrong.

The Benjamin Report in its entirety, however, was not a benign document. And Crile, not Stringer, Lack, or Colloff, was at the center of its accusations. Sauter sent copies of the fifty-nine-page report, including a two-page section of recommendations that were never made public, to Gene Jankowski and Gene Mater, president and vice president of the CBS Broadcast Group. Sauter later said William Paley, retiring CBS board chairman, and CBS Inc. president Thomas Wyman also read it.

On July 14, Crile finally got his chance to defend his documentary. Sauter had promised to release the results of the Benjamin investigation, but he never agreed to make public the actual document. Instead, he composed a memo. He discussed the document with Benjamin several times, then convened a meeting with Ed Joyce (executive vice president of CBS News), Crile, Wallace, Stringer, and Colloff to determine what the official statement would contain.

The gathering, which lasted far into the night, was far from amiable. Crile, Colloff, Wallace, and Stringer all savaged Benjamin's conclusions. Sauter had already written a draft memo, but was influenced to rewrite it. Primarily, he moved the declaration that "CBS News stands by this broadcast" to the top of the statement, rather than hiding it at the bottom.

The eight-page Sauter memorandum, issued July 15, read much like Benjamin's list of transgressions. After the statement of support, Sauter added, "we now feel it would have been a better broadcast if:

> —it had not used the word "conspiracy";
> —it had sought out and interviewed more persons who disagreed with the broadcast premise; and
> —there had been strict compliance with CBS News Standards.
> . . . We now believe that a judgmental conclusion of conspiracy was inappropriate.

(Sauter would later testify, however, that "the pattern of deception established within the broadcast would justify the use of the word conspiracy.") Sauter went on to detail five "violations of the letter or the spirit of CBS News Standards," but noted that none of them changed the substance of the broadcast.

He said Sam Adams had not been rehearsed for his interview and "has not, as alleged, backed away from the premise of the broadcast." He characterized the *TV Guide* story as "an exploitive attack on a serious, substantive journalistic effort."

Sauter announced plans to create a new position at CBS News— Vice President, News Practices—to prevent any such problems in the future. "We are also planning a future broadcast on the issues treated in the original broadcast," he said.

That same day, Crile was reprimanded. "Our dissatisfaction with the violation of the guidelines was expressed," Sauter said.

Stringer was absolved. Wallace was absolved. The blame seemed to rest squarely on Crile. The producer had been told not to defend himself, to wait for the Benjamin Report and Sauter's statement. Now the lid was off, but no one wanted to hear from him, precisely due to the Sauter memorandum. His credibility had been virtually destroyed.

Fearing such an outcome, Crile had already called Peter Boyer at the *Los Angeles Times* and Tom Shales at the *Washington Post*, offering to tell all. The resulting articles were favorable to Crile's cause, but did not soften the sting of the Sauter memo.

While Crile was feeling persecuted, Westmoreland was shopping for lawyers. He had, in fact, been shopping for some time.

The general wanted to sue CBS from the first, but there were daunting obstacles: the endeavor would cost millions of dollars, and a "public figure" such as Westmoreland faced a strenuous burden of proof in a libel case.

Westmoreland asked former Secretary of Defense Clark Clifford for advice and Clifford urged him not to sue. Famous trial lawyer Edward Bennett Williams also counseled against it. Former Army Secretary Stanley Resor, now a partner at New York's Debevoise & Plimpton law firm, told the general to stay out of court. Senator Barry Goldwater warned him that a libel suit would be extremely costly.

Most of these prestigious advisers agreed that Westmoreland didn't have a prayer—that is, until the *TV Guide* article. Shortly after the story came out, Peter Grace of W. R. Grace & Co. sent Westmoreland to see Godfrey Schmidt of Schmidt, Aghayan & Associates. Schmidt felt that the general just might have a case.

While Schmidt and Westmoreland were working out possible financing, Dave Henderson stepped in with another alternative: Dan Burt of the Capital Legal Foundation, a conservative public-interest law firm. After meeting with the general, Burt offered to take the case for free, and Westmoreland agreed to the arrangement shortly after CBS issued the Sauter memorandum, which became an incredible boon to the general.

On August 10, Westmoreland fired a warning volley. Under Burt's guidance, he wrote a letter to network president Thomas Wyman, demanding that CBS "publish a complete apology, approved in advance by me, in the same manner and the same media in which you advertised the program." The general asked for monetary compensation and "a full retraction, of not less than forty-five minutes' duration" presenting "the actual facts and methods of preparation concerning the story you published. The material in this retraction and the production itself must be subject to my complete approval."

Westmoreland was asking for a video Benjamin Report and more!

Two weeks later, Sauter answered the letter, rejecting the request. "It was obvious he was going to sue," he later said. "We were not in a position to provide the redress he wanted."

CBS didn't give up entirely, however. The Sauter memorandum had promised a follow-up program and the network was indeed planning such a show. In his letter to Westmoreland, Sauter repeated an invitation to appear on the panel show, which was to include CBS commentator Diane Sawyer, Peter Braestrup, author of *The Big Story*, Robert Kaiser of the *Washington Post*, Colonel Gains Hawkins, Sam Adams, George Carver, General Danny Graham, General Davidson, and Westmoreland.

The show, scheduled to air September 15, was canceled on September 7 after Davidson, Westmoreland, and Graham refused to appear. In an unusual and desperate move, Joan Richman, executive producer of the canceled show, wrote a letter to Westmoreland the next day. She asked him once again to reconsider, offering fifteen minutes at the start of the program "to say what you wish to say in the manner you wish to say it."

Westmoreland and Burt turned down the offer. They had already made their decision. On September 13, William C. Westmoreland filed a $120-million libel suit in the U.S. District Court in Greenville, South Carolina, naming CBS Inc., Sam Adams, George Crile, Van Gordon Sauter, and Mike Wallace as defendants.

Crile, meanwhile, was in Central America. When he realized he was in journalistic limbo, he had decided to take some time off from the network.

"I said the hell with it, I'll go do some reporting on my own. Do a piece for a magazine." He headed to Nicaragua with Susan Lyne to report on the beginnings of the Contra War, traveling to Managua and Tegucigalpa. It was in a hotel lobby, while talking to a dentist, that Crile heard about the Westmoreland suit for the first time. He called Colloff, who again asked him to return, this time to meet with lawyers.

5.

The Lawyers

ON September 13, 1982, General William Westmoreland, accompanied by a short, nervous lawyer, returned to the Washington, D.C., Army-Navy Club—the same spot where eight and a half months earlier he had demanded an apology from CBS. The paneled room was jammed with many of the same reporters who had attended the earlier news conference. As the somewhat mismatched pair made their way to the front, the general's newly acquired counsel warily eyed the daunting assemblage of cameras, microphones, and notepads. This was his first libel battle and he was clearly ill at ease. Westmoreland, however, was the picture of confidence. When it was time to begin, he stepped forward with his silver head held high, nodded curtly to the crowd, and calmly explained what he intended to do.

"I am an old soldier who loves his country and have had enough of war," the former commander said. "It was my fate to serve for over four years as senior American commander in the most unpopular war this country ever fought. I have been reviled, burned in effigy, spat upon. Neither I nor my wife nor my family want me to go to battle once again.

"But all my life I have valued 'duty, honor, country' above all else. Even as my friends and family urged me to ignore CBS and leave the field, I reflected on those Americans who had died in service in Vietnam. Even as I considered the enormous wealth and power that make CBS so formidable an adversary, I thought too of the troops I had commanded and sent to battle, and those who never returned.

"Finally, I have dwelled at length upon the tremendous bulwark of liberty and freedom that is the First Amendment to the Constitution of the United States. I now feared that public reaction to CBS as the truth came out might lead to weakening of that bulwark through legislated codes of conduct or other attempts to restrain the media."

These considerations so troubled him that he had given CBS one last chance to offer an apology and a public explanation, Westmoreland said. In a letter, he had asked network president Thomas Wyman for forty-five minutes of air time, a full retraction, and unspecified monetary compensation. CBS News president Van Gordon Sauter's unsatisfactory response—an offer of fifteen unedited minutes in which to state his case—dictated "the long and bitter legal battle I am about to engage in," the general said. ("There was no opportunity in that fifteen minutes to undo the harm unless CBS admitted they were wrong," the lawyer, Dan Burt, later told reporters. "All he would have done would have been to dignify a lie.")

Westmoreland announced that lawyers in Greenville, South Carolina, the town where he had grown up, were at that very moment filing suit against the network. "There is no way left for me to clear my name, my honor, and the honor of the military. Let me emphasize the issue here is not money, not vengeance. If I am successful in this case, as I believe I will be, I will not retain any monetary award for my personal use but will instead donate it to charity." During questioning, Westmoreland said he would donate the money to veterans' groups.

Burt, still visibly tense, scowled at the reporters through his octagonal wire-rim glasses as he answered the other questions, many of which had to do with money. His non-profit, public-interest law firm would cover the general's expenses pro bono, but would need to raise more money fast. Capital Legal's total budget for 1982 was only $850,000, with the Westmoreland case already expected to gobble up more than one third of that sum. The next year, the costs would climb higher. CBS would be forced to invest even more—up to $4 million a year, Burt estimated. "CBS will try to spend us to death," he said. He characterized the case as a contest between David and Goliath.

The complaint filed in South Carolina outlined fifteen accusations the broadcast made against Westmoreland, saying they were "false, unfair, inaccurate and defamatory," adding that "the broadcast in its entirety was unfair, defamatory and malicious in content and tone." One of the charges—conspiracy—it pointed out, is "a crime punishable by imprisonment and fine."

CBS's reaction was swift and brief. In a three-paragraph statement, Sauter said the network stood by the documentary and that "CBS will mount a vigorous defense of this lawsuit not only because we see this suit totally devoid of merit but because it constitutes a serious threat to independent journalism in our society." Sauter also said he regretted that Westmoreland had rejected CBS's offer. "Such a broadcast would be more effective in serving the general's stated goals than the course of action he initiated today. Indeed that offer still stands."

Westmoreland's prediction was correct: CBS was a formidable adversary. The network chose Cravath, Swaine & Moore, one of the biggest and most prestigious firms in the country, to carry its banner into this fray. Westy may have been the commander of a conventional army in the guerrilla war of Vietnam, but in this battle the tables were turned. His champion was a guerrilla warrior and his opponent was the legal analogue of the American Army, with a lot of troops, many generals, and a very fat logistical tail. Cravath's Fortune 500 clients ranged from Royal Dutch Shell to Allied Chemical, Bethlehem Steel, and Time Inc. These were the lawyers who had successfully defended IBM in its decade-long, multi-faceted anti-trust battle with the Justice Department, which had ended when the government, already $50 million poorer due to the case, suddenly bailed out.

David Boies, a forty-one-year-old Cravath partner with a gift for relentless cross-examination, would be the chief lawyer for CBS. Boies had played an important role in the IBM victory during the 1970s, but he wasn't a typical product of the Ivy League attorney factories. In the 1960s, he had spent time as a civil-rights lawyer in the Deep South. Although at least three quarters of all libel cases are settled out of court or dismissed, more and more were actually going to trial. So CBS decided against hiring a First Amendment specialist and went with Boies, a courtroom crackerjack who could try a case before a South Carolina jury and not seem like a foreigner.

With the proven expertise of Boies, virtually unlimited funds, and a small army of aides and researchers, it appeared to some that CBS had the advantage. Of the libel cases that went to court, it was true that between 80 and 90 percent were decided in favor of the plaintiff, but most decisions were reversed on appeal. If defeated, CBS would almost certainly appeal, driving costs into the stratosphere for Westmoreland's tightly budgeted legal team. To make matters worse for the general, in a case such as this one, the libel law put the burden of proof on the plaintiff. In the landmark *New York Times vs. Sullivan*, the Supreme Court in 1964 had decided that free speech was so important that even false and defamatory statements made about the official conduct of public figures deserved the protection of law. To recover damages, an official had to prove that the statement was made with "actual malice," or with "reckless disregard" as to whether the statement was true or false. A subsequent case, *Herbert vs. Lando*, allowed a plaintiff to examine editing practices and try to plumb a journalist's thought processes to discover if such disregard existed. Still, few public officials in the two decades since *Times vs. Sullivan* had been brave enough to take a journalist to court. The burden of proof was formidable. To win, Dan Burt had to prove CBS had acted with actual malice in producing "The Uncounted Enemy." Then he had to convince the jury that Westmoreland was innocent of the accusations made in the program.

Boies took little comfort from knowing that Westmoreland and Burt had a tough road ahead. He recognized from the first it would be foolhardy to underestimate the competition. The Sauter memorandum was a problem for CBS; the Benjamin Report could become a problem; and public relations was already a problem. But more important was the nature of Dan Burt. Burt might be lacking in money and courtroom expertise, but he had plenty of rage. This wasn't just another job for Burt. This was personal.

To Westmoreland's Robin Hood, who one moment describes himself as "a short, foul-mouthed Jew from the streets" and the next confides he is a frustrated poet, CBS and Cravath represented a stratum of society forever beyond his grasp, a private club as far from his origins as the Vietnamese jungles were from the lower-class Philadelphia neighborhood where he grew up. Never mind that he no longer *wanted* to join the club, that he preferred the company of working-class people. Burt saw himself as a perpetual underdog who had overcome his humble circumstances against great odds to become the defender of other little guys. These mighty institutions represented a system that had made his struggle harder. And despite Westmoreland's undeniably patrician status, in this situation Burt saw him as a little guy standing up for his honor. Honor and the idea of fighting for it struck a primal chord in Burt. This was something from his childhood, the lawyer was fond of explaining to reporters.

The son of a butcher who owned a small shop in the Rising Sun district, Burt remembers constantly worrying about money when he was growing up. The family was poor. Nonetheless, "my father would always buy a paper from the newspaper boys and give them a half a buck, or a dollar," he said. "Times were hard, but we had obligations to the poor. To the underdog. That's what I learned. What I learned and try to live by."

"Little Joe," as they called him at the butcher shop, also learned to fight, but always for a principle, he said. He was fascinated with the Old West, reading about Kit Carson, James Bowie, Daniel Boone, the Pony Express, and the Alamo. His real-life childhood heroes—his father and a fishing captain named Holmes Russell—seemed to stand up for their beliefs just as the frontiersmen had. His father once chased and shot a man who tried to rob the store; the older Burt stopped to break up fights between youths on the streets; he kept a loaded gun at home. "We knew where the gun was; we knew where the bullets were," Burt said. "That leaves an impression on you, it really does."

Burt's street-wise ethics didn't help him much in school, where the fighting translated into disciplinary problems and mediocre grades. He appeared headed for a blue-collar life, but one day, while driving a meat truck, Burt had something of an awakening. The "Moonlight Sonata" was playing on the radio; he heard it as if for the first time and made a decision.

"I said that's it. I'm not going to have to shovel shit the rest of my life like my Daddy. My father hated his life. You have to be a butcher to know. It's very cold, coarse. The men are very crude. It's a brutal life. And it teaches you brutality. There is something about tearing flesh that does it."

Burt had never even heard of Harvard or Yale when he enrolled in La Salle College in Philadelphia, but his horizons soon expanded. His grades were good enough to win him a scholarship at Cambridge University in England, where he studied English literature and graduated with the exalted "first" degree in 1966. He applied to Yale law school and was accepted.

"Lawyering, in 1966, was a way to change the world," he said. "What I wanted to do was change the world."

After graduating among the top in his class, he struggled to find his niche, working a year and a half for a Philadelphia firm, then moving to Washington, D.C., to work for the Treasury as "the house radical." He had decided that "the game was played in taxes. If you want equality in this society, the tax system is the way you get it." A year within the government was enough to disillusion him thoroughly, however. He became a consultant to an accounting firm, then took a teaching job at Boston University. By this time, he had been married and divorced twice.

In 1975, he simply gave up trying to fit in. He quit his job, planning to move to Marblehead, Massachusetts, and learn to play the guitar. But some former clients from the accounting firm tracked him down, seeking his help, and he ended up starting a firm specializing in international tax work. Dan Burt, scorner of privileged circumstances, got rich. Stranger yet, he amassed his fortune making deals with the Saudi Arabians.

"It was exciting; it was unbelievably exciting," he said of the boom fueled by oil prices. "It was a gold rush. What I saw in Saudi Arabia we won't see again in this century. The streets were literally paved with money. I saw men with half a million dollars in backpacks because the banks didn't work. It was phenomenal. They were building a whole country out of the desert, nothing but sand . . . and there were practically no commercial laws."

Being Jewish didn't worry him, he said with typical bluster. On the contrary, he found he had a lot in common with the Arabs.

"Frankly, I felt a lot more comfortable there than I have in certain clubs in America. There was a lot of hostility toward Israelis and Jews . . . but the hostility was understood . . . they had a real, territorial reason. But I didn't get the sense of a racial hatred. They're all Semites and we tended to respond the same way. We could do a deal; we could shake hands. Unlike trying to negotiate with lawyers in America, some of them. That's one reason I do a lot of business in England, where they are gentlemen. The code is a street code: 'If you give your word, you keep your word.' "

When the "Mid-East bubble burst," Burt, a self-proclaimed millionaire, sold the business, and in 1980 he returned to Washington, D.C., to become president of the Capital Legal Foundation, a business-oriented public-policy law firm with a "free-market bias." Capital Legal was partly funded by industry, including the American Telephone & Telegraph Co., the Fluor Corp., General Electric, and Twentieth Century–Fox, but tax returns show that the bulk of the money came from a handful of extremely conservative foundations, including the Smith Richardson Foundation, the (Richard Mellon) Scaife Foundation, the John M. Olin Foundation, and the Carthage Foundation.

With an eye on his dream of changing the world, Burt set off to stir up trouble. He enjoyed being outrageous. Despite the reputation of his funders, it was obvious from the first that Burt did not fit neatly into any right-wing box. If anything, he was more of a libertarian. Many of Capital's cases were politically conservative, but Burt was also representing an astonishing number of little guys bucking the system. He went to the aid of the so-called Vermont Knitters, a group of women who made ski wear for Stowe Woolens and wanted to work at home, drawing the ire of the International Ladies Garment Workers Union and big manufacturers. The Department of Labor also objected at first, but Capital helped change the rules. The ILGWU sued, but Burt won.

Capital that year had tried, unsuccessfully, to block President Reagan's decision to prevent a formal default by paying $71 million in interest Poland owed on U.S. bank loans. But the group succeeded in other projects, particularly by defending sixty-five-year-old Simon Geller, who singlehandedly operated a classical-music station in Gloucester, Massachusetts. A group of rich New England broadcasters tried to take over Geller's station when it came time to renew his Federal Communications Commission license. They argued that the license should be revoked because Geller was not broadcasting news and public-affairs programming. But Geller convinced an FCC administrative-law judge to let him keep the station. Then, in a surprise move, the FCC overruled the judge and gave the station to the challengers, one of whom was a former state Republican Committee chairman. Burt was furious. "Some deregulation! Some public interest!" he wrote in his 1982 annual report. Capital Legal appealed the decision in federal court and the court remanded it to the FCC, which late in 1985 finally agreed to let Geller keep his station.

The Geller story drew massive attention from the media. So did a book Burt wrote about consumer advocate Ralph Nader. The scathing diatribe, *Abuse of Trust*, accused the Naderites of foxing the public in much the same manner as corporate America. (Burt later said Nader "did a lot of good in this country . . . he'd just overstayed his welcome.")

Burt's life at forty was going well. He was married to his third wife, Maree Therese Webster, an English woman who came from a working-class background and had left school at sixteen but was now completing a linguistics Ph.D. at Harvard. He owned several homes, including a vacation retreat in Bar Harbor, Maine. His private tax practice was flourishing; his annual income was reportedly more than $600,000.

Perhaps it was the recent spate of successes and the positive attention in the media that led Burt, who as a student had protested the Vietnam War, to align himself with the general who had run it and against the country's most prestigious TV network. Many observers considered the move ill-advised, a too risky step onto the totally alien ground of libel law. They wondered if Capital Legal—Dan Burt plus a staff of five—was equipped to take on the CBS-Cravath machine. But one thing was certain: whatever his chances, Burt did not step softly.

* * *

Boies, on the surface, was nothing like the firebrand Burt. His mind was as orderly as a computerized chess game, projecting scenarios and calculating probabilities at a blinding pace while maintaining exterior calm. Not an icy calm. Just friendly, laid-back self-assurance. If a case aroused passion, it never showed on his face; he kept his feelings as well hidden as a gambler might. He was, in fact, a gambler, zipping off to Las Vegas or Atlantic City to shoot craps whenever possible. When he couldn't leave town, he amused himself playing poker, bridge, or hearts. And while Burt might turn up in a peasant shirt or a belted suit of nubby British tweed, Boies stuck to the boringly correct corporate uniform, usually in navy blue. But inside his suit jackets, on the labels tacked to the linings, was more evidence of the real Boies. This lawyer didn't deck himself out in Brooks Brothers or Hart, Schaffner & Marx. He bought his white-collar duds at Sears. ("I love Sears," he says. "I wear Sears shoes, I have a Sears garden tractor, I have two couches from Sears, I have a washer and a refrigerator from them." He buys his casual clothes at K-Mart.) Boies might be the golden boy of a Wall Street firm, but his path to the top had more than a few similarities to that of his adversary.

The son of a high-school teacher, Boies grew up in Marengo, Illinois, and then Compton and Fullerton, California, where his father worked summers at the neighborhood Sears store (one mystery solved) to supplement his meager wage. After graduating from high school in 1959, he was too poor to go to college. He wasn't even sure he wanted to continue his education. Instead, he married his debate partner and high-school sweetheart at eighteen and went to work on a construction crew. It was after his first son was born that Boies made up his mind to improve his status, but he wanted to get through school quickly—an ambition that came to pass due to his budding flair for strategy and self-discipline. He enrolled at the University of Redlands, half planning to become a history teacher, but when he learned about a program at Northwestern University that allowed students to enter law school after three years of undergraduate work, he moved to Chicago. His scholastic record was remarkable enough to land him, like Burt, at Yale, where he graduated second in his class.

"There came a point in college when it became clear that the only way really to stay in school, and certainly to go on to law school and graduate school, was to get very good grades," he relates. "I couldn't afford to do it without scholarships. I worked most of the way through school."

One of his jobs was in the news business, sort of, editing a weekly paper at a California mental hospital. ("It was entirely put out by patients. I was the only 'outsider' there. It was like a school news-paper; the ones who were on good behavior got to go with me to the printers' once a week, where they actually set it with linotypes.") In Chicago, Boies worked at the Sands Motel from midnight to eight a.m. as a clerk and auditor, six days a week, attending classes at North-western during the day.

With his choirboy good looks (dark blond hair and blue eyes), apparently conservative political leanings (he was president of the Young Republican Club at Redlands), and diligent pursuit of white-collar credentials, Boies could easily have passed for an early Yuppie. But in the social upheaval of the mid-1960s, another side of the aspiring attorney emerged. In 1965, he traveled to Mississippi for the Lawyers' Committee on Civil Rights. He protested the Vietnam War; he took time out to do volunteer work in New York for Robert Kennedy's senatorial campaign. It was also at about this time that his first marriage broke up. After law school, he pushed aside a strong yearning to become a teacher, like his father, and instead signed on with Cravath to learn to be a trial lawyer. Soon, however, his idealism took over and he headed back South to represent civil-rights workers and handle voter-registration cases.

He recalled the experience as exciting and dangerous. Young people living in the South today are conscious that racism still exists, but they don't "have any idea of what it was like twenty years ago," he said. "It's hard to imagine."

Whenever he left the relative safety of Jackson, Mississippi, he always called colleagues before leaving, called again upon arriving, and made sure someone knew the exact route he'd be taking.

He returned in 1968 on behalf of Cravath to represent the families of the students killed at Jackson State College when police "just went and shot up the campus" during the rioting that followed the assassination of Martin Luther King.

"It seemed then the clearest-cut issue I'd ever been confronted with of what's right and what's wrong . . . there wasn't any ambiguity, at least not at that stage. I think the Vietnam War was a lot more ambiguous. People have a right to vote, they have a right to be safe. You're really dealing with the most fundamental civil rights.

"I suppose when you're young you always think the issues are clearer than [you do] when you're older, but from time to time I'll get together with people, both black and white, I worked with then, and they almost universally agree that those were the clearest kinds of battles, the clearest views of right and wrong."

Back in New York, Boies balanced his duties at Cravath with a spate of counter-culture cases, representing students arrested in the late-1960s sit-ins at Columbia University and others "who got busted for various causes." He never seemed to submerge himself completely in the firm. After his successful defense of IBM in the Calcomp antitrust case, he took a sabbatical that coincided with the break-up of his second marriage, switching sides to serve as chief counsel for the Senate Antitrust Committee in 1977. Boies enjoyed the challenge, and when Edward Kennedy became chairman of the Judiciary Committee, Boies followed as chief counsel and staff director. But by the end of 1979, he was ready to leave Washington.

"I'm not that crazy about power and the access to it," he said. "Also, I like practicing law. I like trial law. I like the challenge. The competition aspect of it. I like to be in court. I like trying cases. I like that dynamic. I like the kind of intellectual issues you deal with in large cases. When a really big case goes to court, you're almost always, in one way or another, dealing with a very complex factual situation. You are usually dealing in legal issues that are really pushing beyond [existing case law] in terms of whatever general area of law you're about, libel or whatever."

Boies liked to break new legal ground; it reminded him of being back in law school. He began to represent CBS in a number of tangles, most memorably when Atlanta broadcaster Ted Turner sued the Reagan administration along with the three major TV networks in the media "pool" of newspaper and broadcast reporters who cover the White House, saying they were illegally excluding his Cable News Network. The Reagan administration, in an unprecedented move, then decided to exclude all TV cameras from the White House pool until the problem was solved. On behalf of CBS, Boies sued Reagan, saying the decision was unconstitutional, and quickly won an injunction halting the rule. The suit was settled soon afterward (CNN is now in the White House pool).

The Westmoreland suit, with its assortment of defendants and issues, promised to be a challenge. Many reporters were already speculating that the case might have a chilling effect on journalism, possibly leading to a change in libel laws. CBS was definitely nervous. As CBS president Gene Jankowski told a meeting of the Federal Communications Bar Association, " . . . What is at stake here is the ability of the press to investigate government conduct at the highest levels, and in the most serious matters, without fear of crippling penalty. A decision for the plaintiff could do what no court has ever done— permit a high federal official to recover damages for criticism of actions he has taken in his official capacity. This would be to attack the heart of the constitutionally protected area of free expression."

Capital Legal was indeed trying to narrow the libel law. Foundation associate Jim Moody later told the *Philadelphia Inquirer* that the Supreme Court, through *Times vs. Sullivan*, "nationalized the right of the press to take away your reputation. Just like the press argues it's been chilled, we argue that people's right to seek public office and be in the limelight has been chilled."

When Boies filed a motion seeking summary judgment on May 23, 1984, he argued that the suit should be dismissed because Westmoreland had lived as a public figure for years. "In his capacity as Commanding General in our nation's most controversial war, plaintiff exercised the sovereign's power and enjoyed the sovereign's immunities," he argued. "He cannot now use the sovereign's courts to limit the political and historical debate concerning the propriety of how he used that power."

But Boies went beyond the public-figure argument, even before it was clear whether the case would go to trial. Most libel lawyers worry primarily about proving absence of malice, but Bois planned to follow a much tougher strategy. He intended to show that the charges made in the broadcast were absolutely true and therefore not libelous. He also hoped to find a way to broaden the libel law in the process.

Crile eventually came to trust and respect Boies completely, but in the early days of the lawsuit he had little faith in CBS's intentions to defend him. His interests in the case were somewhat different from the network's, and he had already asked his lawyer, John Vardaman of Williams & Connolly, for advice. Since Westmoreland had sought help from the same firm, Vardaman could not represent Crile, so the producer hired a First Amendment specialist, Victor Kovner of Lankenau, Kovner & Bickford, which represented the *Village Voice* and the *Dial* magazine. For several months, it was unclear whether CBS would pay for Crile's separate counsel, but the network and its insurer finally agreed that they should. (In one of the many ironies of the case, Kovner's assistant was Harriette Dorsen, the sister-in-law of David Dorsen, Burt's co-counsel.)

The Benjamin Report quickly became a liability. As soon as the suit was filed, Burt began demanding that CBS turn over all the materials used in making "The Uncounted Enemy." Although the network eventually handed over the transcripts of twenty-six hours of interviews, it steadfastly refused to surrender Burton Benjamin's disastrous appraisal of the show. The report was an internal document, "privileged material," they argued. But Burt was convinced the study would prove Crile had acted with "actual malice," and the lawyer had no intention of backing down. On November 4, Westmoreland's attorneys filed a motion seeking to force CBS to surrender the report. CBS fought the motion energetically, submitting piles of affidavits from representatives of other media companies, among them NBC, ABC, the *Wall Street Journal*, and *Newsweek*. Boies, however, knew from the first that Burt would win this argument, and, sure enough, the judge in the case ruled in April 1983 that the report was discoverable because the network had already made the Sauter memorandum public. The internal document stopped being confidential, the jurist reasoned, when CBS released a press statement based on the study.

"We are about to see the dismantling of a major news network," Burt proclaimed after the decision. Several months later, the judge went even further, ordering the network to turn over the notes and other materials Benjamin had used in compiling the report.

A more important decision, however, went CBS's way.

When Dan Burt decided to file suit in Greenville, he knew he was taking a gamble, but he expected to hit the jackpot. The lawyer never really wanted the suit to go to court, and by threatening the network with a ballgame played on Westmoreland's home turf he hoped to force an out-of-court settlement. Westy was a folk hero in that part of the world, and a Southern jury was almost certain to take the hard line with a bunch of New York City journalists. Burt said several third parties, presumably representing CBS, did contact him around this time to see if there was any hope of resolution, but all backed off when he told them that the general wanted a cash settlement of at least several million dollars.

CBS, as expected, filed papers with the South Carolina judge arguing that the case should either be moved to New York or dismissed. After all, they said, Charleston was the general's home, not Greenville. What happened next, Burt said, was a key reason for the eventual outcome of the case.

"It was a classic example of the difference between an established organization and a pickup team," he said. "For various reasons, we did not want to go to Charleston. I don't want to discuss them. You pay attention to your client's wishes."

He said he looked very carefully at the venue, discussing it with the lawyers in South Carolina. Everyone agreed there was no problem suing in the district they chose. Wincing at the memory, Burt recalled, "I had a feeling in my gut that it wasn't right."

When he flew down to South Carolina to argue his position before the judge, he immediately saw that he had a problem. "I never had an answer for the basic proposition: what were we doing 250 miles away [from Charleston]? Actually, I had a lot of answers, but none of them were good enough for that judge."

CBS pointed out that in the time it would take Westmoreland to drive round-trip to Greenville, he could fly to New York and back. Also, the general spent so much time traveling around the country, speaking on the Vietnam War, that he was out of the state as much as he was in it. Furthermore, CBS noted, on the night of the broadcast the local Greenville TV station had pre-empted the documentary for a local basketball game.

"It sort of showed that this wasn't the site of the greatest harm," Boies said. "I think there was the feeling that the plaintiff was forum-shopping, that he was trying to find the most sympathetic audience. In a sense, there's nothing wrong with that. Lawyers do that all the time. On the other hand . . . once you fall into that, the judge ends up with a lot less sympathy for you. Maybe a greater willingness to send you up to New York."

On November 18, 1982, Federal District Judge G. Ross Anderson, Jr., transferred the trial to the Southern District of New York in Manhattan, to a courthouse just a few miles south of CBS world headquarters.

Although Burt was dismayed at the prospect of fighting in CBS's backyard and was still hoping for an out-of-court settlement, he didn't act like it. He got to work, using the media to fight the media, a technique he perfected in the months before the case went to trial. While CBS was still deciding how to proceed, Burt suddenly started telling reporters how he was going to topple the network, offering bits and pieces of information that made it appear he might indeed have the necessary ammunition. CBS insiders, he hinted, were ready to come forward to testify against the network. Burt was a colorful character and a good story, spewing forth a string of curses and then mildly quoting Yeats or Shakespeare. The lawyer was pleased to be causing CBS so much trouble and he delighted in detailing for anyone who would listen the humiliations he had in store for George Crile, Cravath, and the network. He seemed to be whipping himself into a frenzy of anger, with the brunt of his wrath directed at Crile.

At the same time, Westmoreland continued his rigorous schedule of public appearances, but refused to discuss the case, even with veterans' groups. "In this matter," Burt was fond of saying, "Westmoreland is a soldier and I am the commander."

Burt really was talking with CBS employees and really did intend to call some of them as witnesses. His key informant, of course, was Ira Klein, who by this time was working on a big non-CBS project, Bill Moyers' series "A Walk Through the Twentieth Century." In August 1982, the month before the lawsuit was filed, Klein decided to confide extensively in reporter Don Kowet. At that point, Kowet was considering writing a book about the case and was in touch with several principals in the story, including Burt. When Burt called Klein a month after the lawsuit was filed, seeking his help, the film editor agreed to talk with him. Klein met eight or more times in New York and Washington over the next year with Burt and his Capital Legal associates, and participated in some fifteen telephone conversations. At one point, the three men—Burt, Klein, and Kowet—met for dinner in New York's Greenwich Village to discuss the case.

Klein has said he doesn't remember the exact details of all these meetings and conversations, but one tape-recorded exchange with Kowet which was eventually made public reveals beyond a doubt his animosity toward Crile. In what he later testified was an "adult conversation," he called his former boss a "social pervert," "devious," and "slimy," while making unflattering sexual remarks about some of Crile's close women friends and other members of the documentary unit.

The CBS hierarchy by this time was trying to do a little public-relations work in the journalism community. Efforts to settle the matter out of court continued until just months before the opening of the trial, but after winning a change of venue the network was less inclined to give in to Westmoreland's demands. Mostly, network officials were busy portraying themselves as guardians of the First Amendment beset by the Extreme Right. In a speech to the National Academy of Television Arts and Sciences, Van Gordon Sauter hinted there was a right-wing movement afoot to use the case as a vehicle to tighten libel law. He singled out a fund-raising campaign by Accuracy in Media, an ultra-conservative media-"watchdog" group, as a prime example of the supposed effort. As a result, Burt rejected the $35,000 that AIM collected for Westmoreland's defense, turning instead to direct-mail solicitation and the foundations that already carried the bulk of Capital Legal's expenses. (Richard Mellon Scaife—whom Crile had attacked in his 1975 *Washington Monthly* story about a crooked tax assessor—eventually picked up the lion's share of the bill.)

In January 1983, Sauter told the annual convention of Sigma Delta Chi, the Society of Professional Journalists, " . . . this is not just a CBS issue. The lawsuit has become a rallying point for people who seek to use it as an instrument for damaging the image, spirit, and aggressiveness of the news media. . . . We frankly feel a certain sadness at the prospect of the general, on the witness stand, facing the documents and the testimony that will sustain the CBS position and in the end do irreparable damage to his reputation. But many of those directing and supporting this lawsuit will have achieved their goals regardless of how the general fares. He is merely the point man in their search-and-destroy mission against the news media. And thus we should not consider this as just a legal matter between a citizen and a news organization. It is part of an ongoing battle waged by those who seek to curtail the freedom of the press in this society. . . ."

Dan Burt was outraged by Sauter's speech, telling one reporter that if the CBS News executive "would like to make that statement somewhere else, like in a street or alley, I'd be happy to take the matter up with him." But, overall, the speech seemed to be a touchdown for CBS. Sauter's remarks were widely reported in the national press. A month and a half later, however, the network was stunned when Sigma Delta Chi announced the winners of its 1982 Distinguished Service Awards. Don Kowet and Sally Bedell, the authors of *TV Guide*'s "Anatomy of a Smear," were honored in the magazine reporting category.

Sauter fired off a protest letter to *Quill* magazine, the society's journal, saying the award-winning article contained several serious errors and inaccuracies "each of which illustrates a shocking disregard for the truth." To bolster his point, he quoted from the letter George Allen had written him after the article appeared, in which Allen said *TV Guide* had taken his remarks out of context by claiming he had urged Crile not to make the documentary. "I did not attempt to dissuade CBS from doing the show and I do not believe the show made a 'mountain out of a molehill,' " Allen had written. *TV Guide* promptly responded by sending *Quill* a transcript of Allen's taped interview with the magazine. Whatever Allen said to Crile, it was clear he had told *TV Guide* that "I kind of objected and tried to dissuade Crile and company. . . . " This was not the last contradiction in the lawsuit over a story about contradictions.

Despite the mud-slinging from both sides, the two gladiators— Dan Burt and David Boies—were beginning to have real respect for each other. "Only the best," Burt said of Boies. "Any man who is into civil-rights fights down in Mississippi and still believes in them, he's first class. If I were in a fight, I would want him on my side. And there's few men or women I would want in that position. I would be very comfortable with him even at my back. And there are even fewer I would want there." For his part, Boies described Burt as "complex" and "highly intelligent," saying the other lawyer's abilities were irrefutably proven by the fact he had already shepherded the incredibly complicated case over so many hurdles.

The Capital Legal team—Patricia Embrey, Kathleen McGinn, James Moody, Anthony Murry, and Richard Riese—was throwing most of its time and money behind the Westmoreland cause, with fund-raiser Kay Daly working non-stop to rally more fiscal support. In addition, Dan Burt hired an outside lawyer to help him with the case, David Dorsen of the Washington firm Sachs, Greenebaum & Tayler. Dorsen, a former assistant U.S. attorney in New York, had been assistant chief counsel to the Senate Watergate Committee and offered the libel experience that Burt lacked. More important, Dorsen was at home before a jury and could take over the tricky task of cross-examining the CBS witnesses if necessary.

The CBS defense team was already plotting how to make Burt's job harder, and its line-up was impressive. At Cravath, the lead attorney was getting help from William Duker, Robert Baron, Randy Mastro, and Michael Doyen. CBS vice president and general counsel George Vradenburg III plus corporate lawyers Ronald Guttman, Douglas Jacobs, and Catherine Flickinger were in on the case. And then there were Crile's attorneys, Victor Kovner and Harriet Dorsen.

By this time, Boies was completely immersed in the Vietnam War. He had transformed himself into a student, and his office at Cravath's towering Wall Street enclave began to resemble a war room, with a map of Vietnam spanning the wall above his sofa.

"I did some reading. I spent some time just with maps and statistics. You know, where the lines were, where the battles were fought. To know where it is; what years were people killed; your side, their side; the bombings."

Before he could begin to take depositions and start work on a planned motion asking the judge to rule in CBS's favor without a trial, Boies needed to understand the order of battle and delve into the maze of Sam Adams' chronologies. The heap of documents Adams had spirited out of the CIA provided much factual evidence, but CBS needed more, much more.

Enter Bill Duker. The discovery process roared into high gear when the Cravath associate was assigned to document duty. For a while he made virtually a full-time job of subpoenaing government agencies, searching for any and all papers that might have a bearing on the case. He wanted to know about the order of battle, enemy infiltration, and the daily military doings in the years associated with the numbers dispute. At the same time, he had to reply to Capital Legal's demands for copies of any documents that CBS turned up, and obtain any relevant papers unearthed by Capital Legal.

Before long, scores of cardboard boxes—packed with hundreds of thousands of pages of seemingly random documents—began to arrive from everywhere: the Army, the CIA, the Defense Intelligence Agency, and the Lyndon Johnson Library. A glance at the contents showed that many of the papers had once been stamped SECRET or TOP SECRET. Now those classifications were scratched through, with a librarian's notation and date indicating they had been released to the public for the first time. As Duker mined this raw material of history that was slowly taking over a storeroom at Cravath, his excitement mounted. The labor, while Herculean, was turning out to be fun. He would sift through a thousand or so pages of boring reports and suddenly find gold: a document that could bolster Boies' arguments or a report that answered fifteen-year-old questions about the Vietnam War. He stumbled across two hefty studies the CIA had prepared for Defense Secretary Robert McNamara in the mid-1960s that were as engrossing as the Pentagon Papers.

In Washington, D.C., in somewhat less luxurious surroundings, a similar quest was under way. Anthony Murry, a Princeton alumnus who had just finished law school, was studying for the bar when the Westmoreland case landed at Capital Legal. Within months, the former legal intern also was transformed into a student of military history. Westmoreland had given his lawyers about ten documents as evidence, but they needed more. Murry started knocking on many of the same doors as Duker, filing request after request under the Freedom of Information Act, but looking for a different body of evidence.

He went to the Center for Military History to see what was available and learned that "no one really had a handle on it," primarily due to the messy way the war had ended. "The Army would just throw stuff in boxes and mail it back from Vietnam. Nobody looked at the stuff and indexed it."

So Murry worked to gain possession of large chunks of this unindexed load, 75 percent of which was irrelevant. He found that the Army was willing to declassify the most documents, with the CIA proving almost as helpful. The LBJ Library in Austin, Texas, also cooperated, but dealing with the DIA and the NSA was a colossal headache. They wanted to "sanitize" virtually everything. Nevertheless, he was shaking loose some important material, including proof that the National Security Agency had been reporting to the White House on enemy strength through its own channels during the period when CBS said the military was withholding the true numbers.

As he dug through the boxes piled in a tiny upstairs room at the foundation, Murry began to assemble the events leading up to the compromise on MACV's official tally of North Vietnamese and Vietcong. He flagged hundreds of pages that would later be entered into evidence. "It was exciting," he recalled. "This was original historical research. It was thrilling to be able to piece together a sequence of historical events unknown to anyone but the immediate participants. I began to anticipate the mail coming every day. It was like Christmas."

As he read, he started to develop an admiration for Sam Adams ("Some of Sam's documents were really outstanding"). The thing that bothered him, though, was that he didn't have enough time to scrutinize any papers except those which could be used as ammunition against CBS. Scanning the bumper crop of declassified material, he saw there was plenty of other information here: plans for secret operations that would have violated treaties, information on MIAs and prisoners of war, the daily field records from important battles. "We cast a wide net because it was the only way to do it, and as a result we got bunches and bunches of stuff."

Like Duker, he saw that the process they had set in motion— opening the doors on a period of history so recent that much was still hidden—might have an impact larger than just the case at hand. He secretly believed he might even stumble across "the truth" about the war.

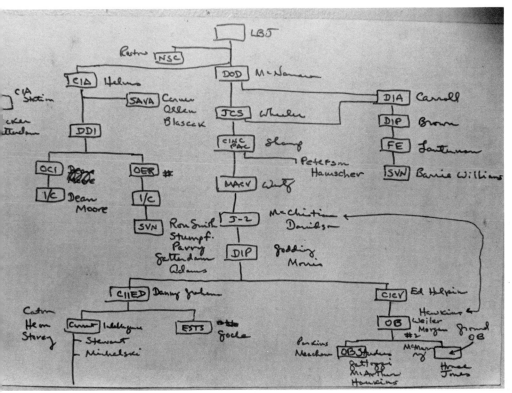

ABOVE   A diagram former CIA analyst Sam Adams sketched on the back of an Algon-
quin Hotel menu to depict the chain of command during the 1967 debate over enemy troop
strength in Vietnam. Similar renderings appear in Adams' voluminous "chronologies."
BELOW   Sam Adams, whose "obsession" led to the CBS documentary.

ABOVE   CBS producer George Crile appearing on-camera during an inter-view for the 1982 documentary "The Uncounted Enemy: A Vietnam Decep-tion." CENTER   George Allen, the CIA's expert on Vietnam and Sam Adams' boss at the Agency during 1967, tells his story for the CBS cameras. BELOW   Colonel Gains Hawkins, an Army intelligence officer who would eventually take the stand on behalf of CBS, tells producer George Crile of the 1967 meetings during which the CIA and the military tried to reach agreement on enemy troop strength estimates.

TOP Retired General Daniel Graham, who headed MACV intelligence during Westmoreland's Vietnam years, scoffs at charges that any enemy troop strength numbers were altered in 1967 and 1968. CENTER The CBS cameras capture General Westmoreland in a tight closeup, nervously licking his lips, during his interview for "The Uncounted Enemy." BELOW General William Westmoreland listens at a news conference he called on January 26, 1982, to counter the charges CBS made in "The Uncounted Enemy."

ABOVE   Mike Wallace in June 1970, returning from Vietnam, where he was on assignment for "60 Minutes." BELOW LEFT   CBS producer Burton "Bud" Benjamin's internal report on the documentary was sharply critical of some of producer George Crile's methods. BELOW RIGHT   Journalist Hodding Carter challenges the thesis of the CBS documentary in the April 21, 1983, edition of his PBS show "Inside Story," titled "Uncounted Enemy: Unproven Conspiracy."

ABOVE   David Boies, the Cravath, Swaine & Moore attorney representing CBS in the libel suit retired General William Westmoreland brought against the network, outside the U.S. District Court in Manhattan in November 1984.   BELOW   Westmoreland's attorney, Dan Burt of the Capital Legal Foundation *(left)*, heads for the courthouse with former Secretary of Defense Robert S. McNamara, a witness for the general.

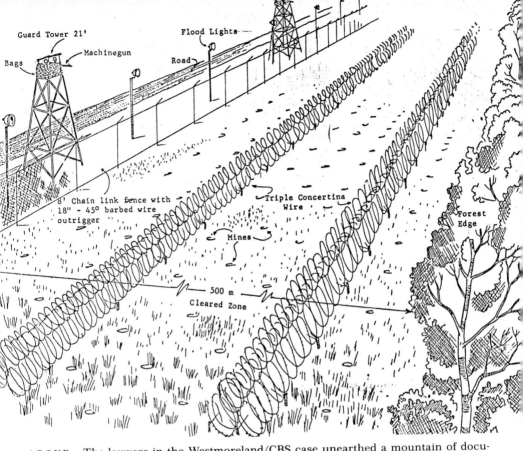

Guard Tower 21'
Machinegun
Bags
Flood Lights
Road
8' Chain link fence with
18" - 45° barbed wire
outrigger
Triple Concertina
Wire
Mines
Forest
Edge
500 m
Cleared Zone

ABOVE The lawyers in the Westmoreland/CBS case unearthed a mountain of documents, including this Army sketch of the proposed "McNamara Line" between the two Vietnams. BELOW General Joseph McChristian, Westmoreland's former intelligence chief, leaves court in February 1985 after delivering testimony that badly hurt his former commander's case.

ABOVE   CBS producer George Crile (*left*) hurries from the courthouse with John Scanlon, the public relations adviser CBS hired for the trial, in January 1985, shortly after the network began to present its case.   BELOW   Sam Adams (*center*) and assorted relatives leave federal court in January 1985 on one of the days he testified for CBS.

General William Westmoreland addresses the National Press Club in Washington, D.C., in March 1985, the month after he suddenly dropped his case against CBS.

Part Two

The History

6.

Revelations: War and Policy

TH E lasting legacy of the Westmoreland-CBS trial is its contribution to the historical record of the Vietnam War. Besides un-
earthing 500,000-plus pages of highly classified government documents, lawyers for both sides interrogated many of the senior officials
of the Kennedy and Johnson administrations under oath about high-
level policies. This questioning was often argumentative, sometimes
combative. Unlike journalists conducting an interview, lawyers de-
posing hostile witnesses put up with little shilly-shallying. They're out
to prove a point and will press fiercely to make it. Lawyers can compel witnesses to answer, journalists can't.

David Boies said after the trial that the Westmoreland case was
the best argument he could think of for keeping intact the sometimes
maligned discovery process. Critics charge that lawyers use the discovery rules to go on purposeless fishing expeditions. They also say
large law firms like Cravath, backed by large corporate clients such
as CBS, use the expensive fact-finding system as a means to grind
down less well-heeled adversaries.

Capital Legal's Anthony Murry agreed with Boies. Although in
the Westmoreland case he was somewhat hobbled by limited funds,
Murry learned to use the Freedom of Information Act skillfully and
concluded that the discovery process is "what democracy is all about.
Current attempts to limit the use of the Freedom of Information Act
are mostly manifestations of the bureacrat's natural desire to cover
his ass and a preference not to have his decisions scrutinized."

Thanks to Murry's digging, and that of Bill Duker and Bob Baron
at Cravath, Swaine & Moore, many decisions made during the course
of the Vietnam War are now open to public scrutiny. "That's the way
it works in an open society," Murry said. "It would be harmful in the
long run to limit the reach of this kind of action. FOIA acts as a check

on a bureaucratic irresponsibility, especially if it's the Department of Defense, the Central Intelligence Agency, or the National Security Agency."

As for the underpinnings of history turned up in the fight with CBS, he said, "People can look at this and make analogies to current situations. We can look at the rationales [made then] with a more critical judgment. The true usefulness of history," Murry said, "is to be able to make judgments. That's why we read Thucydides."

The paper search was only part of the pre-trial battle. Because each side was seeking to prove the "truth" of its case, the lawyers had to hunt down the men who had created the paper: the civilian and military high command of the war. The fact that two self-made men of modest birth, Dan Burt and David Boies, could haul the mighty into witness rooms and compel them to talk about the Vietnam War is also a testament to the U.S. constitutional system. Nowhere else in the world would such an action even be contemplated.

Some of these officials, such as Walt Whitman Rostow, Johnson's loquacious national-security adviser, had already made their views on the war well known through interviews and books and were quite willing to testify. Others, particularly former Secretary of Defense Robert S. McNamara, had kept silent on the war since leaving office and were reluctant witnesses. They were forced to go on the record, in part, by a press-relations tactic of Dan Burt's that backfired.

In mid-December 1983, Burt held a news conference in Washington, D.C., to parade some of the evidence he had accumulated against CBS. To bolster his preview of coming attractions, Burt produced sworn statements from a veritable Who's Who of former officials of the Johnson and Kennedy administrations. For the most part, these testimonies were long on opinion and short on fact. They primarily symbolized a closing of ranks of the Vietnam War's old guard—Dean Rusk, Robert McNamara, former CIA directors William Colby and Richard Helms, former Saigon Ambassador Ellsworth Bunker—behind Westmoreland. These men saw in Westy's case a chance to defend an old comrade while delivering a hard blow to the media.

Their statements confirmed the general's integrity, but skirted the facts of the case. In his three-page affidavit (prepared, like many of the other statements handed out to the press that day, by Burt or his associates at Capital Legal), McNamara simply said, "It is inconceivable to me that MACV arbitarily reduced estimates of enemy strength as a result of this or any other dispute." He added that he had told CBS producer Crile, " . . . I do not believe it would have been possible for the military command in Vietnam to engage in a conspiracy to suppress or fake intelligence on enemy troop strength and, if such a conspiracy had existed, I do not believe it could have been kept from myself or the President."

Although brief, McNamara's statement was a radical move for the chief civilian architect of America's early Vietnam War policy. Since leaving Johnson's service on February 28, 1968, to head the World Bank, McNamara had not uttered a word in public about the war. This short statement, which McNamara thought was the end of his involvement in the case, would ensnare him in something he had avoided for twenty years—a full-scale public airing of his views and knowledge of the war.

Due to their own naïveté about the legal system or to lack of forthrightness by Burt—probably a combination of the two—the men who stood up for Westy with their December 1983 statements soon found themselves compelled to break their silence. Once an individual files an affidavit in a lawsuit, he is liable to cross-examination, allowing the other side to depose him about the allegations made in the affidavit before the trial begins. A deposition is sworn testimony that can be admitted at a trial. But, according to Capital Legal's Murry, the real purpose of a deposition is to find out what a witness at a trial is going to say. The key difference between trial testimony and deposition testimony is that there is no judge overseeing the proceedings to act as a buffer between the lawyers and, in McNamara's case, an extremely reluctant witness.

McNamara, the ultimate whiz kid from the Ford Motor Company who tried to run the Pentagon like a well-ordered corporation, thus found himself unwillingly pitted against David Boies, a relentless questioner who had honed his skills in Mississippi courts as a civil-rights lawyer. It was no contest. First, Boies had the law on his side. Second, it was a field he had played on and excelled at for years. So, on March 26 and 27, 1984, the man who chose not to talk was forced to break his silence in an austere conference room (littered with the remnants of the popcorn Boies eats almost insatiably) at CBS's offices at 1800 M Street in Washington, D.C.

Shortly after the questioning began, McNamara angrily interrupted Boies, saying, " . . . I want it clear on the record that you are extracting these answers from me against my wishes. I told Crile that I have never spoken on Vietnam. I have no intention of doing so. There are two reasons for my reluctance to do so. These are events of twenty years ago. My memory is imperfect. I do not believe that a participant should be judge of his own actions or the validity of those actions."

McNamara then told Boies that because of these strong convictions, " . . . in the mid-1960s I asked that the *Pentagon Papers*, what came to be known as the *Pentagon Papers*, be assembled and be available for scholars and historians as raw material to re-examine the decision-making process of the Vietnam War.

"Any answers I give to your questions today are being supplied solely because I understand . . . understand from you that I am required by law to give them."

Boies calmly confirmed that McNamara was "under legal obligation to answer the questions that I ask you." But, at the same time, Boies, an avid history buff, could scarcely contain his excitement at the chance to satisfy his intellectual curiosity, possibly even on topics beyond the immediate scope of the case. And gambler Boies relished the chance to peek at what might be his opponent's hole card.

McNamara, still wishing he could remain silent, once again told Boies, "I would quite frankly refuse to answer them if I thought I had a legal right to refuse them. I do not wish to engage in a discussion of my views or anybody else's views of the Vietnam War." He said the public has "a perfect right" and "obligation" to examine the decision-making process of the war, but added, "I do not believe that I am qualified at this time to be participating in that process and I will resist to the limit of my legal right any effort to draw me into it."

Despite this fierce resistance to go on the record, McNamara, both in his deposition and in his testimony later given at the trial, was direct in his views on the war—a war he testified he knew could not be won even as he was directing it. McNamara said that although he and President Johnson had a "very, very close, extraordinarily close personal relationship," there was a "considerable period of time we disagreed about the conduct of the war. I continued to try and serve him loyally. He continued to hold me in extremely high regard. We eventually came to a parting of the ways."

McNamara's disagreements with his commander-in-chief were "over details of the conduct of the war. I recall specifically that at the time we disagreed over a period during which a bombing halt should extend; over the targets of particular bombing operations."

The divisions between the President and his Secretary of Defense went further than details, however. "I think there was probably a difference of view as to the general progress of the war and possibly even the way in which it should be continued," McNamara said. " . . . I can tell you my view was that it was unlikely that the war could be won by military means." Asked to put a date on this opinion, McNamara answered, " . . . I certainly held that view at times in 1966, if not earlier." This was quite a revelation. U.S. troop strength in Vietnam at the time was being bolstered considerably. Westmoreland was asking for and getting—from McNamara—more and more ground and air units. Pressed by Boies to explain this startling disclosure, McNamara said he had been "skeptical as to whether a military victory could be achieved and I believed considerable emphasis should be put on developing what was called a political track, which would lead to negotiations with the North Vietnamese. . . . The view that a political track should be developed to complement the military action I held early on and I don't want to put a date on it other than to say that it was probably as early as 1965 or earlier."

McNamara repeated this testimony in court on December 6, 1984, the first time he talked about the war in public since he had left office in 1968. Speaking to a courtroom packed with journalists and their bosses (sitting in one of the press rows next to *Newsday*'s Murray Kempton was Katherine Graham, chairman of the Washington Post Company and an old friend and confidante of McNamara's), McNamara, slicked-down hair only slightly thinned in a decade and a half, told what he had kept secret during his tenure as Defense Secretary: "I did not believe the war could be won militarily."

During cross-examination, McNamara revealed that he and Westmoreland had had "major differences of opinion" about various strategic options. This was vividly illustrated by a TOP SECRET–SENSITIVE memo from McNamara to LBJ on May 19, 1967, that Boies introduced into evidence. This memo examined how the government might respond to a request by Westmoreland for an additional 200,000 troops.

Titled "Future Action In Vietnam," the 1967 memo starts out by stating, "All things considered, there is consensus that we are no longer in danger of losing this war militarily." That, as the memo makes clear, is not the same as winning. One key impediment to winning, in McNamara's view, was the South Vietnamese. "Little has been done to remedy the economic and social ills or the corruption from which popular VC support stems." Furthermore, the South Vietnamese government (run by the military) was not representative, in his view. "The government has launched a program of national reconciliation but with limited success so far. We hope that efforts in this direction will improve when an elected government is installed in Saigon, but there is little ground for optimism."

Two years of bombing North Vietnam had not moved that country toward the negotiating table—Johnson's fervent hope. Massive U.S. ground support had not moved the North toward reconciliation either. "Hanoi's attitude toward negotiations has never been soft or open minded," McNamara told LBJ.

"The Hanoi leadership has apparently decided that it has no choice but to submit to the increased bombing. There appears to be no sign that the bombing has reduced Hanoi's will to resist or her ability to ship the necessary supplies south. Hanoi shows no sign of ending the large war and advising the VC to melt into the jungles.

"The North Vietnamese believe they are right; they consider the Ky regime [in South Vietnam] to be puppets; they believe the world is with them and that the American public will not have staying power against them. . . . They probably do not want to make serious concessions, and could not do so without a serious loss of face."

McNamara then examined two alternative courses of military action. One involved a stepped-up campaign of bombing the North coupled with a large increase in the U.S. troop force in the South, a plan advocated by Westmoreland and the Joint Chiefs of Staff headed by General Earle Wheeler. McNamara countered this with a suggestion of his own, which called for a limited increase in troop strength and a strong push toward a negotiated settlement.

Westmoreland's plan would require calling up the reserves and increasing the Defense Department budget by $10 billion in 1968. McNamara said its proponents argued that "such deployments will hasten the end of the war. None of them believes that the added forces are needed to avoid defeat; few of them believe that the added forces are required to do the military job in due course; all of the proponents believe that they are needed if that job is to be done faster."

Westmoreland, according to McNamara, saw a correlation between increased troop strength and speedier victory. "General Westmoreland had said that without the additions the war could go on for five years. He has said that with 100,000 more men the war could go on for three years and that with 200,000 more men it could go on for two."

Such a course of action would not necessarily hasten the end of the war, McNamara contended, and it could spark such an upheaval at home, primarily due to the mobilization of the reserves, that "there would be irresistible pressure for stronger action outside South Vietnam. Cries would go up, much louder than they already have, to 'take the wraps off the men in the field.' The actions would include more intense bombing—not only around-the-clock bombing of targets already authorized, but also bombing of strategic targets such as locks and dikes and mining of the harbors against Soviet and other ships. Associated actions impelled by the situation would be major ground actions in Laos, in Cambodia and probably in North Vietnam—first as a pincer operation north of the DMZ and then at a point such as Vinh."

McNamara warned that the nuclear genie might not be contained if the military got its way. "The use of tactical nuclear weapons and area denial radiological-bacteriological-chemical weapons would probably be suggested at some point if the Chinese entered the war in

Vietnam or Korea or if U.S. losses were running high while conventional efforts were not producing desired results."

McNamara as dove, a position some of his critics dismiss as a revisionist approach to Vietnam War history, comes through clearly in this memo. Discussing pressures for increased bombing of the North, he argued that, while the paramount concern about the increased bombing was the cost in pilots' lives, "an important but hard to measure cost is domestic and world opinion: There may be a limit beyond which many Americans and much of the world will not permit the United States to go. The picture of the world's greatest superpower killing or seriously injuring 1,000 non-combatants a week while trying to pound a tiny, backward nation into submission on an issue whose merits are hotly disputed is not a pretty one. It could conceivably produce a costly distortion in the American national consciousness and in the world image of the United States, especially if the damage to North Vietnam is complete enough to be 'successful.' "

The "most important risk" of an escalation, however, was communist reaction, McNamara believed. Mining the harbors, which became a constant demand of hawks throughout the war years from President Kennedy to President Nixon, "would place Moscow in a particularly galling dilemma as how to preserve the Soviet position and prestige. . . . The Soviets might, but probably would not, force a confrontation in Southeast Asia . . . [but probably] should be expected to send volunteers, including pilots, to North Vietnam; to provide some new and better weapons and equipment; to consider some action in Korea, Turkey, Iran, the Middle East, or most likely, Berlin, where the Soviets can control the degree of crisis better. . . . "

China, a constant concern of both the military and the civilian high commands at this stage of the war, "might view the harbor-mining as indicating that the U.S. was going to apply military pressure until North Vietnam capitulated, and that this meant an eventual invasion. If so, China might decide to intervene in the war with combat troops and air power, to which we would eventually have to respond by bombing Chinese airfields and other targets as well."

Ground actions in North Vietnam, a contingency Westmoreland and the Joint Chiefs constantly planned for, would cause China "to respond by entering the war with both ground and air forces," McNamara said. "Ground actions in Laos are similarly unwise. . . . In essence, a brigade will beget a division and a division a corps, each calling down matching forces from North Vietnam into territory to their liking. . . . We would simply have a wider war. . . . "

In summing up the two courses for LBJ, McNamara said, "The war in Vietnam is acquiring a momentum of its own that must be stopped. Dramatic increases in troop deployments, in attacks on the

North or in ground actions in Laos and Cambodia are not necessary and are not the answer. The enemy can absorb them or counter them, bogging us down further and risking even more serious escalation of the war."

He told the President that the course advocated by Westy and the Joint Chiefs "could lead to a major national disaster; it would not win the war, but only submerge it in a larger one." While increasing troop strength modestly, which McNamara backed, "likewise will not win the Vietnam War in a military sense in a short time, it does avoid the larger war, however, and it is part of a military-political/pacification-diplomatic package that gets things moving toward a successful outcome in a few years."

Until the Tet Offensive, when Westy again asked for more troops, the course of the war followed McNamara's limited-escalation suggestions—30,000 troops, restricted bombing, etc.—rather than the more radical path suggested by the Joint Chiefs.

McNamara took pains to buttress with facts his opinion that the war could not be won. He had brought a businessman's mind to the Pentagon, had installed a layer of former business-school types to oversee a Pentagon bureaucracy he distrusted, and when it came to assessing the Vietnam War, McNamara again turned outside the Pentagon—to the Central Intelligence Agency.

As McNamara later testified at the trial, he wanted an assessment of military progress by an organization totally separate from the military. "There was constant agreement about all aspects of the elements of enemy strength, and therefore as I say, I had asked the President for special authority to ask the CIA for special service . . . to check independently the figures from my own sources, Defense Intelligence Agency, MACV and so on."

McNamara quickly added that he did not doubt "the honesty of the reports coming to me from the military," but simply "wanted an independent check."

The independent reports the CIA gave McNamara in August 1966 and May 1967 were two extraordinarily prescient memos—if documents with the heft of metropolitan phone books can be dubbed "memos." Through dint of sheer analytical brilliance, the reports accurately assessed the facts and then forecast that, no matter how great the U.S. force of arms in Southeast Asia, the Vietnam War was unwinnable.

Prepared by the Office of Research and Reports, the Office of National Estimate, and the Special Assistant for Vietnamese Affairs in the Office of the Director of Central Intelligence, these two TOP SECRET CIA documents, declassified for the first time during the discovery process of the Westmoreland-CBS case, gave the U.S. leadership the same kind of early warning that the country had had, and ignored, when a primitive radar site in Hawaii tracked incoming Japanese airplanes on December 7, 1941. The difference between the two warnings is that at Pearl Harbor the leaders had only minutes to act. The CIA's admonitions, if McNamara and Johnson had heeded them, might have saved years of fighting a war that almost turned the United States against itself.

The first CIA report, "Memorandum: The Vienamese Communists' Will To Persist," dated August 26, 1966, scrutinzed every aspect of the war, ranging from the effects of the ROLLING THUNDER bombing campaign on morale in the North to the daily logistic requirements of the NVA (North Vietnamese Army) and VC forces in the South to an examination of the lessons the North Vietnamese had learned in fighting the French. The eight summary chapters, the twelve annexes, and the hundreds of pages of charts in this report debunked most of the "facts" the U.S. military cited to show that America could win the war. The report stated, and then backed up with abundant data, that bombing in the North was a strategic failure which actually aided the Vietcong cause. It found that literally no amount of bombing on the Ho Chi Minh Trail—the enemy's main supply route, which went from North Vietnam through Laos—would keep the North Vietnamese from moving the few supplies needed by their forces in the South. It discovered that, despite the seeming numerical superiority of U.S. and allied ground forces, in terms of actual combat troops the two sides were almost evenly matched. It also exposed and confirmed one of the war's dirty little secrets—that multi-national oil companies doing business in the South routinely aided the Vietcong by paying "taxes" to the enemy, letting the VC take a portion of an oil truck's load. This practice, plus purchases of petroleum products in Cambodia or at local gas stations, took care of all of the VC's POL (petroleum, oil, lubricants) needs.

The United States built much of its military strategy around bombing the North, the Trail, and targets within South Vietnam itself. The skies above both parts of Vietnam were so abuzz with airplanes that the military kept an airborne command post aloft twenty-four hours a day to act as a traffic cop. The year McNamara received this report, the Danang airbase surpassed Chicago's O'Hare as the busiest airport in the world.

No aircraft was too small, too large, too old, or too unconventional for this effort. Marine pilots flying o–1 observation planes over rice paddies south of Danang conducted "bombing" raids against small villages with hand grenades; Navy pilots in venerable World War II radial-engined A-1 Skyraiders roared off carriers steaming in the Gulf of Tonkin to drop their payloads on trucks traversing the Ho Chi Minh

Trail in Laos; Air Force F-105 Thunderchief pilots routinely attacked (and too routinely were shot down as the "Thud" racked up the worst loss record of the war) bridges and oil dumps in the North; while the awesome eight-engined B-52 flew 2,400 miles from Guam to attack practically every type of target in both North and South.

Controlling this multi-billion-dollar air war was a chain of command that stretched from the rice paddies to the White House, with Johnson and his Cabinet personally selecting, and often anguishing over, targets in the populated cities of the North. Less politically sensitive targets were selected by methods that ranged from hunches to sophisticated computer and radar-assisted technology. Lowly grunts in the field, from the handset of a simple backpacked radio, could and did direct the unleashing of awesome bomb loads while FACs (forward air controllers) constantly orbited the Laotian portion of the trails, calling in strikes by jet aircraft against foot-slogging Vietcong porters. Sophisticated radar-bombing systems (including a top-secret one in Laos) took control of high-flying B-52s, toggling the bomb loads without the crew even having to touch a switch. Eventually, the United States dropped more bombs on the two tiny Vietnams than all the combatants in the Second World War expended. But it wasn't enough, and Robert McNamara knew that in 1966.

Slightly more than a year after full-scale bombing started, the CIA told McNamara that "The air strikes . . . have created problems for the Communists, but in both military and economic terms, the damage inflicted so far has probably not exceeded what the Communists regard as acceptable levels. . . . In both financial and material terms, the cost inflicted on North Vietnam by allied air attacks is more than covered by other Communist countries. . . . Air attacks conducted under the present rules of engagement almost certainly cannot stop North Vietnam activities essential to the support of the Communist war effort."

The Joint Chiefs and hawks in the Senate had been arguing with Johnson and his advisers that if those rules of engagement—designed to avoid hitting civilian targets, Soviet ships, and supply lines in China—were relaxed, then the United States would no longer be "fighting with one hand tied behind its back." The CIA analysis, however, said this was a false conclusion. " . . . Intensified attacks would have little impact in halting either essential imports or the flow of petroleum necessary to sustain the logistic pipeline to South Vietnam."

Yes, the CIA admitted, the United States could literally bomb the North back to the Stone Age, as some hawks demanded. But such attacks designed to bring what little modern industry there was in Vietnam "to a standstill" could backfire because "demand for internal distribution for the industrial sector would be eliminated. The loss of demand for petroleum for the industrial sector could permit the allocation of most of the available petroleum to the transportation of military supplies, food and other essentials such as civil defense items and medicines. This transport capacity would be supplemented by the use of primitive transport."

At the same time, bombing wasn't cost effective for the United States, particularly with the inflation caused by Johnson's "guns and butter" strategy factored in. According to the CIA, damage caused by air attacks against the North from the start of the war through the date of this report had been minimal—$86 million in total bomb damage, of which only $34 million directly affected the military. Results did not improve with experience either, the CIA said. "Damage to military facilities and equipment during the first five months of bombing in 1966 amounted to only $7 million, and was exceedingly low when compared to 1965. . . . The bulk of this loss consisted of destruction to aircraft and naval craft. . . . The average monthly damage to military facilities and equipment amounted to about $1.3 million."

In sheer dollar costs, the United States suffered more of a loss from the bombing campaign than the North did. Although the Air Force still has not declassified month-by-month aircraft losses during the Vietnam War, it does confirm annual losses. According to the Air Force Historical Branch, 224 aircraft (from all services) were lost over North Vietnam in 1966. This works out to an average of 18 planes a month, or roughly 90 aircraft for the first five months of 1966. One of the most expensive planes in the U.S. air fleet at the time was the McDonnell Douglas twin-engined F-4 Phantom, which cost $4 million. The U.S. lost 81 F-4s in 1966 for a monthly average of 7, or roughly 35 F-4s in the first five months of the year, putting the total dollar loss for this type in that time period to about $140 million, or twenty times the value of the damage inflicted against the North. No price can be put on the lives of the pilots killed or those who were captured and imprisoned.

Bombing didn't work as a terror weapon either. As Hitler found out during the London blitz, a campaign of intimidation from the sky tends to strengthen the enemy's will.

"Initial response of the North Vietnamese population to the US/GVN [Government of Vietnam] bombing was characterized by a high degree of patriotic enthusiasm," the report found. "The air attacks in a large measure have been a strong force for unifying the population in its resistance to the U.S. 'aggressors.' " The CIA did observe a "waning of popular enthusiasm" in the North as the bombing intensified, but warned that any decline in civilian morale "is not likely in the near future to deprive the leadership of freedom to pursue the conflict in the manner it chooses."

In July 1965, McNamara made one of his periodic inspection tours of Vietnam and received some bad news about how ineffective the bombing campaign was on the Vietcong and North Vietnam Army supply efforts. A declassified TOP SECRET transcript of a July 16, 1965, briefing in Saigon by Westmoreland, Ambassador Maxwell Taylor, and Joint Chiefs of Staff chairman General Earle Wheeler reveals McNamara questioning whether the United States could ever stop the supply flow.

After being told by Wheeler that the enemy was meeting most of its needs by moving only fourteen tons of supplies a day into the country, McNamara said, "The chances of stopping that by aerial attack are rather small."

In the same discussion, Ambassador Taylor (who had been President Kennedy's personal military adviser and chairman of the Joint Chiefs before being tapped to replace Henry Cabot Lodge, Jr., as Ambassador in 1964) displayed the kind of naïveté about the enemy's capabilities that would hobble the U.S. approach to the war for years to come. "It is amazing to me how the VC can bring all their people into the country and support them with so little effort when we have such a hell of a time supporting ours," he said.

McNamara, who was beginning to realize the true nature of the enemy, replied, " . . . They are taking the country over on 14 tons a day. To be real strict we can assume that they can take over even more of the country on 28 tons a day." He then summed up the simple reality the United States would face for the rest of the war. "It's pretty cheap warfare for them, so we had better learn how to do it. In order to stop the meager supplies of 14 tons per day it would take tremendous activity on the ground, which up until now we didn't have. The question is how the VC can get along with so little supplies when it takes the U.S. forces so much to support themselves."

In its 1966 report, the CIA confirmed McNamara's worst suspicions. Although the bombing campaign against the Ho Chi Minh Trail would continue unabated for the rest of the war, the CIA concluded that no amount of bombing could effectively stem the supply flow. In fact, the CIA said, the bombing helped the North Vietnamese by forcing them to improve this system.

The North built so many new roads that the CIA reported that "The net effect of the expansion in 1966 has been to provide an alternate route for every road that existed prior to the end of 1964."

The elementary math of the Vietnamese supply requirements just would not bend to any amount of bombing. The CIA estimated that the VC/NVA had a total troop strength in South Vietnam in mid-

1966 of between 260,000 and 280,000, which included 118,000 regular troops. These troops required about 159 tons of supplies a day, but only 20 tons a day had to be acquired from outside South Vietnam.

"These external supply requirements are small and their fulfill-ment requires only a small percentage of the capacity of the supply routes through Laos," the CIA said.

That capacity was immense, considering the terrain, weather conditions, and almost constant bombing the VC/NVA had to endure. "The current uninterdicted capacity of the infiltration network in the Laotian Panhandle for truck movement to points within a few miles of South Vietnam is about 400 tons a day in the dry season and 100 tons a day in the rainy season. Come rain or come shine, this capacity ranges from 5–20 times the current external logistic requirements of the current Communist forces in South Vietnam and from 2–7 times the probable external requirements under current estimates of the probable buildup of the Communist forces by mid-1967."

The awesome U.S. air machine found itself in the absurd posi-tion, according to this CIA analysis, of dropping more tons of bombs than the enemy was moving as supplies and still not being able to halt the flow. In December 1965, the United States sent 8,000 sorties (a sortie is one aircraft on one mission) against the Trail, dropping some 16,000 tons of bombs—"4,000 more tons of bombs than the VC/NVA were capable of moving in 30 days at a maximum daily average of 400 tons a day."

"In spite of this attack the level of truck traffic moving South during the same period—29 trucks a day—was twice the level of the same period one year earlier." No wonder the CIA determined that "the Laotian supply network must be regarded as relatively invulner-able to conventional air interdiction."

To counter the damage done against this important road network by expensive planes dropping iron bombs, the North Vietnamese used the oldest and simplest of Asian resources—manpower. Human sweat was the North's secret weapon.

The prodigious North Vietnamese engineering effort was sup-ported by 20,000 to 25,000 men in the Laotian Panhandle organized into a series of work camps responsible for particular segments of road. These workers were amazingly efficient, considering that they worked under conditions never faced by the average U.S. highway-repair crew. The CIA said, "Photography reveals the clearing of land-slides caused by bombings on route 92 within 3 days and repairs to interdicted portions of route 110 within 3–4 hours. Moreover the repairs have been carried out while the road system was in stage of considerable expansion."

As a result of this expansion and the establishment of permanent repair camps, the CIA said, "the Communists in the Panhandle are better able to counteract the bombings now than they were a year ago."

Another problem with trying to bomb the North back to the Stone Age was that in repairing damage the country was in the Bamboo Age. To replace bomb-damaged bridges, North Vietnam used an ancient but effective tool. According to the CIA study, "bamboo, the universal building material of Southeast Asia, is used extensively in construction of temporary bridges."

The CIA reports also revealed that the Vietcong and regular North Vietnamese Army had no problem meeting their petroleum needs in the South because they got their supplies from the same sources as everyone else in the South did—oil trucks operated by the multi-national oil companies doing business in South Vietnam.

The CIA said that the Vietcong's petroleum-supply requirements in the South were minimal, "being needed primarily for confiscated vehicles, motorized junks in the Delta region, generator equipment at command posts, and in some crude arms factories." The Agency then confirmed a bit of wisdom summed up in a grim joke popular with U.S. infantrymen: "Q. What's the safest vehicle to hitch a ride on in Vietnam? A. An Esso oil truck; the VC lose their aim when they see one." The CIA found a good explanation for this joke: "The VC obtain supplies from taxation of the content of petroleum tank trucks in the VC/NVA controlled areas of South Vietnam, seizure of petroleum supplies and purchase from local gas stations or in Cambodia."

A Royal Dutch Shell spokesman said, when asked about this practice in 1984, that so long after the war there was "no way to know" what the truck drivers did. An Exxon (formerly Esso) spokesman vehemently denied the implications of the report. Exxon "takes strong exception [to reports] that we in any way supported or gave any comfort to the Viet Cong. We forbade any of our employees from co-operating with the Viet Cong." But, he added, 80 percent of the deliveries of the fuel provided by the company to U.S. and South Vietnamese outposts were handled by independent Vietnamese contractors, and "Certainly we were aware that VC roadblocks halted trucks and tried to exact payment of petroleum goods en route to the customers." The Royal Dutch Shell spokesman said "a substantial portion" of Shell Oil deliveries also were made by private contractors and emphasized that the company "had no control over what those contractors did to ship the petroleum."

After United Press International ran stories on the McNamara Report in 1984, a former government inspector who oversaw petroleum distribution called UPI and said that the VC "taxation" of oil supplies went further than the CIA report said. In fact, he claimed, it amounted to outright payment by the oil companies directly to the enemy. It was a well-organized, routine procedure, he said, asking that his name not be used because he still works for the government.

"I had an office in the Esso Building," he said. "I received all the payment documents personally for my review and approval. We got a regular letter from the National Viet Front imposing a tax . . . and we paid that, the oil companies."

But the former inspector emphasized that he had been dealing with the Vietnamese representatives of the oil companies.

*   *   *

Westmoreland continued to press for more troops to fight this wily opponent—more Marines for the provinces closest to the DMZ in I Corps; more elite Army airborne divisions for the Central Highlands; more conventional divisions for the lowlands; more Koreans, more Thais, more Aussies, and more New Zealanders—all the countries besides the United States whose troops made up the Free World Forces (FWF) facing the communists.

But, according to the CIA analysis, just mixing more troops into the Vietnam stew was not the answer. The well-supplied American Army, which had beaten the Germans in World War II as much by the wealth of its supplies and support troops as the grit and determination of its infantryman, was an insanely fat creature to fight an enemy that lived on rice and constructed mines from dud U.S. ammo.

To defeat these jungle will-o-wisps, Westmoreland fielded an Army that included troops charged with doing nothing other than operating PXs that resembled department stores (the officer in charge of the Danang PX in 1965 was awarded a Bronze Star for his efficient management of that facility) or setting up mobile laundries.

Westmoreland also counted among his Free World Forces the crews of Navy refrigerator ships packed to the gunwales with sides of beef, and Army disc jockeys spinning "The Ballad of the Green Berets" for a growing network of Armed Forces Radio stations. Even television would soon come to serve the troops in the first TV war. In the Tet Offensive of 1968, MACV became the first military command in the history of warfare to have an entire mobile television station and studio captured by the enemy. The support troops had support troops—a veritable army of high-paid civilian construction workers, directing an even larger force of poorly paid Vietnamese laborers, who built the infrastructure the American Army needed to go out and hunt guerrillas: piers, roads, airfields, and direct-dial long-distance telephone systems.

These support troops were so far removed from the reality of the war and the grunts fighting it that in rear areas, such as the Danang airbase, air-conditioned enlisted-men's clubs run by and for these support troops wouldn't allow foot soldiers in the door. Too dirty. Too violent!

According to the CIA, instead of possessing the troop advantage, Westmoreland in reality didn't have enough combat troops. On paper, his army was numerically superior to the enemy: 300,000 American troops by the end of 1966, increasing by mid-1967 to 470,000 (plus South Vietnamese and other allied forces), versus a VC/NVA force that numbered between 118,000 and 280,000, depending on who was doing the counting. The CIA conceded this simple mathematical superiority. "In absolute numerical terms the Communists cannot hope to match present and projected allied force commitments," the Agency said in its 1966 report to McNamara. But the CIA added an important caveat:

"However, it is extremely unlikely they feel any need to do so. An analysis of relative force levels shows that the apparent present free world superiority of six to one over VC/NVA forces is largely eliminated when one compares the relative ratios of actual maneuver battalions—i.e., tactical combat troops available for commitment to offensive ground operations. The present ratio of allied to Communist maneuver battalions is nearly one to one. If present estimates of allied and Communist force projections are accurate, by mid-1967 the Communists will have a slight advantage in this critical ratio. The Communists almost certainly feel that if they can maintain a maneuver battalion ratio in this range, they will be able to prolong the struggle indefinitely and wear down the U.S. will to persist."

Huh?

In other words, despite speeded-up draft calls that were tearing apart the fabric of U.S. society, the Vietnam War was an even match in 1966. Westmoreland was trying to hunt a light, swift, jungle-smart enemy with a weird sort of dog—a ten-pound terrier with a fifty-pound logistical tail. "Only about one-fifth of the total allied army and Marine Corps troops are committed to engaging and destroying the enemy in offensive operations," the CIA reported. "Thus of a force in June 1966 totaling slightly over 218,000 Army and Marine ground forces only 44,200 represented troops in maneuver battalions. Over 157,000 troops were involved in indirect combat support, logistics, construction, engineering, security and other support tasks. . . . The Communist forces, on the other hand, have to commit only 18,000 troops or a little over 15 percent of their regular forces to combat support compared to over 80 percent for Allied forces."

No wonder McNamara gave up hope of a purely military victory and opted for hopes of a negotiated settlement. If the CIA was right (and history has proven it so), then the United States was incapable of beating the VC/NVA on the ground or in the air—no matter what the Joint Chiefs of Staff said.

According to TOP SECRET cable traffic declassified during the Westmoreland-CBS discovery process, by the beginning of 1967 the military had begun to believe that it had the enemy on the run. For example, in a February 17, 1967, cable, Wheeler told both Sharp and Westmoreland that "my report to Highest Authority [Lyndon Johnson] upon my return from South Vietnam in mid-January can be summarized in a few short sentences:

"The adverse military tide has been reversed, and General Westmoreland has the initiative. During 1966 we battered the enemy badly in both North and South Vietnam. The military situation will improve still further during 1967 just as it improved in 1966. The enemy can no longer hope to win the war in South Vietnam. We can win the war if we apply pressure upon the enemy relentlessly in the North and in the South." Wheeler added he had recently had a "most interesting conversation" with McNamara and that "it seems he is receptive to increasing our military pressure."

By April 1967, Westmoreland—at the White House pleading for more troops—was less optimistic. According to notes taken by Mc-Namara aide John McNaughton of a conversation between Westmoreland and LBJ on April 27, the general held out the grim possibility of a longer war if he did not get more men. "Without these troops (the 2⅓ additional divisions plus 5 squadrons, making a total of 565,000 men in South Vietnam) we will not be in danger of being defeated, but it will be nip and tuck to oppose the reinforcements the enemy is capable of providing."

But, Westmoreland added, a key goal had been met: the United States had reached the "cross-over point," killing or capturing enemy troops faster than they could be replaced. Johnson then asked Westmoreland, "When we add divisions, can't the enemy add divisions? If so, where does it all end?" The concerned President, seeing his popularity eroding the longer the war continued, his Great Society held hostage to the speedy resolution of a conflict thousands of miles away, asked, "What if we do not add the two and one-third divisions?"

Westmoreland replied, "The momentum will die, in some areas the enemy will recapture the initiative. We won't lose the war, but it will be a longer one."

While Wheeler was telling Johnson that the United States had "battered the enemy badly" in 1966, the quiet analysts at the CIA delivered to McNamara a far more pessimistic study. The second of the fat memos to McNamara, delivered in May 1967, confirmed many of the conclusions reached in the first. "Although we now possess substantial advantages in tactical mobility and awesome firepower the enemy has more than kept pace with our buildup in terms of infantry units," the CIA said, adding, "and [he] has managed to improve his fire support capability."

Yes, the CIA reported, buildup of U.S. ground forces had hurt the enemy, but the enemy had still managed to hit back, hard. "Communist losses in the first quarter of this year have risen 70 percent above the monthly averages for last year. U.S. losses have increased by over 90 percent, however. . . . On balance, the enemy's strategic posture in the main force war appears to have improved somewhat during the past year despite the allied buildup. . . . The ratio of enemy to friendly infantry battalions has grown from a level of 1 to 2.16 to about 1 to 1.65."

The air war had not affected the Vietcong–North Vietnam Army resupply capabilities in the past year either, the CIA said. "We have noted sustantially increased expenditure of ammunition of all types— particularly mortars and recoiless rifles—in all sectors, and a more plentiful supply of heavy weapons, including new types.

"These have occurred despite an intensive sea blockade, the over-running of substantial arms and ammunition caches and apparently effective air attacks on some depot areas."

In the meantime, the richest country in the world was having supply problems. A TOP SECRET April 6 cable from Wheeler to both Sharp and Westmoreland said, "Headlines in all newspapers today play up air munitions shortage in SVN. Even worse, contact made with several key Congressmen reveals that some of them take the attitude that we are over-extended in our military commitment to the point that we are and will be unable to support adequately our present forces and surely cannot support additional forces.

"As you well recognize, such feelings endanger continuation of the buildup of forces which we have planned and are striving mightily to execute."

Wheeler added that in his view the real problem was not the shortages, but the press coverage. "While I do not advocate in any degree concealing the truth from proper authority or accepting less than full support of our troops in combat, I cannot help viewing with concern sensitive information falling into the hands of those with no need to know who readily convert the information into harmful headlines."

Besides a bomb shortage, other cable traffic uncovered for the Westmoreland-CBS trial revealed that Westmoreland also faced a pilot shortage in the Army. Since much of the Army's tactics in Vietnam was built around the helicopter, this was as serious as the munition shortfall cited by Wheeler. In a January 1966 cable to Sharp and the Joint Chiefs, Westmoreland said that "all aviator sources have been exhausted and nearly 500 RVN [South Vietnamese] returnees are being recycled as replacements. . . . It is understood here that the formation of Army aviation units for CY 66 deployment above those now approved is impossible."

Munition shortages or not, the CIA, as it had done a year earlier, firmly stated that the bombing could not, did not, and would not serve as an effective means of cutting the enemy supply lines. "We estimate that current interdiction means are incapable of reducing the capacity of overland lines of communications below the current requirements of forces that the enemy now has in the South, or even a slightly larger force level.

"We are not confident that the blockade is effectively interdicting the movement of supplies by sea. . . . The intensity and persistence of enemy operations suggest that, although our operations may temporarily disrupt his logistical system locally, it is generally adequate to support actions on a scale and tempo at least as great as any mounted in the past."

The CIA also disputed Westmoreland's thesis that the magical "cross-over point" had been reached and wondered if it was an achievable goal. While conceding that enemy losses had increased dramatically, with some 24,000 of the enemy reported killed in the first quarter of 1967—about 70 percent greater than the average loss rate of 1966—the CIA estimated that the VC/NVA could continue despite these losses. They "have the capability to replace manpower losses at a rate higher than the present loss rate being inflicted on them, although probably at some overall cost in quality."

Finally, addressing itself once again to the "Bomb 'em back to the Stone Age" advocates, the CIA estimated that such a tactic was also unworkable. " . . . Even if further bombing were to eliminate modern industry entirely, the economy could still function at levels adequate to supply the bulk of the population's simple needs and to service and repair lines of communications.

"The elimination of modern industry would leave unaffected the half of the country's industrial capacity which is in small factories and handicrafts shops capable of supplying simple farm tools, some machinery and parts and processed foods and textiles."

Even in the Stone Age, it seemed, the North would have the ability to continue.

7.

Revelations: Rusk Remembers

DURING the Cuban missile crisis early in John Kennedy's Presidency, Secretary of State Dean Rusk summed up the situation succinctly: "We're eyeball to eyeball and the other fellow just blinked." Dean Rusk didn't mind going eyeball to eyeball with David Boies; he just didn't want anyone to know what happened. Although the former Secretary of State readily signed an affidavit to help General Westmoreland, he did not want his deposition to become part of the public record. Like McNamara, Rusk—the only Cabinet member to serve from the day Kennedy took office, January 21, 1961, until Johnson turned the Republic over to Richard Nixon eight years later —decided to shun publicity after leaving office.

With rare exceptions, he kept that privacy, breaking it only for a series of newspaper interviews after the Pentagon Papers were published in 1971 and brief television appearances in 1975 after the fall of Saigon. Since leaving the State Department, Rusk has pursued a relatively obscure career as an academic, teaching at the University of Georgia law school as the Sibley Professor of International Law.

Likewise, he almost succeeded in keeping a low profile in the Westmoreland-CBS case, becoming the only witness to have his deposition sealed. A federal judge in his hometown of Athens, Georgia, accommodated the request, which was prompted, says CBS lawyer Boies, by Rusk's worry that the news media might exploit the testimony. Rusk was particularly concerned that the videotaped version would be sensationalized by CBS. The judge agreed, and Rusk's on-the-record comments about the Vietnam War remained sealed until mid-April 1985.

That month the *Village Voice*, recognizing the potential historical significance of the deposition, started legal action to make it public, and Rusk relented, signing a consent order to have the seal removed.

The agreement made his testimony part of what Judge Pierre Leval called "the unique and rich" record that is the legacy of the trial. Rusk has since slowly returned to the spotlight. During the tenth anniversary of the fall of Saigon, he even agreed to be interviewed by Reuters, the British wire service.

CBS lawyer Boies readily admitted that his questioning of Rusk went somewhat beyond the case at hand. "I took Rusk's deposition for two days, and after the first day I must confess I had probably most of what I needed," he said. "The opportunity to sit with him and talk with him about the war and his role in the war and his perceptions of the war was just fascinating."

Boies and Rusk had much in common—a love of learning and teaching. This quest took Rusk, a self-described "Georgia farm boy" born in rural Cherokee County in 1909, far from the farm. His father, Robert, had intended to be a minister, but gave it up due to throat trouble and moved the family to Atlanta, where Rusk attended public schools and then Davidson College. His academic achievements won him appointment as a Rhodes Scholar. He then went on to teach government and political science at Mills College in Oakland, California, from 1934 to 1940. He served in the Army during World War II, rising to the rank of colonel.

After the war, he joined the State Department as assistant secretary for UN affairs and later for Far Eastern affairs. In 1952, he headed back to the private sector, leading the Rockefeller Foundation for nine years until President John F. Kennedy tapped him for Secretary of State.

Those two days the scholar-turned-diplomat spent with the teams of lawyers from both sides (along with two lawyers from the Central Intelligence Agency who monitored the conversation in the name of the "national interest") at Athens' History Park Inn gave scholars of the Vietnam War much to ponder. In his deposition, Rusk knocked the pins out from under some of the accepted historical "truths." For instance, Rusk swore Lyndon Johnson had told him he had decided not to seek another term in office long before the President stunned the nation with the announcement on March 31, 1968. During a nationally televised speech that evening, Johnson revealed, as expected, that the bombing of North Vietnam would be cut back in an effort to draw Hanoi to the negotiating table. But after delivering his prepared remarks, the embattled President stared into the camera and dropped this bomb: "I have concluded that I should not permit the presidency to become involved in the partisan divisions that are developing in this political year. . . . Accordingly, I shall not seek, and I will not accept the nomination of my party for another term as your president."

Instant analysis at the time and subsequent histories ascribed

Johnson's decision to several political factors: the growth of the anti-war movement, particularly demonstrations at the Pentagon the previous summer; Eugene McCarthy's strong showing in the March 12 Democratic primary, in which the relatively unknown anti-war candidate polled almost as many votes as Johnson, who had been elected four years earlier with the largest plurality in history; and the decision by the junior Senator from New York, Robert F. Kennedy, to run against Johnson (and the war) on March 16. *The New York Times*, which reported in the next morning's editions that Johnson had hinted at a single term in office as early as 1964 but that none of his aides had taken him seriously, also listed the erosion of the President's control over Congress as a prime reason.

Boies had been questioning Rusk about the period between January and March 1968 when he asked, "There came a point somewhere in that time frame when President Johnson decided not to seek re-election, correct, sir?"

Rusk replied, "He decided that much earlier. He had told me . . . that he would not run again and that he would have to announce it no later than March in order that other candidates would have a chance to come forward."

Boies pressed on, asking Rusk to recall the date of the discussion, and the former Secretary of State said, "Back in 1967, the middle of the year sometime."

A somewhat incredulous Boies, who in 1968 had been an ardent backer and admirer of Robert Kennedy, then asked Rusk, "Is that fact, that is, you proceeded on the assumption he would not run again, reflected in any written records, contemporaneous of the period?"

"I am not aware of any," Rusk said.

History, for the most part, co-signed the analysis of that night in 1968, blaming Johnson's decision squarely on the Vietnam War and the anti-war movement at home. Eighteen years later, *Time* magazine, in its April 15, 1985, issue marking the tenth anniversary of the fall of Saigon, put it simply: "Vietnam toppled a lot of dominoes in American life. It forced Lyndon Johnson out of the White House. . . . " In the same article, the magazine asserted, "In a sense the war in Vietnam has dictated American political life for a generation. But for the war, Johnson might have served two terms. He might have made his great society work. . . . "

But Rusk said the war had had little to do with it. "When he talked to me about it, he said 98 percent of what he had on his mind was his health," the former Secretary of State recalled, capturing Johnson's characteristic melodrama in describing the scenario the President feared. "He talked about Woodrow Wilson lying there paralyzed while Mrs. Wilson was trying to run the Cabinet. He talked about the people in high positions of responsibility who were ill at the time, like Winston Churchill, Anthony Eden and John Foster Dulles and he said that he simply was not going to inflict that upon the government or his own family." (Johnson, who returned to his beloved LBJ Ranch in the Texas hill country near Austin after leaving office in 1969, suffered a severe heart attack in April 1972 from which he never recovered. He had another heart attack on January 22, 1973, died, and was buried on the ranch.)

General William Westmoreland, in his memoirs, *A Soldier Reports*, says Johnson asked him in November 1967 if U.S. troops in Vietnam would suffer morale problems if he decided not to run again. "His health, he said, was 'not good,' and he was weary. Lady Bird and his two daughters wanted him to retire. . . . He had obviously made up his mind," Westmoreland wrote.

But Rusk had known of the President's decision even earlier.

Reliving the day of the announcement, Rusk said, "I had worked on the final draft of that speech . . . and then got on a plane and headed to New Zealand. When I was halfway across the Pacific one of the White House aides called me on the plane's telephone to say to me that the President wanted me to know that there would be an additional final paragraph on that speech and I knew immediately what that final paragraph would say. I appreciated the call because that would mean when I landed in New Zealand I wouldn't be caught by surprise by his announcement, and he was thoughtful enough to let me know in advance."

Boies continued to press Rusk as to whether Johnson gave any other reason—particularly the war—for his decision not to run. "Yes, he, uh, the words in which he announced . . . he would not run again, he left it open for people to believe that somehow his decision turned upon Vietnam, but my own belief all the way through was that 98 percent of what was in his mind when he decided not to run again was his health and not Vietnam."

As the questioning continued, Rusk disagreed sharply with McNamara, and even took a pot shot at his former fellow Cabinet officer. Asked if he had read any materials connected with the case, Rusk answered, "Oh, I read the opening parts of Secretary McNamara's deposition, until I got bored and stopped." Rusk, unlike McNamara, believed that the war could be won militarily. Speaking of the early war years, Rusk said. "I thought it was entirely possible to deny the . . . achievement of the North Vietnamese goal through military means."

But the North was able to stiffen its will to continue the battle due to anti-war sentiment in the United States, Rusk argued. "In 1967 and '68 other signals were being sent to Hanoi. If we had heard that there were 50,000 demonstrators . . . around the headquarters in Hanoi demanding peace we would have thought that the war would have been over and we probably would have been right. But they could see fifty [thousand] or 60,000 people demonstrating around the Pentagon and there were times when their propaganda would quote some of our own senators back to us."

He then added a familiar refrain from the war years: "Some of those people, whatever they intended to say, in effect said to Hanoi, 'Just hang in there gentlemen and you will win politically what you could not win militarily.' I suspect the authorities in Hanoi made that judgment and at the end of the day they were right in making that judgment."

Rusk knew first hand about college demonstrations. His car was stoned by students after a speaking engagement at the University of Wisconsin while he was Secretary of State. Rusk was treated so rudely during an appearance at the University of Indiana that 14,000 students later signed an "apology" petition.

Gradually, Rusk told Boies, growing sentiment against the war affected even his own family. "It was my judgment that whatever one might think about those demonstrations on college campuses and things of that sort during the first half of 1968, people at the grass roots, like my cousins from Cherokee County, Georgia, finally came to the conclusion that if we could not give them some idea as to when this struggle was going to be finished up, that we might as well get out of Vietnam."

Rusk disparaged McNamara's contribution to the history of the war, the Pentagon Papers, and in his discussion with Boies revealed how tightly compartmentalized the Johnson administration really was. Asked if he had been aware of the Pentagon Papers, Rusk replied, "I became aware of them when I read *The New York Times*," referring to that newspaper's publication of a large portion of the documents and analysis leaked by former McNamara whiz kid Daniel Ellsberg.

A somewhat dubious Boies then said, "To me it is very strange as to why the then-Secretary of State first heard of the *Pentagon Papers* when he read *The New York Times*."

Not strange in a bureaucracy, Rusk explained. "Apparently a set of the *Pentagon Papers* was delivered to the office of the undersecretary of state two days before President Nixon's inauguration and they did not under those circumstances bother to tell me.

"Some time before that, apparently somebody in Secretary McNamara's office asked my office to make available to them documents in the State Department on Vietnam and I apparently readily said yes, but I had no information as to what the *Pentagon Papers* were all about and why they were being prepared, who the analysts were, or why they were given instructions not to talk to principals such as myself."

In Rusk's opinion, the Pentagon Papers do not serve history well. "There is still an unfinished piece of business for somebody to prepare for future historians a realistic and truthful account of what the *Pentagon Papers* were all about [and] why they were prepared," he testified. "As you may know, they were never approved by the Department of Defense. They're just dangling there."

On the second day, as Boies' examination of Rusk was winding down, the questioning again focused on the Pentagon Papers, with Rusk (who said he had had to buy his own set) admitting he had never even read the complete work. "I scanned through them to satisfy myself that in general the documents which were used in the *Pentagon Papers* seemed to be authentic documents. Although the basis for selection of these particular documents out of the thousands and thousands that were available might have raised some questions about what criteria were used, I also looked at a number of those comments by the so-called analysts, the prose sections, and I found that a number of them left a great deal to be desired in terms of accuracy and care and preparation, but I didn't go through the entire set. . . . "

In an age in which many government officials depart with truckloads of documents entrusted to their care (and sometimes tie them up in litigation for years, as did Richard Nixon and his former aides with his presidential papers), Rusk has a refreshing view of whom the items actually belong to: the American people. When Boies subpoenaed Rusk, he directed him to bring to the deposition any and all papers relating to the case. Rusk arrived empty-handed, and, as he told Boies, for good reason. "As far as I am concerned there is no such thing as the 'Rusk Papers.' . . . My view is that whatever those papers were they were in connection with official government business and they belong to the government of the United States and I did not take anything away with me."

He told Boies if CBS wanted his "papers," the network should check the archives and various presidential libraries, prompting Boies to ask if there might be any unofficial repository of papers from Rusk's term in office.

"There may be some individuals here and there who did what I deplore—namely squirrel official papers away in their homes, getting ready to write a book after they leave office," he replied. "I decided when I first joined President Kennedy that I would never write memoirs and I announced it at the time. I don't know, these papers might be lying all over the place, but I don't know where they are and who has them."

He then sharply condemned people who appropriate government documents for personal use, naming former Attorney General Robert Kennedy as a prime abuser. "I deplore that. By legislation, we ought to make it clear that these are government papers, belonging to the government. One example I can give you, if you're looking for an example. When Mr. Robert Kennedy was attorney general he stored away a good many papers involving foreign policy. Upon his death I was told that these papers belonged to his wife Ethel instead of the government of the United States. I believe she put them in the JFK Library, so no great damage has been done, but that is one example of the kind of things that might happen."

Rusk also offered interesting insights into the alignment of "hawks" and "doves" within Congress and how these two groups viewed members of the Johnson administration. "These people on the flanks were passing each other by and were occupying each other's rear, and some of the debate was, uh, missed the point. For example, Secretary McNamara and I talked to different audiences when we went down to Congress. When I would go to the Senate Foreign Relations Committee and present the administration's point of view, I would sound like a hawk. When he went to the Senate Armed Services Committee and presented the same point of view, he sounded like a dove. So, a good deal of this was determined by the nature of the audience and what their reactions would be. But, uh, I think it was not up until 1971 or so that the Southeast Asia Resolution was rescinded by Congress."

Throughout the deposition, Rusk gave Boies-the-history-buff everything he had hoped for—a history lesson, relating the spirit of the country during the Vietnam War to World War II experiences and extrapolating these lessons into the present. Asked to explain the diminishing support for the war in the first half of 1968, Rusk answered, "I think the primary reason was clearly that we could not tell the American people when this thing was going to be over. It was not like an organized battle as in World War II where you could see the lines advancing steadily. . . . After so many years of effort there, a good many people at the grass roots decided that if we could not tell them when it was going to be over, and there was no way that we could in good faith, then we might as well abandon the effort. The American people are very impatient about war."

Boies then challenged Rusk, who considered former General and Secretary of State George C. Marshall his mentor, to cite a historical precedent for this analysis. Rusk responded with no hesitation.

"After World War II, Secretary [of State] Marshall told me that in the argument between the British and the Americans as to whether we should go in through Normandy or in through the soft underbelly of Europe, through the Balkans as Churchill put it, [it] was pretty well decided in the American mind, because of the feeling of our leadership, that we should get it over as quickly as possible," he said. "Before the very institutions of our society melted out from under us and we could no longer support the war effort; that our education system was drying up, the professions were drying up, our economy was all askew, and that going in through Normandy appeared to be the quickest way to terminate the war.

"We could not postpone the war indefinitely for what appeared to be post-war political advantages. So, I think here is something on the record on that, that the American people are impatient in a war situation—and they should be. I valued that part of the traits of the American people."

During the questioning, Rusk also revealed that outgoing President Dwight D. Eisenhower recommended to incoming President John F. Kennedy that the United States invade Laos. Boies had asked him to explain the status of the conflict in Vietnam when he became Secretary of State, but Rusk instead launched into a discourse about the country that stretches along its northwestern frontier. "On the day before Mr. Kennedy's inauguration, President Eisenhower met with him, with about three people on each side. On that occasion, President Eisenhower recommended to president-elect Kennedy that he put forces into Laos. As President Eisenhower put it, with others if possible, alone if necessary."

Rusk went on to explain that "Laos was the scene of the most active military operations at that particular time. The North Vietnamese were moving into Laos in considerable numbers, and so, when President Kennedy took office, we looked very hard at that situation."

But, Rusk said, " . . . It was a very forbidding prospect, it was a landlocked country. The terrain was very difficult and there was little indication that the Laotians, if left alone, had any interest in killing each other." Instead, the United States chose the diplomatic route, through the Laos Conference of 1961–62, to remove all foreigners— "the North Vietnamese, ourselves, the French, anybody else—and let the Laotians manage or mismanage their own affairs as a little island of peace there in Southeast Asia."

Committing U.S. forces, however, was ruled out. "When President Kennedy decided not to put troops into Laos he said that if we have to make a fight for Southeast Asia, we'll have to make it in Vietnam," Rusk said. "The failure to get any performance by the North Vietnamese on the Laos accords of 1962 was a very bitter disappointment for President Kennedy and undoubtedly had a lot to do with his thinking in terms of building up our support for the Vietnamese in South Vietnam."

Eisenhower's personal assistant, Wilton B. Persons, kept notes of that pre-inaugural conversation between the two Presidents and they generally confirm Rusk's assertions. According to Persons's notes, recently declassified by the Eisenhower Library in Abilene, Kansas, "Senator Kennedy stated he would like to have the basic unclouded decisions with respect to Laos and get the advice of the outgoing administration on them." Persons then recorded, "The President [Eisenhower] stated that unilateral action on the part of the United States would be very bad for our relations in that part of the world and cause us to be 'tagged' as interventionists." Later in the discussion, according to these notes, "Senator Kennedy asked the President which he would prefer, coalition with the Communists to form a government in Laos or intervening through SEATO [the Southeast Asia Treaty Organization]. . . . The President pointed out that unilateral intervention on the part of the United States would be the last desperate effort to save Laos, stating that the loss of Laos would be the loss of the 'cork in the bottle' and the beginning of the loss of most of the Far East."

Kennedy then asked Eisenhower's Secretary of Defense, Thomas Gates, if "we could intervene in Laos militarily with success. Secretary Gates replied that he was pessimistic about the political situation but that we could handle the military situation successfully if we did intervene."

Gates warned against unilateral action, according to Persons. "He indicated that the only optimistic plan would be to operate through SEATO, but Laos must make the request and that, to date, Laos has refused to do this."

Eisenhower's Secretary of State, Christian A. Herter, also kept notes of this meeting. According to his notes, also recently declassified by the Eisenhower Library, Herter told Kennedy "that the chances of working out a political solution depended in large measure on the status of the military situation. I then pointed out that the legal government of Laos had the right at any time to formally request the assistance of SEATO. . . . "

Herter added that if such a request was made, it would be "the solemn obligation of the signatories to go to the assistance of Laos and I felt we had no choice but to honor that obligation even though we knew the British and French hoped such a request would never be made."

As Rusk told Boies, Kennedy decided to leave Vietnam's neighbor alone—a decision that would haunt the United States all during the war as the military chafed at its inability to halt North Vietnamese infiltration of men and supplies along the section of the Ho Chi Minh Trail that wound through Laos.

8.

To Slay a Dragon

TRYING to sever the Ho Chi Minh Trail by bombing proved about as effective as a knight of yore trying to kill a dragon by cutting off its limbs and then watching in horror as two, three, even more grew to replace the severed member. The mythical dragon the Trail had become didn't breathe fire; instead it absorbed all that the United States spat from the skies. With each assault, the creature grew stronger and tougher, snaking more and more tentacles from the supply centers in the North into the vulnerable underbelly of South Vietnam.

This dragon particularly frustrated the United States because most of its body lived, roamed, and grew in supposedly neutral Laos, although neutrality did not shield the country long. All it did was add the United States Embassy in Vientiane to the chain of command that directed the air strikes. Ambassador William Sullivan, the U.S. delegate to the 1961 Geneva Peace Conference, had to approve every target in Laos, causing further frustration for Westmoreland and his boss, Admiral Sharp, who already had to get White House approval for air strikes on targets in North Vietnam. Documents declassified in the discovery process of the Westmoreland-CBS libel case reveal for the first time the extraordinary lengths the U.S. went to fight the Trail.

These newly declassified government papers disclose that the niceties of neutrality went up in smoke as air operations in Laos, code-named STEEL TIGER, intensified, trying to keep pace with the ever expanding dragon. Soon, B-52 bombers were unleashed against the Trail, droning non-stop back and forth from the idyllic isolation of Guam with the relentless frequency of Washington–New York air shuttles. Each of the eight-engined monsters released a deadly cargo of 100 750-pound bombs on every flight, and eventually the U.S. air armada dropped 2,235,918 tons of ordnance on the Trail—more tonnage than was expended in the entire Second World War.

The reason for the ferocity of this attack is that "trail" became a misnomer as the North stepped up its movement of men and materiel to match the U.S. escalation. Primitive in origin, the Trail eventually grew into the equivalent of a jungle superhighway. Traversing the trail never was an easy journey, although conditions improved remarkably from the early days when elephants shouldered most of the North's supplies. Laos, "the Kingdom of Elephants," soon became almost elephantless as the beasts were slaughtered in air strikes. Pachyderms gave way to trucks, and trucks required not a trail but a road system, as the CIA told Secretary of Defense Robert McNamara in its TOP SECRET 1966 and 1967 reports. And as the dragon grew, so did the United States determination to slay the creature. Westmoreland and his superiors wanted more bombing and begged for authorization to use almost any conventional (non-nuclear) weapon.

Cable traffic declassified for the lawsuit revealed for the first time the depth of this obsession and the tactics the military urged Sullivan to approve. Eventually, Sullivan agreed to fighting the dragon with fire. In a TOP SECRET March 20, 1966, cable to Westmoreland, Sullivan discussed the use of napalm against the Trail, indicating that the Prime Minister of the Royal Laotian Government, Prince Souvanna Phouma (whose half-brother, Prince Souphanouvony, nicknamed "The Red Prince," headed the Laotian communist forces), concurred in its use. "We have just sent you a message concerning use of napalm in Laos," Sullivan wrote. "The rules . . . [governing the use of napalm in Laos] are drawn from State-Defense Message 602 of March 24. . . . I confess I am a little perplexed about the exact intention of the . . . message. Literally interpreted, it seems to permit napalm only against fixed RLAF [Royal Laotian Air Force] targets in the STEEL TIGER area and not, repeat, not against truck convoys moving on the roads. However, because the wording is ambiguous, I have made no direct attempt to define it further in my message to you." Thus, Sullivan obliquely told Westmoreland that he could use this ambiguity to his advantage when he wanted to use napalm.

Souvanna Phouma, according to Sullivan, had no problem with using this jellied fire against North Vietnamese trucks traversing the Trail in his country. "I did in my message 1024 of March 25 (copy to you) point out that Souvanna agreed with our desire [to] use napalm against trucks. . . . This met with resounding silence on Washington end of line."

Ambassador Sullivan left defining the rules of war in Laos up to military commanders in Vietnam and Hawaii. "From the tactical commander's point of view, I'm sure [Westmoreland] would feel much more comfortable if his rules were more closely defined. If you and your airmen feel such a refinement is merited, I will be glad to seek it from State-Defense. If you feel satisfied to roll along with the current ambiguous definition, I am willing to play it that way also."

MACV was not content with just bombing Laos. Documents uncovered by CBS and the Capital Legal Foundation revealed an escalating effort by Westmoreland and Sharp to convince both Ambassador Sullivan and their civilian superiors in Washington that U.S. ground activities were needed, ranging from infiltration by small Vietnamese or Thai reconnaissance teams accompanied by American advisers to a full-scale U.S. invasion.

This obsession with Laos pre-dated both the bombing campaign and the introduction of regular U.S. ground forces into Vietnam. In an August 25, 1964, TOP SECRET memo, Brigadier General W. E. DePuy outlined "alternate courses of action for the conduct of cross-border operations into Laos which will satisfy the limitations imposed by the Aug 20 Udorn conference." During the conference, held at the U.S. Air Force base in Udorn, Thailand, the State Department set parameters for operations in Laos at a time when few Americans knew what their country was doing in Vietnam, let alone Laos.

The operations planned by MACV at that time involved only Vietnamese troops, but, as DePuy said, " . . . U.S. advisers may accompany when deemed desirable." The objectives of these early operations presaged the ones to follow in the coming months and years: " . . . to deny the use of the Laotian Panhandle as a safe haven for the Viet Cong, to [intercept] the flow of men and equipment from North to South, and to achieve tactical successes in reconnaissance and offensive operations of limited scope. . . ."

The South Vietnamese would assign four eight-man reconnaissance teams, four airborne ranger companies, and three "irregular" companies to these operations, DePuy said. While many of these troops would initially engage in reconnaissance, MACV planned more ambitious operations for the airborne rangers and their U.S. advisers. Those companies were to "infiltrate, by parachute, into the Techepone area of Laos; to engage such targets within their capability that will cause the maximum disruptive and interdictory effect, and to be exfiltrated by helicopter."

As the Dragon grew, so did MACV's desire to choke it, diplomacy be damned. The Westmoreland-CBS papers included numerous high-level cables in which Westmoreland and Sharp discussed cross-border reconnaissance operations in 1966–67 conducted under the code name SHINING BRASS. In July 1966, Westmoreland cabled Sharp urging extension of "SHINING BRASS to include an area 5,000 meters in depth from DMZ south along the border to the present authorized zone of operations . . . to permit short notice use of the recon teams . . . in conjunction with maneuvers of other forces in Quang Tri province [Vietnam] for the purpose of locating and directing air attacks against enemy troops."

In a TOP SECRET Jan 20, 1967, cable to Earle Wheeler, chairman of the Joint Chiefs of Staff, Sharp argued that initial results from these SHINING BRASS patrols called for even more. "The success of SHINING BRASS operations is attributable to the presence of U.S. personnel and the tactics that have been developed. The SHINING BRASS program has been an increasingly valuable asset to the intelligence effort. . . . We should have greater freedom of action in the current SHINING BRASS zone. . . . Since there is little doubt that the Communists control the SHINING BRASS area, recommend that all restrictions be removed for operations. . . ."

Sharp's recommendations were not adopted and Westmoreland continued to complain. "Employment of the SHINING BRASS exploitation force is limited to one platoon," Westmoreland cabled Sharp on February 14, 1967. In this TOP SECRET message, he said, "Relief from this restriction to allow multi-platoon size operations would enhance the exploitation capabilities of SHINING BRASS in profitable targets on routes vulnerable to ground interdiction. A example of the benefits to be gained was in SLAM III, from 29 January to the present. Two deep helicopter infiltrations permitted concentrating forces to search adequately what has been proven to be a major supply area and terminus of infiltration routes into SVN. The ground forces found and destroyed or evacuated Chinese radios and ancillary equipment, weapons parts, over 1,200 mortar rounds and 700 rounds of 12.7mm MG [machine gun] ammunition."

That's not all this penetration accomplished, Westmoreland said. "Acting on SHINING BRASS information, 7th Air Force delivered (through 10 February) 350 tactical air sorties resulting in 209 observed secondary explosions and numerous long-burning fires." Westmoreland explained that "Relaxation of the artificial restrictions now in effect will permit use of this same technique in other areas of Laos where similar success is to be expected."

Westmoreland found the human costs of these clandestine penetrations of Laos acceptable. Only one U.S. soldier had been lost. State Department intransigence held back even greater results from SHINING BRASS, Westmoreland complained to Sharp and Wheeler. He suggested that Wheeler take the case for expanded SHINING BRASS operations directly to President Johnson.

Two days later, Sharp, in a cable to both Westmoreland and Wheeler, discussed the SHINING BRASS restrictions from the political as well as the military perspective. This cable traffic, as well as other "back channel" messages handled outside the normal military communications system, indicates that throughout the war these military commanders kept slipping over the line that had always been drawn between generals and their civilian leaders—policy that theoretically belonged to the civilians.

In his February 16, 1967, TOP SECRET cable, Sharp agreed that restrictions on SHINING BRASS were "based primarily on political considerations. The importance of these considerations is recognized, but difficult to accept unless the military threat is kept in proper perspective."

He suggested Westmoreland work on Ambassador Sullivan. "It is imperative . . . to convince Bill Sullivan that we need his support in convincing Washington . . . ," Sharp wrote.

These arguments worked. On February 23, Wheeler cabled his two battlefield commanders that "You will receive tonight or tomorrow authorization agreed at highest level meeting to conduct expanded operations against North Vietnam and Laos." After delineating added targets for both the ROLLING THUNDER bombing campaign and additional naval gunfire targets in the North, Wheeler said that SHINING BRASS operations would lose some of their restrictions with "The width of the northern sector . . . expanded from 5 kilometers to 20 kilometers. Helicopters may be used to the full zone of the depth of operations. . . . Exploitation forces of up to 3 platoons in size may be deployed."

A declassified TOP SECRET report of a CINCPAC (Commander in Chief, Pacific) Infiltration/Interdiction Conference held July 25–27, 1967, reveals another series of covert Laotian cross-border operations. When these operations, nicknamed PRAIRIE FIRE, began in September 1965, they involved twelve-man reconnaissance teams and were envisioned to include battalion-sized forces. By the time the CINCPAC report was written, PRAIRIE FIRE operations had expanded to more frequent, longer, and deeper penetrations of Laos by the twelve-man teams.

According to this CINCPAC report, the basic cross-border operating unit was a "Spike" team consisting of three U.S. Special Forces personnel and between seven and nine Asian mercenaries. This team was "transported to target areas in H-34 helicopters escorted by a pair of helicopter gunships and two A-1 aircraft. . . .

"The mission of the team is to find targets for destruction by air or ground attack," CINCPAC said. "Air strikes are directed through a forward air controller who supports the team."

Field experience with the PRAIRIE FIRE teams, the CINCPAC report said, led "to the development of the SLAM concept—seek, locate, annihilate and monitor. . . . The PRAIRIE FIRE units seek and locate targets in a specific area. When located, the targets are struck severely by Arc Light [B52s] and Tiger Hound [other strike aircraft] forces. PRAIRIE FIRE units monitor the enemy's attempt to escape and the intelligence is used for complete destruction or continuous follow on strikes.

"In addition, the PRAIRIE FIRE teams complete destruction of material targets, capture prisoners and assess damages. PRAIRIE FIRE and SLAM operations have been so successful that the enemy has . . . diverted sizeable formations of combat troops to defend his storage areas and to attack PRAIRIE FIRE units. . . . "

The Dragon, however, consumed PRAIRIE FIRE the way it absorbed everything else the U.S. flung at it—fighting fire with fire. The operation forced the North to beef up support of its troops in Laos. Eventually, the North Vietnamese were "supported by heavy concentrations of anti-aircraft weapons which make helicopters, FAC, and prop-driven air operations extremely hazardous," the CINCPAC report said. "Future PRAIRIE FIRE operations will have to take into account the fact that they are no longer facing service troops or casual infiltrating units. . . . They must now be prepared to fight well-disciplined and experienced combat troops."

These NVA soldiers, the CINCPAC study concluded, would thwart the effectiveness of the PRAIRIE FIRE teams. "There are still missions for PRAIRIE FIRE to perform, but missions in heavily defended areas must make maximum use of deceptive measures, stealth and surprise; and they must be of short duration. PRAIRIE FIRE units do not have the staying power needed to cope with trained, NVA combat troops."

Never mind that the North Vietnamese had essentially check-mated PRAIRIE FIRE operations, the U.S. military hatched a grander scheme to slay the Dragon. This plan—an invasion of Laos—harked back to the man Westmoreland still considered a mentor, Dwight D. Eisenhower.

In November 1966, Westmoreland dispatched a cable to Sharp suggesting a corps-sized invasion of Laos, dubbed OPERATION FULL CRY. Westmoreland asked to brief the higher-ups in Washington. Sharp, who rarely disagreed with Westmoreland's plans for smaller operations, thought this one politically unpalatable. In a December 14, 1966, TOP SECRET cable, Sharp told Westmoreland, "I frankly view implementation of any concept such as FULL CRY as a rather remote possibility at this time, particularly when it involves deploying across international borders."

In a January 1967 TOP SECRET cable to Sharp, Westmoreland outlined another Laotian invasion plan dubbed FIRE BREAK, on which he had briefed his boss the previous month, "a combined paradrop and helioborne threat [Westmoreland wore the wings of both an Army aviator and a paratrooper; throughout the war, he favored both these specialized branches, always on the lookout for ways to employ their unique capabilities] . . . to An Loc complex in the Laotian Panhandle. This concept included the rehabilitation of Route 9, which runs parallel to and south of the DMZ." But after further study, Westmoreland concluded that FIRE BREAK was "not practical at this time in view of the cost of the effort required to establish credibility and in light of stated national policy."

By mid-1967, Westmoreland and Sharp decided to try to turn over the Laotian problem to the South Vietnamese allies, who at this stage of the war looked more and more like surrogates, if somewhat untrustworthy ones. According to the CINCPAC Infiltration/Interdiction report, OPERATION SOUTHPAW was conceived to "provide for conducting ground or airmobile operations across the Laos border by regular South Vietnamese units up to brigade strength. . . . The operations would be short duration, 3 to 7 days. No publicity would be given the operations and appropriate precautions would be based on current intelligence verified by PRAIRIE FIRE forces. . . . This plan is in the initial phases of preparation and co-ordination. The subject has been broached to Gen. Vien, Minister of Defense and Chief of Joint General Staff, RVNAF [Republic of Vietnam Armed Forces], who reportedly is receptive to the idea."

Notes taken by presidential assistant Tom Johnson of a White House meeting on July 12, 1967, reveal that increased U.S. ground activity in Laos merited high-level attention. These notes, declassified for the Westmoreland-CBS case, but originally stamped LITERALLY EYES ONLY, detail a verbal briefing by McNamara for an audience that included, among others, President Johnson, Dean Rusk, CIA director Richard Helms, and national-security adviser Walt Rostow. Tom Johnson's record shows that McNamara "proposed that there be an increase to battalion-size operations in Laos."

In December 1967, Westmoreland again tried to persuade Sharp and the Joint Chiefs to authorize large-scale U.S. ground operations in Laos. In a December 3 TOP SECRET cable, he outlined plans for OPERATION YORK, in which two brigades of the Army's 1st Air Cavalry Division and one brigade of ARVN (Army of the Republic of Vietnam) airborne would assault NVA base camps in South Vietnam's A Shau valley. The MACV commander observed that this would require a "shallow penetration of the Laos border area," but he reasoned, "It is important to emphasize that the border area is imprecise and heavily jungled, natural access is from RVN not Laos. . . . Penetration of Lao territory would be minimal and limited to essential and immediately adjacent terrain. Steps can be taken to minimize publicity and, as required, to list the entire operation as the battle of A Shau."

This suggestion was somewhat akin to saying Mexico could invade San Diego without anyone noticing or, if someone did, could explain it away with "Hey, what does a few miles difference make this close to the border?" Nonetheless, Westmoreland argued that "protests, if any, from the RLG [Royal Laotian Government] or elsewhere could be dealt with on the basis of necessary maneuvers and fires to protect the security of the A Shau force. . . . Withdrawal of ground forces from the salient would bear out this statement."

By early 1968, the plans for YORK evolved to include "full participation of U.S. ground forces" in the Laotian incursions, according to a January 6, 1968, TOP SECRET cable from Westmoreland to Wheeler. This, Westmoreland contended, made sense tactically as well as politically and diplomatically!

"U.S. ground force participation quite likely would make it extremely difficult to abide by a no public disclosure prohibition," he admitted, but "In the latter respect there may well be advantages to a positive and publicly reasoned approach to these operations." He argued, in fact, that the U.S. could win a political advantage by invading a neutral country. " . . . I would reaffirm the desirability of U.S. ground force base extensions of the A Shau operation; not so much to enhance the tactical success of that limited venture, but rather to establish political precedents for subsequent operations."

Two days later, Westmoreland hatched his boldest plan to fight the Dragon on the ground—OPERATION EL PASO, " . . . A corps-sized operation astride the most critical choke points in the vicinity of Highway 9 to block enemy troop and logistic movement through Laos during the next dry season in the Lao Panhandle. . . . A planning date for D-day is 1 October 68," Westmoreland cabled Sharp and Wheeler on January 8.

He certainly had provocation. For months, the Trail had seethed. The wide-awake Dragon spewed full NVA divisions into the South, surrounding important bases like the Marines' isolated Khe Sanh outpost. Tet, the most sacred holiday in the Vietnamese calendar, was just twenty days away. So was the traditional Tet cease-fire.

But Westmoreland didn't ponder that Vietnamese holiday or cease-fire when he sent this cable. He wanted to finally choke the Dragon. "Looking forward to future operations, I believe the only completely effective method of interdicting enemy movement through Laos, is to deploy forces into Laos, to cut off the enemy's access to the South."

To do this, Westmoreland formulated a sweeping plan which remained classified until the libel case unearthed the records of this grand scheme. He didn't want to fool around with clandestine PRAIRIE FIRE teams anymore or beg for permission to send in a battalion to harass the North Vietnamese Army in its base camps for a few days only to retreat hastily across the border before the press caught on. EL PASO would be a grand operation on the scale an Eisenhower would appreciate.

Westmoreland planned to hurl the best of the American and Vietnamese armies against the Dragon. He planned to assign his elite ground forces: the 101st Airborne division, spearhead of the invasion of Europe; the 1st Air Cavalry Division, an outfit with so many helicopters it could almost turn the midday sky black with its machines; and the ARVN Airborne Division, the best, the toughest troops in that country's often woefully inadequate army.

This crack force, once it met and defeated the enemy, could then enjoy the delicious irony of using the Trail as its own, Westmoreland suggested. " . . . One possibility is to withdraw south by [the] Ho Chi Minh Trail to destroy enemy logistic stocks and enter SVN in Kontum Pleiku area."

Westmoreland's Trail strike force couldn't swing into action immediately, however. Logistics, which for the U.S. Army in Vietnam came before tactics, demanded immediate attention. "Logistic support of the operation will be Highway 9, secured by III MAF [Marine Amphibious Force], as well as by airlift and air drop into Laos. New C-130 airfields at Quang Tri, and Khe Sanh, improved port facilities at Dong Ha, Cu Viet and the new port complex at Hue/Phu Bai will enhance the logistic support operations thru I Corps area. Highway 9 to Khe Sanh will be established as an all-weather road," Westmoreland projected in his January 8, 1968, cable.

Despite Westmoreland's enthusiasm for this operation, Sharp doubted its feasibility. He cabled MACV on January 25, 1968, that, "Political overtones notwithstanding, the many military problems of such an operation militate against any course of action that advocates large scale operations in Laos at this time. The tactical advantages our forces presently enjoy would be negated by an extensive movement into Laos, especially a deep penetration as far as Techepone. Additionally, adverse weather could severely limit our reinforcing capability, tactical air support, and movement of supplies. Conversely, enemy forces would be operating in an area that has long been used to stockpile supplies."

Sharp also worried about the dead and wounded that could be expected from such an ambitious scheme as EL PASO. "Abnormally high casualties during such operations could be exploited by the NVA and constitute a major propaganda victory detrimental to the U.S. and Vietnamese morale.

"In the aftermath of the operation, friendly Laotians might be subjected to reprisal by enemy forces and a concerted effort likely would be aimed to eliminate our Tacan sites [radio navigation towers beaming signals used by U.S. aircraft to locate their positions automatically]. . . ."

Sharp did see some merits in Westmoreland's Laotian invasion plan. "On the positive side—a significant defeat of major NVA forces in one of their sanctuaries could provide friendly forces with a major psychological victory and demonstrate to NVN [North Vietnam] the futility of continued support of war in the South."

Nevertheless, Sharp shrugged off Westmoreland, telling him at the end of the message that the EL PASO plan goes "beyond our present concept of operations in SEA [Southeast Asia] and our capability at this time. . . ."

Undaunted by this criticism, the day before the 1968 Tet New Year holiday, as the North Vietnamese moved into position for the massive Tet Offensive that would shake U.S. confidence in ever winning the war in South Vietnam, Westmoreland fired off another cable requesting a "go" for EL PASO. This six-page cable detailed exactly how OPERATION EL PASO would work and what it would accomplish. It is obvious that Westmoreland—increasingly frustrated by a foe he could see, track, and even bomb, but not engage in a fair fight across a border that the enemy blithely ignored—saw EL PASO as his chance to stage a set-piece battle, maneuvering armies on a World War II scale that would once and for all break the Dragon's back.

The mission of EL PASO, Westmoreland confidently told Sharp, would be to conduct an "airmobile-airborne-ground assault to seize key choke points in the vicinity of Route 9, destroy enemy base areas, supply and logistical facilities, and block enemy infiltration through the Laos Panhandle. . . ."

In laying out the assumptions for this operation, Westmoreland did suggest a drastic change from past U.S. actions in that country. It would "take place with approval of the recognized government of Laos. Facilities and areas under control of the RLG [Royal Laotian Government] will be available for support only if prior agreement is reached with RLG for their use."

Another assumption, and a factor that the U.S. military leaders constantly assessed throughout the war, was the China card. So, Westmoreland said, EL PASO would go only if "there is no China intervention into Laos."

Westmoreland planned on a D-Day of October 1, 1968, the end
of the monsoon season, and split the operation into three phases,
starting with a logistical buildup. This would require:

> Sections of Routes 1 and 9 must be improved. Airfields
> in RVN, pipelines and necessary depot facilities must be
> built and stockpiled with the requisite supplies. III MAF will
> secure areas for construction and supply activities. . . .
> Assault forces of the Corps will be positioned in staging
> areas shortly before D-Day.
> Phase II (Assault and Consolidation). After initial ob-
> jectives have been seized the buildup of tactical forces will
> expand to extent of logistic capability. Construction activi-
> ties within Laos will be initiated concurrently with initial
> tactical operations. Priority of MACV tactical air support
> will be to the provisional Corps. All NVA reinforcements will
> be interdicted as far to the north as possible. Search and
> Destroy missions will be conducted on a continuing basis to
> limit operational capabilities while Corps is in Laos.
> Phase III (Withdrawal). On order, the EL PASO forces
> will withdraw to the east to forward support bases in RVN;
> the provisional Corps may be disestablished and individual
> units will be reassigned. . . .

Westmoreland envisioned integrating on-going unconventional-
warfare operations into EL PASO, including the PRAIRIE FIRE teams
and the CIA's "secret army" in Laos. Air bases in Thailand would
furnish tactical air-support missions for EL PASO.

If the Joint Chiefs approved EL PASO, Westmoreland thought he
could meet the enemy on the ground in Laos and possibly defeat him.
He faced only one problem: the Tet holiday of 1968 didn't turn out
to be much of a holiday for MACV or South Vietnam.

Less than twenty-four hours after Westmoreland dispatched his
grand plan for fighting the Vietcong–North Vietnam Army in Laos,
the enemy launched its own grand attacks—the offensive known
simply as Tet. An estimated 80,000 VC/NVA troops stormed cities and
villages the length and breadth of South Vietnam. Over the next days,
weeks, and months, they penetrated the U.S. Embassy compound in
Saigon; held the Marine forward combat base at Khe Sanh in a state
of virtual siege, and occupied Hue.

Fighting this battle became Westmoreland's first priority. Visions
of carrying the war to the enemy in Laos bowed to the reality of the
situation in South Vietnam. EL PASO ended up on the back burner. In

June of 1986, Westmoreland, who turned over command of MACV to General Creighton Abrams in June 1968, still believed in the operation. He said, "EL PASO could have been executed as planned in 1968 and should have been. The Tet offensive had seriously weakened the enemy and the U.S. and RVN posture in Vietnam was never stronger."

9.

To Cage a Dragon

WHILE Admiral Sharp, Westmoreland, and the Joint Chiefs cranked out plans to cut the Ho Chi Minh Trail by bombing or conventional ground warfare, Secretary of Defense Robert McNamara hatched a bizarre scheme—medieval in origin—to contain the creature.

Just as European kings in the Middle Ages threw up castle walls and dug moats as a final defense line against enemies real or imagined, McNamara decided to erect a wall of his own across the Trail. If the most intensive bombing campaign in history couldn't halt the relentless march of a primitive people, possibly a physical barrier connecting a series of forts could.

Since one of the key issues in the Westmoreland-CBS trial was infiltration from the North, the amount of declassified TOP SECRET material on this barrier system runs into thousands of pages, revealing in great detail one of the weirder ideas of a surrealistic war, "the McNamara Line."

Like many other supposedly brilliant ideas conceived by Americans in their part of the Vietnam War, the McNamara Line evokes déjà vu. In 1966, the year McNamara started to push and prod the Pentagon bureaucracy to build him a wall, U.S. troops newly arrived in Vietnam marveled at the remains of French forts scattered about the country, mini-Maginot Lines standing in mute testimony to the fact that the guerrilla just swims around walls of concrete and steel.

But McNamara didn't plan a wall that vaguely recalled the failed tactics of World War II. He envisioned the best barrier American money and scientific expertise could devise, backed up by electronic systems to make it doubly impenetrable. Cost was no object.

General Earle Wheeler, chairman of the Joint Chiefs of Staff, made this quite clear in a March 22, 1966, memo defining the basic parameters of the McNamara Line:

> The Secretary of Defense has requested me to have the Joint Staff assess the requirements to establish an iron-curtain counter-infiltration barrier across northern South Vietnam and Laos from the South China Sea to Thailand. He has established the following assumptions:
>
> a. Dollar cost will be disregarded.
>
> b. Political aspects will not be assessed.

Wheeler proposed that the barrier, at its most basic, include "a belt of suitable width completely cleared of all trees and shrub growth, defended by two or more barbed wire barriers and appropriate mine fields, supplied with mutually supporting watch towers and night lighting arrangements extending along Route 9 from the South China Sea to the eastern border of Thailand."

General Harold K. Johnson, Army chief of staff, quickly endorsed the barrier concept. In a memo sent the same day as Wheeler's, Johnson said the Army had already prepared "a concept for establishing a physical barrier across the Laos Panhandle" and passed the plan along to Wheeler.

This memo, a "talking paper" prepared for Johnson by a Major Kretzer at McNamara's request on February 4, 1966, cast doubt on court testimony McNamara later gave concerning his dovish instincts. For, as this memo shows, in 1966 McNamara examined almost any tactic to halt infiltration, including the use of radiological-chemical warfare weapons.

Kretzer proposed erecting a physical barrier stretching along the axis of Route 9 from the South China Sea to the Mekong River. He estimated that five divisions (75,000 to 100,000 troops) could secure the area in six months and that it would take another year to construct the Line itself. The barrier would include 500-meter-wide cleared strips fenced in with barbed wire; a road on the inner side for use of patrols; and watch towers erected every 400 yards of its march from sea to mountain.

Kretzer also suggested a grim but effective alternative to barbed wire:

> a. Seed the cleared strip with atomic dust (radioactive isotopes). This method is not considered practical at this time. By 1980, it is estimated that sufficient radioactive isotopes would be available to saturate 150 square miles.

    b. Saturate the cleared strip with persistent chemical gas. Disregarding political restrictions, this method is feasible. Mustard gas has prolonged persistency and could be used at a cost of approximately $5,000 per kilometer for a strip 200 meters wide.

The McNamara Line would consume supplies with a Brobdingnagian appetite, according to Kretzer's memo. He projected that building the line would take 244 engineer-battalion months at a cost of $116 million. The line would consume 7.5 million anti-personnel mines, 3.3 million anti-tank mines, and 7 million board feet of fence posts. To turn night into day, the line would sport 72,000 floodlights and 1,800 twelve-inch searchlights powered by 120 100-kilowatt generators pumping juice through 2,360 industrial-type electrical transformers.

While the Joint Chiefs developed plans to build him an "iron curtain," McNamara decided to farm the barrier problem out to the kind of people he trusted most: academicians, intellectuals, or—in the pejorative term used by the generals—"eggheads" working for the Pentagon-funded Institute for Defense Analysis. The IDA's Jason division (named after a British research group that in World War II came up with a number of scientific breakthroughs, including radar) on August 30, 1966, sent McNamara the results of their "Summer Study," which determined that "In the realities of Vietnam . . . the barrier must be imposed and maintained mainly by air."

This report, based on the research of M. Goldberger and W. Nierenberg, put a twentieth-century high-tech spin on the age-old concept of a wall, with microelectronic sensors replacing bricks and mortar. For a variety of reasons, including the Tet Offensive and the sheer impracticality of stringing barbed wire across two countries crossed and crisscrossed by a variety of armies and guerrillas, McNamara abandoned plans to erect much of the original Line. But he did build this sensor wall which, when coupled with specialized munitions, probably changed the nature of warfare forever.

As the Jasons planned it, the air-supported anti-infiltration barrier would consist of two parts, an anti-foot-traffic barrier and an anti-vehicular barrier, each backed by its own system of sensors and weapons. The Jasons suggested devising land-based adaptations of the acoustic sonobuoys the Navy used to track submarines. These sensors, air-dropped along the Trail, could track men moving on foot or trucks moving alone or in convoy, and distinguish between all three. They would then transmit data to orbiting Navy P2v patrol aircraft, which could call in air strikes.

The Jasons also proposed "seeding" a variety of unique munitions along the Trail, lying in wait for an unsuspecting foe. These included "button bomblets," aspirin-sized explosives designed more to activate the sensors when stepped on than to cause casualties. The bomblets were backed up by "Gravel" mines, slightly larger, irregular-shaped anti-personnel mines.

These munitions theoretically "self-sterilized"—that is, after a number of days or weeks they would automatically deactivate. This feature was needed to prevent the enemy from using the air-dropped bombs and mines as the raw material of booby traps and to ensure that friendly troops, such as the PRAIRIE FIRE teams or CIA-backed Lao irregulars, could, from time to time, safely enter the area of the barrier.

Finally, the Jasons proposed that vehicular traffic detected by the sensors should be attacked with SADEYE-BLU26B cluster bombs.

Building and maintaining a high-tech Maginot Line was an expensive proposition, the Jason "Summer Study" concluded. "The cost of such a system has been estimated to be about $800 million per year," the report said, "of which by far the major fraction is spent for GRAVEL and SADEYES."

Just as the physical barrier required hardware in mind-boggling proportions, so did the air barrier. "The key requirements would be (all numbers are approximate because of assumptions which had to be made regarding degradation of system components in field use, and regarding the magnitude of infiltration): 20 million GRAVEL mines per month; possibly 25 million button bomblets per month; 10,000 SADEYE-BLU26B clusters per month; 1,600 acoustic sensors per month and 68 appropriately equipped P2v patrol aircraft; a fleet of about 50 A-1s or C-123s for Gravel dispensing (1,400 A1 sorties or 600 C-123 sorties per month); 500 strike sorties per month (F4C equivalent) and sufficient photo reconnaissance sorties, depending on the aircraft, to cover 2,500 square miles each week. . . ."

Existing state-of-the art equipment couldn't answer the challenge of the barrier. "Even to make this system work, there would be required experimentation and further development for foliage penetration, moisture resistance, and proper dispersion of GRAVEL; development of a better acoustic sensor than currently exists (especially in an attempt to eliminate the need for button bomblets); aircraft modifications. . . ."

The Jasons, like consultants in other, more benign fields, invoked the first rule of consultancy in this report: they pushed for a follow-on contract. They recommended that the Pentagon follow up the "Summer Study" with a full-time task force, and also suggested that any further development include a system-designs group which would "of necessity be very close to the headquarters task force." They handily noted that "IDA, by virtue of its Washington location and experience, seems a suitable place to manage this effort."

McNamara bit. On September 15, 1966, he appointed Air Force Lieutenant General Alfred Starbird as head of Joint Task Force 728, which would develop the barrier system. Despite the Jasons' recommendation for a strictly air-supported barrier, in a memo that day McNamara asked Starbird to build him a physical one also. He made it clear that the barrier was no flighty scheme in a war filled with chimeras. The barrier was "to be designed, produced and put in place as a matter of highest national priority . . . [with] the objective of having the system installed and in operation by Sept 15, 1967."

To prevent bureaucratic snafus or delay in building this iron-and-electronic curtain, McNamara removed Starbird from the chain of command. "In carrying out your duties as director of the Joint Task Force, you will report directly to me," McNamara ordered, "and are authorized direct contact with the JCS, the military services and subordinate organizations. . . . Implementation will involve political affairs and matters of concern to ISA, the State Department and foreign governments; you should therefore keep Mr. McNaughton (ASD/ISA) [Assistant Secretary of Defense/International Security Affairs] fully informed and call on him for assistance as necessary in those areas. I expect you to make use of an advisory group of non-governmental experts. . . . You are to feel free to call on me as necessary for resources, guidance, decisions and other assistance."

The Joint Chiefs, possibly out of joint because of the carte blanche McNamara gave Starbird, reacted quickly and diplomatically, albeit somewhat skeptically, to McNamara's new toy. In a September 16, 1966, memo, they first praised the concept, then tried to undermine it. "The Joint Chiefs recognize the historic use of barriers and the potential inherent in this concept," they wrote. "The imaginative use of technology and surprise can contribute considerably toward solving the infiltration problem." But they wanted to gain control of Starbird—and the whole scheme—by shackling him to the chain of command: "It is requested that the project definition as developed by General Starbird be submitted to you through the Joint Chiefs of Staff."

They let Sharp and Westmoreland shoulder the onus of opposing the plan, saying, "CINCPAC [Sharp] questions the practicality of the concept as presented. The Joint Chiefs of Staff appreciate and share the concern behind his reservations. . . ." They also wanted to ensure that McNamara's grand plan did not interfere with their war. "It is important that logistical support for the barrier be of a scale that precludes diverting critical munitions and strike forces from other combat operations."

Wheeler, via a back-channel message, then suggested Westmoreland make it clear that if McNamara wanted to build a wall, he should find a separate army to do it. "As you know, JCS hold view that resources to support barrier must be in addition to those now available or programmed to support activities in S.E. Asia," Wheeler cabled Westmoreland on October 20, 1966. He requested, "It would be helpful if you, without reference to this message, could include in your reply to Starbird your comments on force considerations."

Westmoreland played along. In a November 24, 1966, message to Admiral Sharp, Westmoreland said while it "might be desirable to construct a barrier to enhance . . . surveillance and early-warning capabilities . . . I harbored no thought of a static airtight barrier constructed within a rigid time frame. Nor did I visualize deployment of large forces to support a barrier per se. . . ." During a visit by McNamara in October, he said, "We were asked to prepare a plan to support a fixed barrier . . . [but] the plan was predicated on the need for additive forces to prevent degradation of MACV's overall mission capability. . . . Economy of force must be exercised in connection with deployments south of the DMZ. The density and type of deployment must be governed by the enemy situation as opposed to arbitrary barrier requirements. It is not my intention, nor has it ever been, to displace in-country forces of the magnitude required to meet total barrier requirements."

The Jasons' "Summer Study" group had predicted a battle over the barrier, but it thought the foe would be the North Vietnamese, not Westmoreland and the Joint Chiefs of Staff. On December 11, Starbird sent McNamara a proposal calling for procurement of materials for the physical barrier, and asked to prepare and test, preparatory to Vietnam deployment, a mine- and sensor-laying unit of forty-seven aircraft and 2,900 men. He also wanted permission to begin limited construction on five air bases for the barrier forces. On December 17, at McNamara's direction, Starbird met with Westmoreland to get his opinion on these plans.

In a draft of a message to McNamara (which Starbird first sent to Westmoreland), he reported that the MACV commander was "opposed to committing firmly to barrier undertakings, either ground or air-supported, unless additive forces are provided for the purpose."

Furthermore, according to this TOP SECRET cable which surfaced during the Westmoreland-CBS discovery process, Westmoreland did not "consider it prudent to tie down current or programmed forces to man a fixed linear barrier, particularly when the enemy situation and infiltration pattern through the eastern portion of the DMZ does not warrant such action at the present time."

Westmoreland didn't display much enthusiasm for the air-supported barrier either, according to this message, which said, "He favors selective use of special munitions as available to augment existing program in Laos and considers it unwise to place heavy reliance on unproved, untested munitions within a pre-set time frame."

Despite these strenuous objections, Starbird and the Jasons—now operating under the cover name of the Defense Communications Planning Group (DCPG) and ensconced on the grounds of the Naval Observatory in the posh Embassy Row section of northwest Washington—still had a hole card for their barrier plans, now code-named PRACTICE NINE.

In a December 22, 1966, memo to McNamara, Starbird quoted huge chunks of Westmoreland's objections while at the same time delineating the immediate moves needed to meet McNamara's timetable.

McNamara's reply to Starbird on January 5, 1967, was short and forthright:

> 1. You are directed to undertake preparation of an anti-infiltration capability for Southeast Asia. . . .
> 2. This memorandum is your authority to task the Military Departments for accomplishment of their contributing efforts, in accordance with your overall schedule of readiness.

With this bureaucratic equivalent of a blank check, Starbird and the Jasons could order up men and materials, mobilize fleets of aircraft, order development and manufacture of weapons mundane or bizarre. Anything they needed to build McNamara's Line, they could have.

They never built a McNamara Line stretching from the South China Sea to the Thai border, manned with watch towers every 400 meters and seeded with mustard gas and radioactive dust. Tet and the changed tactical situation in Vietnam prevented it. They did, however, build the world's first totally electronic battlefield, harnessing powerful computers, microelectronics, and bizarre weaponry in a Strangelovian reality weirder than science fiction.

The DCPG tapped the best technology America could produce in an effort to conquer the Trail with science. Sandia National Laboratories—a super-secret New Mexico high-tech installation operated since 1945 for the government by the American Telephone & Telegraph Co. on a no-fee basis—ingeniously adapted Navy submarine-detection sonobuoy technology to the rigors of land warfare. Disguised as jungle flora, complete with fake stems and leaves, these sensors rained down on the Trail, where their acoustic ears could electronically distinguish between enemy foot and vehicular traffic.

Equipped with mini-radio transmitters, the sensors passed the data along to the next element in the electronic battlefield—an aircraft orbiting the Trail and equipped with sophisticated receivers capable of monitoring hundreds of the listening devices. For this, the Jasons decided to use a squadron of hump-backed Air Force EC-121s, an extensively modified version of the venerable piston-powered, four-engine Lockheed Super Constellation, a long-range marvel whose airline service was cut short by the introduction of Douglas and Boeing jets.

The EC-121s, each manned by thirty or more technicians, could circle above the Trail for hours without refueling. They served as relay stations between the sensor fields and the brain of the operation—a pair of International Business Machines Corp.'s most advanced computers. These IBM 360s would process the sensor data received from the EC-121s, making sense out of the seemingly random activity on the Trail.

Human analysts would then use this intelligence to guide quick-reaction air strikes against large North Vietnamese convoys or to build a data base for the future sowing of button-bomblet minefields. If all these elements worked when deployed in Southeast Asia, the United States would possess the smartest killing machine in the history of warfare.

As development continued, the Jasons fine-tuned various pieces of the electronic battlefield at locations throughout the United States, including Eglin Air Force Base in Florida, where a test of the self-inactivating button bomblets went awry, leaving thousands of the active explosives scattered about a beach that had to be evacuated.

The traditional military commanders continued to resist both the physical barrier and the electronic battlefield, as indicated in a TOP SECRET message Admiral Sharp sent Westmoreland on May 5, 1967. Referring to the November 1, 1967, start-up date for the McNamara Line, Sharp complained, "We can expect there will be further diversions of resources as we approach the Nov. 1 date. The directed use of funds for upgrading LOC's [lines of communication] and improving ports in I Corps is another example of taking support for Practice Nine 'out of our hides.' "

Despite the complaints of both Sharp and Westmoreland, the DCPG electronic-warfare team—blessed by a man the military could not control, Robert McNamara—came close to meeting its deadline. By December 7, 1967, the world's first electronic battlefield stood ready for service under the new code name MUSCLE SHOALS (changed in June 1968 to IGLOO WHITE). A squadron of the specially modified Navy SP2v patrol planes needed to seed the sensor fields had been moved to an Air Force base at Nam Thong, Thailand, along with the

EC-121s. An Infiltration Surveillance Center (ISC), housing the IBM 360 computers and their acolytes, had been set up at another air base in Nakhon Phanom, Thailand.

The MUSCLE SHOALS/IGLOO WHITE system went on line at a propitious time. As testimony at the Westmoreland-CBS trial later revealed, the National Security Agency had entered the intelligence battle over the Trail, reporting a massive movement of men and equipment in the waning months of 1967. These were not just random replacements for the war farther south. They were well-equipped North Vietnamese army battalions starting to mass near the isolated Marine outpost of Khe Sanh, abutting both the DMZ and the Laotian border. (The CBS documentary and network witnesses at the trial alleged that by the end of 1967 the Trail had become a veritable jungle freeway with some 20,000 men a month in transit.)

In late November 1967, Navy crews piloting SP2v aircraft of Korean War vintage deployed the first anti-vehicular electronic sensor field in the history of warfare. This effort, code-named MUD RIVER, covered hundreds of square miles of Laotian jungle in an area running from slightly above the sixteenth parallel north to midway between the seventeenth and eighteenth parallels some thirty miles inside Laos. In early December, the EC-121s started orbiting the newly emplaced sensor fields. The IBM computers in Thailand hummed away, ready to spit out target data for the analysts.

Westmoreland's staff prepared a "command history" each year and these histories, declassified for the trial, offer an excellent contemporary perspective on the war. The command histories carefully detail the development of the electronic barrier system. As Westmoreland's 1968 MACV history described it, "The first weeks of operation in MUD RIVER were extraordinarily hectic. MUSCLE SHOALS was a very complex and new assemblage of equipment, facilities, concepts and procedures . . . rushed into the field while still definitely in R&D. . . . The interdiction campaign into which it had been injected had only recently entered an unprecedentedly dynamic new phase—five to ten times the pace of the previous year. . . . The early weeks were inevitably a nightmare of fault[y] detections, analysis and correction; design oversight discovery; procedure revision; interface clarification and human error due to inexperience."

The novelty of the project, McNamara's personal interest, and the fielding of a brand-new concept in warfare also affected the first weeks of operation. "Over and above all of these diversions," the MACV history said, "the extraordinary national interest in the project resulted in a flood of distinguished visitors and innumerable urgent messages questioning, recommending and requesting data and explanations."

Despite these expected problems with breaking in the system, the electronic battlefield worked. The MACV command history said, "The sensor did respond to passing trucks (among other things), the EC-121s did pick up the sensor signals and relay them to the ISC and the computer-assisted ISC-analysts did derive usable movement reports. . . . The fundamental premise underlying the system was proven —it was feasible, in a combat environment, to air-emplace and monitor a large sensor field and relay the sensor outputs in real-time to a remote center for analysis and exploitation."

The DCPG planned to install another sensor field, code-named DUMP TRUCK, to monitor foot traffic east of the MUD RIVER field near the DMZ and the border, but the North Vietnamese inadvertently offered an even better combat test of this system with their siege of Khe Sanh. Because of the huge enemy buildup at Khe Sanh, DUMP TRUCK countered an invasion instead of infiltration. The second sensor field deployed in the history of warfare quickly became a tactical tool used by small-unit infantry commanders.

Westmoreland ordered deployment of the sensor field to the Khe Sanh area on January 19, 1967, and by January 25 more than 150 sensors were operational, relaying data on the siege to the number crunchers in Thailand. The analysts quickly relayed their interpretations back to the Marine fire-support control center at Dong Ha and to a targeting center at Khe Sanh, which, in turn, directed air or artillery strikes against sensor-detected troop concentrations.

This successful baptism by fire quickly changed the generals' opinion of what the Jasons had wrought. As the MACV command history said, "Throughout the siege these reports contributed timely and pertinent tactical intelligence not available from any other source. On a 24-hour, all-weather basis they provided from monitored points throughout a wide area, useful information on personnel and vehicular movements, on concentrations and general levels of activity and on firing sites. The speed and success of this system adaptation to a completely different tactical application from that originally envisioned was a dramatic demonstration of the flexibility and versatility inherent in the MUSCLE SHOALS concept."

The duration of the Khe Sanh siege—not at all appreciated by the Marines who lived through it—allowed fine tuning of the electronic-battlefield system. In fact, in the aftermath of Tet, with both the U.S. military and South Vietnam reeling from the aftershocks of the North Vietnamese country-wide attack, the success of MUSCLE SHOALS was one bit of positive news.

"During February and March a significant evolution occurred in the way sensor reports were utilized at Khe Sanh," the MACV command history said. "In the beginning, well-defined targets for artillery and air strikes were scarce and Marine Targeting Officers were unfamiliar with the operating characteristics of the sensor field. Individual movement reports were responded to by artillery or air strikes against the sensor location given in the Spotlight Report—in essence, the originally contemplated 'Infiltration Barrier' reaction. Although a definite improvement on blind harassing and interdiction targeting, this tactic was inherently limited in effectiveness by the time delay in the reporting system (30 minutes and up from sensor reports through DUTCH MILL [the data-processing and analysis center in Thailand] to Khe Sanh) and by unresolvable uncertainties in sensor locations and target separation." Thirty minutes is not long, but to the besieged Marines at Khe Sanh it wasn't good enough.

Less than two years from the time of conception, MACV managed to mold the world's first electronic battlefield to the demands of a fluid tactical situation. According to the MACV command history, "As the siege progressed, potential targets became plentiful and the Marine Intelligence and Targeting staff became familiar with the sensor field, its capabilities and its limitations. At this stage, firing (or bombing) at every indication of movement would have been a relatively unproductive utilization of strike resources. Greater payoff lay in the development of particularly lucrative targets for massed and co-ordinated artillery and air strikes. The sensor reports came to play a key role in this decisive action."

Due to staggering losses, the Marines abandoned patrolling beyond the firebase shortly after the siege began, forfeiting the intelligence that commanders have historically relied upon to learn the disposition of an enemy force. The sensor fields bridged this intelligence gap, and, according to the MACV history, the electronic ears —while no substitute for patrol—went a long way toward providing desperately needed tactical information.

The sensor fields and the interpretation provided by analysts working at data consoles in air-conditioned huts two countries to the west allowed commanders, MACV said in its historical evaluation, to "anticipate the enemy's overall plan of attack, to pinpoint and functionally categorize his concentration areas, and to deduce timing patterns in his supply and assault activities. Against this background, the available artillery, tactical air and B-52 firepower could be concentrated on selected areas to achieve maximum results. In many cases, the proper timing of attack on a selected target was essential. As an example, a known assembly area for the reserve regiment in an anticipated enemy assault plan became an extremely profitable target for pre-planned massed fire—but only in the brief interval between positioning and jump-off."

The Jasons' electronic ears delivered the intelligence that made this split-second timing possible, the 1968 command history said. "In instance after instance, in night and fog, sensor-derived activity patterns provided the 'now is the time' cue for strikes. This mature exploitation of MUSCLE SHOALS as a complement to other intelligence and targeting techniques, rather than as a stand-alone trigger for reflex response, became a major guidepost for future applications."

Khe Sanh also served as the combat proving ground for another kind of sensor system, this one put in place by hand. This system, code-named MICROTALE, used sensors carefully positioned around the garrison, sending data directly to observation posts at Khe Sanh. This gave the Marines almost instantaneous access to the resulting data. The MACV command history said the MICROTALE experiment was "a valuable complement to the wholesale data handling techniques of the basic MUSCLE SHOALS approach. It lent itself well to many anticipated tactical situations."

Although the sensor developments were the most touted part of the electronic-battlefield plan, specialized munitions played an important role during the Khe Sanh siege. "A further contribution of the MUSCLE SHOALS project in this time frame was the successful laying of more than a million gravel mines on the Laotian roads and another million on the approaches to Khe Sanh. Some casualties are known to have been inflicted. However, evidence to date is not indicative of a significant operational impact in either area."

After three months of snaring data from the sensor fields around Khe Sanh, the ISC analysts in Thailand developed such familiarity with the area and the enemy movements that they could fine-tune the information they passed on. For example, instead of reporting every instance of large-scale movement to the airborne command post (ABCC) directing the air armada over Khe Sanh, the ISC analysts first evaluated new tracks against the pattern of total activity. They then fed the location of the most lucrative targets to the ABCC, which directed strike aircraft against only prime targets.

During April and May of 1968, the electronic-battlefield system directed attacks against the Achilles' heel of the Trail—truck parks, repair facilities, storage and transshipment areas. The sensor systems specifically seeded to monitor these jungle equivalents of Phillips 66 Big Rig Truck Stops were so successful that, according to the MACV command history, analysts in Thailand could eavesdrop on the repair-shop activity relayed by the EC-121s. "One successful drop . . . yielded several days of bustle and banging from what was obviously a busy truck repair station." Sensor strings scattered about several of these facilities allowed the ISC to determine the busiest. The ISC then guided aircraft from the 7th Air Force to the jungle pit stops filled with the most trucks.

After three months of operation, the ISC data base on the portion of the Trail near Khe Sanh developed to such an extent that, for the first time since the war began, the United States could ascertain in detail the North's pattern of operations.

In April 1968, pressure on Khe Sanh slackened. Westmoreland, visiting Washington that month, ordered the Army's 1st Cavalry Division to relieve the Marines at their beleaguered outpost. Though many ordinary Americans viewed the siege of Khe Sanh and the Tet Offensive as proof the United States was losing the war, the military insisted Tet was a victory.

Victory, in a sense, did belong to McNamara, the Jasons, and the DCPG. The successful combat trial of the electronic battlefield at Khe Sanh won over even the biggest doubters—Westmoreland, Sharp, and the Joint Chiefs of Staff. The MACV command history concluded that one significant result of the MUSCLE SHOALS operation was "the broad surge of command interest in the tactical potentials of sensor derived intelligence."

While enthusiastic about expanding the electronic-battlefield system, Westmoreland questioned some of the weapons used in MUSCLE SHOALS, particularly the supposedly "self-sterilizing" GRAVEL bomblets. Often, they failed to sterilize, backfiring on friendly troops. According to the Research and Development section of the 1968 MACV command history, "the first generation GRAVEL mine, the XM-27, caused some anxiety, primarily because its self-neutralization system was unreliable and several unfortunate incidents occurred before the magnitude of the problem was fully realized." Westmoreland said he was "reluctant to accept munitions which self-sterilize or destruct for use in areas where friendly forces may be employed in the foreseeable future."

MACV stopped using XM-27 in March 1968, with research and development continuing on similar but more reliable weapons. By the end of 1968, the command history said, "regular GRAVEL, small GRAVEL and MicroGRAVEL mines were in use, the latter so small that they were primarily used as noisemakers, to trigger acoustical sensors. At the same time each category could be given a variety of lifespans so that an area could be made hazardous operationally for the enemy and then safe for friendly forces according to a pre-set schedule."

In April of 1968, Sharp told Westmoreland to work with the DCPG in developing electronic-battlefield plans for a variety of situations in Southeast Asia. Code-named DUCK BLIND, these plans called for evaluation of the electronic-battlefield system in eight tactical applications: combat sweeps; the targeting of enemy troop locations; surveillance of enemy base areas; route surveillance, including waterways; ambush; convoy protection; base defense; and the monitoring of helicopter landing zones. Westmoreland, once strongly opposed to the Jasons and their schemes, embraced this plan, telling his field commanders on May 9, "I am enthusiastic about the potential of sensors and am convinced that we are on the verge of a break-through in acquisition of ground tactical intelligence. . . . Vigorous command emphasis [should] be given to the program for introduction of sensors into tactical operations."

The technology initially lagged behind these plans, according to the MACV command history. There were not enough radio frequencies for all the planned sensor fields, creating interference between sepa-rate fields monitored by the EC-121s. Demand for the sensors created shortages. Despite these problems, the sensors proved valuable in a number of applications, including ambushes, targeting, convoy pro-tection, route surveillance, and LZ [Landing Zone] monitoring.

Development of the electronic-battlefield technology continued so rapidly that by November 1968 the new head of the DCPG, Air Force Lieutenant General John Lavelle, reported to the Joint Chiefs that a whole new generation of equipment was about to make its way to Southeast Asia, employing the best IBM computers—two 360/65s, which replaced the slower 360/40s. Communications would improve, with new sensors able to operate on 640 channels instead of thirty-one. In place of the lumbering EC-121s, a mix of light drone and manned aircraft code-named PAVE EAGLE would monitor the sensor fields. Balloon-borne antennas and unmanned ground relay stations would improve monitoring of hand-emplaced sensors.

The DCPG designated Sandia Labs as the chief sensor-develop-ment facility, and its scientists designed a multitude of new devices. Now the ISC could tap into a whole family of sensors, most with com-mon communications modules, cutting both costs and production time. Lavelle told the Joint Chiefs that the electronic battlefield would cost $2.3 billion over a four-year period.

But the results would be worth it. Talking about a Trail-bombing campaign dubbed COMMANDO HUNT, Lavelle predicted that the elec-tronic battlefield would do to the Trail what all other U.S. efforts had failed to do: markedly impede truck traffic. "I believe that the poten-tial for increased operational effectiveness is being realized because of the closer real time relationship between sensor derived intelligence and strike operations. [Air Force] plans call for hitting movers day and night, but as we know, mostly at night, and through sensor de-rived information, determine where they turn off just before dawn, then hit the occupied truck park areas during the day. I am confident that truck traffic through the Laotian Panhandle will be reduced significantly."

Sensor development continued throughout the war, with the individual services jumping on the concept with plans of their own. Some were absurd and unworkable, such as a "people sniffer" that supposedly would detect North Vietnamese troops by sniffing out their urine. Unfortunately, the people sniffers could not tell the difference between animal and human urine, and the North Vietnamese, aware of the sensors, counteracted this particular bit of technology by liberally spreading animal urine in the jungle to attract the U.S. "sniffers" and strike aircraft.

Like the bombing campaigns that preceded the electronic battlefield, sensor-directed air strikes would not daunt the North Vietnamese. However, as Michael Maclear wrote in his history of Vietnam, *The Ten Thousand Day War*, "Human endurance had prevailed on the Trail—but only just. Perhaps for the last time in a conventional war, man had outlasted or outwitted the machines. The Trail veterans, as General Westmoreland said, were a tough, persevering bunch and perhaps the terrors of the Jasons were nothing compared to those of nature on the Trail itself."

10.

Insights: Bizarre Plans, Bizarre Weapons, Bizarre Problems

L I K E the crews of massive tuna trawlers, the lawyers handling the discovery process on both sides of the Westmoreland-CBS case cast a wide net, hauling in tons of classified government documents that offer fresh insights into the United States' Vietnam War policy and issues. Some of these historical tidbits, such as McNamara's memos to President Johnson, detail policy struggles at the highest level. But many others offer a peek at some of the more bizarre episodes that occupied the military and civilian leadership.

In a Cravath, Swaine & Moore storeroom with a spectacular view of the Statue of Liberty, one cardboard box yielded the minutes of a 1966 discussion in which Army Chief of Staff General Harold Johnson suggested bombing Peking to quickly resolve the Vietnam War. In southeast Washington, D.C., meanwhile, a similar nondescript box stowed on an unused desk at Capital Legal Foundation's office one block from the home of the commandant of the Marine Corps held cablegram after cablegram from the highest levels of the military, debating whether *Playboy* bunnies should be allowed to visit the troops in 1966.

This regiment of cardboard boxes held secrets small and large. A document questioning the inordinately immense amounts of hair spray sold by the PX system to an almost womanless American Army was dovetailed with a report disclosing that Dr. William McMillan— the brilliant chemist General Westmoreland borrowed from the University of California at Los Angeles to be his scientific adviser— enlisted the help of the U.S. Forest Service to figure out how to start forest fires, rather than prevent them.

Some of these leftovers from the Westmoreland-CBS trial are of only the most subtle historic merit, awaiting scrutiny by scholars anxious for any piece of paper that will help answer the "whys" and "hows" of the Vietnam War. Others are frightening, embarrassing, or both.

Take the TOP SECRET minutes of a briefing for Army Chief of Staff Johnson held at Westmoreland's Saigon headquarters on April 18, 1966. After a discussion of the anti-infiltration-barrier program, these minutes said Johnson commented "that operations within [South Vietnam] seemed to consist largely of 'mopping up the floor' rather than 'actually shutting off the spigot' through which infiltrators into SVN are known to pass. This was a clear implication, in CSA's [Chief of Staff, Army's] view, the program within SVN was not going after the source of the problem. He even went so far as to suggest Peking as an appropriate target."

China was a key ingredient for another briefing given for Johnson a few months later in Saigon by Westmoreland's intelligence chief (and a key witness for CBS in the trial), General Joseph A. McChristian. At this July 30, 1966, session, McChristian reviewed aerial reconnaissance operations, including two flown by the Strategic Air Command (probably using high-speed, high-flying, super-secret Lockheed SR71 "Blackbirds," although this memo did not disclose the type of aircraft). One of these flights, code-named TROJAN HORSE, was high-altitude reconnaissance of Laos, North Vietnam, and Cambodia. "A second high altitude SAC photographic project," this memo said, "is called BLUE SPRINGS. This project is targeted against Northern North Vietnam and Southern China." One probable purpose of these high-flying photo missions was to determine exactly what supplies and industries were stashed in China. After the bombing campaign against North Vietnam began, China had become a safe haven for industry, schools, food, munitions, and the trucks needed to keep the Trail operational.

The best reconnaissance the Air Force could offer, of course, wouldn't stop infiltration down the Trail or defeat the enemy on the ground in Vietnam. Many of the documents unearthed in the discovery process focused on specialized weapons to deal with a special foe operating in the strange environment. For example, according to the Research and Development section of the 1966 MACV command history, while Smokey the Bear, symbol of the U.S. Forest Service, exhorted Americans to prevent forest fires, the Forest Service that year helped the U.S. command in Vietnam figure out how to start them.

The reason for this interest in forest combustion, the command history said, was to "deny the VC/NVA the concealment afforded by the jungle." With MACV stymied in its efforts to start a really hot fire in the very wet jungles of Vietnam, the Secretary of Defense told the Advanced Research Projects Agency to "determine the specific jungle-moisture content conditions under which there was the greatest possibility of destroying jungle/forest by fire, and the quantitative reduction in jungle-moisture content that could be achieved through defoliation. The U.S. Forest Service was called on to perform this work and a team of technicians in the field of forest fuels began work on this project in January 1966."

In March 1966, MACV conducted a test, under the code name PINK ROSE, using M-35 bomblets to set fire to a portion of the Chu Pong mountain forest in South Vietnam. The 1966 command history reported that "All phases of the test were conducted under optimum conditions at precise times and with spectacular delivery accuracy, but heavy flames were not observed and fire storms did not develop." (Asked in the summer of 1985 to check on this Forest Service involvement in the Vietnam War, a spokesman for that agency said he could locate no records referring to PINK ROSE and/or any other jungle-burning operation.)

Fighting a modern war in a jungle environment served as impetus for yet another weird weapon-development plan hatched by MACV in 1968. Jungles were not exactly helicopter-friendly, with the dense foliage impeding the Army's much vaunted "air mobile" concept. So, according to the 1968 MACV command history, the Army "sought a means of creating HLZs [helicopter landing zones] in heavy jungle containing trees 150 feet tall and 36 inches in diameter. The desired requirements were that the created HLZ must contain neither large stumps, nor craters and, hopefully, would be large enough to accommodate three to five helicopters."

Calling this a "taxing R&D problem," MACV and the Air Force began searching for the kind of bomb to do the job and the type of aircraft to deliver it. "Some thought was given to the temporary expedient of using A-1Es, F-4s and F-105s to deliver the 2,000-pound M-84 bomb and using the F-105 to deliver the 3,000-pound M-118." But, the MACV history said, "It was obvious from the beginning that sufficient accuracy would not be achieved with these aircraft."

American Telephone & Telegraph Co.'s Sandia Labs subsidiary came up with a novel weapon: the BTV. "It suggested building a huge 43,000-pound bomb composed from a liquid petroleum tank and triggering device left over from the atomic stockpile. This Big Test Vehicle (BTV), as it was called, would be six feet in diameter, 244 inches long and have a blast capability equal to 20 tons of TNT. Moreover, according to the Air Force Weapons Development Laboratory at Kirkland AFB, New Mexico, the bomb could be made quickly, inexpensively and could be carried by the B-52." Whether or not this BTV was ever used cannot be determined from these declassified files, but the MACV command history said "a test program for the BTV was set up in CONUS [the continental United States] with the planned climax to be a series of live tests in a Montana forest. At the end of 1968, however, these tests had not been concluded."

While awaiting results of the BTV tests, the R&D experts came up with what they thought would be a "reasonably good solution, though not an entirely satisfactory one." This involved adapting 1950s Cold War bombs to a 1960s hot war. "A supply of more than 200 M-121 10,000-pound bombs, created specifically for the now obsolete B-36 bomber, was carried in the Air Force inventory. Combining ingenuity and imagination, the experts found that the bomb could be effectively carried and dropped by the CH-54 helicopter (Sky Hook) and, in a palletized version, by the C-130 transport. In both instances, however, the bomb was parachute stabilized and carried a 36-inch extended fuse to ensure detonation just above the ground."

Despite all this "ingenuity and imagination," the 10,000-pound bomb did not turn out to be an ideal jungle destroyer, the command history reveals. "In tests conducted in CONUS and SEASIA [Southeast Asia], some problems became evident. In the first place, the CH-54, while capable of impressive accuracy, had only a daylight VFR [visual flight rules] capability. Also it was particularly vulnerable to ground fire. The C-130 had all-weather, day or night capability, but lacked the accuracy of the CH-54. Accuracy could be of prime importance as shown by one live drop wherein the bomb was only 25 meters off target; however because the bomb fell on the side of a ridge, the landing zone created was not useable."

MACV also discovered in its tests of this ultimate weed-cutter that the goal of creating an LZ capable of handling three to five helicopters was not feasible. The 10,000-pound bomb did clear an area without craters or stumps, but it was only about forty or fifty meters across. "The blast, however, did render it possible for one helicopter to land immediately and, with minor engineering efforts, the HLZ could be expanded to accommodate three helicopters in about two hours."

MACV and the 7th Air Force opted for basic chemistry to try to slow down infiltration on the Trail in a plan code-named COMMANDO LAVA. This plan proposed using chelating compounds to make the Trail slippery at key locations. According to a TOP SECRET briefing paper delivered at the CINCPAC Infiltration/Interdiction Conference in July of 1967, COMMANDO LAVA was "a new concept in LOC interdiction that utilizes chelating compounds to destabilize soil at selected choke points. The program was conceived by CAS [the CIA], which supervised C-130 aerial delivery tactics at Eglin AFB and subsequent experimental application on two LOC targets in southern Laos. Based on the initial results of the Laos tests, 7th Air Force was asked to develop a test program and a plan for operational employment of air-dropped soil destabilization compounds."

By the time of the conference, two targets in Laos had had the dubious honor of being the first in the history of warfare to be pummeled with chelating agents, but the slow turboprop converted cargo-carrying C-130s were worse for the experience. " . . . The delivery aircraft . . . had received numerous hits from enemy groundfire." Due to hazards to the aircraft and their crews, the briefing paper said the commander of the 7th Air Force should put further chelation tests on "temporary hold" until the aircraft could be better protected. General Westmoreland, briefly mentioning the project in *A Soldier Reports*, said "no substantial evidence was ever found that it proved effective in deterring movement."

As MACV tapped the best scientific minds in the United States to devise strange and specialized weapons that could be adapted to the requirements, topography, and climate of Southeast Asia, the Vietcong indirectly benefited. In addition to supplies that came down the unstoppable Trail, the VC and North Vietnamese Army gained another almost unlimited source of supplies—the United States and the South Vietnamese Army. Some were stolen by the VC working on the expanding U.S. rear-area bases. Others were recovered on the field of battle.

But to build the weapon most feared by the U.S. troops, the VC only had to recycle what the Allies fired at them. Even under ideal conditions, a certain amount of ordnance doesn't detonate, but in Vietnam the U.S. dud rate went far beyond normal assumptions. And, as the MACV 1967 command history said, "Statistics prepared on the dud rate of U.S. munitions during 1967 indicated that because of the enormous amounts of munitions used by [the Allies], a dud rate of even one percent was excessive. This conclusion is particularly significant when coupled with the fact that more than 50 percent of the mines and booby traps found in SVN during 1967 were made from dud U.S. munitions."

A message drafted by Lieutenant Colonel James Stuart for Westmoreland and sent to all his commanders in October 1967 offered truly grim statistics on the dud problem. "Mines and booby traps continue to cause a significant portion of our friendly casualties. In 1966 approximately one-third of friendly casualties were caused by this means and it appears that this casualty level will continue for 1967." Westmoreland warned that the United States was indirectly to blame for the deaths and injuries. "Dud U.S. munitions are a prime source of material for VC manufacture of mines and booby traps. Even with an assumed low dud rate, the high volume of U.S. ordnance results in a large amount of dud munitions. In addition to artillery, grenade and aerial bomb dud sources, the BLU-3/B bomblets have had an excessive number of duds due to the requirements of a hard surface for detonation."

Tactics also contributed to the dud-booby-trap equation. Throughout the war, U.S. artillery batteries expended tons of ammunition on Harassment-and-Interdiction (H&I) missions. Fired primarily at night, these H&I missions were not directed against any specific target. Instead, they rained down shells on map co-ordinates that intelligence reports (often no more than educated guesses) determined as apt locations for VC activity. Since H&I rounds hit points where there were no Americans, the VC easily harvested the duds from these missions. As the SECRET October 1967 message said, the risk to American troops from this practice was greater than the rewards: "H and I fire programs continue to be reviewed in view of the volume of fire and low kill ratio as opposed to the high number of friendly casualties from mines and booby traps."

These high casualties resulted from the nature of the Vietnam War itself. Unlike World War II, where huge armies fought precisely planned battles against known adversaries, the war in Vietnam consisted, for the U.S. and its allies, of constant small-unit patrolling against an unseen and unknown foe. These were tension-filled patrols because of the mines and booby traps, made even worse by the idyllic landscape and seeming innocence of the people.

As the U.S. presence in Vietnam increased, so did the talent of the Vietcong for crafting booby traps. On patrol, nothing could be taken for granted. Even the most benign objects could, and often did, explode. Paths were avoided at all costs even if villagers were walking ahead of a U.S. patrol. Locals knew the location of mines. The Americans didn't. The VC booby-trapped virtually everything—trees, shrubs, bushes, roads, houses, animals, tins of food, wells, and even bodies. Soon, for U.S. troops, particularly those in the northernmost section of the country, the fear of booby traps became almost as debilitating as the explosions.

A SECRET study in the November 1967 issue of the Southeast Asia Analysis Report—a magazine-like publication prepared by the SEA Programs Directorate of the Office of the Secretary of Defense— confirmed that the growing dud problem was at the heart of the booby-trap situation, compounded by "unobserved air and artillery attacks." In 1967, it estimated, "We are dropping and firing 35,000 tons of ordnance a month (worth $40 million) at an enemy we can neither see nor gather data that proves we are inflicting significant damage." But the analysts did have "sufficient evidence to conclude that the enemy is reclaiming a portion of about 800 tons of dud explosives we estimate are expended each month. The Viet Cong use these duds to manufacture mines and booby traps, which they use against our troops."

Looking closely at the situation, this study determined that the most vaunted weapon of the war—the ARC LIGHT strikes conducted by B-52s "pickling" (dropping) 1,000-pound bombs from an altitude of 35,000 feet or even more—was also the most random. "Ninety percent of all ARC LIGHT sorties (B-52Z) are considered unobserved. By their very nature, high altitude drops on suspected enemy troop and supply concentrations cannot be observed." The U.S. had a slightly better ability to direct and observe artillery fire, but even so, the study said, 45 percent of all artillery shells expended were unobserved, and 35 percent of all shells fired in South Vietnam during the period were used on H&I missions. Only tactical air strikes, usually directed by either ground or air forward air controllers, had a solid majority of their missions observed—90 percent.

With dud rates running as low as 2 percent for artillery, growing to 5 percent for the B-52 strikes and 20 percent for air strikes, the Vietcong had a huge crop of easy-to-harvest munitions from the unobserved ordnance. Between January and June of 1967, this study estimated, of the 34,173 tons of munitions a month the United States expended in unobserved strikes, the VC were able to harvest some 814 tons of ammo worth $1.4 million that could easily be turned into mines and booby traps. The tragic absurdity of the situation was brought home by the U.S. command's estimate that the VC/NVA forces had a "total monthly munitions requirement of 300 to 450 tons a month." Or, to put it quite simply, the United States was furnishing the enemy with twice as much as he needed to blow American troops to bits.

From January to June 1967, the SEA study said, 17 percent of all U.S. casualties were caused by mines and booby traps—539 Americans dead and another 5,532 wounded.

The VC put great emphasis on dud collection. They even offered rewards. "Some skeptics state it is too difficult and too dangerous for the VC to waste time doing this [collecting duds]; this is clearly not the case," the study said. "Reclaiming U.S. duds is not a small size effort nor is it localized to any area of SVN—it is an overall VC objective. Of course, it greatly simplifies VC logistical problems." These were not a people ready to turn swords into plowshares.

Another startling conclusion of the SEA study was that, despite the primitive state of its arms industry, North Vietnam had a far lower dud rate than the United States. In the only area the United States could accurately measure—the Demilitarized Zone—the North Vietnamese Army had a minimal dud rate, less than one percent.

Despite all the evidence, the analysts said they could not recommend that all unobserved fire missions be stopped. "However, we can conclude that it does lead to large numbers of friendly casualties (mainly through VC retrieval of duds) and it should be minimized. Troop commanders at all levels must realize that unnecessary missions may cause more harm than good. The cost to the taxpayer is only a minor part of this, the cost in friendly lives and limbs is the major factor."

The U.S. munitions profligacy also negated another part of the American war effort that had to be measured in terms of lives lost: the bombing campaign against the Trail. "We are solving a significant part of the VC logistical problem for him, thereby reducing the effectiveness of our interdiction program," the study said.

The study made several recommendations, including beefing up quality control and reducing the use of ordnance with high dud rates. One suggestion, however, would be ignored due to intra-service rivalry: the use of B-52s only "where the intelligence makes the pay-off clearly worth the cost." This suggestion, like many other rational suggestions made during the war, ran into what could be called the "generals' lobby," or, in this case, the "bomber generals' lobby." While the average draftee viewed the Vietnam War as an unsolicited test of endurance, professional officers viewed it as a chance to "punch their tickets" for promotions and experience. No matter how many American lives could be saved by restricting B-52 strikes, a cutback would not and could not happen in a Pentagon ruled by ambition.

This left the grunts with the grisly but accurate final suggestion made in this study: "Conduct an educational campaign to apprise our troops of the dud problem." The SEA study even suggested a slogan for this campaign: "The life you take may be your own."

The Westmoreland-CBS papers—just like the pages of any good war novel—also offer moments of comic relief. A series of high-level messages coordinating the planned visit of *Playboy* bunnies to Vietnam evokes the mad scene of a fictional bunny visit and riot in the Francis Ford Coppola movie *Apocalypse Now*. These cables also indicate how public relations dictated even those issues only peripherally associated with winning the war.

In a September 27, 1966, cablegram to Army Chief of Staff Johnson, Westmoreland discussed the problems that came up when a *Playboy* visit was canceled. Westmoreland said he did not want to "overdramatize a relatively straightforward issue," but pointed out that "the show in question was accepted by MACV on the basis of an outstanding rating" although "subsequently we were advised that because of concern over adverse publicity which could accrue from mothers, religious organizations and other groups, it had been decided the show would be canceled."

In view of this potential adverse publicity (which had not materialized after a 1965 visit by "Playmate of the Year" Jo Collins),
Westmoreland had already agreed that the Department of the Army
would tell *Playboy* not to come. But in his message to Johnson, Westmoreland said it should be made clear he was not the spoiler. "In view
of the fact that MACV was, and is, able to accept the unit, our response stated that if, in DA's opinion, the show would result in adverse
publicity, we were in agreement with the DA cancellation decision.
No concurrence was accorded the proposal that MACV inability to
accept the show be cited as the reason for cancellation."

This request did not reach the minion in the Pentagon who sent
a telegram to *Playboy* publisher Hugh Hefner, stating, "The commander of the U.S. forces in Vietnam has informed this office that
they will be unable to accept the *Playboy* magazine entertainment
unit as previously scheduled."

This telegram, Westmoreland said, "misrepresented" his position
because it conveyed the impression "that I personally signified inability to accept the entertainment unit." Westmoreland told Johnson
he considered this serious business. "This matter assumes particular
importance in the interest of keeping faith with the entertainment
world, which has contributed so richly to the morale of our servicemen in Vietnam."

In a cable to Westmoreland the next day (September 28), Johnson told Westmoreland, " . . . I agree your position on the cancellation
of the *Playboy* entertainment unit has been misrepresented." Then
Johnson blamed the mix-up on that oldest of military excuses, the
snafu. "A determination was made . . . that the decision to cancel the
show should not be put on the basis of adverse publicity or standards
of decency and good taste since these points were arguable and since
Playboy would undoubtedly exploit them in order to bring pressure to
bear for a reversal of the decision." So, Johnson added, "the staff felt
if *Playboy* Magazine was informed that MACV was unable to accept
the entertainment unit as previously scheduled without further explanation, there would be less basis for public outcry."

Johnson added that when conveying this message to Hefner, the
staff had "erred" in using the phrase "The commander of U.S. forces
in Vietnam." But, he said, "this phraseology is not uncommon in
communications with the civilian sector." Johnson then asked Westmoreland to accept whatever heat might be generated by *Playboy*. "I
do not feel it wise to correct the record now. It is generally accepted
by the public that operational, political and other factors require
changes in plans pertaining to Vietnam. The absence to date of any
appeal from *Playboy* would seem to indicate such conclusion on their

part. However, should a strong protest be received, the situation would require evaluation."

Johnson ended his message with a request that Westmoreland accept the *Playboy* skirmish like a good trooper. "I regret the position in which you have been placed and ask your indulgence in sitting tight for the moment to see if this one will blow over. We'll not make the same mistake again."

Playboy bunnies weren't the only important side issues facing Westmoreland in 1966. He also had Mixmaster and hair-spray prob- lems. As a TOP SECRET cable from Joint Chiefs chairman Earle Wheeler shows, regulating these PX goods required the attention of two high-ranking generals. The problem, it seemed, was that although the United States never did "win the hearts and minds" of the Viet- namese people, it succeeded handily in addicting them to American consumer products.

Wheeler's April 9, 1966, cablegram focused more on the potential black-market implications of these PX-funneled goodies than on their socio-economic impact within South Vietnam. "Secretary [Cyrus] Vance [Deputy Secretary of Defense] just informed me that we have troubles coming up in the form of misuse of PX supplies. He states that pictures in congressional hands show three blocks of Vietnamese shops and vendors near Saigon PX selling such items as Mixmasters, blankets and other goods obviously obtained from American sources."

Wheeler warned Westmoreland that "Mr. Vance anticipates a sizeable scandal implicating military personnel, facilities and sup- plies." This scandal—one of many PX scandals throughout the Viet- nam War—resulted in part from the same kind of overkill the United States applied to bombing the Ho Chi Minh Trail. Wheeler, who told Westy he was "surprised" at the pounds per day per man of PX supplies, asked, "Has anything concrete been done to your knowledge to the end of providing supplies on a more austere basis? In this con- nection, I am advised that the State Department inspector who recently visited Vietnam discovered that 500,000 cans of hair spray had been dispensed through the PXs in a brief period, despite the fact that the supported female population is very small."

By November 1966, McNamara had decided to apply the same management techniques to the PX system that he had instituted in the rest of the Pentagon, as shown by a message from Army Chief of Staff Johnson to Westmoreland. Commenting on a recent McNamara trip to Vietnam, Johnson said "he indicated that the management of the exchange system in Vietnam needed substantial improvement. His first reaction was to obtain the services of a civilian merchandising consultant to go immediately to Vietnam and develop independent findings and recommendations to improve the system." This was pure McNamara—consultants and "independent reviews" became the hall-mark of his stay in the Pentagon. Consultants could brainstorm development of an updated Maginot Line and evaluate infiltration on the Trail. They could also fix PX systems.

Westmoreland also had time to ponder semantics, as illustrated by a December 5, 1967, message he sent to both General Wheeler and Admiral Sharp, commander-in-chief of the U.S. Pacific forces. This cable came at a time when the North Vietnamese were pouring forces down the Trail for the upcoming Tet Offensive and the siege of Khe Sanh. As enemy generals laid the groundwork for the assault they believed would win the war, Westmoreland, at least in this message, was preoccupied with nicknames that might give his command bad press.

Westmoreland told Wheeler he had "strong" objections to adopting a Pentagon-mandated system of giving nicknames for operations in Vietnam beginning with "Banana," "Barbara," "Bandy," or "Banjo." "As the directive for this system states," Westmoreland wrote, "nicknames are employed for administrative convenience or for morale or for public information purposes. I do not see where morale or public information purposes can be served reasonably by giving combat operations, where Americans are fighting valiantly, nicknames beginning with Barbara, Banjo or Bandy. News media would ignore or possibly ridicule operations nicknames such as 'Banjo Royce,' 'Bandy Truscott' or 'Barbara Echo.' They have neither cogent meaning nor dignity."

To preserve dignity (and avoid ridicule), Westmoreland suggested that "from the standpoint of identification and history, major operations should be tied generally to geographical locations, or given significant nicknames which instill pride in the participants or pay due honor to noteworthy personalities or places." Emphasizing that the war belonged to the Vietnamese, he added, " . . . I intend to increasingly assign Vietnamese nicknames to U.S. operations which are in direct support of pacification. Other U.S. operations not directly connected with pacification would continue to be given meaningful and dignified nicknames."

Wheeler fired back a message the same day endorsing Westmoreland's strong nickname stance. "I agree with Westy's analysis of the nickname situation with respect to combat operations in Southeast Asia. . . . There is much to be said for giving our operations significant nicknames which have dignity and cogent meaning to the participants and the public. Using names of noteworthy personalities or places has considerable merit. Westy should also be free to use Vietnamese nicknames for operations in direct support of pacification."

So, six weeks before the Tet Offensive would drastically alter the American public's perception of the war, Westmoreland did win one small PR battle. Never in the course of the conflict would American troops be asked to sacrifice themselves in an operation named after a banana!

11.

Insights: Cambodia and MIAs

B E S I D E S detailing the U.S. rape of Laotian neutrality, the classified documents unearthed in the Westmoreland-CBS case also offer fresh insights into similar assaults on Cambodia—a once peaceable kingdom whose 500-mile common border with Vietnam provided such a sanctuary for the Vietcong that eventually the United States would have no compunctions about turning most of it into a free-fire zone, neutrality be damned.

The Laotian and Cambodian borders were not the only artificial lines on the Earth's surface that bothered the MACV commander and his superiors in Honolulu and the Pentagon. The U.S. brass also spent the early war years planning and replanning invasions of North Vietnam above the DMZ. The mound of classified material collected for the lawsuit gives a glimpse of some of these plans.

The Westmoreland-CBS papers also shed new light on one of the lingering issues of the Vietnam war—the fate of American soldiers and airmen still classified as missing in action, or MIA. Several documents cast considerable doubt on North Vietnam's repeated claims that it cannot account for the MIAs. The captured Vietcong papers, referred to in U.S. intelligence memos, reveal that the North, like the United States, had an obsession with record-keeping, focusing much of its reporting efforts on keeping track of American prisoners.

But, unlike the United States, which dotted the Vietnamese landscape with bases holding rear-echelon paper-shufflers and supply men, the North Vietnamese preferred to stash their service and support troops across the border in Cambodia—a country led by the stubbornly neutral Prince Norodom Sihanouk. Depicted in some Western news reports as a jazz-playing, womanizing playboy (all true), Sihanouk was also an extremely effective and respected leader who managed to cast off French colonialism in 1954 without a war. When the United

States entered its own war in Indochina, Sihanouk went to great lengths to ensure his country would not be swept into the fray as a U.S. pawn.

He steadfastly refused to permit American troops in "hot pursuit" of Vietcong to cross his country's border. At the same time, he came to an uneasy accommodation with the Vietcong that ultimately turned Cambodia into a broken and battered victim of the Vietnam War.

In 1966, the Vietcong–North Vietnamese Army sanctuaries inside Cambodia more than bothered Westmoreland. To him, they were a dagger pointed at the heart of South Vietnam. Unable to attack the supply bases, arms caches, and communications centers in Cambodia, he implored his superiors to at least let him peer behind enemy lines with aerial surveillance. A series of cablegrams among Westmoreland, Admiral Sharp in Hawaii, and General Wheeler in Washington, D.C., dealing with covert aerial reconnaissance of Cambodia, fits into the pattern of official U.S. lies William Shawcross reported in his book *Side-Show: Kissinger, Nixon and the Destruction of Cambodia.* The cables from the Westmoreland-CBS case, however, pre-date by three years the documents Shawcross discovered.

These cables also reflect the bombing pattern Shawcross discerned: how one limited air mission could soon lead to another and then another. The conventions of neutrality and respect for another nation's sovereignty are quickly forgotten in the pursuit of short-term military gains.

On June 2, 1966, Wheeler raised the question of aerial spying in a cable to both Sharp and Westmoreland, complaining, "For several weeks now we have been trying mightily to obtain State [Department] concurrence for air reconnaissance of Cambodia . . . which MACV requested and CINCPAC endorsed." Unfortunately, Wheeler said, the State Department was engaged in a "dialogue" with Sihanouk and use of "aerial recon would jeopardize their success in this direction."

But Wheeler said the tactical situation (six U.S. Army infantry battalions were operating along the border at the time) warranted up-to-date intelligence because "there [are] sizeable forces debouching from Cambodia into the plateau area."

To goad the State Department into action, Wheeler suggested Westmoreland send a "strong message" to Sharp "outlining the VC/NVA situation as known to him and reiterate his need of timely and accurate intelligence of enemy activity. It may be that such a message, endorsed by CINCPAC, will at least get us a one-time authorization for a reconnaissance mission." Wheeler, naturally, wanted more than just one mission, as he told Westmoreland and Sharp: "This will not satisfy your need, however, it would get your foot in the door."

Westmoreland sent the suggested message and on June 11, 1966,

Wheeler authorized the first—but far from the last—aerial penetration of Cambodia's neutral skies. In a TOP SECRET LIMDIS (Limited Distribution) cable to Westmoreland and Sharp, Wheeler "authorized one-time photo coverage" of Cambodia, limited to no more than twelve flights operating at 10,000 feet and above.

He then started the chain of official lies, writing, "This operation is extremely sensitive politically and every effort should be made to avoid public disclosure. Release of information necessary for planning and execution should be held to a 'strict need to know.' Pilots and observers should be carefully selected for experience and maturity. They should be briefed to claim navigation error in event of capture."

Wheeler told officials to stonewall the press on the recon operation, code-named DORSAL FIN. "Should an incident occur and response to press inquiry become necessary, your response should be confined to the statement 'We are aware of the incident and are investigating.' No other release is authorized without prior clearance and should be forwarded for co-ordination to JCS."

The subterfuge grew. In a June 25 TOP SECRET message to Sharp and Wheeler, Westmoreland said that DORSAL FIN procedures were established so "aircrews will take off in the apparent mission of flying near border. . . . This will . . . provide a cover story for plausible denial."

By December, the first twelve recon missions had been flown and, like addicts, the military asked for more. They got their fix, with CINCPAC authorizing another twelve missions on December 9. By 1967, DORSAL FIN flights had become quite routine, with the Joint Chiefs authorizing "up to ten missions per month over the entire DORSAL FIN area" as well as authorizing medium-altitude recon flights.

About eighteen months after the DORSAL FIN flights began, MACV's intelligence section reported another kind of Cambodian air activity—the tiny Cambodian air force was doing something that not even the North Vietnamese dared, sending its planes into South Vietnam. According to a CONFIDENTIAL MACV J-2 intelligence report, "since 29 Nov [1967] there has been a series of violations of SVN airspace by [unidentified] aircraft flying out of Cambodia." These incursions included both "high performance" jets and French-built Alouette helicopters, the report said. The 7th Air Force launched intercepters against these unidentified and presumably unfriendly airplanes, but never caught one.

These are extraordinary reports. Despite the fact that the United States had assembled in South Vietnam and Thailand the mightiest air armada in the world, the minuscule Cambodian air force was able to penetrate the skies of South Vietnam with impunity. What would have happened if the North had used its air power? This was a contingency U.S. planners always considered. In fact, the first regular U.S. ground troops dispatched to Vietnam in 1965 were Marine Hawk anti-aircraft batteries set up around the Danang airbase.

Westmoreland, meanwhile, was frustrated. Reconnaissance flights over Cambodia to take pictures of the enemy were no substitute for bombing. Although tactical considerations suggested that attacking the hideouts was necessary to win the war, diplomacy and national policy blocked such a move. Westmoreland found himself in the same position as General Douglas MacArthur, who a decade earlier in Korea had been faced with threats from Chinese troops operating across an international border. Like MacArthur, Westmoreland pressed his case that tactics should overrule matters of diplomacy. Unlike MacArthur, he did not tangle publicly with his President.

But, as cables declassified in the Westmoreland-CBS discovery process show, the generals struggled mightily to bend the policymakers to their way of thinking. Take the series of messages Wheeler, Sharp, and Westmoreland exchanged concerning "hot pursuit" of Vietcong forces in the so-called Parrot's Beak area of Cambodia. Westmoreland thought the hottest kind of pursuit leading to the huge concentration of VC troops and logistical support bases could be supplied by high-flying B-52 ARC LIGHT sorties. The politically astute Westmoreland first convinced U.S. Ambassador to Saigon Ellsworth Bunker that this was a good idea, as shown in his December 4, 1967, TOP SECRET LIMITED DISTRIBUTION message to Wheeler. "The heavy concentration of enemy in the tri-border sanctuary presents a most lucrative target that should be attacked by fire at the earliest opportunity. Because of its importance, I want to send the following message but desire to pass it on to you to solicit your comments before doing so. I have discussed this with Ambassador Bunker who agrees."

This was a strongly worded argument directed to the civilian bosses of the war, Defense Secretary Robert McNamara and Secretary of State Dean Rusk, in favor of hitting the North Vietnamese, hard, in Cambodia. After pointing out that a full North Vietnamese division had encamped in the Parrot's Beak area, Westmoreland said that intelligence reports showed this division to be a relatively easy target to hit and hurt. "Reports state that the enemy units are not disposed in an alert or defensive posture; rather they are utilizing their Cambodian sanctuary to rest, regroup and reconstitute openly and unmolested. There is no evidence of heavy bunker construction."

Westmoreland argued it would be easy to hide the B-52 strikes and artillery barrages he proposed. "The situation . . . presents a unique opportunity for the 'pursuit by fire concept.' The area is remote; the border is ill-defined; there are no known civilians in the area or Cambodian presence; the delivery of fire is easily concealed from scrutiny; and more significantly, the enemy's dangerous activities fulfill all the criteria for substantiating the hot pursuit concept."

He then asked for a huge amount of firepower. "Request earliest approval to attack this concentration of enemy force by employing B-52 strikes for sustained period of at least 72 hours. High intensity tac [tactical] air strikes and artillery fire from Ben Het. Approval of B-52 strikes is particularly urged since exposure of this action would be minimal, and this weapons system will provide maximum surprise. B-52 strikes only at night would be acceptable."

Westmoreland followed up on this message December 16, outlining the lucrative targets he expected to hit in Cambodia. "An intelligence and targeting group has developed a list of 195 targets in the objective area. In Cambodia there are 75 targets, the major elements being the HQ element B3 front, HQ element, 1st NVA Div, 32d Regt, HQ and 1 Bn 40th Arty and logistical elements with an estimated strength of 2,400. In Laos there are 105 targets. . . . "

Westmoreland wanted to hit these targets with a "saturation by fire effort. . . . This would include B-52 strikes on headquarters of the 1st NVA Division, headquarters elements of the B3 front and the 32d Regiment in the Cambodian Panhandle. Concurrently, artillery would fire on targets within the same area using predicted fire techniques on a pre-arranged schedule for the estimated 90 minutes duration of the B-52 strikes. . . . During the initial two hours and 33 minutes it is estimated that four targets would be struck by B-52s, 70 targets would be struck by 4,000 rounds of artillery and four targets would be struck by tac air with four sorties each target."

On December 19, Admiral Sharp endorsed the tactical soundness of Westmoreland's plan in a message to both Saigon and Wheeler at the Pentagon. But Sharp cautioned that the "political situation vis à vis Cambodia will probably not permit execution of the plan at this time. If situation should change recommend early authorization."

Stymied by political factors over which he had no control, Westmoreland sent another message on December 26 to both Sharp and Wheeler, arguing that the practicalities of the situation far outweighed the risk of violating Cambodia's borders. "I think it is worth repeating that the border in this area is ill-defined and traverses rugged, jungle-covered terrain which stretches great distances. The border is indistinguishable by air and the ground. It is not marked by readily identifiable terrain features. Night B-52 strikes and artillery firing only at night would minimize the risk of compromise of operations. Moreover, there appears to be a good probability that attacks under these conditions can be made without publicity."

By early 1968, Wheeler had discerned a change in the political climate, according to a January 3, 1968, cable he sent to Sharp and

Westmoreland. "Sihanouk's recent remarks regarding use of U.S. troops on Cambodian soil have started some discussion here on the desirability of using U.S. forces. . . . The thought has been expressed that recent events in connection with Cambodia might indicate that the political climate is changing sufficiently to allow consideration of employing U.S. forces. . . . "

Given this kind of encouragement, Westmoreland fired back another cable, again asking for permission to use U.S. forces in Cambodia. Referring to the large number of regular NVA troops concentrated just across the northern South Vietnam border, Westmoreland argued, "Current rules of engagement provide the enemy with a decided advantage in allowing him to strike across the border and withdraw, knowing full well we will not pursue and destroy him on Cambodian territory." Because of this situation, he said, "I believe it is appropriate . . . to initiate pursuit of . . . forces into the Cambodian base areas with maneuver elements, supported by artillery and tac air as the opportunity occurs."

Such "hot pursuit" would give the United States political leverage, Westmoreland reasoned. "There are also psychological advantages," he wrote. "By demonstrating our willingness to conduct cross border forays in pursuit of his forces, the enemy's assessment of the value of the Cambodian bases would diminish and the pressure to convene at the conference table would increase."

But by January 14 the massing of NVA troops all along South Vietnam's borders had caused Westmoreland to reevaluate his plans for attacks near or across the boundary. And when the enemy unleashed its Tet Offensive two weeks later, Westmoreland was busy enough without adding a Cambodian campaign. At home, Lyndon Johnson—already under fire for his conduct of the war in South Vietnam—and his advisers did not want to add a Cambodian invasion to their troubles. Richard Nixon, the man who won the Presidency with his promises to end the war, would be the one to extend the conflict further by authorizing a joint U.S.–South Vietnamese invasion of Cambodia on April 30, 1970.

In addition to his goal of fighting the enemy lurking in Cambodia, declassified documents from the lawsuit disclose Westmoreland had ambitious plans to invade North Vietnam—a possibility also considered by Secretary of Defense Robert McNamara.

In August 1967, Westmoreland submitted a plan for a combined airborne-airmobile-amphibious assault north of the DMZ, code-named BUTTSTROKE. Sharp then proceeded to develop such a plan on his own, code-named FRISCO CITY. While Westmoreland endorsed the concept of this plan, the previously classified cable traffic shows it was also subject to the continuing tug-of-war Westmoreland conducted with his nominal military boss in the Pacific, Admiral Sharp. In an October 13, 1967, message to Sharp, Westmoreland took issue with plans to have this operation directed by anyone but himself.

Westy said that any such invasion would "simply be an extension of the operations being conducted in Northern I CTZ. These operations would be, in fact, a temporary extension of the northern battle area, in which my forces would be redeployed by sea and airlift in the conduct of a tactical maneuver to outflank the NVA position along the DMZ. Such operations have to be completely integrated with operations launched from I CTZ against the DMZ. Therefore I request that I be assigned full responsibility for planning and executing the operation. Any other arrangement would complicate immeasurably the command relationships, and require intricate coordination with out-of-country commanders."

Westmoreland recommended that FRISCO CITY, which was targeted at the North Vietnamese town of Xom Lap, a few miles north of the DMZ, be conducted by the Army's 1st Cav Division, the 1st Marine Division, three Vietnamese airborne battalions, and two Vietnamese marine battalions—a force of some 50,000 troops that no ambitious general would want to give up to anyone else.

During the fall of 1967, each side in the Vietnam War pressed plans to deal the other a stunning defeat. While the North was sending thousands of men down the Trail for an all-out offensive at Tet, Westmoreland continued to formulate his invasion scheme. Sharp didn't buy all of Westmoreland's plan, particularly the inclusion of South Vietnamese troops in the initial assault or even in the planning process. South Vietnam may have been an ally, but it apparently was not to be trusted. Again, political considerations entered into discussions between these two military men.

In a November 3, 1967, cable to Sharp, Westmoreland said, "From a strict military point of view, I share your concern for including RVNAF forces in the initial assault. However, unilateral U.S. invasion of NVN could leave us open to severe worldwide criticism of broadening the scope of the war without the full support and consent of the GVN."

Because of this, Westmoreland argued, "I consider RVNAF participation in any operation of this type desirable for political and psychological reasons. To conduct this operation without Vietnamese participation would also be a blow to the new government and to their national pride. . . . Finally, the conduct of an important thrust into North Vietnam without Vietnamese participation would evoke serious criticism abroad and at home where a large body of opinion now exists that RVNAF is not carrying its share of the load in battle."

Planning for the amphibious assault continued—just as the North Vietnamese continued their parallel preparations for an assault on the South at Tet. In fact, the North Vietnamese buildup was viewed as a tactical plus by the invasion planners. Just days before the North launched the Tet Offensive, Sharp sent Wheeler a message (January 27, 1968) endorsing Westmoreland's plan for an operation against the North (now code-named DURANGO CITY) because "The NVA buildup assessed by Westy . . . would certainly leave the enemy vulnerable in the coastal area north of the DMZ."

But the day after Tet (January 31), Wheeler sent Westmoreland a message disapproving of this plan. Instead, Wheeler told Westmoreland to develop a deception plan that would make the North think the United States was going to counter the Tet Offensive with a bold strike of its own. This was no light order. As Wheeler told Westmoreland, the deception plan was developed after "discussion with Highest Authority," cable-ese for President Johnson, who, during Tet and the siege of Khe Sanh, was to take his role as commander-in-chief quite literally.

On February 9, with much of South Vietnam still under attack, with fierce fighting in Hue, the city closest to the DMZ, Westmoreland sent his suggestion for an amphibious feint, code-named OPERATION PACIFIC, to Sharp.

This cablegram is a prime example of the historical legacy of the Westmoreland-CBS trial. Vacuumed up in Capital Legal's wide-ranging series of Freedom of Information requests, it details the capabilities of one of the most highly classified units in the entire American military establishment, Navy Beach Jumper Units (BJUs), which have nothing to do with jumping beaches, but a lot to do with the spooky never-never land of communications deception techniques.

These Navy units—based during peacetime at Norfolk on the East Coast and at San Diego's famed "Silver Strand," Coronado Island, on the West Coast—used radio waves to convince a foe he was under massive attack. Operating radio, tape-recorder, and computer-packed semi-trailers, the BJUs could simulate radio traffic from an entire division.

As Westmoreland told Sharp, the ruse to convince the North an invasion was under way across the DMZ would be elaborate. If it worked, of course, it might take the heat off the South. It would include planned movements of troops within South Vietnam and easy-to-spot maneuvering of amphibious assault ships south of the DMZ. This amphibious shipping, Westmoreland said, "can utilize the capability of the BJU to simulate embarked Marine units by use of communication deception. This appears to be more credible than the alternative of conducting the operation without BJU capability. In this regard, it seems desirable to attempt to portray to the enemy the idea that additional troops from out-of-country have joined TF-76."

But these plans were also canceled. Finally, in March 1968, as Johnson and his advisers were considering what course the war should take in view of the Tet Offensive, Sharp once again urged an invasion of the North. "I suggest that we need to think and act in an aggressive and determined and offensive manner. Westy and I have recommended that we create a feint of an amphibious landing in North Vietnam. Recommend that we lift the current restrictions on this operation and carry it out at the earliest possible time. Further, we should decide now that we will carry out a combined amphibious and air mobile campaign against North Vietnam as early as the weather and the current situation permits. . . .

"It seems to me that we are at the cross-roads. We have a choice of using our military power at full effectiveness with the provision of the necessary forces, or we can continue a campaign of gradualism and accept a long, drawn out contest, or we can retreat in defeat from Southeast Asia and leave our allies to face the Communists alone. The choices are not easy, but seem obvious. We have made frequent and liberal efforts to negotiate, all to no avail. Now we need to get tough in word and deed, the only policy that the Communists understand."

The mass of material declassified for Westmoreland's legal campaign against CBS was filled with plans-that-might-have-been— paper exercises not relevant to the fighting of a real war. Scattered throughout this haphazard record, however, are scraps of information that relate to the present—slim leads that shed light on the Americans still recorded as MIAs, Missing in Action. These almost two-decade-old documents give lie to some of today's headlines, which claim the North Vietnamese government cannot find or account for the majority of the more than 2,000 Americans still listed as missing, with a simple mark setting them off from the other names that march across the stark black face of the Vietnam Memorial in Washington, D.C.

These documents reveal that the North Vietnamese military bureaucracy—just like the American military bureaucracy—had a mania for writing things down, and in the case of captured or killed Americans, the records were meticulously kept. According to the MACV 1967 command history, the North realized early in the war the value of using U.S. POWs, KIAs (Killed in Action), and MIAs as political bargaining chips.

The command history reported, "The Viet Cong were instructed to identify dead U.S. personnel, strip the body of all identification, and then bury them in unmarked graves. The location of the gravesite, along with the identification of all personnel effects taken from them were to be sent to higher headquarters. Captured VC documents continually stressed the importance of taking U.S. prisoners and burying the U.S. dead in unmarked graves as a political tactic to bring pressure to bear on the U.S. at the 'proper time.' "

According to Anne Griffiths, executive director of the League of Families of MIAs and POWs, these MACV reports—unknown to her until they turned up in the trial discovery process—provide some of the earliest "concrete" evidence that the VC kept complete and accurate records on captured or killed U.S. servicemen. She said that these records "clearly show that early in the war the Vietnamese had a firm policy on documenting Americans." The existence of these records, Griffiths added, makes it hard to believe statements that Vietnam cannot locate the remains of any more missing Americans.

The Westmoreland-CBS papers also offer insights into the political use the United States made of its prisoners. Following his dramatic announcement in the spring of 1968 that he would not seek re-election, President Johnson pursued peace initiatives with the North with the same ardor he pursued the war. He restricted U.S. bombing of the North while peace talks in Paris were going on, and he expected some quid pro quo from his adversary, particularly on infiltration. But the North did not respond, according to U.S. intelligence estimates. And Johnson needed proof.

So, according to a SECRET-SENSITIVE briefing paper prepared for General Wheeler on November 25, 1968, Johnson ordered the Marines to capture a North Vietnamese Army soldier infiltrating the DMZ. "On 20 Nov Highest Authority authorized squad-size patrols into the southern half of the DMZ over period 24 Nov 3–Dec 68 to capture some prisoners to prove positively that it is the NVA (or VC) who are violating the DMZ. (For Use in Paris) Platoons south of DMZ back up the 'Snatch' patrols. USMC 'Snatch' patrols made no contacts in DMZ on 24 Nov."

Vietnam was the kind of war—as this "snatch patrol" memo illustrates—where the lines between tactics adopted for purely military gains and tactics adopted in hopes of diplomatic gains blurred. That is probably why in early 1967 Johnson seriously considered appointing Westmoreland to serve as Ambassador to South Vietnam as well as commander of all U.S. forces there. A document uncovered by the paper sleuths at the Capital Legal Foundation had the details.

On February 26, 1967, Earle Wheeler, chairman of the Joint Chiefs of Staff, sent a cable to Westmoreland, saying, "Over the weekend Secy McNamara told me that discussions were renewed concerning the merits of your being designated as Ambassador to Vietnam. He emphasized to me that no repeat no decision has been reached; indeed State is casting about for suitable candidates."

Wheeler added that McNamara was considering two possibilities: have Westmoreland resign his commission and be appointed Ambassador as a civilian with appropriate legislation at the time or later "which would restore your rank" or "be designated by the President as his personal representative and Ambassador as well as commander, U.S. Forces Vietnam."

Wheeler told Westmoreland that his preference was for Westmoreland to be both Ambassador and MACV commander. But, he added, McNamara thought Westmoreland in that role would "devote too much time to the day-to-day running of the war to the detriment of executing the heavy responsibilities in the political and economic fields which would fall on your shoulders as ambassador." Wheeler said he told McNamara that the role model for Westmoreland as soldier-statesman should be the general who had directed the last two U.S. wars in Asia, Douglas MacArthur. " . . . I personally consider what we need in Vietnam is an operation of the MacArthur type wherein you would plan the strategy, both on the military and non-military fronts, insure co-ordination between the two and devote your principal energies to the weakest segment of your operation."

Wheeler followed this cable up with another SECRET "back channel" message on March 3, 1967, relating that "Secretary McNamara informed me this morning that there was a long discussion last night between Highest Authority, Secretary Rusk and himself concerning the assumption by you of additional responsibilities." Rusk, Wheeler said, expressed "concern at the prospect of a complete 'militarization' of our senior structure in South Vietnam . . . " while McNamara "counseled against installing you as ambassador in civilian status. . . . "

Politics in South Vietnam scotched any further exploration of this new role for Westmoreland, as a March 10 cable from Wheeler to Westmoreland made clear. "I learned this morning from Secretary McNamara that the proposal to give you overall control in South Vietnam by making you ambassador as well as commander-in-chief is almost surely dead."

This would mean just too many military men involved in the fight for a country trying hard to prove it was more democractic than its foe, Wheeler explained. "The reason, as I understand it, is strong reluctance to make a military man under any guise Ambassador at a time when the GVN is steadily moving toward an elected government, particularly since this government will undoubtedly have as its president a military man."

While Wheeler thought MacArthur might be a good role model for Westmoreland, the MACV commander already had another role model for whom he felt great affection: Dwight D. Eisenhower, former President and, just as important, a former West Pointer. The Pentagon and the White House periodically briefed Eisenhower at his home in Palm Desert, California. During these briefings, Eisenhower often offered prescient observations on the war, but also indulged his status as an "old soldier."

After one of these briefings, on March 21, 1966, Army Lieutenent General A. J. Goodpaster cabled Westmoreland that Eisenhower "would be very happy sometime to see an operation called 'Abilene' [the former President's birthplace]." Westmoreland quickly replied to Goodpaster that he should be "alert to initiation in the next several weeks of Operation 'Abilene' . . . and pass on to general Eisenhower appropriate information."

While thousands of the cables in the Westmoreland-CBS papers generally have all the literary flair and excitement of a Sears catalogue, a few popped up that offer a glimpse of Westmoreland the man. In early March 1968, following the public-relations debacle of Tet and Westmoreland's appointment as chief of staff of the Army, the outgoing Army chief, Harold Johnson, cabled his congratulations.

On March 3, 1968, a tired Westmoreland cabled back:

"Knowing full well the demands placed upon your time these past four years, I suspect commiseration may be more appropriate. . . . I step onto the merry-go-round with no small amount of trepidation, particularly in view of the scarcity of brass rings this carnival season."

Sixteen and a half years later, as the general and his lawyers prepared to step into the courthouse on lower Manhattan's Foley Square, brass rings would be equally scarce.

Part Three

The Trial

12.

Skirmishes

W H I L E the lawyers plowed through a treasure trove of Vietnam documents that dwarfed the Pentagon Papers, enough side battles ignited for several lawsuits. Many of these confrontations involved the infighting that accompanies every major case but rarely meets the public eye: deposition taking, document discovery, and pretrial motions. This dross of the American legal system enriches lawyers, but seldom generates headlines. The combative Burt, however, used much of this legal spadework to attack CBS, adroitly leaking to favored reporters selected government and CBS documents and depositions. It was soon apparent that the case was going to be tried in the court of public opinion as well as the courthouse on Foley Square.

In the months before the trial opened, both sides indulged in name calling, but Burt was the undisputed champion of using the low road to take the high ground. Burt and his conservative backers could not resist accusing CBS of liberal bias. CBS, and to a certain extent David Boies of Cravath, Swaine & Moore, turned this around and branded Burt and his money men as right-wing ideologues who had "captured" General Westmoreland and his case for their own narrow purposes.

Occasionally, however, the two sides concurred on an issue. They agreed, for instance, to videotape most of their depositions due to the advanced age of some of the witnesses and federal trial rules that make it difficult to compel third-party witnesses to appear for a trial if they live outside the district in which it is held. It was the first time ever in a federal trial that videotaped depositions were used so extensively. As a result, in addition to printed transcripts, the trial's historical legacy includes a visual record of much of the high command of the Vietnam War under oath.

And the adversaries in the case over the fairness of the press agreed on something else—the unfairness of the press covering the case! Burt directly challenged reporters on their supposed bias or the biases of their publications. CBS, for its part, often viewed criticism as unwitting sabotage of the First Amendment.

Along the way, the case collected enough characters and subplots to stock a TV mini-series. Lowly Army historians, the Macmillan Publishing Company, and the super-secret National Security Agency were drawn into its disputatious web, along with the Defense Department and individually the Army, Navy, and Air Force; the Clerk of the House of Representatives; two seemingly live-in CIA agents; a reclusive builder of mini-submarines; enough secretaries, undersecretaries, and presidential advisers to staff a Third World government; and enough retired generals, colonels, and enlisted men to fight several brush-fire wars.

As the attorneys test-fired their ammunition before going to trial, it sometimes appeared they were preparing to present the Vietnam War with the original cast—David Boies at one time even contemplated carrying his search for evidence to Hanoi.

In the midst of this pre-trial maneuvering, Hodding Carter, host of "Inside Story," a press-analysis program on the Public Broadcasting Service, was conducting an investigation of "The Uncounted Enemy" that would cause CBS, Crile, and Mike Wallace almost as much grief as the *TV Guide* article.

CBS decided to co-operate completely with Carter, and Crile was more than ready. Ever since the *TV Guide* article was published the year before, Crile had believed the best defense against press criticism and the lawsuit was a strong offense. His bosses did not agree. They muzzled Crile and rarely replied to Burt's charges, which received widespread publicity. Calls to the CBS corporate public-relations department were met with a stiff "no comment." Requests for documents and papers related to the case were answered with directions to the Clerk of the Court's office.

Crile viewed the decision to talk to Carter as the beginning of his public salvation. Carter seemed likely to give the beleaguered network news division a fair shake. He came from a long and distinguished journalistic tradition. In 1946, Carter's father won a Pulitzer Prize for a series of anti-racism editorials he wrote as editor of the *Delta Democrat-Times* in Greenville, Mississippi. His son displayed the same zeal when he became editor of the paper. Invited by another Carter (Jimmy, the President) to change jobs, Hodding went to the State Department. There he gained national recognition during the Iranian hostage crisis when, as the official State spokesman, he appeared on television more often than Mike Wallace.

Carter had been an early champion of Crile's documentary. Five days after it was aired, he praised the show, writing in his *Wall Street Journal* column on January 28, 1982, that it "rendered an important public service."

After conducting his own probe, however, Carter did a complete turnabout. Concluding the resulting "Inside Story" edition—"Uncounted Enemy: Unproven Conspiracy"—on April 21, 1983, he told viewers: "History may yet decide there was indeed a conspiracy in Saigon to fake the numbers. But at this point the evidence is less compelling, the witnesses are more contradictory, and the possible conclusions less obvious than the documentary suggests.

"CBS is entitled to its opinion. But we're entitled to a more balanced presentation. Even if you're sure of guilt, there's a vast difference between a fair trial and a lynching. It's a distinction that was badly blurred when CBS made 'The Uncounted Enemy: A Vietnam Deception.' "

Crile agreed with the word "lynching." But he thought Carter was the man with the rope. CBS heaped on Carter the same kind of criticism that *TV Guide*, Westmoreland, and Burt had leveled. The network said "Inside Story" had used creative editing, quick cuts, selective presentation of parts of recorded responses, and clever narration to distort the truth rather than tell it. Of Carter, Crile said, "He did to us what he claimed we had done to Westmoreland."

Like Westmoreland with CBS, Crile found that no one at "Inside Story" wanted to listen to his complaints. He said he called Ned Schnerman, Carter's executive producer, asking for a meeting to explain how his interview had been improperly edited. Schnerman, according to Crile, conferred with Carter and then refused.

One of the "Inside Story" 's complaints about "The Uncounted Enemy" was that the show excluded certain key figures such as former Johnson adviser Walt Rostow. On "Inside Story," it was Mike Wallace who was omitted, but he never even got the chance to be left on the cutting-room floor.

At the beginning of the program, Carter said, "Two words before we start. One is about an unseen witness who played a central role in the broadcast: Mike Wallace. He was not available to our cameras."

Wallace was incensed. This statement made it appear he was ducking "Inside Story". He was so angry that he called from Managua, Nicaragua, where he was on assignment, to explain the situation to a reporter. "Carter never tried to get in touch with me. . . . I never had one word with Hodding Carter. I did have an appointment with ["Inside Story" producer] Rose Economu, but it had to be rescheduled. I told them I would be available prior to their broadcast."

Boies called the "Inside Story" piece "the television version of the *TV Guide* story. . . . [Carter] covered the same issues raised a year ago. It was not as if he was making a new contribution." Boies also questioned Carter's research. By the time "Inside Story" started working on its show, Cravath had already dug up literally a ton of documents. The papers were offered to Carter and his team, but Boies said they weren't interested. "We had all the boxes of documents in one room for them. All they did was take some camera shots."

Like *TV Guide*, Carter questioned CBS's decision to use Sam Adams as both a paid consultant and an on-camera interviewee. Carter, however, had potential financial conflicts of his own that were not disclosed to viewers. Like many programs on PBS, "Inside Story" existed on the largesse of corporate underwriters who paid the bills in return for a "bulletin board" identification at the end with their logos briefly displayed on the screen.

At the end of "Inside Story," only one logo appeared: the General Electric Co. That same logo also appeared on checks Dan Burt put into the Capital Legal Foundation bank account—some $55,000 from 1981 through 1983. Press critic Carter didn't like to answer questions about his funding. During an interview several months after the broadcast, Carter became as wary as George Crile. His friendly Mississippi drawl disappeared. So did the calm that had become his trademark during the hostage crisis. Bouncing out of a chair in his cluttered Washington office, Carter yelled, "Hold it! Hold it! Someone get me a tape recorder. I've got another George Crile here!" He then stopped talking.

Once the tape recorder arrived, Carter grudgingly spoke. He said he was "totally ignorant" of the fact that GE funded both him and the Capital Legal Foundation, adding that the company "has carefully distanced itself from our editorial product." Still, in an era when "follow the money" is a journalistic imperative, it seems a press critic should be especially careful to reveal any potential financial conflict.

Carter conceded that the show's introduction, saying Mike Wallace was "not available to our cameras," did not fully describe the situation. Carter said it was "my understanding that for the longest time, going down towards the conclusion of a tight-ass schedule, that Mike suggested a date that was not available to me. . . . When I was available, he was not available. . . . We could not get a mutually satisfactory date."

But he did not agree with Crile's complaint of unfairness. Instead, he took another shot. "The image George Crile has is accurately portrayed. For sheer arrogance, George Crile has few masters." Carter also dismissed Boies' criticism. "All the depositions were not available to us," he said.

Despite the heavy criticism, or perhaps because of it, "Inside Story" 's examination of "The Uncounted Enemy," like the *TV Guide* piece before it, went on to be honored by its peers, winning an Emmy.

"*TV Guide* got a Sigma Delta Chi award, Hodding Carter got an Emmy, and I got a libel suit," Crile recalled ruefully. "For a time, it seemed as if no one in the press was interested in hearing our side of the story."

* * *

Despite the "Inside Story" flap, by the middle of 1983 Crile had been "resurrected at CBS," returning to work as a producer-reporter on a documentary about the Nicaraguan Contras. But with just three weeks to go on the story he hoped would redeem his reputation, Dan Burt hit again. The attorney discovered, and then proceeded to tell the world, that Crile had violated yet another CBS News guideline in the preparation of "The Uncounted Enemy" by secretly tape-recording a telephone interview. And the interview wasn't with just anyone. Crile had taped former Secretary of Defense Robert McNamara, a man so elusive, so zealous in not speaking out about the Vietnam War, that in two decades no journalist had ever managed to get the man on the record.

"Dan Burt struck in *The New York Times*," Crile recalled. "He stirred McNamara up and McNamara denounced CBS. . . . Looking back on it, my instinct is that CBS felt . . . this is just too much. So they scrapped the Nicaragua documentary and I was suspended at that point. With pay. That was a very, very devastating moment. Because I was twice done in."

McNamara said later that if anyone was done in, it was McNamara.

George Crile was no ordinary journalist hoping for the interview of a lifetime when he dialed McNamara's number. He was the socially well-connected George Crile whose wedding McNamara had attended in 1968. This association undoubtedly helped Crile get through to the former Cabinet member. Mike Wallace also helped Crile scale McNamara's wall of silence. "Mr. Wallace knew Mr. McNamara far better than I did." The call, which dealt briefly with the theme of the documentary, probably took place sometime in May 1981, although Crile in his deposition couldn't remember exactly. After listening to the pitch, McNamara agreed to a strictly off-the-record personal interview on June 16, 1981, in Washington, D.C.

Before making the trip, Crile called McNamara again, without Wallace, but with his tape recorder running. "I used the tape recorder as a backup in the event that Mr. McNamara might be talking faster than I could keep up with pen and paper," Crile explained, adding that he taped the conversation because " . . . I wanted to make sure that I would have as accurate a record as possible of the conversation." Such taping was not illegal in New York state, but the practice was taboo at CBS.

Crile followed his June 16 visit with another phone call to McNamara on July 2. He said all these conversations covered similar ground. As the notes from the July 2 phone call indicate, Crile did not get very far. "I'm not going to give any evaluation or judgments about Vietnam at all," McNamara said. "Reason one, my memory is very bad; and secondly, I was a participant and I don't believe that participants should evaluate their own roles."

Crile said he forgot about these conversations and the tapes. In September 1982, as he scoured his office for documents, notes, and other materials he had to provide to Burt in the discovery process, he didn't find the cassettes containing the McNamara interview—or other tape cassettes containing surreptitiously recorded conversations with former Supreme Court Justice Arthur Goldberg; former Undersecretary of State George Ball; General Matthew B. Ridgway; and Brigadier General Winant K. Sidle, the MACV information officer who had conducted the daily Saigon press briefings known as the "Five O'Clock Follies."

Burt had an inkling the tapes existed. He originally asked Boies about their existence in January 1983, but let the matter rest until early June, when he sent Boies a letter saying that he had a "witness" (identified by Don Kowet in *A Matter of Honor* as Ira Klein) who could testify that the McNamara tape was kept in the lower left-hand corner of Crile's desk.

On Sunday, June 12, Burt sent Judge Pierre Leval a letter saying he believed that "more than five" phone calls had been taped by Crile during preparation of "The Uncounted Enemy" and that these tapes had been destroyed. On Monday, June 13, *The New York Times* reported the charges Burt had made in his letter to Leval. The newspaper also quoted Boies, who said Burt's allegations were a "deliberate falsehood."

But before these charges hit the press, Crile found the tapes during a thorough, weekend-long search. The tape with the McNamara, Ball, Ridgway, and Goldberg calls was in a trunk in his home. The Sidle tape he found on a shelf underneath his lower-left desk drawer.

The taping incident, a personal disaster for Crile, turned into a public-relations Waterloo for CBS and Boies. McNamara was angered to the point where he decided to forgo his privacy and come to Westmoreland's defense, and it was Boies who inadvertently helped push McNamara into the general's case. He told *The New York Times* that McNamara "probably knew he was being taped." At his deposition, McNamara told Boies that "I was absolutely incensed, both at the fact that I had been taped without my permission and I was incensed by your statement. . . . I was absolutely incensed by the whole procedure and out of that came one or two calls to Mr. Burt and during that conversation I think he asked whether I had seen the program. I said no. Then, he said, did I believe Westmoreland had conspired to deceive the President and me as the program presumed and alleged. I said no, and he said would I be willing to say that in support of Westmoreland, and I said yes."

When Burt deposed Crile, the taping episode took on a new dimension as he tried to use it to impeach the producer's credibility. The effort took two and a half days and filled 338 pages of transcript. Burt's incredibly detailed questions about Crile's desk, its construction, how he used it, where he placed the tape recorder, and where he placed his pen and pencil turned this expanse of the trial record into probably the most exhaustive examination of a desk in the history of jurisprudence.

The Sidle tape, Crile kept insisting, must have accidentally fallen behind the drawer, making it impossible to find without a thorough search. Burt, sure he could trip Crile up, asked increasingly niggling questions, culminating in this exchange:

BURT: How much clearance is there between the top of the panel and the bottom of the drawer above?
CRILE: I have no idea.
BURT: Is it a big clearance or a little clearance?
CRILE: I really don't know.
BURT: We will measure it. Would you tell me how if there was a panel at the back of the drawer and if the drawer was dark you could see in back of the panel onto the floor of the desk where you say you found the tape?
CRILE: I didn't say it was dark.
BURT: Is there any light in the back of your drawer?
CRILE: It's light in the office.
BURT: How far off the floor is your bottom left-hand desk drawer?
CRILE: I can only guess.
BURT: Guess.
CRILE: A foot, perhaps.
BURT: Is there any source of light radiating from one foot off the floor of your office?
CRILE: No, it's a standard floor.

Burt spent much of these two and a half days trying to prove that Crile knew of the tapes all along and was aware of their location.

He didn't succeed. Zeroing in on Burt's assertion that a "witness" was prepared to testify that his left-hand desk drawer contained tapes, Crile said, "I didn't know who was talking to you or what they had done, whether they were breaking into the office, whether they were going through my files or whether you were operating on misinformation. . . ."

Like many other issues large and small in the Westmoreland-CBS case, the explanation of why Crile couldn't find the tapes and how Burt knew about them remains shrouded in mystery. Did Crile hide the tapes? Did someone known to Burt first remove them and then replace them? These are questions that not even the voluminous record can answer.

*   *   *

Consigned to reportorial limbo by CBS, Crile went back to Nicaragua to continue working on the stories he had uncovered there with hopes of selling a piece to his old journalistic home, *Harper's*. While Crile concerned himself with present-day battles in Central America, Boies prepared to do battle with Westmoreland.

Indeed, the pre-trial deposition process, where each side got to grill the other, bore an uncanny resemblance to combat. Although conducted with a veneer of civility, the depositions were true guerrilla encounters: verbal probes followed by frontal assaults, a quick retreat when the other side seemed to be gaining tactical advantage, then new forays on other weak points.

At 9:30 a.m., April 4, 1983, Boies sat down with Westmoreland in Capital Legal's offices for the first deposition session, kicking off a process that would stretch over a period of months and eventually fill thousands of pages of transcript. After exchanging perfunctory "good mornings," Boies quickly got to the point. "You're suing CBS and certain individual defendants for libel, correct?"

"That's correct," the general said.

Boies then asked Westmoreland how he thought he had been libeled. Westmoreland's answer was simple, succinct, and harked back to the day he took his West Point oath. Honor was the issue.

"I went into a profession that puts a great emphasis on integrity and honor. . . . And, when I saw the advertising, advertisement, which was quite abundant before this particular documentary, and I observed the documentary, it destroyed the one thing I have prided myself in throughout my entire career and, as a matter of fact, throughout my entire life.

"I asked for an apology, it was not forthcoming; so, I had to resort to the action that you have mentioned," he said, adding, "The centerpiece [of the documentary] of course was [the charge of] conspiracy."

The dishonor the documentary brought him among the military and veterans was particularly painful, Westmoreland said. After "The Uncounted Enemy" was broadcast, Westmoreland said, he had received much mail, pro and con, but vividly recalled "a veterans' publication that indicated in a headline that they were going to insist that charges be preferred on me. Another was a letter that I received from a veterans' organization in Pittsburgh giving me an ultimatum in order to explain my actions or they were going to go to Congress and ask that I be condemned. . . ."

Westmoreland told Boies of a painful encounter in an airport, when he met a soldier on leave from Germany who had seen the show. Everyone in the soldier's company, it seemed, had gathered to watch the documentary via Armed Forces TV. "He was a Vietnam veteran and he didn't accept it, but he said all the young soldiers accepted the validity of the uh, thrust and the purpose of the program," Westmoreland said.

In this first day, Boies delved into the central theme of the show —that certain categories of enemy irregulars had been arbitrarily reduced in the MACV order of battle. Westmoreland explained the irregulars away, saying "the homeguard types, the self-defense and the secret self-defense, they were basically poorly armed, if armed at all, and their capability was basically confined to putting in pungy stakes and they were women, old men and young boys. And they were not a threat, they did not belong in the enemy strength figures." The "women, old men and young boys" explanation became a familiar refrain.

Although Boies was an adept interrogator, Westmoreland quickly mastered maneuvering on the lawyer's battlefield. Had the general been libeled by Mike Wallace? Boies wondered. Westmoreland answered, "He was the mouthpiece of the program. . . ."

Boies also did something at this session that he probably would not do at the gaming tables. He tipped his hand. Westmoreland had already indicated he had brought the suit because he considered the use of the word "conspiracy" libelous in connection with his role as commander of American forces in Vietnam. But a key issue in the CBS defense was that the documentary referred to a "conspiracy at the highest levels of American military intelligence." Westmoreland hadn't been an intelligence officer and he was never directly named as a conspirator in the documentary. Boies tested this angle on Westmoreland, but the general would not let himself be outfoxed.

BOIES: Do you see where there is a reference there to a "conspiracy at the highest levels of American military intelligence"?

WESTMORELAND: Yes.

BOIES: Now, that doesn't say the highest level of the military command, does it, sir?

WESTMORELAND: . . . Mr. Boies, the program had my picture on it innumerable times—riding on a jeep, decorated by the president—almost in every segment of the show there was Westmoreland there. Words are one thing but impressions by pictures are another. And that is what influences the American people. They came out of that show with the impression that I, the commander, was behind this so-called conspiracy.

Boies, like Burt, took side trips into minutiae, asking, for instance, if Westmoreland had ever made notes and wondering if the pages of notes had been turned over in discovery. Westmoreland answered, "Gosh, it wouldn't be any pages at all, I just, uh, would read something and if I had a little piece of paper in my pocket, I would just scribble it down to help me remember it."

Boies jumped at this statement like a trout at a fly and decided to pursue the subject in an exercise as crazy as Burt's assault on Crile's desk. The stenographer's description of Westmoreland's actions made this exchange seem even weirder:

BOIES: Do you have any of those notes at the present time?

WESTMORELAND: I may have some, I don't know (commences to search pockets, producing notes). These I put in my pocket. For this deposition in this item (tenders paper to attorney Burt)—which was passed out at my press conference, which was a very good summary.

BURT: Would you like to introduce that into the record, then, since you have asked for it?

BOIES: If you wish.

WESTMORELAND: I have, uh, (search of pockets) I have some notes here which I just scribbled and put in my pocket, apropos of the administrative service troops—which are extracted from the SNIE [Special National Intelligence Estimate]. (Examination of various notes from pocket) And uh, then here are some notes apropos of the Tet Offensive and the number of provinces that were struck by fire, or were assaulted in varying degrees. I doubt if anybody can read these, but I certainly have no objection to your trying. I mean, they were only a memory aid. And here, in my pocket, two telephone calls I've got to return—and let's see if I can find anything else. (Search of pockets) Here is a bill—

BURT: I think, general, that we can probably say this is adequate. Mr. Boies, would you like for the general to do a strip?

WESTMORELAND: Here's a bill—let me see what else, if I've got anything else.

Boies couldn't resist asking historical questions about the Vietnam War that had little to do with the libel suit. He wanted to know more about the bombing of Cambodia. Westmoreland said that if the military had been running the Cambodian bombing operations instead of Henry Kissinger and Richard Nixon, it wouldn't have been kept secret. "We would prefer it to be overt. . . . But we understood why the Administration had to keep it covert . . . because of the international embarrassment. . . ."

Returning to the numbers battle, Boies pressed the general on whether he or his command had deliberately underestimated the foe. Westmoreland said the problem was due more to the nature of the enemy than any deliberate distortion or cover-up. He told Boies: "Nobody knew what the enemy strength was in Vietnam. It was a matter of estimates and guesstimates. What the actual strength was—I mean nobody knew, nobody knew. Nobody knows precisely to this day. But we've got a better feel now than then."

Boies also used the deposition process to scout out another order of battle—Westmoreland's associates and financial backers. CBS maintained that the libel case was an attack by the political right, so Boies spent some time trying to reinforce this theory. The pursuit led to the cross-examination of Dave Henderson, Westmoreland's public-relations man. The Henderson deposition didn't further Boies' knowledge of any right-wing conspiracy, but it did increase his knowledge of unusual economic theories propounded by a builder of mini-submarines.

Dave Henderson, who doesn't mind being labeled a conservative, is so affable that not much gets him riled, even an interrogation by David Boies. The CBS lawyer failed to uncover a right-wing cabal hiding behind Henderson's public-relations firm, but he did learn a lot about the National Dividend Theory.

Henderson told Boies he knew Westmoreland because the general had served as chairman of the National Board of Advisers of the Fiscal Policy Council, which Henderson represented. Boies wanted to know more about the group, although Henderson's attorney, Stephen Boynton, wondered what relevance a discussion of economic theories had to a libel suit, a documentary, or the Vietnam War. Boies blithely sidestepped this, replying, "I think the relevance is reasonably apparent."

What Boies didn't know is that Henderson loves to talk about the theories espoused by the Fiscal Policy Council. He's more than a PR man, he's a true believer. Jumping in after Boynton's objection, Henderson said, "It will take a great deal of time to tell you, but I would be happy to tell you. . . ."

Boies pondered this, then asked Henderson to "give me two representative economic theories, if that will help you shorten. . . ."

He got them.

"The principal thrust of the Fiscal Policy Council was in the analysis of a proposal called the 'National Dividend Plan,' " Henderson said. "And it is a reasonably complicated theory which is now in legislative form, and—although not enacted. Perhaps that short answer will suffice."

Boies said, "Well, if you could tell me what the National Dividend Theory is—briefly—I think that would suffice."

"Well, it is a concept that would declare a moratorium on additional spending by the federal government for a five-year period of time, to allow the phasing in of several items," Henderson said. "One would be the creation of a national profit-sharing trust fund which would accumulate at 20 percent of the corporate revenue, corporate tax revenue collections and would be set aside in this trust fund.

"There would be an elimination of the double tax on corporate dividends. There would be a freeze—not a freeze, but a limit, a ceiling —placed on corporate tax collections at the current level of 46 percent. . . . Tax collections would be distributed on a per capita basis to all registered voters as a national profit-sharing method, but . . . only . . . after any amount of existing federal deficit was removed from the trust fund itself."

Henderson said Westmoreland was under a $1,000-a-month retainer to act as a spokesman for these policies and to help lobby Congress. Boies, now knowing more than he had ever wanted to know about the National Dividend Theory, had one more question for Henderson. Did Westmoreland understand these economic theories? "Thoroughly," Henderson answered.

But Henderson wasn't finished. He went on to tell Boies that the dividend theory was the brainchild of millionaire John Perry, Jr., who had inherited a group of sixteen daily and ten weekly Florida newspapers started by his father. (Perry sold them in July 1969 for an estimated $70 million, according to *The New York Times*.)

Perry, also an oceanography buff and an inventor who was appointed by President Johnson in 1967 to the Commission on Marine

Science, Engineering and Resources, put much effort into trying to turn the economic tide.

His dividend plan was presented to the Senate Finance Committee in May 1968 by Kentucky Republican Thruston B. Morton, and throughout the 1970s Perry's Fiscal Policy Council tried to garner support. At the same time, Perry was developing mini-submarines and an underwater laboratory and habitat "with separate living and work rooms and a garage for midget submarines," according to the Fort Lauderdale, Florida, *Sun-Sentinel*. Whatever the eventual fate of Perry's submarines, his dividend plan never got afloat.

By the time Boies took Henderson's deposition, the Fiscal Policy Council had all but folded, although Perry retained Henderson (and through him Westmoreland) to advance the National Dividend Theory on Capitol Hill.

* * *

Henderson's presence on the Westmoreland team underscored a glaring deficiency on the CBS side. Crile and Wallace had competent lawyers, but the network was losing in the court of public opinion. In the eighteen months since the broadcast was aired, Westmoreland and Burt had managed to build a constituency in the media, a constituency that regularly fired rounds at CBS.

Every time the CBS lawyers tried to score a public-relations coup, it backfired. In late August 1983, the Cravath document searchers uncovered a "smoking gun," a September 10, 1967, cable that Boies said vindicated the documentary. It was a report CIA Vietnam expert George Carver sent from Saigon to Richard Helms, the Agency's director, which seemed to directly implicate Westmoreland in putting an artificial cap on the number of enemy carried in the MACV order of battle. A "variety of circumstantial indicators . . . all point to [the] inescapable conclusion that General Westmoreland . . . has given instruction tantamount to direct order that VC strength total will not exceed 300,000 ceiling," Carver had written. The cable said that the "rationale seems to be that any higher figure would not be sufficiently optimistic and would generate unacceptable level of criticism from the press."

Carver, who in 1983 was a fellow at Georgetown University, reacted swiftly. With assistance from Burt and Henderson, he publicly attacked Boies' release of the cable, claiming it had been "jerked out of context." He said it was just one in a series of cables to Helms. On September 13, 1967, for example, Carver said, he had wired Helms:

"Westmoreland most cordial and receptive. Said he agreed with most of my observations and could see the clear logic behind both sets of figures, which were really not far apart. . . . "

Burt said that Boies, by releasing only one message, had come up

with a smoking gun, but the barrel was "aimed at CBS." He speculated that CBS had chosen to focus on the single cable and claim victory as a ploy to distract the press from the "damaging nature" of the
other messages. Not true, argued Boies, saying he merely had become
frustrated because the other side persisted in trying the case before it
went to court.

Salvation for CBS—at least in the press—was at hand, however.
The network finally decided to hire John Scanlon, a public-relations
expert, whose only job would be to hawk the network's side of the
issue. Scanlon is a Bronx-born Irishman of ample girth and good
cheer, a devilishly happy leprechaun grown to Falstaffian proportions
who had spent eleven years of his youth in a Christian Brothers
seminary. Scanlon had the media contacts to get CBS's story across. In
1975, in the midst of New York City's fiscal crisis, he had worked as
the public-relations adviser to Lazard Frères partner Felix Rohatyn,
head of the Municipal Assistance Corporation, the state agency set up
to "save" the city. In that position, Scanlon had come to know numerous reporters, locally and nationally.

Scanlon also had political contacts. He had worked as an assistant to New York Mayor John Lindsay and had been active in the
anti-war movement in Brooklyn, where, in the late 1960s, he had met
Jim Noonan. A Marine Vietnam veteran, Noonan assisted Scanlon
for the duration of the Westmoreland-CBS case.

"A Scanlon type was imperative," said Van Gordon Sauter, CBS
News president and an executive vice president of the CBS Broadcast
Group. "There is a considerable amount of publicity surrounding a
TV trial. We learned that in the L.A. case [when Dan Rather took the
witness stand in another libel suit against CBS]. It should not have
been a surprise to us. We needed someone to deal with the onslaught
of the media. We were not staffed or designed to handle a trial."

Scanlon did more than just field reporters' questions. He became
an impassioned advocate, using almost any tactic to defend the network. This included, but was not limited to, running down the opposition. It also included covert and overt combat with reporters who
Scanlon thought did not cover the story fairly or accurately. Scanlon's
role as one of the chief supporting players on the CBS team would
eventually be examined and debated in the press.

But in October 1983, Scanlon had a monumental task to complete before he could really go to work. He had to familiarize himself
with the issues. "So, all Noonan and I did from October to December
was read the documents and the court papers," he recalled.

By December, Scanlon and Noonan had mastered the issues and
documents in the case well enough to mount a media operation against
Burt. Westmoreland's lawyer gave them the opening they needed by

calling a press conference on December 27, 1983, in Washington, D.C., at the somewhat down-at-the-heels Hotel Washington.

This was the news conference at which Burt made public the affidavits he had amassed from the military and civilian leaders of the war, including Robert McNamara, Dean Rusk, and former CIA directors Richard Helms and William Colby. These names guaranteed a lot of ink, Burt knew, and the timing was ideal. In the week between Christmas and New Year's, the federal government, the biggest generator of news in Washington, is all but closed for the holidays.

Burt booked a room at the Hotel Washington for his news conference. Scanlon booked a room down the hall. Then he got busy calling reporters to tell them there would be not one but two handily located December 27 events concerning the Westmoreland-CBS suit. Scanlon's competitive streak extended to the smallest details. "We'll have a bigger room and better Danish," he promised.

Burt's conference didn't deliver as much as it advertised—particularly when compared to the full court press Scanlon mounted on behalf of CBS. Westmoreland, who can be incisive, humorous, candid, and his own best defense when dealing one-on-one, came across as wooden. Burt was keeping the general under tight control, allowing him to say little. Westmoreland managed to get out one good quote, calling the mounting evidence against CBS "shocking." But the cables and affidavits distributed to the press reinforced his assertion only superficially.

No sooner had Westmoreland finished parrying with the fifty-plus reporters, camera crews, and technicians than the cameras' red lights winked on in the room down the hall. John Scanlon, attired in a symphony of Irish tweeds, calmly told the crowd, "The management of CBS News fully endorses the subject and the conclusions of the documentary."

Boies then took over the podium, coolly predicting the case would be dismissed because "the broadcast was true." This would be the heart of his defense, he said, although he would also show that CBS prepared the documentary without legal "malice." But, he confidently asserted, "I don't think this case is going to come to trial. . . . I think it will be dismissed as a summary judgment."

There would be numerous PR battles ahead, but this was the turning point. George Crile marked the day as the beginning of his public redemption.

"Until Scanlon arrived on the scene, our hands were tied," Crile said. "CBS wouldn't let me defend myself. But once he was hired and David Boies decided to go on the offensive, everything started to change."

Scanlon made sure Crile had ample opportunity to defend his

work. The next PR target was Don Kowet, co-author of the *TV Guide* article, or, more specifically, the book Kowet had written based on the article. Scanlon did not wait for *A Matter of Honor* to hit the bookstores before mounting his attack.

The book was scheduled for publication in May 1984, but on February 2, shortly after the Macmillan Publishing Company ran an ad in *Publishers Weekly* heralding the book, Scanlon wrote to the company's editor-in-chief, George Walsh, expressing "deep concern." Scanlon vilified Kowet, saying he was "guilty of highly questionable journalistic practices in the preparation of his *TV Guide* article. . . . 'Anatomy of a Smear' was bad journalism which, I fear, can only be a bad book."

The Scanlon-orchestrated blitzkrieg against Kowet's book would build on this theme during the next months. The letter to Macmillan obliquely warned the publisher of the coming PR campaign. "If the book is published without speaking to the substance of the broadcast, I can assure you that we will use our considerable skills to point out its failures," Scanlon wrote. He did give lip-service to Macmillan's right to publish. After all, it wouldn't be kosher for CBS's hired gun to promote the network's cause in a First Amendment case by assaulting someone else's freedom of speech. "I truly believe that Mr. Kowet is entitled to his opinions and conclusions, and you are entitled to print them," Scanlon wrote, but added, "I do hope, however, that you will look closely at Mr. Kowet's work and prevent him from repeating the distortions and outright misrepresentations that characterized his *TV Guide* article." Scanlon, who had not yet seen the book, then attacked the magazine article by citing other stories that questioned its accuracy. Because the *TV Guide* piece questioned the accuracy of a CBS documentary, Scanlon's letter became a twice-removed mirror.

Walsh didn't reply quickly enough for Scanlon, who fired off another missive on February 14. This one said, in part, "I assume that you have received my letter . . . offering access to all the depositions taken to date. . . . These depositions demonstrate most clearly that the substance of the documentary is accurate. . . ."

This letter crossed in the mails with Walsh's February 13 reply to Scanlon's first letter.

Walsh politely told Scanlon to buzz off. "Macmillan rejects your many unfounded allegations and ad hominem attacks on Mr. Kowet," Walsh wrote, adding, "Macmillan has thoroughly reviewed the material in Mr. Kowet's book from both editorial and legal viewpoints. Moreover, in the course of writing the book, Mr. Kowet reviewed and considered the depositions and affidavits taken or submitted in the Westmoreland case."

On February 16, Scanlon shot back, "It is difficult for me to be-lieve that you considered my positions about the Kowet book in any serious fashion. It is equally extraordinary you would suggest that Mr. Kowet has responsibly reviewed and considered the depositions and affidavits . . . since the discovery process has not yet ended."

Undaunted, Scanlon decided to go for the flanks, organizing CBS executives in a letter-writing campaign against the book. The letters, ostensibly directed at Macmillan, became fodder for the charge Scanlon led into the ranks of book reviewers. According to the *Wall Street Journal*, these letters were sent to more than fifty book re-viewers. In a curious move, Scanlon's cover letter borrowed from the language of libel law. He called *A Matter of Honor* "reckless and malicious."

Although Macmillan did not back down, the book did have its flaws, which became apparent as May 1984 approached. Many of the CBS complaints centered on Kowet's use of "reconstructions"—that journalistic technique in which the omniscient writer allows the reader to literally peer over a character's shoulder, although the writer was never near the character's shoulder or any other anatomical part when the described event took place.

Some of the characters Kowet reconstructed had trouble recog-nizing themselves. As Mike Wallace told Macmillan in his letter, "I am somewhat at a loss to express my anger, my bewilderment . . . at various allegations, re-creations and inaccuracies in Don Kowet's book. It is laced with them."

Robert Chandler, senior vice president of administration at CBS News, said he was "astonished and dismayed at [Kowet's] portrayal of my innermost thoughts and of conversations in which I never par-ticipated. I have never met with Mr. Kowet, nor have I spoken with him. Yet he appears blithely to have attributed to me thoughts, con-cerns and conversations which he never bothered to check."

Andy Lack, the former CBS Reports executive producer, pointed out another problem. "Since Mr. Kowet, as far as I know, never met me, that . . . would account for the description of my slick black hair, narrow-set eyes, icy smiles and hats I have never owned or worn."

Kowet even managed to draw the Olympian ire of Abe Rosenthal, executive editor of *The New York Times*. Kowet devoted an entire chapter of his book to "Inside Story" 's critique of the documentary. This included a reconstruction of a phone call Mike Wallace allegedly had made to Rosenthal about a *Times* preview of "Inside Story" by *Times* reporter Frank Prial. The article ran in the paper on April 23, the day the program aired.

"That afternoon," Kowet related, "a CBS source said Wallace

telephoned A. M. 'Abe' Rosenthal . . . a social acquaintance of Wallace. Wallace complained to Rosenthal that by publishing Prial's article before Prial even screened the broadcast (review cassettes were not available due to last minute revisions) the *Times* was both publicizing and prejudging the truth of [Hodding] Carter's allegations about the documentary."

The next day, the *Times* published an Editor's Note (the first in the paper's history) which, in essence, apologized for the Prial article.

Asked to comment on the scenario as related by Kowet, Rosenthal said, "It's absolutely untrue. A total falsehood. Mr. Wallace never called me."

Wallace's reaction was even simpler. "Bullshit," he said.

Kowet stands by his account, claiming that two CBS sources provided him with details of the Wallace-Rosenthal conversation. The reliance on "re-creations" and unnamed sources, he said, was due to the refusal of almost anyone at CBS to co-operate with him. For this he partly blamed David Boies, saying no one at CBS ever returned his phone calls except Mike Wallace, who "told me point-blank, categorically, that he would not do an interview."

Wallace admitted turning Kowet down, saying that by the time Kowet called him it was too late for anything he said to appear in the book.

Many of the book's details relied on the memory of film editor Ira Klein. But, as far as Kowet was concerned, Klein was an unimpeachable source. "Everything Ira Klein has told me has checked out," he said. After the Scanlon-generated media onslaught, Kowet felt much as Crile had following the *TV Guide* article and the "Inside Story" piece. "As far as I'm concerned, CBS News was trying to destroy my credibility as a journalist," Kowet said.

Macmillan finally decided to fight back. On Sunday, April 22, the company issued a press release accusing CBS of engaging in an "unprecedented and shocking attempt to chill" Kowet's book. The company said that, prior to publishing *A Matter of Honor*, it had received a "seemingly orchestrated series of letters" from CBS officials accusing Kowet and Macmillan of "various journalistic lapses, inaccuracy, distortion and outright falsehood."

Macmillan added that while CBS "postures itself as only wanting to set the record straight," the campaign against Kowet's book "should be viewed in the context of the Westmoreland litigation. CBS apparently fears that the public will learn the full story behind the making of the documentary. CBS's attacks on Kowet and Macmillan are ironic for a company that is brandishing truth and the first Amendment as its defense in the Westmoreland case. While stopping short of outright threats . . . CBS has created by innuendo and the carefully selected use of 'buzzwords' familiar to First Amendment lawyers, the impression within Macmillan that Kowet and Macmillan will have to face legal consequences if the book is published."

This impression was reinforced, the publisher said, by CBS urging Macmillan and its lawyers to review both the contents of the book and the *TV Guide* article. "CBS has apparently sought to divert the media's attention from the book's true purpose. *A Matter of Honor* is a journalistic investigation of a documentary and its highly controversial aftermath; it is not a defense of General Westmoreland nor his reputation but of the right of anyone to receive fair and accurate treatment in the media."

Macmillan accused CBS of attempting to try the case in the press and revealed that it had discovered Scanlon was planning to sabotage Kowet's promotional tour. The company urged CBS to hand over the notes from Burton Benjamin's internal investigation, saying they "might end definitively the dispute over who here is telling the truth."

CBS continued to resist giving Dan Burt the Benjamin notes throughout the trial, and Scanlon went ahead with his anti-Kowet campaign. Macmillan had scheduled Kowet to tour the country publicizing the book. Wherever he went, Scanlon endeavored to send Crile. The first public debate was on "All About TV," a public television broadcast show produced at WNYC in New York City and sold to other public stations around the country.

Although CBS took a risk in letting its most vulnerable defendant engage in unrestricted debate with one of his principal accusers, Crile relished the opportunity. It was like being freed from prison. "I had been waiting more than a year to challenge Don Kowet in person. We moved our way through the country, and when we got to Chicago, Kowet just backed down and discontinued his book tour. He couldn't support any of his claims. In the end, he wouldn't even agree to appear on the Christian Broadcasting Network when he was informed I would be given a chance to reply in a following segment."

In mid-1985, Kowet, happily working at the *Washington* (D.C.) *Times*, said this whole period "was very difficult for me and very difficult for my family." Scanlon and CBS were "killing me," he said, but added, "Really, nothing in the book was challenged by CBS. Once [the case] started to develop, reporters laid off me."

Scanlon defended the assault on Kowet's book in a characteristically flip fashion. "You want to know why? You want a quote? I'll give you one. I don't like Kowet's book because it's a waste of trees."

Kowet paid a personal price for his Vietnam obsession. *TV Guide* fired him in 1983 when he said he would like to write a book about the case. David Sendler, the magazine's editor, confirmed firing Kowet and said the magazine had decided to "adopt a neutral stance" in the controversy. Nonetheless, Kowet and *TV Guide* would play one more significant part in the case. And, ironically, it involved the surreptitious recording of telephone interviews. During his research for the *TV Guide* article, Kowet had taped a number of interviews, including one with CBS executive vice president Howard Stringer.

Burt learned of the existence of the tapes, subpoenaed them in May 1984, and then immediately handed them over to Peter Boyer of the *Los Angeles Times* and Dave Tabacoff of ABC's "World News Tonight." The resulting news stories dealt CBS another embarrassing setback in the public-opinion arena by revealing Stringer's apparent lack of confidence in Crile. Stringer, who had listened to a barrage of Kowet's allegations, seemed quick to put some distance between himself and the producer, referring to Crile as his "nemesis." He went on to say: "You just got to hire the right people. . . . Yeah, you can fuck up from time to time, I suppose, but you have to have the right person doing it and you got to watch them along the way. . . . "

On the tape, Stringer said he and Roger Colloff had both been "suspicious" of Crile, adding that "George is a very bright guy" but he is "kind of an ideologue and I think that in a sense it's got to be controlled in a way. . . ."

In an interview with the *Los Angeles Times*, Burt characterized the tapes as "a bombshell" that would discredit the CBS defense. He said the tapes showed "that, as a matter of law they [CBS] were malicious. They didn't believe the broadcast was true."

Stringer further embarrassed himself by telling Kowet, "I don't believe generals as a matter of course, having worked for them."

Burt's bombshell created a new firestorm around Kowet, sparking charges that he had engaged in the same kind of loose journalistic practices for which Crile had been condemned. At least three times on the tape, Stringer asked Kowet if the conversation was off the record. Each time, Kowet assured him it was. Furthermore, Kowet had violated the unwritten journalistic code that a reporter never, never turns raw notes over to a court.

Kowet's quick response to Burt's subpoena proved to be a problem for *TV Guide*. The magazine had already refused to turn over any material related to the case. The tapes were not even Kowet's property, Sendler said, since he had conducted the interviews as a salaried *TV Guide* employee. When the story of the tapes broke, Sendler considered what legal action the magazine might take, but, after considering various options, decided the situation was moot.

Kowet, meanwhile, saw no similarity between his tape recordings and Crile's taping of McNamara. "I had not promised Stringer confidentiality," he said. "And I was not going to resist a subpoena in defense of a network that orchestrated a publicity campaign to kill my book."

Stringer, like McNamara, had been unaware he was being taped and had had no intention of being quoted. "Good Lord, I'm not that stupid," he said. "I certainly did not choose my words with care, but when Kowet called me I was really pissed. . . ."

Stringer also complained that Burt had chosen to give Boyer and Tabacoff only the portions of the Kowet tapes that would prove most embarrassing to him and to CBS. Left out of the news reports were qualifying remarks he made to Kowet, such as: " . . . When you get that many people on television, spilling their hearts out this long after what happened to them or what they felt happened to them, it isn't necessarily the whole truth or nothing but the truth, but the fact that they do it, and they can be collected, is an extraordinary comment on these times."

As for Stringer's remark about generals, news reports ignored the context in which it was offered. An Oxford graduate and a British subject, Stringer had been working at CBS only a matter of months in 1965 when he received a draft notice. Friends urged him to move back to England, but he answered the call, completed basic training, and was shipped out to Vietnam for a year's tour with the Army's 720th MP Battalion. Because of his education, Stringer could have sat out the war in a cushy billet on Westmoreland's staff. He was offered such a position, but chose instead to stay with his MP outfit.

*   *   *

While battling Burt in the press, the CBS legal team was battling the Central Intelligence Agency and the House of Representatives on another front, trying to force them to turn over documents important to the case. This effort, which began early in the discovery process, continued until two days before the case was settled.

Although the CIA furnished thousands of pages of material for the trial, it refused to turn over some documents the Cravath lawyers considered vital to their defense. A U.S. district court would not force the Agency to comply, so Cravath sought help from the federal appeals court in Washington, D.C. Some of the CIA papers had been deposited with the House of Representatives, raising interesting constitutional issues. Article I, Section 6, Clause 1 of the Constitution generally prevents court examination or subpoena of congressional speech, records, or deliberations.

At the same time, CBS was seeking to videotape the deposition of former CIA director Richard Helms. Helms had refused and the district court had backed him up, but CBS appealed, pitting CBS's freedom of speech versus Helms' right to privacy under the First and Fourth Amendments.

Finally, CBS asked the appeals court to consider whether an arcane bit of common law known as the "deliberative process privilege" allowed the CIA to withhold a TOP SECRET internal history of the Vietnam War called the Palmer Report, as well as the notes of morning meetings Helms had held during his tenure as CIA director.

Cravath argued that lack of access to the Palmer Report, Helms' minutes, and the documents the CIA had given the House Select Committee on Intelligence (the Pike Committee) during its 1975 hearings on the numbers controversy would seriously limit CBS's ability to defend itself against Westmoreland.

A key issue in the case was the integrity of the "compromise" reached between the CIA and Westmoreland's Vietnam command on the number of enemy listed in the Special National Intelligence Estimate (SNIE) 14:3:67. Boiled down to basics, this document created two classes of enemy: regular North Vietnamese and Vietcong forces, and another category consisting of various types of irregulars—those ubiquitous "women, young boys and old men" who supposedly presented no threat to U.S. forces.

As the documentary reported, Sam Adams had argued for inclusion of these irregulars in the order of battle, which would have increased drastically the recorded number of enemy the U.S. faced in Vietnam.

CBS claimed in its appeal:

"The compromise reflected in SNIE 14:3:67 was in fact an almost complete abandonment by the CIA of its own figures in favor of the military command's drastically lower estimates of enemy strength. Plaintiff claims that the military figures reflected in SNIE 14:3:67 represented a good faith position rather than a politically motivated position that plainly ignored the best available information. . . . The lack of access to contemporaneous CIA documents such as the minutes and the CIA documents provided for the Pike Committee's examination severely handicaps CBS's ability to respond to plaintiff's claims concerning the CIA's position."

The network argued that the House's privileges should be waived because records leaked from the Pike Committee backed up the contentions of Crile's documentary regarding the juggling of the OB figures. (On February 16, 1976, the *Village Voice* published "The Pike Papers," a special supplement containing much of that body's final report, which had been leaked by CBS newsman Daniel Schorr.) The leaked report said, in part, "The validity of most of the numbers was significantly dubious. Unfortunately they were relied on for optimistic presentations. . . . General Westmoreland used such figures to support his contentions that the enemy's guerrilla force is declining at a steady rate.' "

Cravath argued that holding back the House-CIA papers undermined the network's "ability to defend itself. . . . CBS cannot fairly be required to pay damages for criticism of a high government official's conduct if information important to its defense is withheld pursuant to governmental exercise of uniquely governmental privileges."

In this appeal, CBS claimed it needed to videotape Helms' deposition because it had reasons to doubt his veracity. In 1977, after Helms pleaded "no contest" to a misdemeanor charge of failing to testify fully and accurately to a Senate committee, the former CIA director had boasted to the press that he did not feel at all "disgraced" but would "wear his conviction like a badge of honor."

CBS said, " . . . Helms' record indicated that he may believe he has the right, indeed the duty, to dissemble, if a full and accurate answer would reveal matters that he believes it undesirable to reveal. . . . Thus a videotaped record of his deposition was necessary to ensure an accurate and trustworthy record."

These issues were still unresolved when the libel trial began. But on Friday, February 15, 1985, Boies headed for Washington, D.C., to finally press these cases before the court of appeals. But he did not do as well in front of the appeals panel as he did before Judge Pierre Leval in New York City. The judges constantly interrupted his arguments, questioning his points of law and fact. The cool, unflappable lawyer was flustered. He seemed unsure of himself for the first time since the libel battle began.

It didn't matter. Three days later, on February 18, a settlement in the Westmoreland-CBS case was announced. Asked about the status of the appeal case, Boies gave an answer appropriate for many of the issues raised in the larger litigation: "I suppose it's moot." (In the fall of 1985, the appeals court ordered Cravath to pay Helms' legal fees.)

* * *

Because of the sensitive nature of the documents involved and the high-level government officials called as witnesses, the opposing legal teams soon found uninvited guests at practically every deposition: two lawyers from the Central Intelligence Agency and one from the National Security Agency (NSA). These three legal spooks attached themselves to the case like sullen pilot fish and stayed with it until the last day, listening, observing, presumably making sure that no national-security secrets were breached.

The NSA, so secret that the act establishing it was classified, soon found itself in an unfamiliar and uncomfortable position. With the development of computers and high-tech communications, the agency has assumed an increasingly important role in U.S. intelligence. It spends most of its time eavesdropping on the radio traffic of governments and armies, intercepting the raw material of intelligence. But it does not appear in court with any regularity.

In July 1984, when Burt filed a brief with Judge Leval showing for the first time how he planned to fight CBS, much of it was based on the fact that an agency he referred to only as "Source X" had provided both military and civilian leaders with extremely accurate information about North Vietnamese infiltration into the South, disputing a key thesis of the documentary that Westmoreland had deceived his superiors. "Source X," of course, was the NSA. After the trial began, witness after witness reported that they had indeed received pertinent order-of-battle information from "an intelligence agency located somewhere in the Baltimore-Washington area," another oblique reference to the NSA. Since the NSA is hardly the kind of organization to willingly let its employees take the stand, it ended up signing an unusual stipulation agreement that provided the public with a rare insight into the agency's capabilities.

James Bamford, author of *The Puzzle Palace*, a very unauthorized history of the agency, said he'd never heard of the NSA making such an agreement before. "Usually when they get involved in a case, they go in to the judge with ten pages stamped TOP SECRET, arguing that any disclosure about the NSA could mean the end of the country. They never volunteer information. Usually, as in the Pentagon Papers case, they try to suppress it."

In Westmoreland vs. CBS, however, the NSA disclosed a great deal in the factual admissions it filed with the court, revealing how expert its electronic eavesdropping had been in the 1960s. The NSA, these documents revealed, was tracking North Vietnamese infiltration electronically prior to the Tet Offensive.

As the agency said in its October 15, 1984, filing with the court:

"NSA began to report the movement of elements of two NVA divisions and three NVA regiments toward South Vietnam. The first report of the movement of any of these elements was made in mid-November 1967. NSA did not report the troop strength of these units as that data was not available, but NSA did report the type of unit. . . . Reporting . . . continued until the units arrived in South Vietnam or staging areas in the DMZ and Laos in late 1967 or early 1968. These units were included in the MACV OB summary dated February 29, 1968."

The NSA did not say exactly how it had tracked these units. It could have been done from ground-based listening posts operated by its affiliated agency, the Army Security Agency, located in Hue in northern South Vietnam or from facilities in Cambodia, Laos, or Thailand. (The agency has been listening to military radio traffic in mainland China from such posts in Okinawa and Taiwan since the late 1950s.) It could have used EC-121s packed with communications gear, orbiting above the Trail, or, more likely, a sophisticated satellite system.

Whatever the method, it got even better, the NSA said in its court filing. "In the early part of 1968, following the Tet Offensive . . . NSA began to provide for the first time data on the number of personnel North Vietnam dispatched to South Vietnam, either as replacements for casualties suffered by, or as augmentation to, units already deployed in or near South Vietnam. NSA began to report this data to MACV and other concerned departments and agencies in Washington and elsewhere in the spring of 1968."

Because the NSA did not begin to report numbers of troops until after Tet, it conveniently was excused from revealing more of its methodology at the trial.

At first glance, it is easy to see why Burt considered the NSA his secret weapon. The statement seems to destroy the documentary's assertion that Westmoreland was faking infiltration figures. After all, if the agency was monitoring North Vietnamese traffic on the Trail and reporting this to everyone in Westmoreland's chain of command, how could the general engage in a conspiracy to conceal a fact that everyone already knew?

CBS, however, hoped to use the NSA stipulation to prove that raw communications intelligence is about as useful as raw sewage. Boies contended that only Westmoreland's command could meaningfully tie together all this information and that only MACV was charged with producing the total infiltration picture.

One section of the stipulation shored up CBS's theory that the NSA information was not very important. "Unlike some other intelligence agencies," the agreement read, "NSA is not authorized to combine and assess intelligence data to produce overall estimates or answers to questions such as total NVA/VC troop strength, total infiltration into South Vietnam or any other questions requiring a compilation of data.

"Consequently, at no time prior to the Tet Offensive did NSA (including COMINT [communications intelligence]) provide an estimate of total infiltration into South Vietnam nor, with respect to the time prior to the Tet Offensive did NSA (including COMINT) provide data from which a recipient of NSA (including COMINT) data could produce such an estimate by relying exclusively on NSA (including COMINT)."

The two parts of the NSA statement created enough ambiguity to allow each side to pick and choose paragraphs or sentences to prop up its argument. Burt could, and did, argue that Westmoreland wasn't deceiving his superiors about infiltration because NSA furnished them with information. Boies could take the same statement and dismiss the importance of the NSA information by claiming that it meant nothing without interpretation.

But neither side could press the NSA for any clarification of these ambiguities. They had signed a protective order with the court, which was then sealed and filed. This sealed document ordered that "Any evidence to be offered at the trial relating to the NSA, the sources . . . from which NSA collects and anlyzes intelligence data . . . shall be limited to the facts contained in the Stipulation of Facts. . . ."

Another sealed part of this document bound the parties to agree that "No evidence shall be offered at trial relating to the circumstances under which, or reasons why, following the Tet Offensive, NSA began to provide data on the number of personnel North Vietnam dispatched to South Vietnam as replacements for casualties or augmentations of units already deployed. . . ."

The NSA screwed the lid down even tighter with the final part of the order: "Paragraph 5 of this protective order shall not be disclosed by the parties except to the attorneys, paralegals or witnesses, and only when necessary for purposes of litigating this case. For this reason, the protective order shall be filed under seal by the Clerk of the Court."

So, like much evidence in the libel trial, the NSA smoking gun ended up as more of a cap pistol. Although the NSA's disclosures may have been unprecedented, the agency walked away with most of its puzzles intact, free from further questioning at the trial.

*   *   *

In the days before court convened, even Cable News Network was swept up in the legal fray. CNN wanted to bring its TV cameras into the courtroom and it had two tough obstacles to overcome. Although forty-one out of fifty states allow cameras, rules in both the Southern District of New York and the entire federal judiciary explicitly forbid photography of any kind.

To sidestep these strictures, CNN asked Judge Leval to permit coverage of the case on an experimental basis in the public interest. The news network promised to keep obtrusiveness to a minimum by using only one television camera and one still photographer with two cameras. No logo would identify the camera crew as representing CNN, and the coverage would be shared with all other news organizations on a pooled basis. Neither side objected to CNN's petition for coverage, and the general heartily endorsed it. George Vradenburg III, CBS's chief in-house lawyer, said in a letter to CNN that he, too, would go along, although he would prefer to await a ruling on a pending request by twenty-eight news organizations to cover all federal trials.

CNN filed its request with Judge Leval in August 1984. Leval delivered his answer on September 19. It was both a ringing endorsement of the need for television coverage of federal trials and a denial. Leval wrote, "The public's legitimate interest in obtaining the information it would receive is beyond dispute. Courts play a vital role in American life, in adjudicating civil disputes sometimes affecting the rights of huge classes, trying criminal indictments and interpreting the laws of the land. The people should have an opportunity to see how the courts function."

But, whatever arguments he could come up with, Leval ran smack into the concrete wall of the federal rules. "Believing that I have no discretion in the matter in the face of those rules, I deny the application, in spite of its merit," he concluded.

Armed with Leval's positive statements, CNN quickly appealed the coverage issue to the U.S. Court of Appeals in the Second Circuit, located in New York. By not allowing cameras in courtrooms, CNN argued, the First Amendment rights of the public were abridged. Judge James L. Oakes, however, demolished that argument. "There is a long leap . . . between a public right under the First Amendment to attend trials and a public right under the First Amendment [to see those trials] televised," Oakes wrote. "It is a leap we are not yet prepared to take."

Still, CNN did not give up. On March 1, 1985, it took the case to the Supreme Court, although the Westmoreland-CBS trial had, by then, been over a year. "It is not only the right to cover this trial—which has now been settled by a stipulated dismissal—that is implicated here: if this trial may be placed off-limits to all television coverage, however unobtrusive and acceptable to all participants, then so may every trial."

But the Supreme Court evidently was not impressed. In June 1985, it dismissed the appeal without considering it, ending at last the string of legal sideshows generated by the Westmoreland-CBS suit.

*   *   *

While CNN battled to cover the trial, David Boies was working to eliminate the need for a trial. On May 23, 1984, he filed a mountain of paper with Leval, asking him to throw out the suit. This Motion for Summary Judgment included a 379-page "memorandum" arguing for dismissal, a 612-page collection of affidavits, a 117-page analysis of the supposedly undisputed facts in the case (even the most adversarial of lawyers can agree on some issues), and a 379-page collection of exhibits, including TOP SECRET CIA documents that Boies contended proved the truth of the broadcast.

Two months later, Burt fired back the legal equivalent of a sixteen-inch artillery shell. The July 23 Capital Legal reply included a 363-page motion opposing Boies' filing, backed up by a 524-page collection of affidavits, documents, and Burt's analysis of the undisputed facts.

Leval spent the summer wading through this material and on September 24 ruled against Boies. While Boies had put much stock in use of the "truth" defense, Leval made short work of it. He said, "The principal bulk of defendant's voluminous briefs is dedicated to the point that summary judgment should be granted because what was stated in the documentary was true. . . . It is sufficient answer that plaintiff offers evidence to the contrary. I express no views on the persuasiveness of the proofs offered by either side.

"Summary judgment must be denied if there is conflicting evidence on any substantial issue," he concluded.

At the same time, Leval struck down some of Burt's pet contentions, including the claim that Crile and CBS were libelous because they had set out to prove a foregone conclusion. The judge suggested that such "bias" could sometimes be a good thing:

"The press is not obliged to satisfy the Platonic ideal of investigation to qualify for summary judgment on the issue of constitutional malice. . . . Reporters, of course, investigate where their suspicions lie. A previously formed belief rebuts as much as it establishes constitutional malice, as it tends to demonstrate sincerity."

Leval ruled that if Westmoreland's position were supported only by "such contentions of insufficient thoroughness, bloodhound-determination and bias," the case should indeed be dropped. But, he noted, the plaintiff "also asserts contentions of dishonesty and willful falsity in the editing and presentation of evidence." Some evidence CBS had used to back up the thesis of its broadcast may have been deliberately misstated, he said.

The instances in question included:

1. The Gains Hawkins "crap" quote. When CBS interviewed Hawkins, a MACV OB specialist, he referred to old enemy-strength figures obtained from the South Vietnamese by saying "these figures were crap. They were history." Leval said that in editing this statement for the documentary, CBS presented it in a context "suggesting that Hawkins was applying the labels of 'crap' and 'history' and worthless to the figures the MACV delegation were sponsoring" at a conference to resolve the OB hassle.

2. Misdescription of the status of and a statement made by another MACV intelligence analyst, Colonel George Hamscher. In discussing Hamscher's role in a conference called to resolve the OB controversy, correspondent Mike Wallace said in the documentary, " . . . The head of MACV's delegation told us that General Westmoreland had, in fact, personally instructed him not to allow the total [estimate of enemy strength] to go over 300,000." As Leval pointed out, "Hamscher was not the head of the MACV delegation, nor even a member of it, nor even under General Westmoreland's command. . . . Moreover, Hamscher did not state that he had received such an order from General Westmoreland."

3. CBS had also misattributed a cable, confusing both the viewers and General Westmoreland. During his interview of Westmoreland, Wallace asked the general if the real reason he removed the self-defense militia from the order of battle in the summer of 1967 was "based on political considerations." Westmoreland answered, "No, decidedly not. That, that—"

Wallace jumped in and said, "I have a copy of your August 20th cable," adding, "As you put it in the cable, you say the principal reason why the self-defense militia must go was, quote, 'press reaction.'"

Leval observed, "The cable to which Wallace referred, however, was not General Westmoreland's. It was sent from Saigon by General Creighton Abrams, the deputy commander of MACV, while Westmoreland was away, a fact concededly known to the makers of the documentary."

These, plus two other similar episodes, raised "triable questions of knowing or reckless falsity to foreclose summary judgment on the issue of constitutional malice," he said.

In other words, the stage was set for what *Newsweek* magazine would call "The Libel Trial of the Century."

13.

The Trial

ON Friday, October 5, 1984, Dan Burt bantam-stepped across a meeting room at the Harley Hotel in New York City and into a blaze of TV lights for the last dueling news conference before General Westmoreland's battle moved to the courtroom. One TV newsman who had never seen Burt before remarked to another, "God, I never thought I'd see the day a guy in a green velvet suit defended a four-star general."

Making his way through the crowd of hundreds of reporters, cameramen, and TV technicians, Burt had the air of a prizefighter leaving the ring after scoring a near-impossible knockout, not that of a wary opponent climbing in with a fierce and untested adversary.

On the surface, Burt had good reason for confidence. He had come close to accomplishing the impossible. Next week, after the Columbus Day holiday weekend, he would present Westmoreland's libel case to a jury of twelve ordinary men and women. Burt had fielded the best that the best law firm in the country could throw against him in the pre-trial period, beating back David Boies' finely crafted (and expensive) "truth" defense.

The live-remote TV vans ringing the outside of the Harley like a herd of tin-toothed behemoths pausing to feed proved that Burt had already won one victory. He had succeeded in using the media to assault the media in a trial about media fairness. Anyone who pulled that off could wear whatever he wanted to a news conference.

Looking out over a podium festooned with a phalanx of microphones, Burt firmly set the ground rules for questioning, letting the assembled international press corps know that he was there not so much to be questioned as to take issue with them.

In the back of the room, near a litter of used coffee cups, CBS PR man John Scanlon worked the press, affably greeting old friends as someone on their side, someone ready to defend the First Amendment. Down the hall, David Boies relaxed in an empty ballroom with a handful of associates, awaiting his turn before the voracious news army—three television networks, all the local New York TV stations, CNN, and a handful of foreign crews.

Graciousness was not Burt's theme that day. When a reporter from WCBS-TV ventured to ask a question, Burt sneered, demanding, "You're from CBS aren't you?" He waxed conciliatory one moment, combative the next. Burt paused once to admit that, while his exchanges with the press before the trial had been "reasonably acerbic . . . there has been remarkably fair coverage of this case to date." A few moments later, however, he wondered "whether the press is going to accurately report the trial. If something improper was done [by CBS], is the press going to be as critical of that as improprieties in the Nixon White House?"

Westmoreland's lawyer said that when he first watched "The Uncounted Enemy" his reaction to the program had been "Oh my God, he [Westmoreland] did it." Burt defended his politics. "I am not now and never have been a conservative. . . . I've been a member of the ACLU since leaving law school. . . . "

Asked how he could bring a libel suit if he believed in the First Amendment guarantees of freedom of the press, he said, "Litigation itself is a form of free speech under the First Amendment."

Behind all this bravado, however, Burt had some real problems. The day before, in the last pre-trial session with Judge Leval, he had dropped a large portion of his case. Burt would not challenge CBS on a key assertion of the documentary: that Westmoreland had conspired to deceive the press, the Congress, and public about enemy troop strength in Vietnam. Instead, Burt would attempt to prove that CBS had defamed Westmoreland on a much narrower issue: that the general had deceived his superiors, including the Joint Chiefs of Staff and the President.

The reporters at the news conference wanted to know why Burt had changed his mind, but the lawyer brushed them off with the explanation, "When you prepare a complaint, you put everything in it." He then added, "The general did not report to the press. . . . "

Sensing a hot story but unable to pry a clearer explanation from Burt, the press mob oozed down the hall to the ballroom, where Boies was waiting to fill in the gaps. Wearing one of his trademark blue Sears suits, Boies casually walked to the podium and wryly observed, "Holding a press conference on the eve of a trial is not an ordinary litigation technique." After the cacophony of questions abated, Boies readily addressed the paramount issue. He said he was "very pleased" Burt had dropped some of his charges.

The decision would "narrow the trial considerably," he said. "The basic thrust of the broadcast was that the public was misled. This is a very different road to travel. . . . What we are seeing here is the crumbling of the plaintiff's case."

Burt had tried to downplay the seriousness of this abrupt move on the eve of the trial, but it was more of a setback than he cared to admit. Almost from the start of the case, Burt and Westmoreland had focused the heat of their assault on the words Mike Wallace had uttered at the beginning of the documentary. Besides referring to a "conspiracy," Wallace had said, "We Americans were misinformed about the nature and size of the enemy. . . . "

In this more limited case, as Judge Leval saw it, Burt would have to prove CBS had defamed Westmoreland by saying the general had deceived "the president and military superior officers, including the Joint Chiefs of Staff." Leval, after considerable discussion in the pre-trial hearing, had suggested that one possible interpretation of Burt's case now might be that Westmoreland, out of duty, had deceived the press, the Congress, and the American people while giving the true story to his superiors. Burt had agreed with this hypothesis, but had told the judge that any instructions for the jury to ignore claims of libel on the counts that the general deceived the American people or Congress would be "very prejudicial."

*   *   *

On Tuesday, October 9, as Burt made his way through the media mob outside the courthouse in Foley Square, he did not look like a man who had given up three fourths of his case. Barging through the TV camera crews and still photographers clicking off shots with machine-gun-fire rapidity, Burt still projected the image of a winner.

Katherine "Kitsy" Westmoreland, the general's wife, also took the horde in stride. The wife of a West Pointer, daughter of a West Pointer, and sister of a West Pointer, she had the mettle only an Army brat and an Army wife could have—the special adaptability that allowed her to dine with Presidents and Prime Ministers with ease although she once had ridden to school in a buckboard at Fort Sill, Oklahoma. She had tasted the best that Army life could offer: world travel, a villa in Saigon, staying in the family quarters at the White House. But she had also faced the toughest, greeting wounded GIs as they were carried off the Medevac transports shuttling between Saigon and Clark Air Force Base in the Philippines, her home after terrorist attacks made even a Saigon villa too uncomfortable.

Army wives learn early to stand by their men, and that's what Kitsy Westmoreland intended to do as she made her way into Room 318 of the federal courthouse, despite the fact she had been "violently opposed" to filing the suit. The courtroom was packed with prospective jurors, the media, lawyers for both sides and their support staffs. But Kitsy—her needlepoint readily at hand in her large bag—wasn't concerned about the mob. "I just figured I would end up sitting next to Wes," she said. "I don't know why. But we had never been in court before . . . and no one told us what to expect."

Her resilience almost deserted her, Kitsy later admitted, when she found she could not sit where she had planned. Worse, she discovered, the bench reserved for family members was also occupied by the Cravath paralegals—representatives of the enemy.

"I was so alone—the press was in front of me and behind me, and I didn't know anyone," she recalled. "I've never prayed so hard in my life. I asked, what would my mother do in a situation like this? And I thought, she'd smile and say good morning. So I did."

Then she pulled out her needlepoint and set to work adjusting to the strange environment that circumstances had thrust upon her. By the end of the trial, Kitsy had come to know most of her companions and, in an atmosphere fraught with personal conflicts, had earned the respect and warm admiration of all in the courtroom, including the opposition.

Westmoreland's entry into the courthouse signaled the beginning of his personal vindication. As the white-haired general in civilian garb made his way through the corridors of the courthouse, the day-in-and-day-out inhabitants stopped to greet him, to give their thanks and encouragement. In one corridor, a porter mopping the floor paused to share his Vietnam experience with the general. In another hallway, a federal parole officer, also a Viet vet, asked for an autograph and voiced his support.

Entering the packed courtroom, Westmoreland made his way through the hundreds of potential jury members and took his seat to the left of the judge's raised desk, alongside Burt and his assistants, who, viewed together, looked like a legal Mod Squad. Besides Burt, the Westmoreland defense team included David Dorsen, the Ichabod Crane–lean Washington attorney on retainer to the defense; Anthony Murry, Capital Legal associate and inner-city black who had, in record time, made the journey from a poor Catholic high school in Camden, New Jersey, to Princeton University, to a benchside seat at the historic trial; and Pat Embrey, a serious-looking young woman lawyer dressed for legal success. The member of the team most startling in appearance was Jay Schulman, a huge-headed man with a white beard and mane who looked, acted, and talked like the last beatnik.

Although Schulman and Burt later had a falling out, Schulman's presence was key this first day, for he was the master—some say inventor—of an arcane art. He was a jury-selection expert.

Courthouse buffs, some members of the press, and lawyers who
dropped in to rubberneck at the start of the trial were startled to see
Schulman on Burt's team. He seemed, from previous cases, ultra-
liberal. His last client had been Kathy Boudin, the former member of
the radical Weather Underground who had been scheduled for trial
earlier in the year for her role in a Brink's armored-car robbery, but
had copped a plea.

Schulman's first clients had been the Berrigan brothers—also
1960s radicals. During their trial in Harrisburg, Pennsylvania. The
Berrigans had asked Schulman, a psychologist, to sit in the courtroom
and observe prospective jurors as the judge quizzed them, using his
training and ability to discern which ones would be sympathetic.
Since then, jury-selection experts have been used in cases large and
small.

Schulman said his politics had nothing to do with his place on
the Westmoreland team. "I work for people I like, I work for people I
think are right. And Westmoreland is right," Schulman said. He
equated Westmoreland's fight against the vast and wealthy CBS with
the battles of individuals of conviction against the government—such
as the Berrigans.

Jury selection in a federal trial is left mostly to the judge, with
the lawyers for each side allowed only limited peremptory challenges.
Leval had devised an extensive series of questions to winnow the
potential panelists down to twelve jurors and six alternates. He
quizzed the men and women about their views on the Vietnam War.
He asked them about their reading and television-viewing habits and
preferences. He probed their knowledge or acquaintance with the
literally hundreds of people and institutions with any tie to either
side of the case.

In two days, Leval put together the seemingly perfect panel. This
group of eighteen men and women had virtually sat out the 1960s.
With only one exception, they had no strong opinion on the war. They
had an amazing lack of knowledge about the people who had run the
war. Leval asked if any of the jurors had heard of Robert McNamara.
No one responded. He tried again, asking the jurors if they'd ever
heard of the Robert McNamara who had been Secretary of Defense
and head of the World Bank. Again, no takers.

The jurors didn't think much of contemporary leaders, either.
During his questioning, Burt asked them to name an American public
figure they "respected highly." None of the jurors could come up with
anyone they respected enough to cite!

Of the six men on the jury, none had served in the military during the Vietnam War. Randy Frost, a twenty-four-year-old college
student and foreman for a cosmetics manufacturer, expressed a

"personal view against the war," but he was the only one who had any opinion about the conflict. The jurors hailed equally from the city and the suburbs, with the commuting jurors coming from Westchester and Rockland counties north of the city. Their ethnic backgrounds reflected the polyglot nature of the metropolitan area. One panelist, fifty-four-year-old Carmen Batista, knew firsthand about wars of revolution. Born in Cuba, she had fled that country in 1964.

The other jurors were M. Patricia Roth, a forty-two-year-old real-estate agent and art teacher with a master's degree; Miriam Lucas, fifty-five, a high-school graduate who worked as a customer-service representative for Consolidated Edison Co., the New York power company; David Lederman, twenty-six, a laboratory research technician with a bachelor's degree; Eileen Miller, thirty, a real-estate acquisition specialist for Citicorp; Myron Gold, forty-nine, an accountant with the Internal Revenue Service and a college graduate; Catherine Ryan, a fifty-three-year-old gift-shop owner; Linda Pasquale, twenty-six, a dental assistant and high-school graduate; Philip Chase, thirty-three, a college graduate and New York State accountant; Michael Sussman, forty-two, yet another accountant; and Richard Benveniste, thirty-two, an insurance underwriter. With jury selection completed, Leval adjourned court for the day and scheduled opening arguments for the next day, with Burt slated to go first.

The next morning, October 11, David Boies was sitting around his Manhattan apartment, talking with his wife, Mary, the head of corporate public affairs for CBS. A friend of Mrs. Boies was visiting from Seattle. "David was so relaxed that my friend just assumed that court had been canceled for the day," she recalled. "She was astonished when David got up and said he had to be in court in a half-hour for the opening statements."

The lawyers and principals for both sides again ran the familiar press gantlet, including CNN's live-remote unit. Producer Nancy Lane —at twenty-five already a seasoned trial producer due to her supervision of CNN's coverage of a sensational rape trial in New Bedford, Massachusetts, earlier in the year—busily snared lawyers and witnesses for live interviews in front of her streetside camera. After walking up the three flights of granite steps, everyone wanting to enter the courthouse, four-star general or ordinary citizen, first had to pass through a metal-detector. Three flights up in an elevator and through a series of wide marble hallways, yet another metal-detector stood sentry outside the courtroom.

The high-ceilinged room had metamorphosed overnight— transformed into an ersatz TV studio. The front of the court was ringed with TV monitors. Cables snaked from these monitors to two video-tape players sitting next to Boies on his table and to a video and audio control console on the left of court, manned by two technicians hirsute enough for bit parts in *Hair*. Television physically dominated this trial about television and the first televised war in history.

The trial Westmoreland sought to defend his old-soldier's honor finally began at 10:20 a.m., with Leval telling the jury what the case was about and what it was not about. Looking much like a fleshed-out Mr. Rogers in judicial robes, Leval simply and without condescension laid out the parameters of the case and the issues the jury should consider and ignore:

"We spent two days in which I was asking you questions about what your feelings are about the military, what you feel about peace and war, what your feelings are about the war in Vietnam, whether press criticism of the government is a good thing or a bad thing, what you think about press commentary and freedom of the press, and a number of questions like that, and now I want to say very emphatically that so far as concerns the job of the jury and the job of the judge, those questions are completely behind us, they are no longer a part of the trial, they have nothing to do with this case, and you are not to allow concerns and considerations of that kind to enter into your thoughts while doing your job as a jury."

Despite the emotionalism connected with the Vietnam War, the jury had a really simple task, Leval said. They only needed to decide, based on the evidence presented, "who did what, when and where, what they knew when they did it, what they didn't know when they did it, and what they believed when they did it."

The judge also admonished the jurors, as he would do daily throughout the trial, to ignore press coverage of the case. "Your decision is to be based on the evidence that's received in this courtroom and nothing else," he said.

Standing, facing the jury or occasionally pacing back and forth, Leval spelled out the case: " . . . The elements of the case of a libel brought by a public official, are whether CBS and the defendants in preparing the broadcast made defamatory statements about General Westmoreland; whether the defamatory statements, if they were defamatory, were false; if they were false, whether they were made with knowledge of falsity, whether the statements were made in reckless disregard of the truth or falsity; and whether the plaintiff suffered damage or injury as a result of these statements."

Listening to these remarks, the main characters in the case assumed the postures they would retain, with few exceptions, for the remainder of the trial. Directly in front of the judge was the plaintiff's table, where Westmoreland sat ramrod straight in one of the green leather chairs, listening intently but somehow standing off from the process unfolding before him. Behind this table was the CBS table, where Sam Adams—looking much like the Virginia gentleman farmer he was—scratched copious notes on a yellow legal pad. George Crile, the documentary's producer, in a grayish summer-weight suit, also sat erect, but he often shifted forward to take notes. Mike Wallace looked like the most relaxed man in the courtroom, leaning back, listening, but not with the intensity displayed by Westmoreland.

All paid close attention as Leval walked toward the jury and explained the various kinds of evidence the panel would consider during the trial. The "truth" each side would attempt to prove or disprove in the case was not a simple truth, Leval said. Then he gave them a crash course in the principles of libel law, saying they would have to determine the "state of mind" of various CBS employees at the time they assembled the broadcast. He carefully explained the concept of "reckless disregard" for truth or falsity. Leval used this rather complicated approach to replace a word commonly used in libel cases but which he found inaccurate—legal "malice."

After a brief recess, Burt—decked out in a gray-blue suit with wide stripes and sporting a new haircut that diminished the wild curliness of his hair—stepped forward to launch his formal indictment of CBS. In the moment before he began, the only sound that could be heard in the room was the scratching of the colored chalk used by the TV artists, working in the right front row.

This was Burt's first-ever appearance before a jury. The lawyer had presented his case a number of times to the press, but this time it really counted. He came prepared, speaking almost woodenly from what appeared to be a script placed on the lectern.

"I speak here today on behalf of General Westmoreland, who was America's commander in Vietnam from 1964 through 1968. My own remarks this morning are not—they are not evidence. They are intended only to give you an overview of what happened to General Westmoreland and why he came to sue the defendants. . . . "

Like Leval, Burt let the jurors know that the Vietnam War should take a back seat. "The issue here is very specific and very limited. It is, did General Westmoreland lie to his superiors? Did he order his troops to hide evidence of the enemy's strength from our government?

"I ask you to keep your mind clear of the questions about the war in Vietnam itself as I describe a widely known intelligence debate that CBS converted into an alleged conspiracy through the alchemy of television."

Pointing to the TV monitors, Burt told the jury he would play a series of clips from the broadcast to show how CBS and the "Uncounted Enemy" producer, George Crile, used video sleight of hand. Crile, he said, had "needed a big story, a sensational story he could do himself."

Burt then laid out his interpretation of the genesis of the documentary and its central theme of conspiracy, referring to Crile's story proposal. "Crile's blue sheet used the word conspiracy 24 times in its tale of high crimes by a former well-known official."

Burt played for the jury the first of many snippets of videotape they would see during the next months, a portion of Mike Wallace's interview with Walt Rostow. During this presentation, it seemed that filmed "truth" owed much to editing. In this first piece of tape, LBJ's former national-security adviser told Wallace that the President "was totally aware of the differences in the intelligence community and was particularly aware of the debate."

Burt told the jury that, despite the strength of this statement and the fact that "Dr. Rostow knows better than anyone what the president was told about foreign security matters," CBS "did not use one second of Dr. Rostow's interview in the broadcast."

Venality had motivated Crile to leave Rostow and other interviews on the cutting-room floor, Burt asserted. "George Crile needed a big story. He was ambitious to become a famous correspondent like Mike Wallace. So George Crile pushed aside all the books, cables and documents that belied his tale."

What material Crile did use, he misused, according to Burt. "We will show you how he did it, show you the statements taken out of context, half quotes, misattributions, hypothetical questions paired with lead-ins to make it appear that answers were being given to questions that were never asked, and collapsing multiple events to create events which never existed."

Burt said there was a witness to this fabrication: Ira Klein, the documentary's film editor, who would "describe how Crile created 'The Uncounted Enemy: A Vietnam Deception' with reckless disregard for the truth."

Burt then went through the documentary point by point, showing how, in his view, Crile had skewed it to present a preconceived idea. Bits of television were flashed onto the multiple screens to illustrate Burt's tale. The presentation, however, was marred by technical difficulties. Tapes were miscued or did not play at all. Two large Sony monitors stubbornly refused to turn on, and the technicians rushed about, furiously clicking remote controls. At one point, a technician blurted loudly, "I've got the wrong script, I've got the wrong script."

Crile hadn't got the supposed "facts" he presented right either, Burt said. He charged CBS with failing to interview Ambassador Robert Komer, Westmoreland's pacification chief. "One of the things he [Komer] will testify about is the report containing evidence that CBS said General Westmoreland suppressed. A copy of this report was found in Ambassador Komer's Vietnam files in the course of our preparation for this trial."

Burt also used CBS footage to indict the network for its failure to interview General Phillip Davidson, Westmoreland's intelligence chief. He played a segment from Wallace's interview with Westmoreland, when the MACV commander suggested that CBS talk to Davidson. Wallace told Westmoreland, "General Davidson is a very, very sick man. We want very much to talk to him." Not only had Davidson beaten cancer, Burt told the jury, but in 1981 he had been willing to be interviewed and easy to find. The lawyer promised that Davidson would testify "he received no call, no letter from CBS."

Burt said Crile had "ambushed" Westmoreland when he asked the general to come to New York for an interview. "Only the night before his interview was Westmoreland given a letter listing the five points to be covered, the fourth of which contained a reference to the Order of Battle controversy," he said. "It is no wonder then when you see General Westmoreland's interview—and you will—you will see an ambushed, angry and frustrated 68-year-old man forced back on a 14-year-old memory of events that played a comparatively insignificant role in the war he was fighting."

The jury would have a chance to assess firsthand the tricks of television and how they had worked to indict Westmoreland unfairly in the documentary, Burt said. "Many of us are accustomed to accepting as reality the images and sounds we see on television screens— particularly younger people who have grown up with television all their lives. I will show you how those images are cut, spliced, put together to make the appearance of reality which never occurred."

When Burt started to play another portion of Wallace's interview with Westmoreland, Boies stood up to object, asking to approach the bench. Leval agreed, beginning the first of the numerous "sidebar" conferences that broke the trial up each day. The sidebar is literally that—the portion of the judge's bench farthest away from the jury. There the lawyers could wrangle over points Leval did not want the jury to hear. These exchanges were transcribed by the court reporter, who also moved to the sidebar.

Boies asked for the first conference because, just as Burt did not approve of Crile's editing, Boies did not approve of Burt's editing. "What happened is you cut it at an earlier point than the description of the segment you gave us originally," Boies complained. Burt admitted this, but said he had advised Boies of the changes in writing, adding that if Leval desired, he would play the part of the clip that had been omitted.

Since the conference came so close to lunch, Leval decreed a one-hour-and-fifteen-minute recess. Television, however, did not give Westmoreland a lunch break. The general ducked out the side door, hoping to avoid the camera-crew mob parked on the front steps, looking like a hydra-headed, multi-eyed beast of prey, bristling with antenna-like microphones on long poles. This camera creature spotted Westmoreland as he strolled up the street and across the square. With the cry "There goes Westmoreland!" the lumbering horde gave pursuit.

After lunch, Burt told the jury he was going to put the pieces of the documentary back together for them so they could see exactly what Crile had done. He explained, "When you make a documentary, you film lots of interviews and then you take those interviews and cut them. When you put the cuts that you have taken out, when you put the fragments together, from the long and whole entire interviews, the question is: are you faithful in that assembly process to, in fact, what you are told?

"If you are not, you can make what never occurred appear to happen," he said. Burt then demonstrated his point by showing parts of CBS's interview with one of its key sources—Colonel Gains Hawkins, chief of order-of-battle intelligence at the Combined Intelligence Center, Vietnam. This interview, and the way it was edited, had been dissected in Don Kowet's book. It was one of the questionable points Judge Leval had cited when he refused to dismiss the case.

The portion of the Hawkins interview that was included in the broadcast made it seem as if Westmoreland had ordered him to reduce the number of guerrillas carried in the OB; another quote from the same interview conveyed the opposite meaning. After playing the tape, Burt said, "As you saw, Colonel Hawkins said that he was not told to go back and reduce any numbers. He was told to review it, take another look. He didn't want to put words in General Westmoreland's mouth. But CBS put those words in his mouth in the broadcast and you will see that."

Burt played sequences in which he claimed CBS, by careful editing, made General McChristian and Richard McArthur seem to be saying things they hadn't really said. He then turned to Hawkins' quote that the figures were "crap." Burt seemed to relish saying "crap" in a federal court, repeating it four times within several minutes.

This portion of the Hawkins interview, Burt said, was "the high point of the CBS broadcast. CBS is going to show you an anguished Colonel Gains Hawkins apparently confessing on camera that he was defending MACV estimates at the Langley session that he did not believe in. . . . But Hawkins wasn't talking about the estimates he took to Langley [for a conference on the OB]. He was talking about the old estimates for the home guard and the political cadre MACV inherited from the South Vietnamese in 1966."

Burt ran the tape, saying, "What Crile did was to drop the first 18 words in Hawkins' answer in order to fabricate Colonel Hawkins' damning confession. . . . "

Taking his lead from Leval's summary-judgment ruling, Burt then turned to the Abrams-Westmoreland cable duplicity. He showed the jury another portion of Wallace's interview with Westmoreland, pointing out, "What Mike Wallace said about the cable was false. The cable Mike Wallace had right in front of him was not General Westmoreland's cable. . . . Wallace was reading from a cable clearly stating it was from . . . General Abrams. . . . "

Point by point, Burt savaged the CBS show. When he finally asked for a ten-minute recess, Boies grabbed the opportunity to talk to the judge at the sidebar. With the jury absent and much of the courtroom audience on its way to a coffee break in the courthouse cafeteria two flights up (emblazoned with the sign LET US CATER YOUR NEXT PARTY), Boies asked for a mistrial.

Burt's "use and misuse of evidence and argument goes far beyond anything that is permissible in an opening statement to the jury," Boies argued. " . . . Mr. Burt has gone beyond what he told the court and he had told me was the basis of his case in terms of a deception of the President and the Joint Chiefs of Staff and Westmoreland's superiors. He has repeatedly gone into the area of the extent to which the public was misled. He has repeatedly gotten into the area he told the court and the court indicated was not appropriate, which was the area of consequences of the deception or the attempted deception.

"He has repeatedly referred to whether or not the Tet Offensive was a surprise or not, which was specifically one of the things he said yesterday he was not going to do and which we again discussed this morning."

What really galled Boies, however, was Burt's self-serving editing of the documentary, particularly the use of Hawkins' "crap" quote. Burt, who at this stage apparently saw the trial as a battle over which lawyer could edit the miles of tape and film to the best advantage, replied, "Mr. Boies is free to put his broadcast on."

After listening to Boies' objection, Leval said, " . . . I guess my answer is that if Mr. Burt has taken unwarranted liberties and made improper . . . suggestions . . . by the way he has cut the quotations and clips of the film, you will have the opportunity to show him to have been a liar."

The judge said he would tell the jury to take statements made in the opening arguments "with a grain of salt," but he denied Boies' motion for mistrial.

(Later, after court adjourned for the day, Boies was still irritated by Burt's display and said "he's lucky he did not have to follow CBS News guidelines." Crile chimed in, saying, "It's amazing that lawyers in a legal proceeding like this can trick edit." But Mike Wallace had no complaints. "He's editing it very effectively to sell a point of view.")

As the recess ended, Leval asked Burt if he planned to touch on "whether the president was prepared for the Tet Offensive and whether the president was deceived. Is there any more in your opening statement on those subjects?"

Burt replied that the broadcast did touch on Tet.

Boies objected to this, pointing out, "What the broadcast says . . . is the surprise came from the size of the Tet Offensive, not the Tet Offensive itself. . . . There's never been any doubt that people were advised that there was going to be a Tet Offensive and indeed the broadcast says that."

Leval said he intended to "tell the jury that the issues of whether the president was surprised or whether the president and the Joint Chiefs of Staff got accurate information from other sources is not an issue in this case. . . . The libel suit is about the issue of whether General Westmoreland attempted to deceive and I certainly recommend that you stay clear as you can of anything that has to do with the question of whether an actual misperception occurred because . . . it has a great capacity to confuse and misdirect the jury."

The lawyers left the sidebar and Burt resumed his position at the podium, telling the jury they would see another piece of tape and hear "Dr. Rostow telling Mike Wallace that the President knew all about the Order of Battle debate . . . and that debate did not distort the President's assessment of the war."

Burt asked the technicians to start playing the tape, and then inadvertently cued it to a section where Rostow discussed Tet. Leval ordered the tape cut off, and Burt hastily apologized. Leval told the jury to disregard what they had just seen, explaining that the trial was about libel, not Tet.

Summing up the case ahead, Burt said, "In the course of this trial . . . you will hear many people testify that when [CBS] aired its broadcast they either knew the broadcast was false or were recklessly indifferent to its falsity. You will see evidence from official documents that what CBS said was false. . . . All I ask of you as this trial begins is that you keep an open mind. The broadcast is a powerful work of fiction that creates the illusion of wrong where none existed."

Once again, Burt reminded the jurors that the Vietnam War was not on trial. "The issue in the case is very important, but it is also very simple. It is not whether the Vietnam War was good or bad. It is whether General Westmoreland lied to his superiors, whether he lied ultimately to his commander in chief, the President of the United States."

*   *   *

Now it was Boies' turn. As the Cravath attorney began to speak, the differences between the two advocates were dramatically apparent. Burt, despite his stiff presentation, seemed propelled by controlled fury. Boies carried himself with a relaxed, natural air. Although this was his first libel joust, the courtroom was his habitat. Boies was a trial attorney.

Even the way the two men played the videotapes underscored their differences. Burt had technicians on the sidelines punch the buttons, and he got flustered at the glitches. Boies kept the equipment on his table and played the tapes himself. If anything fouled up, he just shrugged it off.

In his opening, Boies briefly rebutted Burt, telling the jury, "I want to emphasize . . . that you ought to look at the facts and you ought to look in my statement, and I would suggest in his, not at the characterizations that we use, not at the words we use, but what are the facts." For the next several weeks, he said, they would only hear Burt's side of the story. He asked the jury to "keep in mind . . . the kinds of questions that the facts I am going to show you raise, so that you have in your mind the kinds of questions that you expect those witnesses to answer.

"Mr. Burt gave you some suggestions as to the things you might look for. If I could, for those of you who are going to keep notes, I would like you someplace in that note pad to draw a line and above it write 'Witnesses who testified that CBS knew the program was false.'

"You may recall that Mr. Burt said you're going to hear a lot of witnesses, many witnesses, come in and testify that CBS knew that the program was false. That's not so." Boies told the jury to focus on two questions as they listened to Burt's witnesses. "One, was the broadcast true? And two, what was CBS's state of mind about that broadcast?"

Having defined his view of Burt's case, Boies paused to criticize his opponent's editing. "I am going to try and play, in sort of a catchup fashion, some of the portions of the broadcast that Mr. Burt did not play. We have a situation where Mr. Burt is complaining that CBS, in putting together the documentary, unfairly edited some of the interviews." But, Boies said, he had "sort of a complaint" that Burt "unfairly edited some of those interviews, and indeed, the broadcast itself, when he was presenting it to you, and I am going to try and go through and show you some of those things."

Boies discussed Walt Rostow, the first "witness" in Burt's video-tape presentation. He said he would play a portion of the Rostow interview that would rebut the portion of the same interview Burt had played.

Standing next to the video players on his table, Boies leaned over, slipped in a tape, and punched the PLAY button. One juror said, "Could you turn it up?" Another added, "Can't hear." Boies smiled, admitting, "I can't either. My client is an expert in this. I am going to try again."

The tape played, and the jury saw Rostow tell Wallace, "No, I didn't know about it," referring to the question of whether or not Rostow knew that General Westmoreland refused to dispatch a cable drafted by his intelligence chief, General McChristian, which sharply raised the number of enemy troops in Vietnam carried in the OB.

Boies countered almost every piece of Burt's tape with segments of his own, carefully weaving these film clips into his counter-argument. He played the full opening of the broadcast, letting the jurors hear Mike Wallace say that CBS had documented evidence of a deception. Then Boies told the jury:

"Now you recall that Mr. Burt said, well this was an idea that was fabricated by CBS. 'Fabricated' was his word. That this was something that CBS just made up, that somehow CBS or George Crile, out to make a name for himself, constructed this theory, this idea, this false idea, Mr. Burt would say, that is expressed here in this program.

"Mr. Burt didn't explain a lot of things. One of the things he didn't explain is what possible incentive Mike Wallace would have to go along with a false idea like that. . . .

"What did Mike Wallace conceivably have to gain, at the pin-nacle of his profession, a man who has received every broadcasting award given, a man that's received more than ten Emmys, to risk that kind of reputation with an idea, a program that he knew was false?"

Boies was more relaxed than Burt, but he, too, had a flair for drama. Cued up on one of his tape recorders was a beauty of a scene designed to bring down the opening-act curtain—a speech delivered by Senator Robert Kennedy in 1968, shortly after the Tet Offensive began, questioning the administration's assessment of the number of enemy troops the United States faced in Vietnam. Footage of this speech was in the CBS archives Crile had used to research the docu-mentary, and Boies believed that was enough of a lever to invoke the romantic Kennedy image for his defense.

Boies told the jury, "The kinds of questions that this program raises are the kinds of questions that have been raised without answers since the beginning of the Tet Offensive. While the Tet Offensive was still under way, while fighting was still going on, less than a week after the fighting commenced, the same kinds of questions that were raised in the CBS documentary were being raised by the junior senator of New York."

Boies barely had time to get that sentence out of his mouth before Leval called the lawyers to the sidebar. "I don't understand why we are going into this," the judge said. "I don't understand why Mr. Burt went into it. . . . This is not a trial about what were the causes of how we fared in Vietnam. I don't understand why we are getting into this question of how many people, whether Senator Kennedy or anybody else said that the public was deceived or now said that the military was unprepared for the Tet Offensive. Is that what Senator Kennedy said?"

"No," Boies answered. "The thrust of Senator Kennedy's remarks . . . has to do with what people were being told about enemy strength in the period immediately preceding the Tet Offensive." Asked how Kennedy's speech related to the case, Boies pointed out what Kennedy had pointed out: the optimistic reports from Vietnam did not square with the intensity of the Tet assault. If those reports were true, Kennedy wondered rhetorically, "Who then is doing the fighting?"

Burt objected. "It seems it's irrelevant what Senator Kennedy said since General Westmoreland was not reporting to him."

Leval, however, swayed toward Boies' argument, commenting, "To the extent that what Senator Kennedy said in the speech is that the military was putting out false figures, to the extent that that is what this says, I think it's appropriate." But, Leval warned, "I am not going to allow this trial to be broadened into some kind of historical inquiry of how we fared in Vietnam, whether we won or lost, what the reasons were. . . . "

He gave Boies permission to play the tape.

A frustrated Burt, well aware of the potential effect the martyred Senator could have on the jury and the press, said, "We continue to object to the use of Senator Kennedy, a highly emotional and well-known figure here."

Again, Leval turned him down, saying, "Senator Kennedy is a perfectly accurate source."

The power of Kennedy's fiery Boston accent, condemning the war and the Johnson administration and questioning the accuracy of U.S. intelligence, silenced the court, achieving exactly the effect Boies wanted and Burt feared. This ghost from the past hammered home the order-of-battle problem better than any argument Boies could assemble.

After the tape was played, Leval again felt compelled to tell the jury, "We are not going to get into a historical inquiry of what President Johnson in fact knew, what the Joint Chiefs of Staff knew . . . what information came to them. The question that General Westmoreland raises by his complaint is whether CBS falsely accused him of undertaking to suppress and distort and conceal enemy strength figures and I am taking pains to try and shut off at the earliest possible moment any tendency on either side to go beyond the issues in this case. . . . "

Boies may not have widened any issues, but in gaining Leval's okay to play the Kennedy tape, he gained a great deal of latitude in arguing his case. The spirit and the fire of the man David Boies had most admired in his life—Bobby Kennedy—probably won that first full day of the trial for CBS.

14.

Standing Up for the General

TRIALS depicted on television shows teem with drama, confrontation, and minute-by-minute eloquence. The same is not true, however, of trials *about* television. Throughout the fall and early winter of 1984, as Burt slowly—too slowly, his critics charge—presented his case against CBS, on many days the most palpable emotion in Room 318 was boredom. Several times, impassioned exchanges briefly shook the courtroom, but these were exceptions. One juror regularly fell asleep within moments of sitting down.

There was a good reason for the monotony. To build his case effectively, Burt had to present a string of experts—ranging from humble colonels to a far from humble former Secretary of Defense—who would testify that the guerrilla threat described by Sam Adams had been no threat at all.

Witness after witness trooped to the stand, gave their bonafides, and intoned the same opinion: the guerrillas with whom Adams had been obsessed—the so-called self-defense and secret self-defense militia and a category often referred to as VCI, for Viet Cong Infrastructure (the equivalent of American support troops)—were just "women, young boys and old men."

On cross-examination, Boies would try to knock this description down, asking the witnesses about the weapons these guerrilla forces carried and their ability to set booby traps. This wrangling over exactly what constituted a guerrilla in a guerrilla war soon resembled a discourse among medieval theologians bent on determining how many angels could dance on the head of a pin.

Contributing to the courtroom malaise was the physical atmosphere. An unduly warm fall, the lack of air-conditioning, and, later, radiators that would get stuck on full throttle made the room stuffy to the point of inducing sleep. Judge Leval repeatedly dispatched his crew of marshals and clerks, armed with poles of the kind found in old-fashioned schoolrooms, to adjust the windows. On one particularly hot day, however, the window pole—by then an essential tool of the trial—had disappeared. Leval took time out to make everyone aware of this. In the middle of a series of announcements to the jury and litigants, he paused and said, "One further and more important item. If anyone has the 20-foot pole needed to open and close the windows, please return it to the courtroom. . . . "

The principals in the case started to settle down to a routine. Both sides hired chauffeur-driven cars, but the Westmorelands often rode the subway from their Upper East Side hotel to Foley Square. While seasoned New Yorkers consider this trip grueling and many out-of-towners find it frightening, the four-star general and his wife found it exciting and rewarding. On these daily jaunts, the general came into contact with his former troops and ordinary citizens who, time and time again, offered him encouragement, often telling him to "Give 'em hell, Westy." When he walked on the street, drivers of garbage trucks and taxis would lean out and shout their support. One day, a well-known TV commentator taking the same train said hello and confided, "I'm for you."

The benumbed courtroom crowd came to life in the hallway outside when Judge Leval declared one of his frequent recesses. Chance and the legal system had thrown together a diverse and interesting group, and the corridor talk was far from boring.

There were the regulars—the press corps with reporters from the television networks, the wire services, and the top newspapers in the country, including *The New York Times*, the *Washington Post*, the *Boston Globe*, the *Philadelphia Inquirer*, the *Los Angeles Times*, the *Wall Street Journal*, and *Newsday*. But the hallway at any given time also was cluttered with much of Lyndon Johnson's White House staff and Cabinet, plus numerous generals and celebrity visitors. Dan Rather dropped in from the state court next door where he was on jury duty. William F. Buckley, Jr., turned up, taking frenzied notes on his portable computer.

The sideshow in the hall also emphasized the contrast between the lead lawyers. Dan Burt, who had cultivated the press corps before the trial, made it clear from the first day that he had nothing further to say. During breaks, he darted off to his command post in a room down the hall. Boies, however, lingered in the corridor, explaining details of the case to reporters.

The witnesses and lawyers for CBS and Westmoreland got along with each other fairly well, probably due in part to Judge Leval's demeanor. From the first, he proved that he was ideally suited to handle the volatile case, conducting himself with style and grace punctuated with flashes of wit. His respect for the law spilled over onto the participants; although Burt for most of the trial seemed to carry a grudge against the CBS defendants—though not against Boies —the relationship between the two sides was cordial, polite, and correct.

Leval also brought another gift to the case: clear, jargon-free, colloquial speech—no small accomplishment in a case fraught with confusing military acronyms and conflicting statistics. Once, during a wrangle between the lawyers over the exact legal residence of a witness, Leval interrupted, asking simply, "Where does he hang out?" On another occasion, while explaining to the lawyers which issues he would not allow them to raise at the trial, Leval said, " . . . we ain't gonna get into that."

And although Leval often indulged the attorneys in their numerous trips to the sidebar to argue about evidence they wanted to introduce, he could endure only so long. On the third day of the trial, after listening to Burt's reasons why a number of documents should be admitted, Leval finally stopped him. "You know, there may very well be pieces that when put together would make all of these admissible," Leval observed. "You are just starting with a piece at the top of a pyramid and you just want to put it up there with nothing holding it up and it ain't going to stay up if nothing is holding it up."

The judge's style extended to his dress. Most days, a jaunty bow tie popped out over the top of his robes. Jogging shoes peeked out from underneath.

Leval was so relaxed that not once in five months did he ever use his gavel to call for order, and this patience extended to the parade of witnesses. Leval treated them all evenhandedly, no matter how monumental their egos, no matter how lofty their former positions. The prize ego of the trial, without a doubt, belonged to Burt's first witness, the academic who had become Lyndon Johnson's national-security adviser, Walt Whitman Rostow.

After being sworn in, when asked to give his educational and professional background, Rostow was the only witness of the trial to announce where he had attended grammar school! (Grades one through seven in Irvington, New Jersey, finishing up at the Worthington Hooker School in New Haven, Connecticut.) Burt chose Rostow and the witness who followed him, Robert Komer, to illustrate that CBS had been lax in covering the flip side of the broadcast's "conspiracy" thesis. Burt planned to use the testimony of these two men to refute the theme of the broadcast as well as indict Crile and CBS for ignoring the opposing point of view.

It didn't work out exactly that way with Rostow, despite Burt's best effort to qualify him as a witness and Rostow's enthusiasm for reciting what amounted to his résumé. Gazing levelly through his wire-rim glasses, his mouth arranged in a careful half-smile, the portly Rostow straightened slightly in his immaculate pin stripes and intoned the number of books he had written, twenty-four; his education at both Oxford and Yale; his service with the OSS in World War II; his study of German V-2 rockets and his work with Gunnar Myrdal in Europe after the war because "my wife and I decided that the tasks of European reconstruction were so great."

Rostow recalled his White House days, noting that his office was "about 30 seconds" from that of the chief executive.

Burt then asked Rostow about a key April 1967 meeting in the White House attended by Westmoreland, Johnson, Defense Secretary Robert McNamara, Secretary of State Dean Rusk, CIA director Richard Helms, and General Earle Wheeler, chairman of the Joint Chiefs of Staff. To Rostow he read Mike Wallace's description of that meeting from the documentary:

" . . . On this day Westmoreland had mostly good news to offer his commander-in-chief. The Vietcong's army, he said, had leveled off at 285,000 men. And, best of all, he told the President, the long-awaited cross-over point had been reached. We were now killing or capturing Vietcong at a rate faster than they could be put back in the field. We were winning the war of attrition."

Burt asked Rostow, "Did you hear General Westmoreland say that to the president in the meeting you have just been describing?"

"That, sir, is not my memory of the meeting or the tone of it . . . ," Rostow replied, pressing his lips together in the chilly smile.

Burt asked Rostow several more questions and then inquired, " . . . Do you know from your personal knowledge whether General Westmoreland was under pressure from anyone to deliver good news on the war?"

"No, sir. He was not under any such pressure," Rostow said confidently.

In order to prove his now narrowed case, Burt needed key figures in the chain of command to testify that they had known about the order-of-battle hassle. Rostow testified that he had first heard of the dispute in January 1967, from George Carver, CIA director Helms' Special Assistant for Vietnamese Affairs.

"After listening to Mr. Carver's description of the differences of view . . . I called General Wheeler and suggested to him that the parties to this dispute, an intelligence dispute, focused on certain elements in the enemy's order of battle—that these should be aired and debated and resolved and that led directly to the meeting in Honolulu, which was the first of four meetings which finally resolved the matter in November."

Burt then asked Rostow to address the other serious charge in the documentary—that MACV had under-reported the size of North Vietnamese forces infiltrating down the Trail into South Vietnam, particularly in the period prior to the Tet Offensive.

First, Rostow instructed his audience in the two definitions of infiltration—the military definition and the President Johnson definition.

"As it was calculated by professionals in MACV . . . it was an estimate that had to be verified from contact, documents, captured prisoners, and there was always a lag. So when we had a published number for infiltration, we knew that this was a number which was going to be revised as more intelligence came in."

But infiltration also had another meaning, Rostow explained.

"Let's say I was talking to President Johnson. I don't think he was terribly interested in exactly the technical definition that was used by the experts. Infiltration, if you were talking generally, was how many are coming in right now or even up there on the trails heading our way.

"That's a very different matter. And there what you were trying to do was to get what is happening now in the flow of men and supplies from the North into South Vietnam. . . . You did not spend your time trying to figure out whether or not they had actually crossed the border. . . . On the most solid side of the evidence, you had intelligence from the National Security Agency."

MACV had also had access to infiltration intelligence from scouts on the Trail, from sensors, and from reports by pilots flying over the route, Rostow testified. He said he believed there "was a supplement to the order of battle summary" that contained this additional information.

Burt then guided Rostow through the material the NSA had already stipulated, getting him to confirm that "starting in the second half of November and building up on a gradually accelerating curve through December and January was evidence from NSA that a very substantial North Vietnamese force, perhaps two divisions and three regiments, were moving down the Ho Chi Minh Trails and by December, we had concluded their major object likely was to be Khe Sanh."

Gripping the sides of the lectern as though it were a steering wheel, Burt asked Rostow whether he had received infiltration reports of 25,000 men a month as early as September 1967. Rostow said the earliest date he could put on reports of an increase in infiltration down the Trail was November.

"In your opinion . . . would have it been possible," Burt asked him, rocking forward for emphasis, "for infiltration in the range of 25,000 a month to have occurred beginning in September of 1967 without that having been reported to you as National Security Adviser?"

"It would have been impossible," Rostow said with absolute certainty.

On this strong note for his case, Burt ended his direct examination of Rostow, casting a sidelong glance at Boies as he sat down.

In his cross-examination, Boies first concentrated on infiltration, asking Rostow to estimate, with the loose method he used when briefing President Johnson, how many NVA troops had been moving down the Trail in December 1967. Without hesitation, Rostow said, "About 20,000."

Boies then got Rostow to admit that the official military reports had not contained the looser definition of infiltration he had talked about earlier, hammering away until finally the almost exasperated witness blurted, " . . . I don't know of anyone who has a firm figure for that [infiltration in December 1967]. . . . "

Boies continued to push, and Rostow finally made a damaging admission. If Johnson had asked about infiltration in 1967, Rostow said, he would have told the President, "Sir, I can't tell you and no one can tell you. It's a hell of a lot higher and we ought to do something about it!"

Rostow said he had not been aware that some intelligence officers estimated North Vietnamese infiltration as high as 25,000 a month in September, October, November, and December 1967.

After wringing this admission from Rostow—a process that took almost an hour—Boies moved on to the order-of-battle debate. Rostow, still composed and self-assured, his white collar crisp, informed Boies he had been aware of the inter-agency argument but had believed that each side operated in "good faith."

But, in a rapid-fire string of questions, Boies elicited from Rostow that his defense of Westmoreland was based on strictly secondhand knowledge.

"Did you ever have occasion to personally discuss enemy strength estimates or issues relating to order of battle with General Westmoreland?" the lawyer asked.

"No, sir," Rostow answered.

"Were you ever present when General Westmoreland discussed enemy strength issues with the President?"

"No, sir."

"Did you ever have a direct written communication between you and General Westmoreland concerning enemy strength estimates?"

"No, sir."

"Were you ever present at any press conference that General

Westmoreland was also present at where enemy strength estimates or issues were discussed?"

"No, sir . . . ," Rostow said, looking somewhat less placid.

Next, Boies wanted to discuss the Tet Offensive. "The Uncounted Enemy" maintained that the ferocity of this assault (and its impact on an American public who until this time had thought the war was going well) was due to the participation of the self-defense and secret self-defense forces, as well as the larger number of North Vietnamese troops that had infiltrated down the Trail.

"We did know that in addition to the infiltration . . . there was a major effort before Tet to mobilize manpower down to 11- and 12-year-olds," Rostow said. "But the question I'm raising is whether they were recruited into the self-defense corps or the guerrillas and I don't know the answer to that."

A few minutes later, Rostow conceded, "Our initial impression, was that, yes, some of the self-defense forces had been thrown into these numerous attacks in the cities and had been rolled up. But that initial impression may not be the historians' verdict."

The next day, Boies finished Rostow off by having him indirectly refute the first strong statement he had made to Burt—that there was no factual basis for Wallace's assertion in the broadcast that Westmoreland had told Johnson in the spring of 1967 that "the long awaited cross-over point had been reached."

To do this, the lawyer used a document from a readily available, non-classified source—the Pentagon Papers. First, Boies set Rostow up by asking if he was familiar with the papers. "To say I am familiar at this stage is an exaggeration," Rostow said, adding, " . . . I have not looked at them since they came out, and that is getting on to be 15 years."

Boies entered the fourth volume of the papers into evidence and asked Rostow to look at a May 19, 1967, memo written by Assistant Secretary of Defense John McNaughton about an April 1967 meeting between General Westmoreland and senior administration officials. That memo said:

"The VC/NVA 287,000-man order of battle is leveling off, and General Westmoreland believes that, as of March, we reached the 'crossover point'—we began attriting more men than Hanoi can recruit or infiltrate this month."

Burt objected. Striding angrily to the sidebar, he told Judge Leval, "Your honor, we had testimony yesterday that, according to Dr. Rostow, Mr. McNaughton wasn't present at the meeting. . . . It's obviously hearsay. There is no evidence that Mr. McNaughton knew what took place."

Despite Burt's objection, Rostow, after relentless questioning by Boies, finally caved in, conceding, "Whoever took the notes, Mr. McNaughton or others, I assume this was an accurate set of notes. I was not present and do not recall a discussion of this kind. I have no doubt about the accuracy of the notes."

Boies was clearly pleased. He had reversed Rostow's strong testimony of the previous day, and scored some important points in the process.

Burt's next witness was former Ambassador Robert Komer, aptly nicknamed "Blowtorch." The genial-looking, mustachioed, round-faced Komer didn't just answer questions; he passionately spewed forth fact and opinion. He briefly gave his background—Harvard graduate; World War II service, where he started as an enlisted man and rose to a lieutenant; thirteen years with the CIA as an analyst and estimator until he went to work for President Kennedy on the National Security Council staff; and a brief stint as Johnson's deputy assistant for national security. Then he described how he had landed the Saigon job.

Komer said President Johnson called him into the Oval Office one day and told him, "Bob, I'm going to put you in charge of the other war in Vietnam."

Komer recalled asking the President, " . . . What's the other war in Vietnam? I thought we only had one."

"That's part of the problem," Johnson replied. "I want to have a war that will build as well as destroy. So I want to put you in charge of a massive effort to do more for the people of South Vietnam, particularly the farmers in the rural areas, and your mandate will be a very extensive one. In fact I wrote it myself."

Komer explained that under this sweeping order he "engineered the devaluation of the piaster" to fight Vietnamese inflation; unclogged the ports; worked on the refugee problem; developed a land-reform program "to give the farmer a sense he had a stake in the struggle"; built up the police forces and improved local security in the countryside.

Burt, who had seemed somewhat subdued since his first witness left the stand, then led Komer into a discussion of the SD, SSD, and VCI.

Komer took Westmoreland's line, saying they had "some kind of vague function for the defense of the hamlet," but he dismissed them as any kind of real military threat. "The booby trap problem, which caused us considerable casualties at most times, was really a matter of trained Vietcong and sapper units—not these women, children and old men—doing rather artful things with unfired 155 artillery shells. . . . "

Komer also disputed both the broadcast's and Adams' thesis that MACV and Westmoreland had ignored the quantification of these guerrilla forces. He said he had never thought MACV had a very good "handle" on "the more shadowy and less military parts of the VC lineup" and that he had gone to Westmoreland with the problem in the fall of 1966.

At this point, Burt tried to introduce as an exhibit a report Westmoreland's intelligence chief, General Joseph McChristian, had sent to Komer dealing with the guerrilla order-of-battle problem. McChristian's study pointed out some of the same problems that Sam Adams struggled with at the CIA. The figures for self-defense and for secret self-dense forces did not reflect the reality of the situation, the study said.

Boies objected strenuously to admission of the document on the "truth" issue, saying there was no evidence it was an official MACV estimate.

Leval, addressing Boies' objection, showed how hard it was to define the word "truth" in a trial concerned with how various intelligence analysts—sitting in air-conditioned quarters far from the smell of smoke, fire, and flesh—counted guerrillas who came and went with the ease and invisibility of the wind.

"How would you reach an issue of truth?" Leval wondered. "What we are talking about is estimates. We are talking about estimates of enemy strength. We are talking about estimates of capability of different kinds of units. There's no such thing as truth. . . . There isn't any definitive truth to be nailed down."

Burt showed Komer another document relating to the numbers controversy. This study by the Saigon CIA station, titled "MACV J-2 Estimate of VC Irregular Strength—Comments," endorsed MACV's methodology of counting guerrillas. It also seemingly poked holes in Boies' case of a "conspiracy" by declaring that MACV's 1967 estimate of irregular troop strength was "the most comprehensive and coordinated effort to date to accumulate meaningful statistics on a frequently shadowy subject. . . . "

Boies objected again, fighting to have this document excluded from the trial record. This piece of paper substantially reinforced Burt's case, particularly since Komer said he had asked the CIA to prepare it as a independent check of the MACV guerrilla study.

At the sidebar, Boies told Leval that admitting the study would be "in error and prejudicial" because it included "characterizations of events" rather than an estimate. Burt, naturally, defended the document. It did more than just buttress his case. It also put General McChristian, Westmoreland's chief accuser in the documentary, into a box. As he told Leval, "We are introducing the report that went to

Komer over General McChristian's cover letter as evidence of what MACV's best estimates were at the time. . . ."

"The defendants say that they will introduce people who say numbers were arbitrarily cut, slashed," Burt said, his hands chopping the air for emphasis. "Defendants also say that General McChristian is, in Colonel Hawkins' words, a white knight serene, and I believe there is either an admission or a statement in a deposition of some of the defendants that General McChristian did nothing wrong.

"If General McChristian did nothing wrong and General Mc-Christian testifies under oath, sworn testimony, that these were his best estimates, nothing was arbitrarily slashed or cut, and we can establish that these estimates were widely distributed, that goes some way to proving that nothing was suppressed and it was a debate over what categories belonged in the order of battle."

Burt won. Leval overruled Boies, and Westmoreland's lawyer, pleased at winning this skirmish, resumed questioning Komer with more confidence than he had previously displayed.

The former Vietnam pacification chief said that before receiving the report in question he had attended two briefings in Vietnam concerned with quantifying the size of the enemy guerrilla force and thought the process "byzantine."

Komer said one problem in evaluating the size of the guerrilla forces had been that the estimates were based, in part, on captured Vietcong documents, which were unreliable for reasons quite familiar to the Americans. He said these documents often "represented the view of higher VC headquarters . . . and inflation of strength figures was not something confined exclusively to our Vietnamese." Komer said that, besides reviewing MACV's analysis of the combat guerrillas, he also had discussed them with U.S. tactical unit commanders, who had dismissed the SD and SSD as an effective fighting force.

Komer related how he had met with George Carver, the CIA's leading Vietnam expert, during the September 1967 Saigon OB conference, and told him he thought the SD and SSD were too "vague and nebulous" to be included in any enemy-troop-strength estimate. He also had told Carver that if the press discovered the differential between MACV and CIA estimates of the SD and SSD, it would create a serious "credibility gap."

Carver had continued to stick to his guns—insisting that the 120,000 or so SD and SSD be included in the MACV published order of battle, Komer said. At a meeting in Saigon to discuss the issue, Carver and General Phillip Davidson, who had replaced McChristian as MACV intelligence chief, were at "a head-to-head impasse," he said.

Komer had had a private dinner with Carver on September 11, 1967, after which he had reported to Westmoreland, " . . . I thought there was room for a meeting of the minds, if we could get the two sides to back off a little from their turf fight. . . . "

At a "full-scale meeting with all the command group," Komer said, "General Westmoreland then spoke up and said that he thought these differences were readily resolvable and he by and large accepted the viewpoint that George Carver had presented."

Asked by Burt to explain, Komer told him that Carver had presented a compromise which "clearly separated" enemy "civilian elements" from the military order of battle. Carver had agreed, Komer testified, to not quantify the SD and the SSD in the order of battle, but instead put them into a separate, narrative section. Carver had agreed that the evidence on the SD and SSD was "very tenuous, and that while at one point we had estimated that there might be more than 100,000 of them it was very difficult to arrive at any valid numerical estimate at that time," Komer said.

After another brief sidebar conference, court broke for the day. The next morning, Burt quickly finished up his examination of Komer, continuing to qualify him as an expert. He asked how extensively Komer had traveled in Vietnam. Komer said he had visited forty-three of the forty-four provinces, missing the one because "there was supposed to be mostly elephants there and it was utterly insignificant from a military pacification viewpoint."

To refute the documentary's charge that MACV also had hidden increased infiltration from the chain of command, Burt elicited testimony that Komer began receiving the NSA infiltration intelligence in November 1967. And, despite Leval's admonition to avoid the subject of the Tet Offensive, Burt had Komer recall the campaign.

Komer said he was "in my house asleep" when Tet began and during the next three days toured the major scenes of fighting, including Danang, Hue, and Dalat. Asked if the enemy attacked with 500,000 to 600,000 troops (a pet theory of Adams), Komer bluntly replied, "If it had been an attack with 500,000 troops, it would have been one hell of a lot more attack than we were enduring at the time."

Burt nodded smugly and began gathering up the papers on the lectern as he framed his final questions. He asked if Komer had ever conspired to suppress or alter information on the size of the enemy.

"No, sir, I did not," Komer said.

To drive home his point, Burt put it another way, asking if Komer had ever received orders not to report on estimates of enemy strength that he might have obtained.

"At no time during my entire association with Vietnam did anyone ever give me any orders with respect to any ceilings or any preconceived conclusions with respect to enemy strength in Vietnam."

Now it was Boies' turn.

The CBS attorney started his cross-examination by asking Komer about the September 1967 Saigon meetings to resolve the order-of-battle dispute. Komer said it was true he had had an obligation to "loyally" support the MACV command position on the numbers, excluding the SD and SSD from the statistical OB. But this was the result of "our previous understanding with Mr. Carver," he said.

Komer agreed that Westmoreland had not wanted the SD and SSD quantified, but could not say when the general took this stance. Generals Davidson and Godding had helped forge this "command position," he said, noting he knew of no MACV intelligence officers who had believed it deceptive or misleading.

Boies then showed Komer a July 10, 1967, cable Carver had sent to CIA director Richard Helms. The message said that releasing increased enemy-strength figures would cause "political" problems for MACV because it would come at a time when Westmoreland was asking for more troops. Carver told Helms he had suggested to Komer that this problem be resolved by a background briefing for the press. MACV would tell reporters that a "quantum improvement in intelligence data . . . gave us [a] much firmer handle on total size of organized Communist structure, military and non-military, with which we have been coping for past several years."

Komer testified it was Carver, and not MACV, who first suggested that the civilian and military elements be separated in the order of battle. When Boies asked about the difference in guerrilla figures contained in the Carver cable—100,000—and the range in the SNIE for guerrillas, Komer told Boies that they were in "the same ballpark."

"It depends on how you define 'ballpark,'" the CBS lawyer commented.

Komer snapped, "All right, sir, the Detroit Tigers' ballpark. . . . Let's have a common understanding, Mr. Boies."

Next, Boies wanted to know whether Komer knew the number for political cadres or administrative service troops in the Carver cable (80,000).

Komer said he had no personal recollection of the numbers. "I wasn't following this with great care. . . . I thought I had other things to do that were more important toward winning the war . . . ," he said.

So it went, with Boies spending the better part of two days in court trying, with little success, to chip away at one of Burt's most credible witnesses.

Boies managed to score several small hits, but after the trial he admitted that Komer was such a "strong" witness for Burt that he was glad when Komer finally left the stand.

The next witness, retired Air Force Colonel Edward Caton, gave an insider's glimpse of a persistent conflict within the intelligence community: daily intelligence versus the more analytical basic intelligence. (As Sam Adams tells it, with some bias, "The current-intelligence types are very much like reporters, and every reporter on earth thinks the guy who is getting the latest scoop, the hottest smoking poop, is the guy who has the real story. And it may be worthless. The current-intelligence types believe this and they tend to dump on the basic-intelligence types. However, in every OB conference I was ever at, you never saw any current-intelligence types. . . . ")

When he took the stand on October 18, Caton quickly made it clear that he had nothing but professional scorn for one of the documentary's chief accusers and CBS's stellar witness, retired Army intelligence Colonel Gains Hawkins.

Caton had joined the Army Air Corps in 1939 as a reconnaissance photographer and had served in Vietnam as chief of the Joint Intelligence Branch (JIB) in Saigon for a year beginning in June 1966. As Caton explained it, the JIB was "charged with determining the organization, the identification of units, the strength of their personnel, and we were primarily charged with military combat units, to keep track of them." Caton had reported directly to General McChristian "on a daily basis, three to four hours a day," and had often briefed General Westmoreland on the order of battle based on "highly classified intelligence."

David Dorsen stepped into the spotlight for the first time in the trial to examine Caton for Capital Legal, asking the witness if he knew anything about Hawkins' branch, the Combined Intelligence Center, Vietnam (known as CICV).

Caton described the section as "a production and training center for the South Vietnamese intelligence divisions." He dismissed the value of the low-classification CICV reports, particularly when compared to the JIB intelligence, which "carried the highest classification levels."

The colonel said the order of battle Hawkins had produced was of little importance, calling it a "reference document." Caton said he would not even call what Hawkins and CICV put out an order of battle. Waving a copy of Hawkins' OB that Burt handed him, Caton derisively commented, "It's just a handle that's put on this compendium. It shouldn't be confused with the military order of battle."

Caton said Hawkins' OB was merely a "sanitized" version of his own more accurate tally. "We would be current and up to date and his, I say, would be outdated. It's a study. It's a study. His is a reference guide."

The witness said he had briefed Westmoreland frequently on enemy strength, but had never heard him say, as the documentary alleged, "What am I going to tell the president? What am I going to tell Congress? What am I going to tell the press?" However, Joint Chiefs Chairman Wheeler had asked such a question after a briefing in Saigon, he testified.

"He was nonplussed at the evidence we had," Caton said. "It had not been presented to him before he left Washington. As a matter of fact, it was collected while he was on the way. . . . "

Dorsen finished up his direct examination of Caton by asking, " . . . Were there any restrictions placed on you . . . as to what you could report of the intelligence you received or developed?"

"To the contrary," Caton answered. "My instructions were to collect everything I could, analyze it and report it."

After a brief recess, Boies cross-examined Caton, who stuck so firmly to his account of Wheeler's remarks that Boies soon changed the subject, asking the witness to look at a monthly intelligence report called a PERTINREP. Boies wanted to know if this monthly report would have served to "augment" the daily intelligence summaries Caton prepared.

"You have to remember this is confidential," Caton answered. "It's a very limited classification. . . . It's fatuous to say it will augment. It does augment, but it doesn't add to anything, because not everything is in there."

In Caton's view, there couldn't have been much of a conspiracy to keep down the numbers of guerrillas in the order of battle. "Everybody in the world was aware of the problems concerned with and providing evidence to substantiate an increase in the numbers," he said. "I don't know anyone in the intelligence community that wasn't aware of this ongoing struggle."

No matter what Boies tried, Caton deflected the direction and tone of the questioning. He did it again when the attorney asked if he recalled being briefed by Hawkins' intelligence unit on the SD and SSD. Caton did remember receiving a briefing on such a "project," which he dubbed a "training exercise." The information CICV had presented at these briefings was "useless. . . . If you can't use it, why bother to remember it? If it gets validated it will be in a published document and I can turn the pages and find it."

Boies then asked Caton if he recalled any MACV briefing at which higher enemy-strength estimates for the SD and SSD were presented.

"No," the witness said.

He asked if Caton had attended any such briefing in May of 1967

—the one at which the markedly higher numbers for the SD and SSD were allegedly first floated.

"Are you saying the Weekly [Intelligence] Estimate Update? [This document was abbreviated WIEU and pronounced at the trial as "whoooo," like a train whistle.] The hell, that was my responsibility."

Boies said he had no more questions.

Luckily for CBS, when Dorsen took over again, asking Caton further questions on redirect, he made a tactical blunder, getting the witness into a discussion of the various categories of guerrillas, including those oft-disputed "women, young boys and old men" who supposedly had had no military capability.

Caton had described Vietcong assassination squads as guerrillas who would enter a village and "take the school teachers and kill them . . . because they were servants of the government." Then he had said the SSD "apparently had some equipment," adding, "They were capable of using passive—"

At this point, Dorsen, sensing that his witness was straying into dangerous territory, broke in nervously and asked, "Utilizing what?"

Caton answered, "Passive devices, using booby traps, satchel charges—am I to respond to your question?" Caton looked at Dorsen, confused, seeking guidance.

Dorsen tried to change the subject, saying, "The question I would like to pursue . . . "

Seeing an opportunity to gain something from this obstreperous witness, Boies sprang to his feet and said, "If he hasn't finished the answer, I would like to have it."

Dorsen turned to Leval in an attempt to get Caton off the hook. "I think my question may have been unclear, your honor," he said.

The question was read back by the court reporter. Caton, sensing he had given something away, answered this time without mentioning booby traps—one of the key points at which CBS hammered away to prove the guerrillas were indeed a military threat. But Boies didn't let Caton off. When it was his turn to ask more questions, Caton had to admit that the SSD used mines.

"They may have had the claymore mines [an arc-shaped device standing slightly off the ground that, when tripped, spewed hundreds of deadly pellets throughout the arc] we had," he said. "They had a similar weapon or bomb [in] which they sometimes just put pieces of nails, cut up portions [of] any scrap metal they could find. . . . It was a shaped charge and it would just blast out at knee, ankle height and you had casualties."

*   *   *

While Boies worked to influence the jury, John Scanlon and Jim Noonan, the network's PR men, pushed the CBS viewpoint to the press. They did this quite artfully—at least, initially.

The image experts followed the first rule of good public relations: don't hide anything. No sooner was a document mentioned in court or a videotape sequence played on the multiple screens around the courtroom than Noonan, Scanlon, or their associate, Sarah Voss, appeared outside the courtroom with multiple copies. Scanlon set up his own command post in an office five minutes from the courthouse. There, an industrial-strength Kodak photocopier and collator spewed forth declassified documents by the ream. In another room, Sal Friscina, a CBS editor loaned on a full-time basis to the defense team, chopped the documentary into whatever bits Boies and the press needed. At the end of every day, CBS would give the CNN "pool" producer the videotapes relevant to that day's testimony. This producer in turn took the tapes to the CNN mobile unit, where they would be zapped instantly via microwave to all the broadcasters, local and network, in New York.

Not only did Scanlon funnel network information to the media, he also helped reporters keep up with what their colleagues were writing about the trial.

Twice each day, the CBS PR department would copy and pass along to Scanlon all articles about the case that appeared in the country's major newspapers and magazines. Scanlon compiled the stories into booklets, which he initially distributed to the Cravath lawyers and the defendants. When the press asked for copies, he had extras made for them. He used a transcribing service to tape copies of all television stories on the trial, and these were available for viewing in his office.

Working closely with Boies, Scanlon also furnished documents that refuted or contradicted material Burt had introduced into evidence on a given day. With the press, there was no Judge Leval to rule on the admissibility of evidence.

A self-admitted trencherman, Scanlon also organized frequent luncheon expeditions to Chinatown or Little Italy—both close to the court. What reporter would turn down the opportunity to break bread with Mike Wallace? This thorough care and feeding didn't do anything, however, to influence the reporter CBS cared about most— Myron Farber of *The New York Times*.

Farber received extraordinarily personalized service from Scanlon and Cravath. Every day, before the slightly built journalist with the long gray hair and beard left his front-row seat in the courtroom to file his story, Cravath made sure he had the transcript of that day's testimony, as well as a complete bundle of documents.

This special treatment didn't sway Farber to take the CBS side. In fact, within a week of the beginning of the trial, Scanlon and Noonan were complaining to other members of the press corps about Farber's reporting on the case. What irked them most was that he usually left the trial between three and four p.m.—often before Boies had had a chance to cross-examine a witness. Thus, Scanlon and Noonan argued, Farber heard only half the story and his coverage reflected this, making Burt's case look much stronger. Scanlon and Noonan even considered taking their complaints directly to the *Times*, drafting a letter to Farber's superiors.

Burt, of course, also catered to Farber. Westmoreland's defense team did not have the deep pockets or copying capabilities of CBS, but every day of the trial Farber started out with copies of the documents Capital Legal intended to introduce into evidence that day. Halfway through the trial, at a meeting with reporters, Burt denied showing Farber any favoritism. But as Burt finished uttering that sentence, who should walk out of the inner recesses of the lawyer's New York office? Myron Farber.

* * *

If the battle for Farber was a draw, the fight inside the courtroom was beginning to tilt in CBS's favor. Behind the bluster, Burt proved to be a less adequate trial lawyer than Boies. He stumbled verbally. He never relaxed. He made such blunders in questioning witnesses that Leval frequently stepped in to guide him. Worse yet, some of his best witnesses were crumbling on the stand under Boies' relentless cross-examination.

Testimony from General Phillip Davidson, a co-architect of MACV's official position on guerrilla categories in 1967, added almost nothing to Burt's case, although he had been billed before the trial as the man who would have known beyond a doubt if there had been a conspiracy. Davidson confirmed that he was indeed alive and that he had never received a phone call from CBS, but when Boies started asking questions, the former intelligence chief's memory seemed to fail him.

"A lot of what our witnesses were giving on the stand was coming as surprises to us," jury expert Jay Schulman said later. "We had our fingers crossed almost all the time. We'd only worked with a handful of our witnesses because they were mighty muck-mucks."

Some of the witnesses were indicting themselves with their own words, making it easy for Boies. The lawyer's favorite trick was to ask a series of questions, get the answers on the record, and then reach into the mound of paper on his desk and pull out that witness' deposition testimony. Boies would show the jury that what the witness had just said—under an oath to tell the truth—did not jibe with the earlier testimony also taken under oath.

Boies had a subtle verbal tic that clicked in whenever he employed this tactic. He would end every question with the word "sir," putting such emphatic spin on that supposed honorific that it came out as a sarcastic bludgeon.

General George Godding gave Boies ample opportunity to hone this technique. Godding, had who retired as a two-star major general in charge of the Army Security Agency—a hush-hush outfit that performed electronic intelligence-gathering functions for the Army and the National Security Agency—was the officer who had headed the MACV delegation to the crucial August 1967 National Intelligence Estimates Board meeting at CIA headquarters in Langley, Virginia.

Godding joined the Army in 1940 and served in Europe, where he was wounded by a mortar shell. At the end of World War II, by then commander of an infantry battalion, he left the Army and finished college. He rejoined the Army and, in 1949, went into intelligence. He did two tours in Vietnam: one in the spring, summer, and fall of 1967, when he served as chief of intelligence production at MACV, and another in 1972, when he ran the entire MACV intelligence operation.

Godding's testimony was necessary to disprove one of the main points of the documentary's conspiracy theory, what Sam Adams called "the smoking gun"—that Westmoreland allegedly ordered his officers attending that August 1967 Langley meeting, including Godding and Hawkins, to keep the total enemy strength below a ceiling of 300,000.

David Dorsen had handled Godding's deposition testimony, so he stepped in to examine the general in court, starting October 25. Godding testified that before he left for the Langley conference, he had had a meeting with both General Westmoreland and General Davidson, who had taken over as head of MACV intelligence from General McChristian several months earlier. Godding remembered it as a relatively straightforward discussion, with Westmoreland making "no comments" on the estimate except to say, "Your estimate is good. I stand behind it. Move out."

Later, Dorsen returned to this meeting with Westmoreland, asking, "Do you recall whether General Westmoreland made any statements that this headquarters will not accept a figure in excess of the current estimate strength carried by the press?"

"No," Godding answered, repeating his earlier testimony about the meeting. Godding said he had recounted the same conversation for Sam Adams in 1979, telling him "there was no ceiling, we carried back our best estimate." Likewise, Godding said, George Crile had called him three or four times before the documentary was aired and asked essentially the same questions about a ceiling on enemy strength that Adams had asked in 1979. Godding said he had told Crile, "There was no ceiling placed on us. Again, I stated it was the best estimate. . . . "

Dorsen finished up his relatively quick direct examination by inquiring whether Godding was "ever asked to do anything that in your view was improper while you were an officer at MACV intelligence during 1967."

Godding's reply was simple and forceful. "I did not," he said.

That was the last simple moment Godding was to have for the next day and a half. David Boies' cross-examination resembled an inquisition. It took the lawyer less than five minutes to trip Godding up with his own words. Reminding Godding that he had been deposed under oath, Boies asked if he remembered testifying during his deposition that the figures he took to the Langley conference in late summer were from the May order of battle.

"Yes," Godding answered.

Boies then asked, "And you said that every time it came up in the deposition, correct, *sir?*"

"That is correct," Godding agreed.

Boies asked Godding if he had also testified that the numbers he had been "instructed to protect and defend" were taken from the monthly PERTINREP report prepared by Hawkins' intelligence group.

"That's correct," Godding said.

Boies repeated the question, this time ending it with a "correct, *sir?*"

"That's what I testified," Godding replied.

Boies shot back, "Is that true?"

Trying to defend his earlier testimony, Godding said that he had thought the enemy-strength figures Boies had shown him during the deposition were from the PERTINREP because they "rang a bell. . . . "

Like a hawk circling its quarry, Boies narrowed his questions on this point until finally the retired general conceded he "was in error" when he said during the deposition that the figures he took to Langley were from the PERTINREP.

Several jurors who had appeared close to dozing off suddenly leaned forward in interest. Other panelists scribbled on their notepads.

From that point on, Godding would have difficulty keeping his trial testimony straight. For example, he confirmed for Boies that when Adams and Crile called, "I told them that I could not quote any figures, I could not quote the categories and that the material I carried back was the best estimate as of that time that I went back to Langley." But just a moment later Godding testified, "I think the way

I stated it [to Adams and Crile was] that the parameters of the May OB were the basis of it [the MACV command position at the Langley conference]."

Continuing to pull pages from Godding's deposition, Boies attacked the man's credibility and poked holes in the plaintiff's case.

In May 1967, General McChristian and Colonel Hawkins had prepared a report called the RITZ study, which showed that the guerrilla and irregular forces the United States faced in Vietnam were significantly higher than the figures carried in the MACV order of battle. Boies asked Godding if he was aware of such a study.

"I am now aware of it," the former intelligence officer said. After a brief recess, Boies asked Godding if he had been aware of the RITZ study during his deposition in April 1983. Godding answered, "I was not aware of it by name at that time, no," adding that he had become aware of the name over the past four or five months "when I started receiving some documents" from the Westmoreland legal team.

Boies then asked, "Is it your testimony that you only learned the name of the RITZ study when Mr. Dorsen began sending you documents in the last three or four months?"

"I didn't say I learned it," Godding replied. "It brought it back to my attention. I was aware of the RITZ study at the time, yes."

This didn't square with the deposition transcript, which Boies produced with a flourish and read for Godding and the jury. During his deposition, Godding had said he "was not" aware that the RITZ study postulated significantly larger enemy-strength figures than those reflected in the May 1967 MACV OB.

Boies kept badgering Godding on this point until Dorsen objected. But Leval allowed Boies to nibble away, asking Godding almost the same question in slightly altered form, again and again.

"Were you aware that some of the studies showed significantly higher figures?" Boies demanded.

"I said I was aware that they were higher," Godding pleaded. "There were many studies . . . but I was aware of them from a peripheral standpoint and these were briefed to General Westmoreland. . . . "

After gaining this admission, Boies zipped through the 348 pages of Godding's deposition, again hoisting the general on his own petard. During the deposition, Boies had asked Godding if he was aware, while preparing the July 30 order of battle, of information showing estimates of a much larger irregular force.

"No, I do not remember anything, any estimates that pushed the irregulars up significantly," the general had said in the pre-trial testimony. Boies asked him again about this statement, framing question after question until Godding finally conceded, " . . . I was aware of the studies, but I did not remember specifically the results. . . . "

Boies followed this line of questioning for about five more minutes and then, probably to the relief of Godding, abruptly asked Leval if it would be a convenient time to break for the day. It was Friday afternoon and Leval readily agreed, wishing the members of the jury a pleasant weekend. He added wryly, "I think I recall that at least one of you is going on a trip. Please come back."

When the trial resumed on Monday, October 29, Boies continued his assault on Godding as though no time had elapsed. The general's answers made Boies' job easy. The lawyer asked Godding: you are "now aware that there were studies in MACV that resulted in higher enemy strength figures, are you not, sir?"

"In certain categories, yes," Godding agreed, but added that "I don't think they were any bombshell or anything like that."

Boies zeroed in on this statement, getting Godding to admit that the McChristian studies indicated there were uncounted guerrilla forces in the range of 100,000. But Godding refused to concede this was sizable.

Boies asked him, "Is that a significant increase, sir?"

"Well, I think that's a matter of how you want to state it," Godding replied. "I didn't consider it as such, no."

"You didn't consider it as such; is that what you said?"

"That's right."

"You didn't consider an increase of 100,000 in enemy strength to be a significant increase?"

"This was a re-evaluation and so forth . . . ," the general began to explain, but Boies broke in.

"My question goes to what you mean by significant," Boies insisted. "I think you have said that you have trouble defining the word significant in this context; is that fair, sir?"

"I don't have trouble defining the word significant," Godding protested.

Later that day, Boies drew Godding into a discussion of the combat capabilities of the SD and SSD. Again, Godding displayed ignorance.

"Do you know what percentage of the self-defense forces were armed, sir?" Boies asked.

"I do not," Godding replied.

"Do you know approximately?"

"To the best of my recollection, very few."

"You say very few, approximately what percentage, sir?"

"I would say somewhere around ten percent."

"Is that based on any study you have ever seen, sir?"

"No," Godding admitted.

"Have you ever talked to anyone who told you that?"

"No, but in combat, in a similar situation, very few of the old men, women and children were armed and I went through the European war and we had the same type of units there, I mean the same type of people there."

Amazed, Boies asked, "Are you saying that you are basing your answer on what you saw in the *European* war, sir?"

"That is the one I am drawing on, yes."

Boies returned again to Godding's deposition, tripping him up once more. Dorsen finally protested and the lawyers went into a huddle with Leval. Endorsing Boies' strategy, the judge commented that Godding "says different things on different occasions, sometimes in close proximity to one another, and they are entitled to be the basis of examination."

The next day, in one of the numerous mini-summations Judge Leval allowed each side, Boies, facing the jury but well aware of Westmoreland sitting just a few feet away, said, "I think the answer to Mr. Burt's question of did Westmoreland lie to his superiors is 'yes.' . . ."

Burt then delivered his summation and turned the next portion of the case over to Anthony Murry. The trimly bearded, quite hip-looking Murry was a natural in front of the jury, cool and articulate although it was the first time he had ever appeared in federal court. He spoke easily, free from the anger that hobbled Burt. "I wasn't even scared," Murry recalled. "It was beautiful. I didn't know how good it was until I had done it. To me it was like driving a Ferrari after a Volkswagen."

Despite Murry's enthusiasm, the next witness for the plaintiff, former Lieutenant Colonel Everette Parkins, had more trouble holding his story together than General Godding.

Although Parkins had refused to be interviewed by CBS for the documentary, he played an important role in the development of the program's indictment of Westmoreland. He was the West Point graduate who presumably had planned to soar to great heights in the Army but, as Mike Wallace said in the show, "had become so incensed by MACV's refusal to send on reports of an enemy infiltration of 25,000 a month that he lost his temper and shouted at his superior." "The Uncounted Enemy" then quoted Colonel Russell Cooley as saying the superior officer, Colonel Charles Morris, had "fired" Parkins for trying to put the report through to higher echelons. Parkins had subsequently told *TV Guide* that CBS had gotten the story all wrong.

Parkins, a World War II enlisted man who was admitted to West Point at the end of the war and then served as an officer in the Corps of Engineers from 1951 until retiring in 1977, denied under questioning that he had ever taken the intelligence report Wallace mentioned in the documentary to Morris. He also denied he had ever estimated that enemy infiltration in 1967 hit 25,000 a month.

Parkins, a balding, round-faced man with a pleasant expression, visibly bristled when Murry asked him about Colonel Morris.

"I disliked Colonel Morris intensely," he hissed. "I feel that the feeling was more than reciprocated on his part." The argument reported in the broadcast, Parkins testified, had come about when "I delivered a message to the headquarters at one time which was not for Colonel Morris. While I was leaving that message Colonel Morris came in, picked it up. That is when we had the violent argument at which I was told I was fired."

In fact, Parkins testified, the only reason he had dropped that particular message off was that he wanted to use his unit's jeep to go to the PX. To get the jeep, he had to deliver the message first.

The addressee, Parkins related, was a Colonel Liewer, but "Colonel Morris picked it up, started reading it and I am not sure what he was talking about, but he made the statement 'that is not what we are reporting' and started being fairly abusive. I am sure, since I have a very pleasant temper, I retaliated a bit with words and it ended up with him telling me that I was fired."

Parkins acknowledged he had had some conversations with Sam Adams in the fall of 1980. By that time, Parkins was retired and working for Borg-Warner as an engineer. He met Adams at O'Hare Airport, near his home in Ottawa, Illinois, and had dinner with him in Oak Brook, where, he said, he told the former CIA man "essentially the same thing" about the argument.

Murry asked Parkins if he was still friends with any of his Army colleagues, and the former officer answered "yes," but said none of them had influenced his testimony.

The lawyer finished his questioning by asking Parkins the question that was, by this point in the trial, a familiar parting shot: "During the time you were at MACV J-2 were you ever told that there was ever any kind of limit on what enemy strength figure you could report?"

Without pause, Parkins answered, "I was not."

Murry then inquired if Parkins was "ever ordered or asked to falsify any intelligence. . . . "

"I was not," Parkins repeated.

Boies strolled to the lectern, glanced briefly at the jury, and

started his cross-examination by asking Parkins whether Colonel
Cooley's statement on the documentary was true.

Parkins said he couldn't answer the question because he didn't
know what Cooley was talking about in the documentary.

Boies tried another approach.

"Well, do you know whether or not you were fired for trying to
get a report through?" he asked.

"I was fired," Parkins admitted, "but not for trying to get a report
through."

"Do you know why Colonel Cooley would say this?"

"I do not," Parkins answered.

Boies told Parkins, "Colonel Morris, here on behalf of the plaintiff, [said] . . . that the reason he fired you was that you refused to obey
an order to do some kind of statistical study; is that true, sir, or
untrue?"

Parkins' mild expression once again evaporated.

"I do not believe that's a true statement," he said coolly. Pressed
by Boies for an explanation, Parkins said, " . . . I figured the reason he
was firing me was because I was quite active in defending myself. I
did not know the substance of the material that he was talking about
because I could not read it at the time he was reading it. . . . I do not
remember what the contents of that document were."

Boies grabbed at this last statement. "You do not remember anything at all about the contents, sir?" he demanded.

"No," Parkins said.

"It's your testimony that you don't remember anything at all
about what was in that study?"

"I do not remember what was in that study."

Boies then wondered why Parkins had bothered to take the
message to Morris at all.

The former colonel stuck to his jeep story, saying, "There was
one jeep in the group and I wanted to use the jeep to go to the PX and
the only way I could get the jeep was to deliver the study which was
due there."

Boies found this somewhat incredible. Dripping sarcasm, he
asked, "You are not suggesting, sir, that you were just acting as a
messenger here?"

"I was acting as a messenger," Parkins confirmed.

"Just acting as a messenger, taking over a study or a message?"

"That's right."

Boies stared at him in disbelief. "That's your testimony?"

"Yes, sir."

"That's your testimony under oath now?"

"Yes, sir."

Boies knew that Parkins' relationship with the study had been more than that of a messenger and he proved it, using Parkins' own words. Picking up a document from the increasingly disorderly mound on his table, Boies showed Parkins a copy of the affidavit he had made on August 3, 1983. The witness said the statements in the affidavit "were true and accurate" when he made them.

Boies then directed Parkins to look at the second page of the document, where he had testified, "Toward the end of 1967 I supervised the preparation of an enemy strength study." Then, as Boies asked a series of questions with the speed of machine-gun fire, Parkins reversed his testimony of only minutes before.

"Do you see that (the sentence above), sir?" the lawyer asked.

"Yes, I do," Parkins agreed.

"That's the study you served as messenger for?"

"That is right."

After gaining this admission, Boies pressed on.

"Let me be sure I understand," Boies said. "We have been talking about a study you delivered to MACV headquarters?"

"Yes."

"You talked about that with Mr. Murry and you talked about that with me, correct?"

"That's right."

"Now, I had asked you before whether that was a study you supervised the preparation of and you indicated you couldn't recall that?"

"That is right."

"Does this at least refresh your recollection . . . ?"

"I cannot remember all the details. . . . If something was presented to me in the proper fashion I would have said I prepared the . . . enemy strength study. I did that every day of the week there."

Boies was enjoying himself. "This is not just any enemy strength study, is it, sir?" he asked. "This is the enemy strength study you took to Colonel Morris?"

"That's what this says, yes."

In the affidavit, Parkins also had said, "To the best of my recollection and belief, Colonel Morris believed that the study should report enemy strength figures lower than the figures I was reporting." So Boies asked the reluctant witness if it was "clear to you now, sir," that the argument he had had with Colonel Morris was over an enemy-strength study.

Parkins looked uncomfortable. "It is not 100 percent clear that we were arguing about numbers," he mumbled. "It was that we were arguing about a study that had been prepared in the order of battle section. . . . I do not know exactly what inflamed Colonel Morris."

Boies continued to hammer Parkins about the study and the argument, asking, "This was not an argument about a personality conflict or about the way you dressed or what you ate for dinner; this was an argument about the contents of a study you brought him, correct, sir?"

Murry, who had been observing the interplay with mounting concern, finally objected. Boies was being argumentative, he protested.

Judge Leval overruled Murry, and Parkins answered the question, saying, "Even though the argument was about the study, it was still a personality clash."

Before introducing the next witness to the jury, Murry showed a videotape of CBS's interview with the former intelligence officer who, along with Westmoreland, played the heavy in Crile's documentary. In his blue sheet proposing the program, Crile had made Lieutenant General Danny Graham's role in the drama quite clear. The section was titled "The Key Conspirator Takes Charge."

Graham, Crile told his bosses at CBS News, "had been in Vietnam only two weeks when he produced the Crossover Memo. . . . The enemy, it announced, was at long last diminishing in numbers. . . . Its thesis was as welcome as it was startling, since it concluded that the war of attrition now guaranteed victory.

"The problem is the report was based on the false premise that there were 285,000 VC and, beyond that, it purposefully excluded the overwhelming bulk of evidence that showed the VC gaining in strength."

In the proposal, Crile depicted how Graham at a Washington conference "summons the two troubled MACV officers (Godding and Hawkins) to a meeting in the Pentagon. There, in a small room adjoining the offices of the Joint Chiefs of Staff he calls on them to openly falsify the estimates of specific enemy units."

According to Crile, Graham, after the Tet Offensive, approached Navy Lieutenant Commander James Meacham, who maintained a computer data base on the enemy, and asked him "to erase the computers, an illegal action akin to burning official records."

The computer episode, of course, ended up in the finished documentary and had since been denied by Graham and Westmoreland in pre-trial news conferences and interviews.

Graham made an easy target because of his personality and unbridled ambition. Pugnacious, salty in speech, and a hard task-master, the officer had earned many enemies and few friends in his Army service. Sam Adams had become one of the enemies when Graham contemptuously dismissed the analyst's theories and, according to the CIA man, broke the cardinal rule of intelligence by "jacking around with evidence."

Watching the outtakes of this interview in the courtroom, it was obvious that Graham would not be a pushover for Boies. The former intelligence chief more than held his own against America's most feared interviewer, Mike Wallace. In one of the only portions of that interview to make it into the broadcast, Graham brusquely dismissed Wallace's question about tampering with the computer, saying, "Oh, for crying out loud. I never asked anybody (to) wipe out the commuter—the computer's memory. I don't know what he [Meacham] —I honestly haven't got any idea what he's talking about."

The silver-haired Graham, unlike some of the former military officers involved in the documentary, was an unrepentant hawk. Since his retirement, Graham has served as director of an outfit called High Frontier, whose primary purpose is promotion of the "star wars" militarization of space. He backed a tough U.S. nuclear stance and flippantly dismissed concerns over nuclear weapons.

In his research for the trial, Boies had found a documentary that he felt put Graham into proper context, and he argued at length with Leval that the tape should be admitted into evidence. On this program, produced by the Arts of Peace Foundation and titled "In Our Defense," Graham was asked about the effect of nuclear weapons. He replied, " . . . If you had enough wits to walk for 59 minutes and then get behind a lilac bush, you wouldn't be hurt by the bomb."

Boies told Leval this "absurd" remark proved Graham would "make virtually any statement to promote what he believes to be the interests of the military. . . . "

Leval, who did not want to inject any more controversial topics into an already wide-ranging trial, flatly denied Boies' request, saying "we would be calling nuclear scientists to debate to what extent one can or cannot find safe cover under those circumstances."

Wherever Graham planned to stand in the event of a nuclear attack, he stood solidly behind his former leader in this campaign. Like Westmoreland, he was an old-style West Point graduate who refused to break ranks. He had already offered to continue Westmoreland's case should his former commander die during the trial. After Graham was sworn in, Murry (who had also conducted Graham's deposition) lost no time in getting this star witness to condemn the key facts in the CBS documentary.

First, Murry wanted Graham's opinion of the Combined Intelligence Center, Vietnam, the place where CBS's chief accuser, Colonel Gains Hawkins, had worked. Graham dismissed it with the same kind of sarcasm used by Colonel Caton.

"To be perfectly frank, CICV was to me bean counters," he said. Graham added he had had "some real difficulties with the CICV product. For one thing, their strength figures would have a lot of mock certainty in it. You would see a figure like a total in Vietnam of 246,113 people or something like that, as if we knew there weren't 246,112 or 246,111, and that was preposterous."

Murry produced a copy of an order-of-battle document prepared by CICV and handed it to Graham, who glanced at the paper and dismissed it with a wave of his hand. This was not an estimate, he said. "This is an order of battle summary, and so long as it's treated as such, then these mock-precision figures I guess are acceptable."

Graham also dismissed the various categories into which Adams, Hawkins, and McChristian wanted to place the guerrillas, saying it was impossible to absolutely determine which ones were self-defense troops, secret self-defense, political cadres, or whatever. Making this differentiation was "a pedantic exercise that bore little connection to reality," he said.

Graham denied that any artificial ceiling had been imposed on enemy-strength figures during his time in Vietnam. He denied ordering Hawkins and Godding to slash strength figures at the August 1967 Pentagon conference. Graham insisted he hadn't even been at the meeting. He also disputed that infiltration in the fall of 1967 had run in the area of 20,000 a month, saying, "There was no indication of that." He repeated his denial of any attempt to erase any data in the CICV computer and said that while he was in Vietnam "nobody asked me to falsify intelligence."

With that, Murry concluded his examination, and Boies took over. From the first exchange, it was clear that Graham would give Boies no quarter.

The lawyer asked, "Do you remember telling Mr. Wallace in words or substance that the people arguing against the MACV position with respect to enemy strength numbers essentially was only Sam Adams?"

"No, I don't remember saying it."

"You don't remember saying that? Is that what you said?"

"If you will—I am sure that you've got the record there," Graham answered, settling back comfortably on the wooden witness seat in a body-language challenge to the CBS lawyer. "You're paraphrasing. Perhaps I did say something along those lines. I would like to see what you say I said."

Boies then decided to press Graham for details of the third Army-CIA-DIA meeting in 1967 to reach a compromise on the order of battle.

"Did anyone ever tell you what the CIA's position was at the September 1967 Saigon conference?" he asked.

The hard-nosed general refused to give an inch. He shot back, "I have difficulty with that question because I never considered that small group of people that were out in Saigon to be carrying a CIA position."

Graham referred instead to the so-called Special National Intelligence Estimate that was issued in November 1967 and contained the final compromise (the one Adams called a "cave-in") reached at the September meeting.

"The only CIA position that I ever saw on this matter is in this document [SNIE 14.3.67], which is signed. This is the opinion of Richard Helms, the Director of the Central Intelligence Agency."

Graham was such a strong witness that Boies desperately wanted to impeach his credibility. In a conference with the judge, the CBS lawyer tried a number of ploys, only to have Murry object in open court. Leval sustained objection after objection.

Finally, Boies found a lever: a memo Graham had written in April 1968 about yet another OB conference convened after the Tet Offensive. In that memo, Graham said, "We note that the CIA analysis is essentially the same as that presented and rejected prior to the publication of the [November 1967] SNIE with the exception of new minor differences with MACV. . . . "

Leval agreed to let Boies use this memo to try to snare Graham. He did.

Choosing his words carefully, Boies asked, "Did the analysis that these representatives of the CIA, who you understood were representatives of the CIA, put forward [at the April 1968 conference] bear any relationship to the CIA's analysis in 1967? . . . "

Unaware of what Boies had up his sleeve, Graham replied confidently, "It was distinctly different from the CIA position that they had taken in the August—in the 1967 NIE."

Boies then asked if Graham knew whether the CIA "came forth with an enemy strength analysis."

"If they did, I never saw it," the witness said.

Boies immediately introduced the April 1968 memo into evidence, demanding to know whether or not it was true when Graham wrote it.

The general answered yes, it was true, but, when pressed to explain the contradiction, he tried to downplay it, saying he was "essentially referring to the Sam Adams analysis. It's unfortunate shorthand to say the CIA analysis."

Boies was ready to shred Graham's believability like a claymore mine. He went in for the kill, asking, "You say that when you wrote this document your use of the term 'the CIA analysis' was unfortunate shorthand?"

But cutting down Graham was no easy task. The witness threw out an answer that caused the attorney to lose his cool. "I did not foresee this court case, so I used ordinary shorthand," he said.

Inexplicably, Boies took the bait, responding, "I suspect there would have been a lot of documents that wouldn't have been written if anybody—"

Leval interrupted Boies almost angrily. "The jury will disregard that comment," he said. Looking down at Boies, he scolded, "Limit yourself to questions, please."

Boies pounded Graham for a grueling hour, asking about the memo and the contradictions in his testimony. Graham continued to insist that his use of "CIA" in the memo really meant Adams. Boies also wanted to know if there had been anyone at the 1968 conference, besides Adams, who opposed the MACV enemy-strength estimates. Graham's answer drew a roar of laughter from the courtroom.

"There wouldn't have been much of a conference if it had been just Sam Adams against MACV. We would have rolled right over him."

Boies asked Graham if he had, as Crile alleged, returned to the United States in August 1967 from Saigon, and he supposedly ordered the slashing of enemy-strength figures. Taking out a transcript of Graham's interview with Wallace, Boies asked the general if he recalled discussing an August trip with the reporter.

"Yes, something about it," Graham replied, but he could not remember what he had said.

In that interview, however, Wallace had said to Graham, "When you went back to Washington for the National Intelligence Estimate —when? in September 1967?"

Graham had answered, "Yeah."

"You'd been in Vietnam for about a month and you went back there?" Wallace then had asked.

Graham again answered, "Yeah."

Confronted with this discrepancy, Graham breezily dismissed it. "I don't think I was listening very closely. . . . Mr. Wallace rattles them off pretty fast."

Boies then handed Graham a letter he had written to General Davidson in April 1975, indicating that he had been in the United States in August 1967. Again, Graham blithely explained away the contradiction, saying he had "misconstrued that with the time I did come back to Washington in April 1968."

Leaving the issue of Graham's whereabouts for the jury to decide, Boies turned his attention to the order of battle produced by CICV, zeroing in on the inclusion of the VCI, or political infrastructure. Graham obstinately refused even to call the document an order of battle.

"Well, did MACV call it an order of battle?" Boies demanded.

Graham shot back, "Some did, some didn't, I for one."

The general then made probably the most salient point of the trial about the inclusion of this nebulous "infrastructure" in a compendium of enemy forces, saying, "Politicians are normally not arranged in battalions, companies and platoons."

Graham's testimony stretched over three days—with much of the time devoted to numerous arguments at the sidebar over which bits of tape from the outtakes of the documentary could be presented. Some of the TV reporters covering the trial began to feel professional concern about this amateur approach to their business. "Out-takes only tell part of the story," said ABC News producer Dave Tabacoff. "You don't know what went on before the interview and you don't know what went on afterwards. Even out-takes can be taken out of context."

While the lawyers argued at the sidebar, the television artists covering the trial grasped for subject matter. One day, the WCBS-TV artist, frustrated by the dearth of drama, swiveled on the front-row bench, shifted her assortment of chalks and charcoal pencils, and set about drawing all the other artists who were dutifully rendering the uneventful courtroom.

Leval found the numerous conferences a waste of the jury's time and always tried to offer an explanation. On the last day of Graham's testimony, after a protracted session delayed the trial for almost an hour after the lunch break, Leval turned to the jury and told them, "Sorry for the delay. . . . Just so that you will know, it was not because anyone was off playing pinochle or something. I have ruled on 22 different disputed issues in the time you have been waiting. . . . "

Graham and Boies spent the last day the way they had spent the first two—locked in verbal combat, each trying to one-up the other. Boies managed to catch Graham in some more minor contradictions. (In an interview after the trial, Boies said the jury had found Graham to be one of Burt's least credible witnesses, but, he admitted, the general did not give ground the way Rostow and Godding did.)

Boies was on the spot. Although he had discredited Graham somewhat, he needed a memorable finish. He paused for a moment, as though weighing whether he could get away with what he had in mind.

"I have just one more subject," he finally said. "You have stated, have you not, General Graham, that you believe we won the Vietnam War?"

The court became hushed. Although Leval had consistently tried to keep the broad questions surrounding the Vietnam War out of this libel case, it looked as though Boies now intended to put the war on trial.

Graham's one-word response broke the silence. "Yes," he said. Murry quickly objected, but Leval, surprisingly, overruled him. Boies continued.

"How long have you held that belief?" he asked.

"I have—I believed from the time of the Tet Offensive that the communist forces had been militarily whipped in Vietnam," Graham said. "To that degree, my view was that we had—that we won that thing."

Graham, who had been slouching casually during much of his banter with Boies, now sat erect, squarely faced the jury, and delivered his own indictment of the war. "My view has never changed that militarily it was won," he said. "Politically it was lost. . . . We made political decisions to withdraw just as we were making great headway, and I think they—even in the end, had the South Vietnamese been supported, they would have survived the assault from the North Vietnamese."

Murry continued to object. Leval finally called the lawyers to the sidebar and asked Boies what he was doing.

"I am not sure I understand the relevance," Leval said. "I allowed the first question about this . . . because I think you're offering it on the subject of bias and credibility."

Boies agreed Leval had indeed guessed his strategy and said if he was allowed to continue with this line of questioning, Graham would "further testify that he believes the press bears a significant responsibility for what had been described as a political defeat in Vietnam. I believe that goes to his bias in the case."

Boies continued, and Graham answered just as predicted.

"When do you believe the United States ceased providing adequate support for the South Vietnamese?" Boies asked.

"Early in '74 when they refused—when they slashed the military assistance budget to South Vietnam so severely," Graham answered.

"Do you believe that the press played any role in what you view as our political defeat in South Vietnam?"

"Yes, I do."

"At what time?"

"In 1974, sir, the time you were just talking about."

Satisfied that he had made his point, Boies finished his questioning of Graham by asking if he thought that the documentary had adversely affected his reputation and honor and also that of the officer corps.

Graham answered "yes" to both questions.

With that, the still-combative warrior left his verbal duel over an Asian war that was gone but not forgotten and returned to Washington to lobby for arms for future space wars.

15.

Westy Takes the Stand

JUST a few days before he was due to testify in his case against CBS, Westmoreland decided to leave New York City for a reunion with his former troops. It was Veterans Day weekend and there were big plans in Washington, D.C., to dedicate a statue at the new Vietnam Memorial. As it turned out, the timing was perfect for a major public-relations triumph. The media zoomed in on the former commander whenever he turned up at one of the official events, using his battle against CBS to symbolize the rough time many Vietnam veterans had experienced since coming home. The general and his wife made the front page of the *Washington Post* and all three network newscasts, including CBS.

Westmoreland seemed unimpressed by the wildly favorable press. He spent much of his time far from the TV cameras, quietly trekking through hotel suites and lobbies to greet the men and women who had served alongside him in an unpopular war.

Wherever he went, the troops yelled their praise for Westmoreland and his lawsuit. Late Saturday night, the general and Kitsy stepped from an elevator into the lobby of the raffish Hotel Washington and were mobbed by hundreds of vets decked out in camouflage clothing and jungle boots. The rowdy crowd was eager to shake his hand, get his autograph, or trade war stories. The general drank up this support with a wide smile, appearing truly at ease for the first time since the start of the trial.

In the basement of the Hotel Washington, meanwhile, a more organized demonstration for the commander was in full swing. A group of veterans who viewed the CBS documentary as an attack on all Viet vets had put together an impressive counterattack almost a year earlier. Operating out of a "Veterans for Westmoreland" booth, the volunteers were raising money for the general's defense and passing out red-white-and-blue buttons emblazoned with the slogan WESTY'S WARRIORS.

The leaders of this effort—Tony Bliss, a lanky veteran who had served with the Army's 101st Airborne Division in Vietnam and then spent eight years on the foreign desk of *The New York Times*, and Bernie Palitz, a graying, gruff, and tough World War II 101st Airborne vet—had already raised $77,000 for the general and planned to contribute even more. The group ran ads in virtually all the military-association publications, and some, such as the *Static Line*, reported each month on contributions made by various units. One $55 donation came from three World War II veterans of the Office of Strategic Services—the CIA's predecessor.

"General Westmoreland had no choice but to sue for libel," the group said in its literature. "His fight is for more than his own honor. It is for all of us—for every veteran and for the military as an institution."

Bliss said the group was formed because a lot of veterans felt their own integrity had been attacked by the documentary. "They also resent the fact that CBS and its PR men have tried to turn this into a battle of the Right versus the media."

One contribution, he said, came from a paratrooper who was injured in a jump. "Westy dropped down next to him and took care of him until the medics arrived."

Another letter on display at the WESTY'S WARRIORS booth was from a veteran named Fagan in Boise, Idaho, who had been in the 101st Airborne. The soldier said he was sending $1 to beat "those CBS anti-veteran scribes. I can't afford to send any more because I'm disabled and I can't work. I believe in you and what you are and stand for and will fight any man who says different. . . . Us paratroopers stick together. Geronimo on your way to victory."

In an interview with the *Atlanta Constitution*, Westmoreland said he was "amazed" by the fund-raising drive. "I did not initiate it, I did not endorse it, but I told them that if that's what they wanted to do I would not reject it. I was touched by it."

* * *

Westmoreland needed the psychological boost he received that weekend. Just a month into the trial, Burt's case against CBS in the courtroom appeared less solid than it had in the months before the trial. David Boies continued to knock down Burt's witnesses by using their deposition testimony to impugn their trial testimony. Or he would use trial testimony from one day to raise doubts about testimony given on a later day.

Few witnesses coped successfully with this tactic, but Colonel John Stewart—one of the few active-duty officers to testify at the trial (he had been the intelligence chief during the Grenada invasion)—proved an equal match for Boies. Stewart had been an intelligence officer in Vietnam in 1967 and 1968 and strongly disputed the documentary's thesis that the self-defense and secret self-defense militia omitted from the order of battle had posed a military threat. The colonel termed them "little more than a motley crew" and an "insignificant" fighting force.

During the second day of cross-examination, Boies tried to knock down Stewart's strong testimony by getting him to put a number on this "insignificant" force. But Stewart wisely refused to play. He told Boies, "You'll get me to say an approximate figure, Mr. Boies, and then hoist me on my own petard. The answer is, I don't recall."

George Carver, the CIA's Special Assistant for Vietnamese Affairs (SAVA) and Sam Adams' boss, did not fare as well, although his direct testimony seemed a strong blow against CBS. An Asia hand with far more experience than Adams (Carver had been born in Shanghai, where his father was chairman of the University of Shanghai's English Department), the former CIA man first praised Adams' "enthusiasm, energy and imagination," but then dismissed his former subordinate as "intolerant" and prone to jump to conclusions.

As Adams took copious notes on a yellow legal pad only a few feet away, the balding, testy, almost gnomish Carver insisted General Westmoreland's command had not hidden enemy-troop-strength data from anyone.

In fact, he asserted, Westmoreland's command had generated so much information that many analysts found it "too much for their in-baskets. . . ." MACV, he added, "never withheld raw data from anyone in the intelligence community."

Besides serving as the CIA's in-house Vietnam expert, Carver had also acted as the Agency's liaison to Defense Secretary Robert Mc-Namara. He had directed the preparation of two key CIA reports that advised the Secretary the U.S. bombing campaigns could not win the war, regardless of the military's rosy predictions. Despite this important role, CBS producer Crile had not interviewed Carver until a week before completing the documentary—a fact that had been driven home in both the *TV Guide* article and the Benjamin Report. Now Burt planned to use it to prove Crile had weighted the documentary in favor of those "witnesses" who backed Sam Adams' viewpoint while ignoring those who disagreed. The lawyer returned to this point again and again while questioning Carver.

Any gains for Burt, however, were quickly dashed when Boies

took over. On cross-examination, the lawyer neatly impaled Carver on his own deposition and also showed that the witness had been extensively rehearsed. Carver admitted he had met with Burt or other Westmoreland lawyers "maybe a dozen, maybe two dozen" times in the year before the trial.

More important, Carver had written critically of MACV's enemy-strength estimates, and Boies eagerly introduced a January 1967 memo—written by Carver—that sounded like it could have been from Sam Adams. He wrote, "We believe the MACV Order of Battle of communist ground forces in South Vietnam, which on 3 January carried the number of confirmed Vietcong, including North Vietnamese at 277,150, is far too low and should be raised, perhaps doubled."

Asked to elaborate, the ex-CIA man testified, "It was an expression of view, and I go on to point out that [of] the four components in the Order of Battle, two of which are already being looked into and two of which needed further address, and I asked the director of intelligence if they would work on the remaining ones."

Carver said he had sent the memo because " . . . I wanted to get their attention."

Mindful that General Westmoreland would take the stand the next day, Boies used this cross-examination to introduce into evidence the scathing memo Adams had written Carver when he resigned as SAVA. In this memo, which established the parameters of the two-decade-long obsession that eventually led to the trial, Adams told Carver:

"The pressures on the CIA and SAVA, I realize, have been enormous. Many of those pressures—but not all—have originated from MACV, whose Order of Battle is a monument of deceit. The Agency's and the office's failing concerning Viet Cong manpower, I feel, has been its acquiescence to MACV half-truths, distortions, and sometimes outright falsehoods. We have occasionally protested, but neither long enough, nor loud enough."

After Carver left the stand, the two lawyers took the opportunity to deliver another set of mini-summations. The trial had now been under way for a month, and Burt told the jury that his case so far reminded him of a part of Gains Hawkins' interview with producer Crile that was not included in "The Uncounted Enemy." Hawkins had said, "George, there was so much noise being made, I don't see how anybody could have been kept in the dark."

"That noise is still being made," Burt said. "Nobody is in the dark now and nobody was in the dark then."

Boies told the jury that although all the witnesses to date had been the plaintiff's, even this hand-picked testimony supported the CBS case. Burt's witnesses, he said, had essentially confirmed "there was a ceiling, an upper limit that MACV believed had to be placed on enemy strength figures."

The drama of the next few days, however, would eclipse any oration either lawyer could devise. General Westmoreland was about to confront his accusers.

*   *   *

As the Westmorelands approached the courthouse on November 15, the general's first day on the witness stand, they were again confronted by a media circus. Television mobile units ringed Foley Square. A mob of still photographers equipped with motor-driven cameras had staked out the broad front steps of the courthouse and the side door. Westmoreland alone would have warranted a throng of reporters, but this was a double feature: the Day of the Generals. One day earlier, Israeli General Ariel Sharon's libel suit against *Time* magazine had started on the first floor of the same courthouse. Sharon, who decided to play along with the press, marched up the front steps in full view of the cameras, but dodged a reporter's request that he compare his trial to Westmoreland's.

The MACV commander, granite jaw thrust firmly skyward, chose the side door, deflecting questions with a terse "No comment."

In the case against *Time*, Sharon claimed the magazine had libeled him by saying he had discussed with the family of assassinated Lebanese leader Bashir Gemayel the need for them to take "revenge" on his killers. The *Time* article then portrayed the Israeli general as being responsible for the Phalangist militiamen's 1982 massacre of Palestinian civilians at two refugee camps outside Beirut. "This was a lie," Sharon's lawyer, Milton Gould, told the jury.

Just as Westmoreland considered the CBS broadcast an insult to his West Point code of ethics, Sharon considered the *Time* article an insult to his Jewish tradition. "My parents were Hebrew . . . they fought for the truth," he told the jury on the day before Westmoreland took the stand upstairs. "We were brought up that way, defending the truth—your truth, the people's truth. That was also what brought me here 6,000 miles away from home to this American courtroom."

Like CBS, *Time* had selected Cravath, Swaine & Moore to handle its defense. Thomas Barr, the Cravath partner heading the *Time* defense team, like Boies, had never handled a libel case. In fact, during much of his stint at Cravath, Barr had directed IBM's defense against the Justice Department lawsuit that Boies also worked on. Boies considers the often intense Barr "the lawyer at Cravath most influential in developing me as a lawyer."

The press had a field day making comparisons between the two cases brought by two generals against two different and powerful news organizations. George Crile saw many similarities and readily offered them to the *Washington Post*.

"Both these generals presided over disasters," Crile told the *Post*. In Westmoreland's case, he said, it was "the only war we ever lost," while in Sharon's case "it was a massacre that happened on his watch."

Shortly after Crile gave his view of generals, Westmoreland took the stand in his case against CBS. Sitting straight as a flagpole and wearing a gray suit with a Vietnam service ribbon pinned to the lapel, Westmoreland told a capacity audience (more people were lined up outside, where U.S. marshals deftly let one person into the court for every one who came out) the particulars of his life: birth in tiny Saxon, South Carolina; education at West Point and the Citadel, a military college in Charleston, South Carolina, whose students took part in the bombardment of Union forts during the Civil War. He then detailed his military career from his first post through his early days in Vietnam.

As he spoke, Westmoreland frequently glanced at Kitsy, who sat in the third row pretending to be engrossed in her needlepoint, snipping off gray and beige threads with the Swiss Army knife she used as sewing scissors. From time to time, she looked up, caught his gaze, and smiled encouragingly, apparently relaxed. But she was gripping the little knife so tightly that her knuckles showed white.

After the biographical sketch, Burt turned the general's focus onto the case. Westmoreland recalled he had spent three or four days a week in the field in Vietnam, talking to officers at every level of command, "all the way down to battalion and sometimes company" level. "I don't recall the word self-defense and secret self-defense coming forth in these briefings," he said.

Burt, who treated Westmoreland with deference bordering on the obsequious, then guided the general into a discussion of the cable General Joseph McChristian had given him concerning these guerrilla troops at the heart of the CBS broadcast. The figures McChristian had brought to Westmoreland would have sharply increased the strength of the enemy the United States faced in Vietnam. Mike Wallace had charged in the documentary that Westmoreland "suppressed" McChristian's cable.

After the fateful message to Westmoreland, McChristian had been transferred out of Vietnam. Wallace had said, "It was at that point, we believe MACV began to suppress and then to alter, critical intelligence reports on the strength of the enemy."

Westmoreland dismissed any connection between the transfer and the cable.

"Well, General McChristian, he wanted a command," he said. "Frankly, he wanted a command in Vietnam. He was an armored officer and we had no armored divisions in Vietnam. And I corresponded with [Army Chief of Staff] General Johnson [and asked] . . . if he could put General McChristian in command of an armored division, and I did receive notice that he would be reassigned to Fort Hood, Texas, and given command of an armored division."

This all had happened in April 1967, Westmoreland testified, well before McChristian came to him in May with the cable.

In the documentary, McChristian had said Westmoreland seemed "quite disturbed" by the higher enemy-strength figures contained in the cable. He had told CBS, " . . . I had the definite impression that he felt that if we sent these figures back to Washington at that time, it would create a political bombshell."

Westmoreland's recollection of this scene differed sharply from McChristian's. He said he had just come in from the field when McChristian arrived with the cable. After looking at it, Westmoreland testified, he had told McChristian, "Joe, we're not fighting these people. They're civilians. They don't belong in the numerical strength of the enemy."

He said he had told McChristian he wanted to "reflect" on the contents of the cable.

"I was not about to send a cable without a briefing. . . . Such a cable, with its numbers, would be terribly misleading and could be misconstrued by people not familiar with this category," Westmoreland testified.

Burt asked if McChristian had disagreed with Westmoreland's decision. The general's answer broke the tension in the court, evoking laughter. "I don't see how he could. After all, I was the commander," Westmoreland answered, with emphasis on the words "I" and "commander."

During his second day of testimony, Westmoreland conceded— as the broadcast had asserted—that he had realized McChristian's cable could generate adverse publicity. But the general insisted he had never used the word "bombshell."

"I am confident I did not use those words," he said. "Bombshell is not part of my lexicon." He remembered telling McChristian, "Joe, if this cable goes in without further explanation it will create a public relations problem."

Asked if he had told McChristian to reduce the guerrilla-strength estimates, Westmoreland answered forthrightly, "I did not."

Having dealt with McChristian's charges, Burt asked Westmoreland to focus on his other main accuser, Colonel Gains Hawkins.

"Did Gains Hawkins ever complain to you?" the lawyer asked.

"He never did," Westmoreland replied.

"About anything?"

"Not that I can recall."

Burt then asked if McChristian had ever complained about any order Westmoreland gave, and the general answered with a simple "No." He gave the same curt reply to questions about whether any intelligence officer in his command had complained about being ordered to alter figures, suppress figures, or distort intelligence—the core of the CBS "case" against Westmoreland in the TV show.

"No," Westmoreland said again and again.

This exchange came right after one of the most theatrical moments of the trial. Burt had asked Westmoreland, "Can you tell me whether when you were COMUSMACV [if] there was any policy in effect whereby you could, whereby a junior officer could complain to you?"

Westmoreland said he had had such a policy and that it extended to even the most junior enlisted man. He then reached into his inside coat pocket—where, as he had revealed during his deposition, little notes to himself and assorted small oddments were often stashed—and pulled out a card, about the size of a playing card, bearing the MACV shield.

Burt made a great show of offering the card into evidence (exhibit 1704) and telling the general, "We will have to mark on it."

"It is my only copy," Westy protested.

"We'll put a little tag on it, a very little tag," Burt assured him.

Boies, who watched the performance with bemusement, did not object.

Westmoreland settled a pair of black-framed, Army-issue reading glasses on his nose, briefly studied the card, and then explained that it had been given to MACV officers and contained fifteen points, most of them concerning tactics and administration. The most important, he said, was, "Make the welfare of your men your primary concern, with special attention to mess, mail and medical care.

"But the second one is: 'Give priority emphasis to matters of intelligence, counterintelligence and timely and accurate reporting,'" he said.

"And then number 13, I shall read it, says: 'Maintain an alert "open door" policy,' open door in quotation marks, 'on complaints and a sensitivity to detection and correction of malpractices.'"

As the jury passed the card around, examining it, Westmoreland explained that every commander in MACV, down to the level of platoon commander, had received a copy.

With this bit of theater, Burt managed to impress on the jury that, despite the charges contained in the documentary, Westmoreland had gone to great lengths to hear complaints of the kind Hawkins said he had raised but could not get heard.

That was not all the drama for the day. Next, Burt asked Westmoreland about a cable CBS had used as a prime piece of evidence against him in its broadcast: the August 20, 1967, message from his deputy, General Abrams, to General Wheeler, chairman of the Joint Chiefs of Staff. In "The Uncounted Enemy," CBS misidentified this cable as coming from Westmoreland to prove he had wanted to hold down enemy-troop-strength figures due to fear of adverse publicity.

In the message, Abrams worried that the press would react strongly to the "inflated" irregular-force figures some intelligence analysts were recommending. "Now . . . the newsmen immediately seize on the point that the enemy force has increased about 120–130,000," the cable said. "All available caveats and explanations will not prevent the press from drawing an erroneous and gloomy conclusion as to the meaning of the increase."

Burt asked Westmoreland if he had written the cable, and the witness replied, "I did not." But the general agreed with Abrams that press reaction to increased enemy-strength figures was of great concern.

Burt asked him why.

Westmoreland thought for a moment, then leaned forward slightly to ask if he could elaborate in his answer. Satisfied that he had a green light, the general launched into a strong attack on the press coverage of the Vietnam War and an equally strong—no, impassioned—defense of the men who fought that war.

"The Vietnam War was unique in many respects, namely that we were fighting an unorthodox enemy halfway around the world, an enemy supported by armies to the north, namely North Vietnam," Westmoreland began quietly.

Judge Leval interrupted, saying, "You're dropping your voice." With that, Westmoreland sat up even straighter, squared his shoulders, and delivered one of the most eloquent speeches of the trial:

"It was also unique by virtue of the fact that the war was territorially confined to the territory of South Vietnam, except for the bombing to the North, which was not my responsibility. In the context of answering this question, this was the first war without censorship, it was the first war ever fought that was covered by television, it was a unique experience for those of us on the battlefield and it was a unique experience to the media. Considerations were given to press censorship and they were ruled out. I did not approve at the time for the initiation of press censorship.

"My troops did a wonderful job. . . . I was proud of them, they were proud of themselves, and properly so. They did a difficult job in this time frame. They were doing it magnificently. They never thought —and I got this everywhere I went—they were getting a fair shake from the media. . . . "

His voice full of emotion, Westmoreland paused for a moment, but the spellbound room kept quiet. Some observers dabbed at their eyes as the general cleared his throat and continued.

"How the war was reported was important to my troops in the field—they got clippings from home—and when they didn't get this credit it was detrimental to their morale.

"At one time I had 500 reporters accredited to my headquarters. They were not organized as a group. Every individual was on his own. There was great competition for lead stories. Most of the stories were very good and accurate, but there [was] a number that weren't. . . .

"Sure, we were sensitive to press reaction. We would have been dumb oxes if we weren't. I felt an obligation to my troops that what they were doing be given the credit they deserved, and to come out publicly with a statement they were fighting over 100,000 more people than we said we were fighting, which was a distortion—the additional people were not fighters, they were not fighters we wanted to do battle with, they were not people we wanted to kill, they were basically civilians—and to come out with a hard figure that was brought about by virtue of adding these people would have been terribly detrimental to the morale of my troops. . . .

"Certainly we were sensitive to press reaction, and it's very logical that we be that. So I certainly agreed with General Abrams' language. I agreed with it then, I agree with it now, and if I had to do it over again I would agree with it."

At the next courtroom break, David Boies conceded to reporters crowded around him in the hallway that, following this performance, he would have to tread carefully in his cross-examination.

"It's very difficult to figure out how to cross-examine a seventy-year-old, retired war hero; you've got to be a gentleman but bring out the truth," he said, lifting his hands in a gesture of mock helplessness. It would be a "no-win situation" if he was either too soft or too hard on Westmoreland.

The general's simple eloquence won him points in the ongoing media battle. *Washington Post* reporter Eleanor Randolph equated the scene with the card to television drama:

"It was a moment that would have warmed Perry Mason's heart in a trial that up to now has featured mounds of dry, 17-year-old documents and men with creaky memories." She then observed, "Clearly, the surprise witness so far in Westmoreland's case has been Westmoreland.

"Among the legal insiders who have followed the trial over five weeks, the general was not expected to do well as a witness. . . . But in two days of answering questions from his lawyer, his well-schooled military bearing has translated into an air of confidence."

The general didn't feel as confident or comfortable as he appeared. In an interview after the trial, he described it as an "odd, strange experience." Although he was at the center of attention on the witness stand, he felt cut off from the judge, cut off from the jury. It took all the control he could muster to keep from acting on what he really wanted to do: to get up, stroll over, and casually discuss the case with them. He wanted to get to know them and let them get to know him. "But there was an iron gate," he said ruefully. "You couldn't be friendly with the judge, you couldn't be friendly with the jury."

On Monday, November 19, Burt let Westmoreland press his case directly against the documentary, Crile, and Wallace. Since the program aired, the general had complained about having been "set up" by CBS. This was his chance to have a jury listen to his story.

It all began innocently, Westmoreland testified. Mike Wallace called and asked his help on a CBS program about Vietnam. The general recalled how he had asked Wallace " . . . is this going to be a 60 Minutes type program? And he says, oh, no, this is going to be an educational and objective program. . . . "

The courtroom audience roared with laughter at this remark.

(In a mid-trial interview, Crile dismissed Westmoreland's interpretation of this phone call as ridiculous. "I was there," he said. "The general broke into straight, old-fashioned deception. . . . The one thing almost anyone in this country knows is if Mike Wallace is calling about the Vietnam War or the situation in Lebanon, it's not going to be an educational broadcast.")

After the laughter subsided, Westmoreland replayed the events leading up to his "lynching" by CBS. He emphasized the lack of candor by both Wallace and Crile as to the real focus of the documentary. When Westmoreland angrily testified that during the interview Wallace and Crile had "orchestrated a scenario so that they would go for the kill," saying, "They wanted to go for the jugular," Boies rose to his feet and objected. He asked the judge if they could talk at the sidebar.

Boies had kept his objections to a minimum during Westmoreland's direct testimony, but this was too much.

"Your honor, I would move to strike the last answer," the lawyer said evenly. "I would also ask the court to instruct counsel for the plaintiff, and if necessary, to directly instruct the witness about some of the speeches he is making. . . .

"I think I have been fairly patient, when we have gone through speeches last week, including him taking out of his pocket a card to demonstrate things he had not previously . . . identified to us, although it was perfectly clear that Mr. Burt was aware of what was coming—the speech about the Vietnam Memorial and what his men told him at that time.

"Now this talk about being ambushed and lynching is highly prejudicial. It is something that is not one or two spontaneous slips, but it is something that has been prepared. I think it is not relevant, I think it is not competent testimony, and I think it's prejudicial. I think we ought to have it stopped, and stopped now."

Burt argued that his witness had not been coached, that his testimony "goes to the obvious pain and suffering and the question of damages." He took aim at CBS's video techniques. "More importantly, sir, on that interview they close-framed him, they put the shots in tight, they got him licking his lips, and that may very well be argued, and I believe I have heard the argument before, that that is evidence of guilt, he was caught, he was trapped, and I think he is entitled to explain what happened."

Leval thought a moment, then said it was "appropriate" for Westmoreland to explain his mental process during the interview. But he added, "I do agree with Mr. Boies that a very large part of the last answer consisted of inadmissible testimony. . . . "

Burt then pressed the judge on whether or not he could guide Westmoreland into recalling how he had felt "rattlesnaked" by Crile and Wallace. Leval pondered this, answering indirectly, " . . . It's appropriate for him to testify as to his confused and unprepared, disturbed state of mind."

Burt continued to take his client through the 1981 interview with Wallace, eventually asking, " . . . Did you communicate [your] state of mind in words or in substance to anyone who was present at the end of the interview?"

Boies quickly objected, but Leval overruled him, saying, "I will instruct the jury afterwards."

Burt repeated the question, and Westmoreland replied, "I said I was deceived as to the nature of the interview and I said 'I have been rattlesnaked.' "

Getting this testimony in was no small victory for Burt. It advanced his cause both in court and in the battle for public opinion. The "rattlesnaked" quote jumped out of newspaper headlines the next day.

At this point, Westmoreland's reckoning was interrupted by another witness, William Bundy, whose tight time schedule required him to testify in mid-November or not at all. As it turned out, LBJ's Assistant Secretary of State for Far Eastern Affairs added little to either side's case.

After Bundy left the stand, Burt switched his focus to establishing the damages—both to emotions and to reputation—the general claimed to have suffered. Over Boies' strenuous objections, Burt managed to introduce articles and newspaper editorial cartoons attacking Westmoreland after the broadcast. (Westmoreland called one cartoon "the most humiliating experience.") He also introduced letters Westmoreland had received after the show aired, including a scathing attack from a Houston woman named Linda Shelton. Shelton had written:

"Your interview with Mike Wallace, Saturday, January 23, 1982, and what I saw on Vietnam appalled me.

"For years the American public resented, even hated Lyndon Johnson for the mismanagement of the war when in reality so much of it was your lack of leadership and lies.

"You ordered our sons, husbands, brothers, fathers, and friends to fight a hopeless battle against insurmountable odds. How could you have such little regard for our young Americans? You knew that these boys were going to their death and so they did.

"You played God with those lives and to this day American parents are still grieving. If anyone ever deserved to be stripped of their so-called honors it is you. You lied to President Johnson and to Congress hoping to buy time and come out a hero. You made the statement that we won the war over there but lost it at home. We lost the war . . . period!

"After seeing that show on TV, I hope the American people never give you another moment's peace. You needed a lot of help in making decisions but refused to listen to the advice of those around you. The aftermath now lies on your shoulders."

After reading this, Burt asked Westmoreland how long he had been in the Army.

"Forty years," Westmoreland answered.

Burt then asked, "General Westmoreland, while you were in uniform did you ever lie to one of your superior officers?"

Westmoreland replied loudly, "Never!"

With that, Burt told the judge, "We have no further questions at this time."

After a short recess, Boies, calmly, almost diffidently, took his turn with the general. He didn't bother with polite preliminaries. Within minutes, Boies was up to his favorite trick, tripping Westmoreland up by finding contradictions.

"I believe that you testified that you did not have a reporting obligation to the President of the United States, correct, sir?" Boies asked. The "sir" was somewhat less cutting than with previous witnesses, but Boies' intent was unmistakable.

Westmoreland answered, "I don't recall that."

Boies then showed him where he had given such an answer during the trial. Next, he asked if Westmoreland remembered briefing LBJ on enemy-troop-strength figures in the Cabinet Room of the White House during a trip to the United States in April 1967.

"I frankly don't remember being that specific," the general replied.

Boies then hauled out an exhibit previously used by Burt, the notes Assistant Defense Secretary John McNaughton had taken of a discussion between the President and Westmoreland on April 27, 1967. In the documentary, Mike Wallace had stated that at that meeting Westmoreland told Johnson "the Vietcong's army had leveled off at 285,000 men. And, best of all, he told the President, the long-awaited cross-over point had been reached. We were now killing or capturing Vietcong at a rate faster than they could be put back in the field."

The McNaughton memo, almost to the word, agreed that this was indeed what Westmoreland had told the President.

Boies gave the memo to Westmoreland and asked him to look at the section referring to the strength figures and the assertion that the cross-over point had been reached. "Do you see that, sir?" Boies asked.

"I do," the general said.

"Did you tell that to the President on or about April 27, 1967?"

"According to those notes I did. I don't, frankly, recall making the statement."

Westmoreland next inadvertently strengthened Boies' case by endorsing the authenticity of the McNaughton memo.

"Do you have any reason to doubt the accuracy of these notes?" Boies asked.

"I have no reason to doubt or not doubt the accuracy," the general said.

Prodded by Boies, Westmoreland finally conceded that the 285,000 figure included the guerrilla forces and that the estimate had been "given to me by my intelligence chief," General Joseph Mc-Christian. After more back-and-forth over this figure and whether or not it had changed after April 1967, Boies asked Westmoreland a question directly related to the documentary's charge of a cover-up.

"At the time you presented to President Johnson the figures that General McChristian had presented to you, did you believe the irregular category, or what you referred to . . . as the guerrilla forces, were substantially understated?"

"What's the date of this now?" Westmoreland wanted to know.

"April of 1967, when you presented this 285,000 figure to President Johnson."

"No—no," the general answered. "I thought—I considered them the best estimate that General McChristian could compile."

Boies then asked if General McChristian or anyone else at MACV had told him prior to the April meeting that they believed the 285,000 figure was "seriously understated."

"Not that I recall," Westmoreland said.

Boies asked Westmoreland if he remembered receiving a report from the Honolulu OB conference in February 1967. Again, Westmoreland's memory failed him.

"I don't recall that I received a report," he said. "I'm quite sure there was a report. I was quite aware of the purpose of the conference." But he added that he could "not recall" receiving either a written report or an oral briefing from McChristian after the conference.

Boies also got Westmoreland to concede that the MACV order of battle included the self-defense and secret self-defense forces, but in his answer the general referred to it as the "so-called order of battle."

Boies wanted to know why the general used that term.

"I say 'so-called' because, in effect, it was a misnomer . . . ," Westmoreland explained. "It was a procedure we had carried over from the Vietnamese."

This "misnomer" continued, Westmoreland said, "up until the Special National Intelligence Estimate had been formulated and published." The general also admitted that the political cadre—more "civilians"—was in the order of battle, adding that "this was a matter we accepted and hadn't really concentrated on yet."

Boies moved on to the next objective.

Earlier, Westmoreland had testified that the purpose of the February 1967 conference was to ensure that everyone was "playing off the same sheet of music." Now the CBS lawyer wanted to know exactly what he had meant by that expression.

Westmoreland answered, "There would be similar criteria . . . so there would not be two or three or four enemy estimates."

Boies then asked Westmoreland, as he had previously, "Was it your understanding that the participants at this conference, as you put it, focused on what category should and should not be included in the order of battle?"

"Well, I did not attend the conference," Westmoreland said.

"But you have a report?" Boies insisted.

The general did not want to go back over this ground, so he tried to end the questioning by saying, "I can't talk in detail about the conference."

But Boies was not ready to quit. He tried to ask if Westmoreland had received some kind of briefing after the conference. Burt objected, but Leval overruled him and Boies set out again to pursue this question. Before he could complete the question, Burt objected again. This time, Leval sustained the objection.

Finally, Boies gave an angry speech, accusing Westmoreland of deliberately forgetting that McChristian had briefed him after the conference.

"General Westmoreland, I suggest to you, sir, that following this conference, General McChristian, your intelligence chief, told you that at this conference the entire intelligence community had focused on what should be included in the Order of Battle and he told you that and I ask you is that not so?"

Burt objected and Leval sustained it "for the future," but he allowed it to be answered "for this question."

Westmoreland drew in a breath and said, "I don't recall what General McChristian told me."

With time that day running out, Boies tried to reconstruct the encounter in May 1967 when McChristian brought Westmoreland the draft cable.

"In the course of discussing that draft cable with General McChristian, did he refer you to the conclusions of the February 1967 conference, sir, if you recall?"

Again, Westmoreland didn't recall. Mercifully for him, court recessed for the day.

The next morning, Boies continued to grill Westmoreland about the OB and the McChristian cable. Westmoreland seemed to have grown feistier overnight. Boies pressed him to admit that he told McChristian the higher guerrilla figures would create a "political bombshell," but Westmoreland refused to back down an inch. With Judge Leval's help, he even managed to hurt Boies a little.

"On your direct examination," Boies began, "you said you were certain . . . that bombshell was not part of your lexicon. Do you recall that?"

"I do," the general said warily.

"And when you said 'bombshell' was not part of your lexicon, did you mean by lexicon, your vocabulary, the kind of words you used?"

"Well, I don't recall using that term, it is not a term that is in my lexicon or familiar to me, or is frequently used. . . . "

Boies then showed Westmoreland a place in his deposition where he *had* used the word "bombshell." Westmoreland peered at the passage with only moderate interest and commented, "Bombshell has been thrown around so much, and I heard it so much during 14 days of depositions with you, Mr. Boies, that you thrust it right into my lexicon."

Somewhat taken aback, Boies said, "Would you take a moment and look back on the questions and look back as many pages as you wish, and tell me when you find the page in which I thrust the word 'bombshell' into your lexicon."

Westmoreland was ready for this one. "Well, I have it right in front of me, I just read it," he said.

"That was your word, right, sir?"

"Yes."

"Now, what I want to do is just keep going back in the questions where you see that."

At this point, Judge Leval, his eyebrows raised almost to his hairline, broke in, demanding, "Over 1,642 pages?"

The Puckish remark broke up the courtroom. As the laughter subsided, Westmoreland explained, as he had on direct examination, that if McChristian's cable "had gone forward without any explanation, it would have been a major public relations problem."

A five-day Thanksgiving recess did nothing to cool the tension between Westmoreland and the CBS attorney. They spent much of the first day back arguing about the accuracy of a chart on enemy-strength figures that the general had shown to President Johnson in November 1967. Burt's first witness, Walt Whitman Rostow, had testified that the 242,000 enemy-strength figure shown on the chart excluded figures for the self-defense forces "and the President was well aware of that."

Westmoreland contradicted both Rostow and Boies.

"I understand this chart, which apparently you don't," he said sarcastically, adding, "I don't know how to say it, Mr. Boies, but you don't know what you're doing."

According to Westmoreland, Rostow also had been out of his depth. Rostow, he said, had misinterpreted the chart, which showed enemy strength of 285,000 at the end of 1966, then declining to 242,000 at the end of 1967. All three sets of figures on the chart excluded the SD, Westmoreland said.

Boies asked incredulously, "Are you saying that the 285,000 figure excludes the self-defense forces?"

"It does. Mr. Rostow made an inaccurate statement. He didn't understand the chart."

Westmoreland seemingly played into Boies' hands as the dialogue about the chart continued. As Boies explained to reporters later, he was trying to prove that Westmoreland's staff had kept enemy-strength figures under 300,000 by first coming up with a total and then skewing the data to meet these totals.

The general explained that after the SD had been dropped from the OB in October 1967, his intelligence chief, Major General Phillip Davidson, had made a "retroactive adjustment" of all the figures in the chart. This, he said, had been approved by the Defense Intelligence Agency.

Sensing a chance to tie up part of his case, Boies continued to press Westmoreland as Burt tried to halt the examination by frantically calling, "Time, please," as though he were a coach in the last crucial seconds of a football game.

"Did anyone tell you that this 285,000 figure, as reflected in this chart, was, as you put it, a retroactive adjustment?" Boies demanded.

"I don't think they had to tell me because I knew exactly what it was," the general said.

Boies then asked, "General Westmoreland, are you saying that this third quarter figure . . . just happened to come out at 285,000?"

"That was strictly coincidental," the general said, deadpan.

"Strictly coincidental?" Boies echoed in obvious disbelief.

"Yes," Westmoreland repeated.

Wanting this exchange to linger in the minds of the jury, Boies told Leval he was done for the day. Throughout the day, Westmoreland had been in constant pain from a chronic back condition that had flared up with a vengeance. That night, the problem worsened and the trial was suspended for two days. When he returned to the stand, Westmoreland lacked vigor and did not joust with Boies at all.

Boies spent much of the day introducing and reading newspaper and magazine articles critical of Westmoreland in an effort to mitigate the damages sought by the general. For example, he read from a 1971 *Time* magazine article in which the chief United States prosecutor at the Nuremberg Nazi war-crimes trials, Telford Taylor, suggested that "Westmoreland could be found guilty of Vietnam war crimes if he were to be tried by the same standard under which the U.S. hanged Japanese General Tomayuki Yamashita."

To show that Westmoreland had been criticized in the press about the OB controversy before the CBS documentary, Boies introduced articles published in 1975 while the congressional Pike Committee was holding hearings on the numbers controversy.

Leval, who usually gave the lawyers great latitude in their questioning, left his Mr. Rogers demeanor at home this day. He kept both attorneys on a short string, and from time to time gave the string a sharp tug. After Boies asked Westmoreland, "You are familiar with the Jack Anderson column, are you not, sir?" Leval interjected, "Are you asking him whether he's familiar with the phenomenon of the Jack Anderson column or the particular edition of it?"

Boies, somewhat surprised, answered, "I'm not sure 'phenomenon' would have been the word that I [would have] chosen. Familiar with the column itself."

After this exchange, Leval let Boies introduce five articles which criticized Westmoreland's handling of the OB issue, but told the jury, "These articles are not received for the truth of anything that is said in them. They are received only as evidence showing what was the nature of General Westmoreland's reputation prior to the playing of the CBS broadcast."

Later, Boies tried to introduce an article from *Saga* magazine that was extremely critical of Westmoreland's role in the enemy-strength issue. Burt objected, arguing that McChristian might have written it under a nom de plume.

This time, Leval brought Burt up short, saying, "So what?"

Burt quibbled, arguing that the *Saga* article was not "an independent, neutral attack" but rather one written by someone with a "motive" to hurt Westmoreland.

Leval shot back, "If Jack Anderson wrote his column because once when he was 11 years old General Westmoreland stepped on his toe, it has no effect on the issue. . . . "

Burt withdrew his objection and Boies continued reading from his collection of unfavorable clippings.

An extract from a book by former Vietnamese Premier Nguyen Cao Ky proved particularly damaging to Westmoreland. Ky charged that the general "must have known all about the strength of the impending attack" of the 1968 Tet Offensive. "I am convinced that the White House did not," Ky wrote, adding, "American leaders in Saigon deliberately issued a string of lies to the White House, in an effort to maintain the impression that the Americans were getting on top of the Vietcong."

Boies was willing to try any strategy to besmirch Westmoreland's reputation in the minds of the jury. During a sidebar discussion, the lawyer told Leval he intended to question Westmoreland about the My Lai massacre because this could refute Westmoreland's claim of an "open-door policy" exemplified by "the little card" that had been produced so dramatically during the general's direct testimony.

Westmoreland's policy, Boies argued, "was not a system that effectively uncovered wrongdoing and I think the My Lai massacre is an example of that."

Leval deemed the inclusion of My Lai in the trial inappropriate, observing that Westmoreland never suggested "an open door policy is a guarantee that no bad thing can happen without its being reported." He overruled Boies, telling him My Lai was "full of prejudice and . . . full of capacity to mislead the jury. . . . "

Despite this admonition, when Boies returned to question Westmoreland, he asked the general about a report on the "Son My incident," which is just another term for My Lai.

Burt objected, but Boies tried to persist, arguing in court that "the fact that this is an investigation of an important incident bears on the significance to be attached . . . to the responsibility of commanders for their commands."

Unswayed, Leval again overruled Boies, saying he was worried about the effect even this discussion would have on the jury.

Although Westmoreland continued to deny that he had tampered with figures to show Johnson that progress was being made in the war, he conceded he had known that the administration, under increasing attack over the war, wanted assurances of progress. But Westmoreland told Boies he hadn't felt any pressure to report progress.

"I would have resented pressure in that regard," he said. "But I was aware, primarily through the Ambassador in Saigon that Mr. Johnson and his Administration were convinced that we were making substantial progress in Vietnam and he wanted hard facts so that the progress would be recognized."

This statement contradicted Westmoreland's deposition testimony, in which he had told Boies he had "never" had the impression that the President wanted hard evidence on progress in the war.

Westmoreland said he had "felt strongly" that including higher figures for the SD and SSD in the order of battle would be "misunderstood by people unfamiliar with intelligence and the components of the order of battle."

Boies then asked, "Did those people include your chain of command?"

"Well, it didn't include Admiral Sharp, because he was at the briefing," Westmoreland said. "It could have been misunderstood, but only temporarily, by the chairman of the Joint Chiefs, who did not follow such detail. But it would have been explained to him."

This seemingly innocuous question, a paraphrase of one Boies had asked several times before, would come back to haunt the lawyer the next day.

The documentary contended, and Boies intended to prove, that part of the "conspiracy" Westmoreland had engaged in was an attempt to hide the real enemy-strength figures from his chain of command, including Admiral Sharp. Although Burt had managed to establish Admiral Sharp's presence in Vietnam during the briefings on guerrilla strength, he had been unable to prove what had transpired. Boies continually challenged Burt and the general to come up with hard evidence—and on the last day of Westmoreland's testimony, Burt did exactly that.

Both sides had pored over hundreds of thousands of pages of Army documents, but neither had been able to find the record of the May 19, 1967, Command Information and Intelligence Conference (CIIC) and a portion of that, the Weekly Intelligence Estimate Update (WIEU). Neither subpoena nor Freedom of Information request could locate this elusive document or free it from the Army's files.

At the last hour, however, Zane Finkelstein, a retired Army colonel who lived in Carlisle, Pennsylvania, home of the Army's records center, managed to find it. Finkelstein, who performed volunteer archival research for the Westmoreland team out of loyalty to his former commander, found a reference to the document in a microfilm list of records.

The Army declassified it on November 23, 1984, just in time for Burt to use it in his redirect examination of Westmoreland on December 4.

Relishing the coup, Burt slowly worked his way to the meat of the memo, establishing that Sharp had attended the meeting—an important point, because if Burt could prove that MACV had briefed Sharp on the higher guerrilla-strength figures, then Westmoreland could not have "conspired" to deceive his superiors, the main charge remaining in the pared-down case.

"General Westmoreland," Burt said, "can you recall whether you testified you were briefed on the revised irregular study and revised political cadres estimates at this CIIC meeting on the 19th?"

"I so testified," the general agreed.

"Did you testify that this was the first time you had been briefed on these revised estimates?"

"I did, yes."

"Has it been your testimony that Admiral Sharp was present at that briefing?"

"It has. Admiral Sharp was present."

Burt then started to hand Westmoreland the newly discovered memo, but Boies, who had been told of its existence only the week before, objected.

The lawyers wrangled about the document's authenticity until Leval finally called them to the sidebar. Boies explained that his objection stemmed from the relationship between Finkelstein and the defense. Burt pointed out that the document, like thousands of others in the case, bore an Army declassification tag, removing any doubt about its authenticity. Boies disagreed, saying the affidavit from Finkelstein should not be admitted without an opportunity for cross-examination.

Leval interrupted, commenting somewhat sarcastically on Boies' objections. "What he [Boies] is saying is that he thinks there's a sufficient possibility that this Mr. or Mrs. Zane Finkelstein, whoever Zane Finkelstein is, forged the document rather than having obtained it in the manner described by the affidavit.

"He is entitled to contest that," Leval admitted, pointing out that "most documents in this case . . . have not been contested as to authenticity. . . .

"I can't bar Mr. Boies," he decided, "particularly in view of the circumstances of this document appearing in the middle of the trial. . . . "

But Leval was clearly opposed to Boies' delaying tactics.

"If the document turns out to have been found among the history record of the Army, as suggested in the affidavit of Zane Finkelstein, I think that while Mr. Boies's battle may be prolonged, I think it will ultimately be a losing one," he said. "Maybe you should take a few minutes to decide whether to pursue it."

Boies took Leval's advice, and he and Burt adjourned to telephone both Finkelstein and Colonel Pasqual, director of Military History at Carlisle Barracks. Returning a bit later, Boies told Leval, " . . . I am prepared to accept that this document was produced from the files of the Army. I still press my objections on other grounds, including lack of foundation and including the fact that this document, which appears to be readily available, was not among the documents that were listed as exhibits pursuant to pretrial orders."

Leval listened to further arguments from both Burt and Boies, questioned Westmoreland extensively about the document, and finally overruled Boies.

Burt, openly pleased at this important triumph, had duplicates of the exhibit distributed to the jury while he produced his own copy with a flourish and read it out loud. As promised, the report showed that Westmoreland and Sharp both had had ample opportunity to consider new enemy-strength figures:

"Memorandum For the Record. Subject: CIIC meeting, 19 May 1967. This memorandum confirms oral guidance issued by COMUS-MACV following the subject meeting.

"A, the advisability of releasing the information presented in a VC Irregular Forces strength in South Vietnam briefing without further refinement was questioned. J-2 [General McChristian] will pull together representatives from IO and J-3 to analyze this study in depth and to determine how this information should be presented, both officially and publicly. COMUSMACV [Westmoreland] requested specifically that those irregular forces that are armed be identified. Additionally the data presented in the political order of battle briefing will be analyzed by this group with the same objectives as the foregoing. COMUSMACV will be briefed on this before the information in either study is released by this headquarters."

Burt then asked Westmoreland what kind of "oral guidance" he had given.

"I wanted to identify the fighters from the nonfighters," Westmoreland said.

Burt then asked if the May 19 briefing on VC irregular strength had numerical estimates, to which Westmoreland answered, "yes," adding that "they were higher" than those MACV published in its monthly OB summary.

"Did Admiral Sharp—was this briefing given aloud, was it spoken?" Burt asked.

Westmoreland answered with a grin, "Oh yes. In English."

Boies hardly bothered to cross-examine Westmoreland about the document. After court that day, he admitted that the Finkelstein memo strengthened Burt's case. In his mini-summation the next day, Boies again avoided the Finkelstein document. Instead, he attacked the general's credibility by briefly recapping the numerous contradictions between what Westmoreland said in the documentary, what he said in his deposition, and what he said at the trial.

"Even if you were to assume that the story told by [Westmoreland] for the first time here at the trial was true," Boies said, "there is no way CBS could be charged with predicting . . . [what he told the network] was not true."

Burt, in his summation of the case to date, viewed it quite differently. He told the jury that the sixteen witnesses heard so far had "demonstrated throughout their testimony that the CBS broadcast is untrue. . . . "

This set the stage for Burt's confrontation with the individual he viewed as the chief villain of the documentary: George Crile.

16.

Crile's Trial

W H A T George Crile later termed an "old-fashioned duel" began when he took the stand on the afternoon of December 5.
Burt had called Crile to testify as a "hostile witness"—one who appears for direct questioning by the opposition—but most of the real
hostility was on Burt's part.

Crile saw Burt's examination as an "all-out fight. Dan was out to
knock me off on the way to greater glory, that is, dismantling a great
American network," Crile said. "But he couldn't do that until he dealt
with me, so I became the object of all his energies. He seemed to decide that if he couldn't break through me, he couldn't mount an effective offensive on the main target—CBS.

"He even made faces at me," Crile said after the trial. Burt's
questions, loaded with sarcasm, seemed designed as much to cut Crile
down as to elicit information. During these hours and days, it seemed
that the duel was between two classes as well as two individuals:
tough, up-from-the-streets Dan Burt, who had had to earn everything
he had in life, versus born-to-the-manor Crile, whose bearing, manner,
and even speech epitomized the WASP obstacles Burt had always had
to surmount.

Burt denied that he had set out to ruin Crile or that he resented
his class. "That's crazy. . . . After all, Westmoreland's also a WASP."
Told that Crile had taken the cross-examination as a personal attack,
Burt replied, "Not surprising. So did Westmoreland," referring to the
documentary.

Burt's visible stress as he quizzed Crile reflected the growing tension within the Westmoreland camp. Jury analyst Jay Schulman began to double as an in-house therapist, stamping out flash fires of
discontent as members of the legal team argued with each other or

bitterly complained about Burt. David Dorsen was surprised that Burt wanted to bear the load himself. He had expected to play a major role in the trial. In a post-trial interview, Dorsen said Burt had surprised him when he announced "he was going to do all the major directs and all of the cross. . . . I told him he was biting off more than he could chew and that I should play a larger role." Anthony Murry was astonished at Dorsen's assessment. "It was no surprise that Dan would handle the majority of the direct examinations. Everyone knew this before we left for New York."

George Leisure, another lawyer who got wrapped up in the trial, questioned the wisdom of calling Crile at all. Leisure's firm, Donovan & Leisure, had wanted to take the Westmoreland case from the beginning, but could not afford to do it on a pro-bono basis. "I thought we should be involved in this case because [Wild] Bill Donovan, head of the OSS [Office of Strategic Services, the World War II precursor of the CIA], founded this firm, and I know he would have been involved." But Leisure did offer his services and that of two colleagues, plus space in the firm's plush RCA Building offices on a contingency basis. As the case progressed, Leisure became good friends with General Westmoreland and Kitsy and, as Schulman puts it, "grafted himself onto the team," showing up in court almost daily.

Leisure argued that by calling Crile in the midst of presenting his case, Burt would lose momentum. Burt countered that without putting Crile on the stand, he would have a hard time proving malice. Most of the testimony from the witnesses so far related only to the "truth" issue.

Burt prevailed. His examination of Crile was a disaster.

Crile countered Burt's attempt to make quick, rapier-like thrusts into his credibility by swathing himself in a cotton batting of verbosity. Burt tried, but couldn't stem this torrent of words. Nor did he seem capable of follow-up when Crile opened himself to attack.

Not once did Burt use the weapon brandished so effectively by Boies, contradicting Crile's trial testimony with his deposition. Also, within days, Judge Leval started to tell Burt how to ask questions and what kinds of questions to ask. The judge had trouble following Burt's line of attack, saying at the sidebar during the first day, "I have found this examination very confusing. . . . I am really at quite a loss as to what the facts are that you are seeking to bring out."

Burt, who seemed to base much of his case on the "evidence" contained in the *TV Guide* article and Don Kowet's book, *A Matter of Honor,* learned that what can be used to pillory in print often doesn't stand up in court. *TV Guide* had based much of its research on the Crile's "blue sheet" proposal for the documentary. This intemperate document may have made Crile appear biased to the readers of *TV Guide*, but Leval soon explained to the jury that a blue sheet, no matter how inflammatory, is not the foundation of a libel case.

After Burt cited several volatile passages from the blue sheet, Leval undid his work by telling the jury, "It is not one of the elements of the case whether preliminary documents might have been prepared in a reckless fashion."

Burt's inexperience in handling witnesses helped Crile win the duel. The producer bested the lawyer by drowning him in a sea of words. Leval repeatedly tried to stop Crile, telling him on December 10, the second day of his testimony, "You are to answer the question that is put to you. You are not to use the opportunity to be on the stand to make speeches or use the question that is given . . . as an opportunity to say things that help your case, which are not responsive to the question. . . . "

Burt would land a few punches, but didn't follow up. Or he would let Crile drone on so long that the thread of his argument was lost. Despite this torrent of words, Crile never came up with a good explanation for why he had not contacted General Davidson for "The Uncounted Enemy." Burt managed to make Crile's excuse that Davidson had been "a very sick man" look ludicrous, particularly for a newsman who had set himself up as an authority on intelligence.

> BURT: Did you call his [Davidson's] home in Texas prior to the broadcast being aired?
>
> CRILE: I attempted to, yes.
>
> BURT: And when you called his home did you understand at that time that General Davidson was on his deathbed?
>
> CRILE: . . . It was the word in the intelligence community at that time that he had that problem.

Since Davidson had already appeared in court, this would have been an ideal opportunity for Burt to follow up and ask which part of "the intelligence community" had told Crile that Davidson was terminally ill. At the very least, it might have allowed Burt to impeach some CBS witness from that intelligence community.

Burt's poor handling of Crile stemmed from the fact he did not understand the difference between pre-trial work and the rigors of the courtroom, some legal observers said.

"Partly he began to believe the image he was projecting, partly he saw David Boies alone doing all these things," David Dorsen said after the trial. "Partly he didn't like to hear me tell him the problems we'd get into. . . . I'd like to know what he thought Crile was going to do when he got up there and started cross-examining him. I don't know what the hell he had in mind."

Dorsen also faulted Burt for not using Crile's deposition, taken a year and a half earlier, and suggested that he had not reread the document before examining the witness. "I think it is accurate to say that Dan did not once use Crile's deposition transcript in the entire seven days Crile was on the stand. And you compare that with what David Boies or I did with the depositions and you get some picture of Dan's inexperience."

In a post-trial interview, Crile, ironically, came to Burt's defense, saying that Dorsen, who had handled part of his deposition examination, was less much effective. "Given my choice, I would rather be examined by David Dorsen than Dan Burt any day. . . . Dan is a tough advocate for his cause." Murry, in a post-trial interview, denied Dorsen's assertions that Burt didn't prepare for Crile's examination. "Dan did a lot of work. He did reread the deposition."

Burt didn't trust Dorsen. He had hired the litigator on the advice of another lawyer, but quickly grew displeased with his work. A year before the trial began, even David Boies recommended that Burt get another co-counsel, saying Dorsen was not a team player. But by that time Dorsen had taken many of the depositions and was intimately familiar with the case. More important, Burt said, he had given Dorsen his word. As the trial progressed, the rift between Burt and Dorsen widened. Schulman said Dorsen felt so frustrated with his bit part in the courtroom drama that he became a self-promoter. "Dan believed, rightly or wrongly, that David [Dorsen] was talking to the press," Schulman said. "It's clear David had come on the case in order to have his chance. Certainly to help win the case, but also to put his name in lights. And Dan was aware of that."

By December, Burt was beginning to feel the pressures of the trial. "There came a time in the litigation when Dan became particularly demoralized, right after the Crile examination," Schulman said, adding that Dorsen saw this as an opportunity. Dorsen began "lobbying George Leisure and others to be allowed to take over the major crosses [and] hostile directs . . . that would come up in CBS's case," Schulman recalled.

In a meeting between Leisure, Dorsen, and Schulman, it was decided that Dorsen should handle the upcoming cross-examinations of George Allen, Colonel Gains Hawkins, General Joseph McChristian, and Mike Wallace, with Burt concentrating on the summation in the case. Burt immediately agreed to let Dorsen take over Allen. Later, he would relinquish Hawkins and McChristian.

A deteriorating family situation contributed to Burt's problems.

The strain of the trial and the physical separation from his wife badly strained the marriage, Burt's third. In addition, Maree did not get along well with either of the Westmorelands, particularly the usually unflappable Kitsy. Maree had asked the general to use his influence to get West Point cadets to participate in a linguistic study for her Ph.D. and Westmoreland said he had called the academy, but learned it was "not practical" for the cadets to participate. There was no evidence anyone was upset, he said, but members of the Capital Legal team disagreed. They said Burt felt hurt and became angry that Westmoreland couldn't do him a personal favor and help Maree, who struggled under a difficult deadline to finish the degree.

Burt also missed his infant daughter, whom he constantly referred to in casual conversations. Eventually, he kept the baby in his hotel room for several weeks.

Midway through his battle with Crile, the judge dealt Burt yet another setback. On December 13, Leval ruled inadmissible as evidence CBS's internal investigation of the making of "The Uncounted Enemy," the Benjamin Report, because it "is largely irrelevant to the issues before the jury and consists in great part of opinion and hearsay of varying degrees of remoteness." This stripped Burt of another way to indict Crile for lack of balance.

In ruling out the Benjamin Report, Leval once again underscored one of the most important but obscure points of libel law: fairness or lack of it is not a proof of libel. Observing that the report traced "various charges made against CBS, primarily by *TV Guide*," Leval then ruled that "These charges address different standards and criteria than those involved in the libel suit.

"Thus the report addressed whether the broadcast was 'fair and balanced' and whether supporters of Westmoreland's side of the dispute were given fair opportunity to respond to the charges of others. . . .

"The fairness of the broadcast is not at issue in the libel suit. Publishers and reporters do not commit a libel in a public figure case by publishing unfair, one-sided attacks. The issue in a libel suit is whether the publisher recklessly or knowingly published false material. The fact that commentary is one-sided and sets forth categorical accusations has no tendency to prove that the publisher believed it to be false. The libel law does not require the publisher to grant his accused equal time or fair reply. It requires only that the publisher not slander by known falsehoods (or reckless ones). A publisher who honestly believes in the truth of his accusations (and can point to a non-reckless basis for his beliefs) is under no obligation under the libel law to treat the subject of his accusations fairly or evenhandedly."

Though Boies called Leval's ruling a "victory," it was only a partial one. The judge didn't totally disallow the report. "I do not mean by this ruling to suggest that nothing in the report may be received. There are interspersed in the text a substantial number of items which would be appropriate for receipt in evidence . . . [and] the great majority of the admissible matter contained in the report are not disputed by the defendants." In other words, the only sections of the Benjamin Report that Burt could use were the ones that Boies had no problem with.

Burt's worst mistake with Crile came much later, on February 7, as Boies finished his direct examination of the CBS producer. After the trial, Crile recalled that moment with admiration for Boies' chutzpah. "David has both the instincts and guts of a river-boat gambler, so when he told me what he was going to do that day, I trusted him enough to agree." The gamble that Boies the lawyer took evoked the kind of risk that Boies the crap-shooter enjoyed: one winner-take-all throw of the dice.

Ready to turn his witness over for cross-examination by Burt, Boies calmly turned toward the jury and threw down a challenge: he asked Burt to show "exactly what there is in the broadcast that is critical of General Westmoreland that the plaintiff believes is false."

Flustered by this directness, Burt asked for a recess. He angrily complained to Leval that Boies was off base in "trying to force" him to pursue any line of questioning. Leval declined to correct Boies, but did tell the jury that "Mr. Burt is entitled to conduct his case as he sees fit and he is not under any obligation to ask questions that are suggested or challenged by Mr. Boies."

Lacking the fire and intensity that characterized his earlier examination, Burt questioned Crile only perfunctorily, ignoring Boies' challenge. Boies considered this was one of the watershed moments of the case, equal to winning the change-of-venue motion.

As the Christmas break neared, Burt had to face another major problem: time was running out and Crile seemed determined to eat up as much of it as possible. By December 19, Burt had used 102 hours out of the 150 hours of court time Leval had allotted to each side—without calling key witnesses such as Mike Wallace and Sam Adams.

In a conference that day, Leval asked Burt if he "still felt well in control" of his time budget. Burt didn't answer directly, but revealed the severity of the time crunch. Burt said he was "seriously considering" dropping Wallace and Adams from direct examination.

Although news reports were less favorable to Burt as he slogged through the examination of Crile, the CBS public-relations campaign continued.

Shortly before the trial adjourned for Christmas, Scanlon's PR firm distributed to anyone in the press who wanted it a scathing attack on Burt from the *Yale Law Review*. In an article, "With Charity for All," Oliver Houck, professor at Tulane University law school, charged that Capital Legal let its major corporate donors, like Fluor Corp., call the litigation tune. Peter Fluor, a vice president and major stockholder of the company that bears his name, Houck wrote, was on the board of Capital Legal. He was, Houck said, a close friend of Burt's and turned to Burt for help in fighting the Occupational Safety and Health Administration over stringent standards of worker exposure to benzene, a carcinogen.

Houck charged that Capital Legal, under Burt, fought in court to ease OSHA's strict benzene standards, implying that Fluor got quite a big return on the tax-free public-interest bucks it donated to Capital Legal.

This was a juicy story, implying that Burt was an enemy not only of the press but of workers exposed to environmental hazards. But the attempt to stain Burt's escutcheon didn't check out.

"We haven't handled any OSHA cases since I came to Capital," Burt said. "Not only that, but Peter Fluor doesn't sit on the board anymore. The right wing doesn't like us as much as they used to. Joe Coors doesn't even give us a dime anymore. That's because the right doesn't like what we did in the Orange Marketing Order case," he said, referring to the landmark decision against the grower/marketing cartel that had long dominated the California orange business.

The Oil Chemical and Atomic Workers International Union, whose fight for safety in the workplace is legendary, didn't know of Burt's involvement in any OSHA cases. Their answer to a question about him was "Dan who?"

Houck, in an interview, admitted he became aware after the article was printed that Burt had not had any involvement in the OSHA case he cited. "But . . . this was a historic study of Capital Legal, and not just Burt's involvement in it. When I wrote the article, Fluor was still on the board."

This attack on Burt was related, indirectly, to the lawyer's running battle with Ralph Nader. Under Burt's direction, Capital published *Abuse of Trust*, a polemic that accused Nader of foxing the public in the same style as corporations.

The source for much of Houck's material on Burt and Capital Legal was Russell Mokhiber, a lawyer with the Nader-affiliated Corporate Accountability Research Group. Mokhiber, whose business card describes him as a "Corporate Criminologist," when asked if he was aware that Peter Fluor was no longer on Capital's board and that Burt had denied ever handling an OSHA case, said, "No, I wasn't. The real issue was the long relationship between Fluor Corporation and Capital. Did Fluor help set up Capital?"

Mokhiber also tried to have Burt investigated by the District of Columbia Bar Association for the unauthorized practice of law. Burt didn't belong to the District Bar—a common practice of Washington-based lawyers. Burt explained that any time he went to court in Washington he was allowed to appear under rules that recognized his membership in the Pennsylvania and Massachusetts bars. (Burt was admitted to the D.C. Bar in 1986.)

According to Burt, Mokhiber's obsessive pursuit of him was fall-out from Capital's book on Nader, a charge Nader has denied in several published reports.

Although Scanlon's mischief was better organized, Burt wasn't above passing along secondhand gossip. In December, an exhausted Mike Wallace checked into a hospital. The trial, constant travel (he'd been to Ethiopia and back), and a separation from his wife (she suddenly moved to Tahiti) had sapped his strength. However, Burt told at least one reporter that Wallace had tried to commit suicide, and that a "source" had offered him copies of the record of Wallace's admission to Lenox Hill Hospital indicating that Wallace's attempted suicide, not collapse, was the real reason.

CBS's vice president for public information, George Schweitzer, strongly denied these charges, indicating that a number of reporters had called with the same query at about the same time.

Amid this gutter fighting from both sides, the Westmorelands continued to display grace under pressure. One of the first bunches of flowers Mike Wallace received in his hospital room bore a simple card signed by the general and Kitsy.

After the holidays, Burt's case ended with more of a whimper than a bang. With time running woefully short, he gave up any hope of putting another hostile witness, such as Wallace, on the stand. Burt chose to finish his assault with Crile's chief accuser, Ira Klein, the documentary's film editor who had served so ably in the pre-trial publicity battle. CBS blamed Klein for feeding ammunition to Kowet for his *TV Guide* article; Klein was a chief source for Kowet's book, *A Matter of Honor*. Burt clearly had planned for Klein to repeat his performance at the trial, but he hustled this important witness through his testimony in less than a day.

Compared to the convolutions of Crile's testimony, Klein's seemed relatively straightforward. Burt had the witness relive his frustrating and eventually maddening crusade to have producer George Crile bring balance to what the film editor perceived as a flawed, skewed work.

Klein testified that he had been turned off by Crile when he complained that the documentary's credibility would be weakened by "not permitting General Westmoreland to have time to present his point of view."

Asked what Crile had to say in response to this suggestion, the boyish-looking, almost baby-faced Klein testified, " . . . Mr. Crile told me he was deciding what was true and what wasn't."

The editor told the jury that Crile at one point admitted "he knew" Sam Adams was "obsessed." He also testified that Crile took unethical short-cuts and sometimes even hoodwinked his bosses at CBS News. He told how, during a screening of an unfinished version of "The Uncounted Enemy," Crile ordered him to shut off the audio to conceal from the CBS brass the last part of Westmoreland's comment on the 1960s "Meet the Press" program when the general had said the Vietcong had the capacity to step up infiltration—a statement that seemed to contradict what Westmoreland told Wallace in a later interview.

During much of this examination, it appeared that Burt was still trying his case by the book. Not the lawbooks, but Kowet's book. To Burt's dismay, however, while Klein alleged that CBS and Crile had lacked balance, fairness, integrity, and even displayed a loose sense of ethics, Leval repeatedly pointed out there was a vast difference between bias and libel in the eyes of the law.

Still following the thrust of the Kowet book, Klein testified to more serious errors by Crile, telling how Sam Adams had told him that Westmoreland's intelligence chief, General Davidson, was as "healthy as a clam" and not ill, as the producer claimed. Klein also recounted how, after the broadcast (and Westmoreland's press conference), Adams had come to his editing room and confessed that "we have to come clean, we have to make a statement, the premise of the show is inaccurate."

Recalling this scene for the jury, Klein said, "I looked at Sam and said 'It's a little bit late' and Mr. Adams said to me that he was telling George all along that LBJ had to know."

Burt then said he had no more questions for the witness and asked for a lunch break.

When court resumed, Boies began his cross-examination of Klein by going for the jugular of his integrity. The lawyer once again used his favorite tactic of impeaching a witness with his own words. In this instance, the trick had a delicious sense of irony. To both discredit and embarrass the witness, Boies used the tape recording that author Kowet had made of interviews with Klein.

Minutes after he began grilling Klein, the witness admitted he had told Kowet that his relationship with Crile during the latter stages of preparation of the documentary was so bad that "I couldn't stand to look at him."

Working from the transcript of the Kowet tapes, Boies then had Klein further damn himself.

"Did you tell this reporter that you believed that George Crile was a social pervert?" Boies asked.

"I believe so, yes," Klein admitted.

"Did you tell this reporter that you were just too good and that bothered Mr. Crile?"

"As I can recall, yes."

"Did you tell this reporter that Mr. Crile was devious and slimy?"

"Yes. I believe that to be so."

Crile wasn't the only CBS staffer bad-mouthed by Klein in the interview with Kowet, the jury eventually learned.

Boies asked the witness, "Did you have similar personal problems with other members of the production team, sir?"

"No," Klein said.

"With any members of the production team?"

"No."

Boies decided to get specific. "Let's take Mr. [Alex] Alben, who you have identified as the researcher," he suggested. "Did you tell the reporter we were talking about here that Mr. Alben was a homosexual?"

Before Klein could answer, a flustered Burt, seeing his prize witness hoisted on a tape recording made by his prize reporter, quickly objected. At the sidebar, Burt argued that Klein's remarks about Alben lacked relevancy. Boies disagreed, claiming the remarks were relevant because they illustrated the "deepseated and vicious bias" of Klein toward CBS, Crile, and others associated with the documentary.

Leval asked exactly what kind of prejudicial things Klein had said. After riffling through the tape transcript, Boies said, "Up here we have Klein laughing about the possibility of Alben becoming another gay CIA agent. . . . "

Leval finally agreed to let Boies continue with this line of questioning, cautioning him not to get into the exact nature of Klein's comments about Alben's sexuality.

Boies then asked Klein if his reference to Alben's sexual preferences had been hostile.

Klein answered, "Absolutely not," insisting any remarks he had made to Kowet about Alben should be understood in context. It was "an adult, casual conversation."

But Boies persisted.

"You knew that Mr. Kowet was a reporter?"

"Yes, I did," Klein answered.

"And you knew that this conversation was designed to result in a story, did you not, sir?"

Klein's answer laid bare an apparent double standard. Some reporters should be allowed to work with complete freedom, without any of the criticism he had heaped on Crile.

"That was Mr. Kowet's prerogative," the editor said, "to work with the material as he saw fit. . . . "

Boies also used the Kowet tapes to defuse one of the most damaging parts of Klein's testimony against Crile. Though Klein had testified he had had two conversations with Crile about General Davidson—one in July 1981 and one later during production—the Kowet tapes contradicted this. "You told Mr. Kowet, did you not, that the last time you ever brought up Davidson's name was in that conversation in July. That's what you told Mr. Kowet, correct, sir?" Boies asked.

Klein answered "yes," but after further questions from Boies said, ". . . I corrected myself . . . subsequent to the publication of Mr. Kowet's book."

Boies had a hard time accepting this answer. Waving the transcript at the glowering witness, he asked, "That's not what you say here, is it?"

Klein tried another weak explanation, but it didn't work and Boies offered in evidence this portion of the Kowet tapes to impeach Klein. Burt didn't object.

Boies then asked Klein a series of questions which established that the film editor did not know much about the business of news reporting, documentary producing, the Vietnam War, or the order of battle and military intelligence.

Klein conceded he had not attended any interviews for "The Uncounted Enemy," had never personally interviewed anyone in connection with a story, had never written a news story or article himself, and was unaware that Crile and Adams had taken notes of interviews that were not filmed. He said he had seen Adams' extensive chronologies, but could not recall actually reading them, did not recall ever reading any Army or CIA documents relating to the broadcast, and had never reviewed any order-of-battle documents although he knew the numbers dispute was the centerpiece of the documentary.

Boies also got Klein to admit that he did not know what the Pike Committee was; that he had never read several books Crile had used in preparing the show, including a West Point textbook covering the Tet Offensive; and had not seen all the filmed interviews in their entirety. And, despite Klein's complaints about the substance of the broadcast, Boies showed that the editor had never discussed the show with Mike Wallace or taken any problem to Howard Stringer or

Andrew Lack during the production, although other members of the documentary unit had done so.

Boies then abruptly halted his questioning. During the break, he explained that, while he could have used more material from the Kowet tapes, they were "just too disgusting and too unfair to innocent people" to be played in open court.

After the break, Burt told Leval at the sidebar he wanted a chance to "rehabilitate" Klein's credibility in his redirect examination. He complained that Boies' cross-examination might have left the impression that Klein was "simply a spoilsport" who disliked George Crile enough to go around making accusations.

Burt told Leval that Klein's remarks about Crile actually reflected "frustration" with CBS rather than any animus toward Crile.

A somewhat skeptical Leval agreed to Burt's request, but limited the questioning to determining "if there is another explanation for the hostility of those comments."

After much maneuvering, with Leval finally having to take over and ask the questions for him, Burt tried to get out of Klein what he wanted.

Leval asked Klein, "Did you also make some comments to Kowet about other persons connected with the broadcast that were not friendly remarks?"

"They weren't meant not to be friendly."

"Well, would you agree that that comment about Mr. Crile was not friendly?" the judge asked.

"Yes, I would agree."

"Now, did you say anything about Mr. Alben that was not friendly?"

"I didn't perceive it as being that way, no."

Klein's testimony about the Davidson incident was equally lame, and again a frustrated Leval took over the questioning.

Both lawyers then followed up with several routine questions and Burt's case was finished. While Boies still considers his grueling cross-examination of Klein a sharp blow to Burt's case, Kowet and Klein view it quite differently.

In a July 1985 interview, Kowet said, "If there's one thing that happened out of this, [it] is George Crile's version of events was discredited. Boies's efforts to paint Ira as bent on revenge failed."

Klein maintains he never had a vendetta going against Crile. "It's all so absurd. . . . I never in any way wanted to hurt that man, even at the time we were making the film. . . . I have never tried to seek celebrity status. I made a conscious decision, considered the negative aspects. Really it was a moral choice."

Klein also maintains that his performance on the witness stand

and the testimony in his deposition reflected only the "narrow" questions asked by Boies, not his actual understanding of the Vietnam War and the order of battle.

"It's interesting," Crile says. " . . . Ira clearly has a powerful, heroic self-image. Ira somehow thinks of himself as representing the true tradition of Edward R. Murrow. But I wonder how he does it from beneath a rock in the editing room, in the dark, windowless room."

With Burt's direct case all but wrapped up, it was obvious that he had lost much of his momentum. Some witnesses—especially Westmoreland—had fared well on both direct and cross-examination. But others Burt had counted on to reinforce Westmoreland's refutation of the documentary had withered and recanted under Boies' blistering counterattack.

The quality of the witnesses, not the quality of the lawyering, was the problem, Boies said later, in a June 1986 interview. "Dan did not do as bad a job as people after the fact are asserting. When we got to trial, I don't think there was any question as to who was doing better, but Dan had a hard time with his direct-case witnesses. They didn't perform the way Dan expected them to. What I don't understand is why Dan didn't stop [ask for a settlement] after the direct case."

The witnesses CBS would put on were stronger than Burt ever anticipated, Boies said.

17.

Boies' Guerrilla War

DURING much of the trial, the Vietnam War seemed an abstract backdrop against which a parade of witnesses passionlessly heaped mounds of testimony and piles of often conflicting statistics. Gradually, the kind of Newspeak favored by military briefing officers during the war filtered into the courtroom. This was a language crafted for speaking easily about war without conveying any of its horrors. The patois of the trial became that curious mumbo-jumbo uttered by bureaucrats, generals, CIA analysts, and Cabinet officers which reduced man's inhumanities to buzz words that masked reality. Dead soldiers became KIAs, while the maimed became WIAs.

In order to prove the CBS case, David Boies needed to break through this wall of abstraction. So he found a couple of ex-grunts to bring the gritty reality of the Vietnam War into the comfortable courthouse on Foley Square. He wanted to *show* the jury how simple it was to construct a booby trap, not just tell them. A little theater was in order, he felt.

As Army recon specialist Daniel Friedman answered the usual questions about his background from the witness stand, telling how he had been wounded twice in Vietnam, Boies, without warning, pulled out a pineapple grenade. As he handed the grenade (tagged as exhibit 1637) up to the witness, Boies quickly said, to the relief of some gasping onlookers, "For everybody's comfort and so I am not swarmed with marshals, I will explain that the charge has been removed."

Boies asked Friedman to explain how a booby trap could be constructed out of such a grenade.

"Very easily," Friedman said as he began to work on the device from the elevated witness chair. Moving his fingers delicately to the cotter pin that held the spoon in, he said, "All you would do is loosen the pin over here, straighten the pin out so it could be easily pulled." After this maneuver, Friedman explained to an intensely observant jury, "There is some pressure on the pin, but not very much. And you would tie a trip wire, a piece of fishing line, a very thin piece of metal wire, almost anything that would be hard to see on the trail—a fishing line was used commonly—you would secure the grenade to the area that you want the kill zone to be in, and you would lace the trip wire further ahead, where your point man might set it off.

"Usually on patrol you would have a point man walking several meters in front of the body of the patrol and he would trip it off—it's usually a three to five second delay on the explosion—and the grenade would cause maximum damage.

"By the pressure of the foot touching the string, this would come out," Friedman said as he pulled out the pin. "The handle would fly off and about three to five seconds later there would be an explosion."

"That's all that would be required to set a booby trap?" Boies asked.

"All you have to do is to be able to tie a knot," Friedman said.

The jury, bombarded for months with testimony about various ways to count various kinds of VC, was fascinated. This testimony carried authority. Not the authority of a rear-echelon intelligence analyst, but of someone who had been there.

Dan Burt had had no hint that Boies planned to stage such a dramatic display, and later he referred to this witness and the next one, who also built a booby trap, as the turning point in the case. "It was the most important piece of evidence in the entire trial," he said. "It was devastating. And it was a total surprise."

In Vietnam, booby traps were the "primary" cause of concern because "they were constantly causing a very, very high percentage of our casualties," Friedman testified. "That's something that you really can't see coming. They were very cleverly hidden.

"An enemy force sometimes you can hear coming. Sometimes an enemy force, we were prewarned it was coming. But there might be booby traps anywhere, any time, and I saw too many of my buddies go down because of them not to be concerned by them."

Before Boies pulled his grenade trick, Friedman had already testified that booby traps had been set by the same people Westmoreland's witnesses had viewed as harmless: the women, old men, and young boys. Friedman described going out on patrol through a supposedly "friendly" village whose residents would wave in greeting. The grunts would often toss out cans of C-rations. On the way back in, though, "very often we were ambushed in or near that same village. For instance, we would take a rocket or hit a mine or receive sniper fire.

"If there was an exchange of fire . . . there would be bodies that we would later recognize to be some of those same people that we saw waving to us on the side of the road, and many of these mines or booby traps that disabled some of our vehicles or some of our foot people were made of those same type of C-rations" that the troops had given the villagers, Friedman testified. David Dorsen, who was handling the cross-examination that day, vehemently objected to Friedman's testimony, but chose poor ground on which to take a stand.

"I think bringing out through individual witnesses the kinds of casualties caused by mines and booby traps is inflammatory," Dorsen protested. "I think it has no real basis in this case. I think to have a witness just talk at some length as to buddies of his that were injured by mines and booby traps is inflammatory and essentially irrelevant and distorts the war, much less the case."

Leval didn't buy this attempt to deflect Friedman's gripping personal testament. He said one of the "most important areas" of the case was the capabilities of the irregular self-defense and secret self-defense forces. Leval said that while there were "all kinds" of doubts about Friedman's qualifications to tell whether the SD and SSD he referred to had been the same force the analysts had tracked and whether the mines and booby traps he had observed "were made by them or someone else, that question is very much open to speculation no matter who is talking about it. I don't see anything wrong with the proposition that a front line reconnaissance person can't describe his experience in these respects."

Later on, Boies had Friedman specifically single out the SD as a threat to American troops, asking, "Can you explain what you mean by self-defense forces?"

"Self-defense forces were an integral part of the irregulars of the Vietcong . . . ," Friedman answered. "They gave the appearance of performing everyday civilian chores. However, they were responsible for many terrorist acts against us and we were able to identify them as such."

Friedman testified that the guerrillas often disguised themselves as barbers, setting up their poles in American camps. But, as he testified, "many times, unfortunately, after the fact, we noticed that they were staking these poles next to petroleum dumps or ammo dumps . . . and when they would leave at night . . . they would leave these poles staking out their area, and we would get hit with mortars that night or rockets, and these rockets or mortars would be very accurate and hit those petroleum fuel dumps or ammunition dumps. . . .

"The Vietnamese civilians did not show up the next day," he said.

Boies also had Friedman, who in civilian life took a job as veterans' counselor for the state of New York, deflect Westmoreland's impassioned testimony that adding 100,000 SD and SSD to the order of battle would adversely affect the morale of his troops. Friedman testified, "I believe it would have been better for my morale to have had a more accurate picture of who we were fighting and what we were up against."

The next CBS witness was Howard Embree, a soft-spoken English teacher at Mississippi State University. Embree, an award-winning West Point graduate, had had one of the toughest jobs in the war: adviser to a Vietnamese Army unit in Quang Tri province, the north-ernmost province of South Vietnam. Embree was a soldier's soldier. He graduated from the academy in 1963 (Westmoreland was the superintendent there during all but Embree's plebe year) and then took Ranger and Airborne training. Posted to Germany, he attended a five-week advanced Corps of Engineer mine-and-demolition school. On leaving Germany, he attended an adviser-training school in Fort Bragg and then the Defense Language Institute in Monterey, California.

During his service in Vietnam from May 1966 through May 1967, Embree testified, he "saw combat more or less continuously," daily encountering "local units, self-defense militia, secret self-defense militia, operating in and around villages."

With Boies' associate Randy Mastro handling the questioning, Embree said the mission of the SD and SSD had been to defend their villages. "And that I would take to include mining, booby-trapping, sniping in the proximity of the village."

The mines and booby traps were "extremely simple" to build, he said. "Anyone in this room could do it. I could teach anyone in this room to do it in the next ten minutes" if he had a "piece of wire and grenade."

Mastro didn't miss a beat. "I just happen to have those things here," the lawyer said.

For the second time in matter of hours, the CBS defense team advanced its case by having a witness build a booby trap on the witness stand.

Within a few minutes, Embree fashioned a trip-wire grenade, saying such a trap would probably be set on a path "perhaps four to six inches, or maybe only a couple of inches off the ground. . . . The first soldier by would, of course, pull the pin out, the spoon would fly off. He would be over there by the time the grenade went off. The grenade would catch him from behind and the next guy, even if he were spaced out properly, would be about where I am, and it would catch him up front.

"So typically, a grenade might easily get two men and would wound them severely or kill them."

This was so common, Embree said, that "It was the most routine part of my day to Medevac two ARVN soldiers who had fallen prey to this thing." He testified that 50 percent of his unit's casualties had been caused by mines.

As Boies had done with Friedman, Mastro asked this soldier to evaluate Westmoreland's opinion of the SD and SSD. Mastro asked Friedman if he agreed with Westmoreland's statement that "we are not fighting those people. They are basically civilians."

Embree answered firmly and without equivocation. "Those people were fighting us and we were trying to fight them. That's what we understood our job to be, and I'm very surprised to discover that General Westmoreland did not know that's what we were doing."

* * *

As the CBS defense moved forward, it became clear that, just as Westmoreland had been his own best witness, Sam Adams would be the best advocate for his position on the arcane Vietnam "numbers game."

While admitting that some people thought he was a "whacko" because of his single-minded pursuit of the OB controversy, Adams took comfort in the fact that history is often kind to those who speak unpopular truths. In an interview midway through his testimony, Adams equated himself with Galileo, who had been excommunicated by the Catholic Church for postulating that the Earth revolved around the sun, and had not been rehabilitated for centuries. "You know, I might be right," Adams said. "And in that case [if] it merely boils down to having been right, why the hell do I pursue such a thing so long? . . . When was Galileo exonerated? Was it last year? Why the hell do they bother? They look silly. That means that until 1983 the guy was really full of it."

Just as Galileo answered to the laws of nature, Adams' duty was to the numbers. It was a duty intertwined with the force Westmoreland had responded to when he chose a military career: patriotism. Adams readily agreed that he and Westmoreland shared a common motivation, but said they each had "a different view of what duty, honor and country is all about. . . . It's a different view of patriotism. What I would like to think I have is a more clear-eyed view.

"I'm not a radical [like] the old Sam Adams, another man who had whacko elements to his character. He was the American equivalent to Lenin. I'm not that type. I was in the United States Navy. I ran boats and stuff. Another thing I'm not is a whistleblower. I did not want to bother with all this goddamned crap of trying to turn people in. It's a pain in the ass."

But, as he said in his testimony, Adams had had little choice. In his view, too many GIs had paid too high a price for the OB intelligence dispute.

"What was at stake at—over this argument was basically our policy in Vietnam.

"If, as I and Colonel Hawkins among many others believed, the enemy was twice as big, we had to do something about that. We had to change our policy, we had to do something else. We could have done a number of things. Two things come to mind. We could have mobilized the reserves and sent more troops and tried to fight this much larger enemy, fight this much larger war that we were in, or we should have tried the other—gone the other route and withdrawn from Vietnam.

"I remember, however, during these proceedings [the various conferences on the OB] which went on through August and into September, thinking these things, and also remembering all the people that were being killed while we were playing with numbers up on the seventh floor of CIA headquarters. GIs were stepping on booby traps, they were being shot, they were being killed by shrapnel, and it was that that was at stake, these kids that were fighting the war. That is what I felt most strongly about."

Like Westmoreland, Adams had made a pilgrimage to the Vietnam Memorial. He said the vision of those names starkly etched in granite had only reinforced his convictions.

When Boies called Adams to the witness stand in early January, he asked him to explain why his "obsession" with the OB was so important.

"Because we lost the Vietnam War," Adams said. "It's the first war, as the program started out, it's the first war we ever lost, and it seems to me that there had never been an adequate reason as how we managed to do it. We're a great big country. Vietnam is a little bitty country. And yet we managed to lose that war. I don't think it's enough to say that the press did it."

The tweedy numbers-cruncher paused for a moment, then recalled his trip to the memorial.

"It's a long block of granite, slabs of granite," he said, "And on that granite are carved 58,022 names. Not all 58,000 of them were killed in action or in combat. Some of them committed suicide, some of them were in helicopter accidents, other things like that. But about 45,000 were killed in combat in Vietnam.

"And I remember when I visited the Vietnam Memorial, I asked myself, as sort of an analyst, how many of those 45,000 who were on those slabs of marble—it isn't marble, granite—of granite, how many of those were killed probably by people who weren't listed in the official order of battle or who belonged to organizations that weren't in the order of battle, and I said to myself, trying to figure the odds, that it was probably at least a third were killed by people not in the OB."

The trial had been going on for three months by the time Adams took the stand, but not once had the documentary been shown from beginning to end in court. Reporters and courtroom regulars had begun to joke about the fate of the "Unseen Documentary," wondering when, if ever, either side would show the complete work.

Boies finally played the entire program on January 14, with Adams on the stand. The lawyer would play a segment, stop, and ask Adams to explain the scene just screened. Adams, looking somewhat professorial in his herringbone jacket, then affably outlined the process, backing it all up with numerous references to people interviewed, their views, his methods, and the historical background. It was a masterful bit of showmanship, with Boies displaying the documentary and its supposedly obsessed progenitor in the best possible way.

At one point, Boies stopped the action with a younger-looking, brown-haired Sam Adams in freeze-frame on the screen. The man on the witness stand was now almost totally gray, dramatically suggesting he had paid a heavy price in his battle for the truth. The Sam Adams going through the documentary point by point didn't come across as a flake. Looking "like a rustic Paul Newman," as the *Washington Post* described him, Adams projected an image of knowledge, stability, and deep concern for his country and its soldiers.

Kitsy Westmoreland, meanwhile, had never seen the complete show and she didn't want to see it this time, either. Each time Boies started up the videotape, she attacked her needlepoint feverishly, scowling in mock concentration and yanking haphazardly at gold- and pewter-colored threads until she could no longer ignore the monitors. When she did glance up, it was only for a moment. She deliberately avoided looking at her husband, who shifted uncomfortably in his seat, occasionally clenching his fists.

"It was all I could do to keep from running up and grabbing George Crile and saying, 'You son of a bitch,' " she later confided.

Westmoreland's attorneys tried to diminish the impact of Adams' testimony, particularly his recollections of who had told whom about what during the various OB conferences. Objecting at one point to "leading" questions by Boies, David Dorsen didn't get far. "I think it's awful hard to examine on conversations that took place 17 years ago and I don't see anything wrong with using trigger words to call his attention to aspects of the conversation. We don't want him to testify who asked for coffee," Leval said.

On cross-examination, Dorsen tried to impeach Adams with his own words. For example, Dorsen had dug up a memo Adams wrote in 1967 that seemingly refuted the analyst's claim that all irregular forces should be included among the combatants listed in the OB. In this message, Adams described the VC militia as "noncombatants." Adams readily admitted writing the memo, but added, "Militia largely did not mix into firefights. . . . As I knew then, they made mines and booby traps." He repeated that the devices had accounted for about one third of all American casualties in Vietnam.

In almost two days of cross-examination, Dorsen managed to punch only a few holes in Adams' story.

"Our goal was to paint Sam as an obsessed, haunted crazy and we failed completely," said jury specialist Jay Schulman. He blamed the fact that Capital Legal was running out of time; he also blamed Dorsen. "An absolutely first-class litigator might have made a difference. But that would have meant going for the jugular. You don't destroy Sam Adams by nitpicking with him about what extrapolation means."

The few points Dorsen scored were eclipsed by Adams' persuasive testimony. The numbers breathed when Adams spoke. He painted word pictures that transported the courtroom audience back to the dusty Vietnamese market town where his pursuit had begun. He took them through steaming prisoner-detention centers and urged them to share his outrage over an apparent distortion that would skew the odds of survival for thousands of American soldiers. He managed to re-create the political climate of the 1960s.

The Vietnam War, after all, had changed a whole generation, he said in a mid-trial interview, reflecting on the "Ahab-like" quest that had led to the trial. "I'm not saying the OB question did it. I'm not crazy." But he said the alleged fakery had had a lot to do with the disillusionment. "You can almost point to a single day, which was the beginning of the Tet Offensive, that the whole thing began to unravel, and you had a generation that began to mistrust the American government.

"The OB dispute is a part of what happened. Because the American government was screwing around with a bunch of crazy-ass statistics. I'm not saying for an instant that the people who did that had bad motives. They wanted to buy time to win the war . . . but it's sort of tragic. A real, honest-to-God Greek-type tragedy, whereby you're trying to do something good and a series of circumstances comes along and precisely what you didn't want to happen happens. . . . That's the nature of my whacko obsession."

Adams, at this point, also predicted that the upcoming CBS witnesses would destroy Westmoreland's case.

" . . . Westy is wrong and he's going to lose," Adams said. "When he filed the lawsuit, my jaw just dropped to the floor. . . . He's just going to back into a twirling fan. And he's doing it, and the chunks are going to start flying in the next six weeks."

The blades of that fan were career CIA analysts and Army officers who had as much a sense of "Duty, Honor, Country," as Westmoreland, Adams said, and were ready to detail the OB cover-up under oath.

They, like Adams, did not mince words.

The first of these witnesses, George W. Allen, former deputy chief of Vietnam affairs for the CIA, said his agency had "sold out" to the military on the OB issue, so that President Johnson had ended up with a Special National Intelligence Estimate of enemy troop strength that was "essentially a dishonest piece of paper, a dishonest document."

Allen, who had spent a total of "two years and 35 weeks" in Vietnam, ending in 1966, testified he had discussed this SNIE with Adams in 1967, telling him the estimate was "the mistake of the century. . . .

"I told him that, as he well knew from his research, that I . . . fully believed that the evidence supported a force of half a million as being the organized communist forces opposing us in Vietnam, and this estimate comes up with—the highest total you could find in the estimate was under 250,000.

"I told him it was misleading because it did not make clear to readers . . . that the total . . . did not include the same categories of forces that had been published in earlier national intelligence estimates on Vietnam. . . .

"It was misleading because it said we couldn't come up with a number for the self-defense forces, we couldn't come up with an estimate. . . . This was not true. This was in fact a lie, it was dishonest, because in the intelligence business we existed to estimate, to give people our informed judgment. . . ."

Allen said he knew in 1967 why the CIA went along with a dishonest estimate. It was the same point made by the documentary. " . . . I told Mr. Adams that I felt the agency had sacrificed its integrity on the altar of public relations and political expediency. . . . "

Late in the morning of his first day on the stand, Allen, who had been wounded in Vietnam, was asked by Boies to give his views on the compromise reached after the September 1967 OB conference. Speaking nervously and trying not to look at Westmoreland, Allen testified that he had told Adams he had been "outraged" and called the compromise a "sell-out." He said MACV's position was "unprincipled" and a "prostitution" of intelligence. Dorsen, not liking the word "prostitution" at all, rose to object, but Leval moved even quicker, interrupting Allen and asking, "Just a second. Are you talking about a conversation?"

"Yes," Allen said.

Leval instructed him, "Stick with what you said to Mr. Adams."

This gave Allen a chance to start all over.

"I told Mr. Adams that I thought this prostitution of the intelligence process was intolerable. . . . I told Mr. Adams I was going to have great difficulty determining how I was going to continue my career as an intelligence officer when developments like this could occur."

The impact of this "prostitution" had been revealed by the Tet Offensive, Allen testified. Shortly after Tet, Allen had gone to Vietnam with an inter-agency task force headed by General Earle Wheeler, chairman of the Joint Chiefs of Staff, where he had found that MACV was still tinkering with the numbers. After visiting all four military regions in the country and talking to a number of U.S. and Vietnamese officials "ranging from the President and Vice President of Vietnam down to battalion commanders and provincial intelligence officers," Allen had concluded that "MACV had originally estimated early in the Tet Offensive that a force of 87,000 men had been involved in, had participated in the offensive."

Allen testified that, judging from his research, this had been a "gross understatement." In fact, Allen said, "I estimated that the enemy force that conducted the Tet Offensive had totaled at least 400,000, given the strength of the attack . . . throughout the countryside." This had dovetailed with Adams' estimates, and Allen said he had determined that the self-defense forces had participated in Tet, refuting MACV's contention that they were non-combatants.

During the afternoon, Bois asked Allen the same series of questions he had asked in the morning, this time establishing that what Allen had told Adams in the 1960s he had also told George Crile in the 1980s. This was a laborious but necessary exercise to prove that Crile and CBS had done their homework before airing the documentary. Boies also had Allen explain why it had been necessary for Crile to interview him twice.

"Why did you hold back on camera?" Boies demanded. "Why did you tell Mr. Crile some things off camera that you were not prepared to tell him on camera?"

"First, I had some feelings of guilt about my involvement in it and was reluctant to . . . publicly acknowledge that guilt," Allen told him.

Allen also charged that the CIA had required him to continue the "whitewash" of the OB controversy in his testimony before the Pike Committee. Though he had been prepared to testify "openly" at the Pike Committee hearings in 1975, Allen said that George Carver, his former boss and the chief of the CIA's Vietnamese branch during the war, had sent him a copy of his statement before the committee so that Allen would know what the "line was to be."

During his research for the documentary, Crile had asked Allen to recount what happened the day he went to testify before the Pike Committee, and Boies had Allen explain this in court. Allen testified he rode to the hearing with CIA director William Colby, who instructed him "that I was to be very careful in answering questions from the committee and not to give them answers that went beyond the point of the question."

Allen testified he had told Crile that at the hearing Colby read a statement which was "an attempt by the agency to watch this one out, to sweep it under the rug, to cover up, not to attack the military in this estimate or estimative process at this time."

Allen said that when it came his turn to testify before the committee, " . . . I played my role on that occasion, I regret to say, of not breaking ranks and conforming to what I now see clearly in my view was a whitewash. And I told this to Mr. Crile as well."

Allen was the point man of a squad of CIA agents Boies used to breach Westmoreland's defense. He was followed by Doug Parry, a low-ranking analyst in the CIA's South Vietnam branch. Ron Smith, Sam Adams' old boss in the same department, took the stand the last week of January, putting the full strength of his experience and credentials behind Adams, Crile, and CBS.

Those credentials were impressive. After graduating from Boston University in 1951, Smith joined the Air Force, which sent him back to school. He received a master's degree in Soviet studies from Syracuse University in 1954 and joined the CIA in 1958. The CIA also sent him to school, to Brown University, where he studied economics for a year and then taught. In the mid-1970s, he spent a year as a resident fellow at the Harvard University Center for International Affairs. Then Smith went back to the CIA to organize a new branch in the Office of Economic Research to focus on the energy crisis. Because of this experience, the CIA detailed him to serve as chief of intelligence for the Department of Energy from 1982 until he retired in mid-1984.

In 1967, Smith was appointed to head the CIA's South Vietnam branch, where he met Adams. While some of Westmoreland's witnesses from the intelligence community branded Adams as a singular obsessive, Smith had an entirely different view. "Sam was one of the finest analysts that I ever worked with. . . . He was always full of vigor, always upbeat about getting the work done, intelligent and co-operative with other analysts and last but not least . . . he was a very good writer. . . . "

Unlike many of the witnesses who testified for either side at the trial, Smith came to court an OB-battle virgin. He testified he had not

discussed the document with Adams since the dispute first arose in
1967 and 1968. But, Smith said, at that time his views had been as
strong as Adams'.

Asked by Boies whether or not he thought the 1967 intelligence
estimate had been honest or dishonest, Smith replied that he had told
Adams at the time " . . . it couldn't have honestly been an honest
depiction of the situation." Pressed by Boies, Smith testified that in
1967 he had told Adams that the OB as it appeared in the SNIE was
"grossly inadequate" and would mislead senior officials. Putting only
the figures Westmoreland's command wanted into the OB was a
"capitulation to MACV's views" and "morally unacceptable," he told
the attorney.

Boies then turned to Westmoreland's role in the OB dispute, asking Smith if he had ever expressed an opinion to Adams about the
general's role in 1967 or 1968. Smith said he had told Adams that
Westmoreland's role was wrong because the general should have let
intelligence analysts "do their work unencumbered." He added that it
was also wrong for Westmoreland "to use the political power he had
at the time to force the thing down our throats," Smith said.

During his testimony, Smith also revealed that the North Vietnamese Army, like the American force, had had its share of paper
warriors. "Fortunately for the analysts," Smith recalled, "the North
Vietnamese Army were great producers of paper." He told how every
infiltrator not only knew the number of his infiltration group, but
actually carried a piece of paper identifying him as a member of that
group with the group number on it.

And the ID cards were just the beginning of the North Vietnamese paper trail, Smith explained. "There were other kinds of
military bureaucratic papers that pertained to these things from which
we could get group numbers, from which we could analyze—they
often gave us the number of people in groups, number of people in
collections of groups, so that there was a great, there was a great deal
of captured documents picked up during this process."

MACV was capturing this bureaucratic dross by the ton and
shipping it out fast. "MACV analysts would receive them the day they
were published . . . we in Washington didn't get them much later,"
Smith said. "They would come in by air pouch—sometimes, depending
upon the way flights came, we would have them in a couple of days
and sometimes a week, but not a long period of time."

This material, plus electronic intelligence received from the
National Security Agency, led the CIA to conclude that in the months
before the January 1968 Tet Offensive the enemy had turned the
infiltration spigot of the Ho Chi Minh Trail wide open. The Agency
estimated that in the five months prior to Tet the North was sending

down 20,000 to 30,000 men a month—a charge made by the documentary and disputed by Westmoreland. MACV analysts, however, claimed that only 7,000 to 8,000 men a month were moving down the Trail.

This anomaly didn't make sense to Smith. Asked by Boies if he thought there had been sufficient intelligence prior to Tet to demonstrate that enemy infiltration was substantially larger than MACV was reporting, Smith answered emphatically, "Yes, sir."

Dorsen tried to object, but was overruled. Smith continued.

"All of these documents are carefully dated, the captured documents are dated, carefully chronicled as to when they were picked up, when they were translated and when they are disseminated, and I had explained that MACV analysts would have them a day—or certainly within 24 hours after they were disseminated and we would have them [within] at most a week.

" . . . As a matter of fact, because we were disturbed at MACV's infiltration analytical reporting [this] was one of the reasons that we went into this analysis, and we took careful note of this factor, when these materials would have been available to MACV analysts."

Dorsen then tried to dent Smith's testimony in a cross-examination that lasted for the rest of the day. Whatever ground he gained was lost by the dramatic testimony Boies extracted from Smith on redirect examination the next day, January 30.

Boies asked Smith once again to recall his discussions with Adams about the OB in 1967 and 1968. Smith's response measurably widened the breach in Westmoreland's case.

"I felt that MACV had misrepresented not only every element of the force structure in a very serious manner, but that, added together, this representation of the order of battle misrepresented the very nature of the war we were fighting."

He said he had also told Adams that public and private dealings with senior MACV officers had convinced him "there was a massive effort to distort these numbers to Washington policy makers that would have been impossible without the leadership of General Westmoreland."

Smith, the quiet analyst who finally came in from the cold, ended his testimony with a succinct condemnation of MACV's use of intelligence. He said he had told Adams that he thought the MACV enemy-strength estimates were "rampantly dishonest."

The next witness, Richard Kovar, had even more impressive credentials. After serving with the CIA almost thirty years, Kovar had retired in 1980, going to work for a book publisher in Alexandria, Virginia. But after two years Kovar had missed his former life and called up an old boss, who helped him get "the best job in the CIA."

In that assignment, which Kovar held until shifting to another, secret, assignment two weeks before the trial began, he put together President Reagan's Daily Brief—"a daily digest of current intelligence prepared specifically for the President of The United States."

In July 1983, while serving in that sensitive post, Kovar sat down and prepared an affidavit which lavished extraordinary praise on Adams and CBS while sharply, angrily, condemning MACV and high CIA officials. The affidavit succinctly traced the history of U.S. intelligence in Vietnam as Kovar detailed his intimate knowledge of the subject.

Kovar started his CIA career in 1954, editing translated transcripts of Hanoi radio broadcasts. He then spent two years at a radio-monitoring station in the Far East, selecting and editing broadcast material from Radio Hanoi, Radio Peking, and Moscow.

From 1956 to 1958, Kovar was posted to the sleepy, colonial Saigon Graham Green described in *The Ugly American*, directing native translators who analyzed broadcast and newspaper material from Hanoi and Saigon.

In 1962, as a brash American President named John Kennedy developed an interest in the Green Berets' novel counter-insurgency tactics, Kovar's Vietnam experience came in handy. He joined the staff of the Agency's Deputy Director for Intelligence, or "DDI" in CIA shorthand. There, from 1962 to 1968, among Kovar's many duties, as he told the court, "my principal assignment was to monitor all cables, memoranda and analytical products relating to Vietnam that passed through the DDI's office."

As the U.S. interest and presence in Vietnam grew, so did the flow of raw intelligence. Despite this increase, Kovar noticed a dangerous information gap. During the early 1960s, Kovar recalled, " . . . I and many of my colleagues at the CIA became deeply concerned about the failure of the U.S. intelligence community to evaluate accurately and methodically the size and nature of the enemy we were facing in Vietnam. I did not know then, nor do I now know, how our first total for the number of communist combatants in South Vietnam was arrived at. . . . We thought it much too low, we knew that it had to be based on incomplete and questionable sources, and we resisted using it as a base against which newer cumulative data would be added or subtracted."

The situation in the early 1960s portended the situation to come. "From time to time we would protest to the military members of our working group about the inadequacy of our data base," Kovar swore in his affidavit, "At the same time, we pleaded for better information and more people to deal with it."

In 1965, as U.S. Marines in battle garb inched their way down nets hanging from the side of the attack transport U.S.S. *George C. Clymer* and into boats waiting to take them to an assault landing on a beach outside Danang, one of the *Clymer*'s former officers, Sam Adams, was starting to analyze the Vietnam situation at the CIA. Kovar remembered his arrival well. "Sam Adams was a godsend to the CIA's intelligence effort on the situation in Vietnam. I believed at the time, and continue to believe that Adams was one of the best intelligence analysts I have ever encountered and, more importantly, one of the most devoted to the objectivity that the CIA purported to stand for."

Backing into the conflict that was to become Adams' obsession, Kovar conceded that Vietnam was initially "viewed at the CIA as an intelligence sideshow. . . . Overworked and undersupported, we too often had been told that Vietnam was the Pentagon's problem."

Heartened by Secretary of Defense Robert McNamara's increasing reliance in the early 1960s on the CIA to counter-balance the Pentagon, Kovar recalled, "We were all the more frustrated . . . when in formal estimate sessions the military . . . insisted upon the adoption of analyses that seemed to us neither objective nor factually based. . . . "

Turning to Adams' 1967 estimates of enemy troop strength, Kovar termed the research "the most thorough review ever done on enemy order of battle." But during the debate over this intelligence estimate, Kovar said, "representatives of the military services used every tactic from horse trading to browbeating in their efforts to induce the CIA to change its position. There was no suggestion that the military representatives had better estimates based on superior analyses or more extensive intelligence source material. Indeed, I am not at all sure that they even pretended to have analyzed the data themselves. They simply insisted that MACV's figures be accepted. . . ."

Recalling the September 1967 Saigon OB conference, Kovar described MACV's success as a victory of force, not reason. "There was no suggestion that MACV had persuaded anyone of the logic of its case; it was simply a matter of asserting its primacy in determining what the figures should be."

Kovar blamed CIA director Richard Helms for the cave-in because he refused to back up George Carver, the Agency's chief negotiator in Saigon. Regarding Helms' cabled instructions to Carver, Kovar said, "I do not recall exactly whether I actually read Mr. Helms' cabled reply, but I know that I and others were aware of its substance. 'Helms punted' was the way it was described: he had opted to accede to MACV's demands."

When Kovar learned of Adams' fight against the MACV numbers, he said, he had admired Adams "above all men" because "He had put his reputation and his career on the line in order to have a bad decision re-examined, and he did so within official channels. . . . "

But after complaining to the CIA's inspector general, keeping the fight in-house, "Sam Adams was put into limbo."

The villain, Kovar said in his affidavit, was one of Westmoreland's star witnesses. "Many of the trails led to Lieutenant General Daniel O. Graham, a man I had known and despised as Major and later Colonel Danny Graham, an upward-climbing careerist who let nothing stand in the way of his grandstanding efforts to win the favorable attention of his superiors."

Kovar contemptuously described Graham as a man of few principles. Graham was "infamous in the intelligence community as a man who would take whatever analytical position he thought would bring him the greatest reward from his superiors and pursue that position doggedly—or change it for another if expedient—regardless of facts, logic or analysis which indicated a contrary conclusion."

Describing his reaction to the "The Uncounted Enemy" when it aired in 1982, Kovar said, "As I watched the story unfold, I found myself cheering much of the time and wanting to weep the rest of the time. For the very first time, I realized with painful clarity that what we had all been involved in was not some abstract academic process but a train of truth versus falsehood that led directly to the debacle of the Tet Offensive. Sam Adams had been right and I and Mr. Helms and Paul Walsh had been wrong." (Walsh oversaw the preparation of the SNIE at the CIA in his position as Deputy Director of the Agency's Office of Economic Research.)

Kovar said the CBS broadcast drove home a searing truth. "It was not just the CIA versus the Army, but ultimately a matter of truth and consequences, and the consequences had been military and political defeat and death and maiming for untold numbers of Americans and Vietnamese."

" 'The Uncounted Enemy,' " Kovar said, "was a great service to the intelligence process—a process which was served so poorly by the CIA and the military alike during the period of the Tet Offensive of 1968. I viewed Sam Adams and George Allen and the others who helped make the documentary as heroes. Indeed, I believe that CBS should rebroadcast the documentary in prime time on each anniversary of the Tet Offensive so that no intelligence analyst, soldier or citizen who watches it will ever let anything like this happen again."

Kovar concluded his affidavit with a paean to Adams and a swipe at his critics. "I want my children and other children to learn from Sam Adams that being right, doing right and seeking the truth can made a difference, a terrible difference. . . . The CIA owes Sam Adams an apology and a medal, and all of us who lack his dedication and failed to support him owe an acknowledgement of our shame."

On the stand, Kovar characterized the enemy's self-defense forces, which MACV had not wanted included in the order of battle, as "the first line of defense" in the South. "These were the people, as I understood it, who harassed and sniped our forces . . . when they patrolled and swept through an area, laid booby traps and ambushes for them. . . .

"As such, these people killed our troops. They inflicted casualties. . . . We counted these people when we found them dead. . . . This was an important, essential element of the Vietnamese communist capabilities for fighting in South Vietnam. . . . "

An intelligence estimate which omitted these troops, in Kovar's opinion, "did not fulfill its purpose. It did not describe or estimate accurately or completely the capabilities of the Vietnamese communists for fighting in South Vietnam."

Asked directly by Boies' associate Bob Baron if Adams was a mental case, Kovar testified: "What Sam did wrong was that he didn't . . . salute and shut up. He didn't close ranks. Not only did he not shut up, he pushed his arguments and he pushed his outrage at the Agency's acquiescence in this process beyond the levels that a subordinate is supposed to go. And that frightened a lot of people and it made people mad."

Kovar was a strong witness for CBS. His affidavit was damning, and the Westmoreland team had to defuse its effect. Kovar gave them a small opening. Dorsen on cross-examination elicited from the witness the statement that "I know that the self-defense militia didn't appear in the final draft [of the SNIE]." That was wrong. They appeared, but not in the main body of the report.

Dorsen used this as a wedge to try to impugn Kovar's credibility, but the CIA man nevertheless was a critical witness for CBS. His affidavit was strong ammunition, particularly against Danny Graham.

As January gave way to February, Boies continued to widen the gap he had breached in Westmoreland's case. His bit of theater with the grenade illustrated better than any spoken testimony the threat posed by the SD and the SSD, and the testimony from Adams and his CIA colleagues significantly bolstered the analyst's credibility. Boies felt that the jury was probably convinced the SD and SSD ought to have been included in the order of battle. The time had come to convince the jury that they had been left out on Westmoreland's orders. The battlefield was prepared for the introduction of Boies' heavy artillery: General Joseph McChristian and Colonel Gains Hawkins.

18.

The End of the Long Gray Line

WILLIAM C. WESTMORELAND put a premium on two things in life: the tradition of the United States Military Academy at West Point, New York, and the honor code that binds its cadets and graduates together. The CBS documentary "The Uncounted Enemy" attacked both. Now the code and the tradition were on trial in federal court, ripping apart the Long Gray Line of West Point graduates spanning two world wars, Korea, and Vietnam.

In the opening pages of his autobiography, *A Soldier Reports*, Westmoreland reflected on his years as a West Point cadet and said that while he appreciated the associations that would last him a lifetime, the "most rewarding" part of his academy experience "was the appreciation and respect I gained for the code of ethics for which the Military Academy stands and which its honor system exemplified."

When Westmoreland graduated in 1936, General of the Armies John J. Pershing, the U.S. commander in World War I and Westy's idol, was the commencement speaker. As the cadets stood stiffly at attention in their dress gray on the green grass of the West Point parade field, Westmoreland remembers, Pershing's "words for young officers were lucid and cogent. Maintain your own morals at a high level, he said, and you will find them reflected in the morals of your men."

West Point graduates, inculcated with this code and its notions of chivalry, became the glue that held the American Army together through peace and war. In 1962, when Douglas MacArthur gave his last speech at the academy during Westmoreland's tenure as superintendent, he eloquently and passionately evoked the unique bond:

"The shadows are lengthening for me. The twilight is here . . . I listen vainly for the bewitching melody of faint bugles blowing reveille, of far drums beating the long roll. In my dreams, I hear again the crash of guns, the rattle of musketry, the strange, mournful mutter of the battlefield. . . .

"Today marks my final roll call with you, but I want you to know that when I cross the river, my last conscious thoughts will be—of the Corps—and the Corps—and the Corps."

One of the unwritten parts of the West Point tradition is that graduates back each other up, help each other out, and rarely criticize one another. (During World War II, non-academy officers derisively referred to graduates as members of the WPPA, the West Point Protective Association.) Westmoreland's former Vietnam intelligence chief, General Joseph McChristian (West Point, 1939), broke with that tradition.

When producer George Crile asked McChristian if Westmoreland had participated in a cover-up of enemy-strength estimates that would have violated any statutes of the Uniform Code of Military Justice, McChristian answered, "Not that I am aware of." Then he broke ranks by adding, "But there's something on a ring that I wear from West Point that the motto is: 'Duty, Honor, Country.' It's dishonorable."

That one sentence in "The Uncounted Enemy," as much as the word "conspiracy" in the opening moments of the ninety-minute broadcast, was a motivating factor behind Westmoreland's decision to sue. After the documentary aired, Westmoreland called his former officer, urging him to join a press conference attacking the show. McChristian recalls Westmoreland told him he had been "hurt" by the statement relating to dishonor. McChristian refused to help, explaining in a Mailgram:

"I have gone over my notes and find that George Crile did tell me that Colonel Hawkins testified that he had been ordered to abide by a ceiling established by you. Knowing this unproven allegation I answered George Crile's question. I'm sorry if my answer hurt you. The allegations in the documentary pertained to actions that took place after I left Vietnam. I feel that the people who were there should help you refute them. If they cannot refute them then I think you, general, should determine who the guilty persons were."

Westmoreland had taken a lot of heat on the war, both when serving in Vietnam and afterward when he toured college campuses. But he could not ignore McChristian's attack. It made a mockery of his life. So, when McChristian took the witness stand on February 6, 1985, he was more than just another witness; he represented the Code and the Corps to which he and Westmoreland owed deep allegiance. The courtroom was packed. Would McChristian dare to attack Westmoreland's honor under oath?

Just before McChristian took the stand, Dan Burt, worried that his case was unraveling, began working behind the scenes to settle out of court. The CBS witnesses seemed to make a good impression on the press, the public, and the jury. Too good. More disturbing, McChristian clearly planned to testify. Before the case went to court, Burt had predicted to reporters that the former intelligence chief would never dare appear. Worse yet, the Israeli general in the courtroom downstairs had just lost his case. On January 24, a jury decided *Time* magazine had indeed published an untruth about Ariel Sharon and the article had defamed him. But the panel found *Time* had not acted with malice and granted no damages.

According to some members of his legal team, Burt was becoming driven by fear. David Dorsen said Burt "was scared to death. . . . Dan also had terrible problems at home. He spoke to Westy about moving back to Washington for the last two weeks of the trial. 'Desperate' is not an inaccurate word to describe his marital situation. It was distracting him, affecting his judgment."

Dorsen said Burt began to meet with jury specialist Jay Schulman every night. "They were sitting around trying to figure out what the jury is thinking. That's bizarre . . . that's fantasy work in the middle of a serious trial."

"Dan was extremely nervous, extremely sensitive, extremely vulnerable," Schulman recalled. "It took him a long time to begin to feel comfortable in the court. Now, Dan is very, very smart—he has as fast a mind as I've encountered in a litigator. But being fast does not compensate for being very vulnerable and very sensitive. I think Dan put on a better show in the direct examination of our witnesses than I would have expected. However, that show was not good enough. Especially when contrasted to David Boies."

Burt also worried that the case was losing the support of Capital Legal's financial backers, his associates said. His manner, which had been abrasive in a "kidding around" way, "turned nasty," Dorsen said. "He started screaming at people. He called himself the commander. He was a field marshal or something like that. It was a very strange performance. . . . He screamed at Westmoreland. Morale was absolutely destroyed."

Westmoreland flatly denied that Burt had ever treated him with disrespect, but admitted the pressure was taking a heavy toll at this point. He began to look haggard as the line of CBS witnesses trooped forward day after day to discredit him. It was one of the most difficult times of his life. "I had to keep telling myself, well, there's nothing you can do about it. . . . I let it go in one ear and out the other, as if it was unreal. I'm certainly not suggesting that I have no emotions. I was restless at night, reflecting. You went to bed at night thinking about it and you woke up in the morning thinking about it. Most every night was a restless night."

His sleep was also affected by persistent back problems and worry over how Kitsy was holding up. "We were both pretty much bushed," he said, recalling that at one point the top figure of his wife's blood pressure shot up to 220 and he rushed her to the emergency room at Lenox Hill Hospital.

Although used to regimentation, the general tired of playing by the rules of the courtroom. It wasn't easy for him to relinquish control to Burt, and he was frustrated that he couldn't talk to the judge or jury. He wished for a more open process, with everyone allowed to speak their piece. "I had no experience in the federal court system. . . . I had a simplistic view that it would be some sort of debate controlled by the judge," he said. Westmoreland had to work hard to keep himself in check.

As Burt negotiated secretly with CBS, he was acutely aware of the strain on Westmoreland. He worried that the general's health would fail. And although Burt was searching for a way out, the tension for both men would double on the day McChristian took the stand.

Judging from McChristian's conflicting pre-trial affidavits, neither side could be sure which way his testimony would go. Westmoreland's former intelligence chief seemed unable to make up his mind whether he would be a loyal comrade-in-arms or the general's Brutus.

In a 1983 affidavit, McChristian recalled his 1977 meeting with Sam Adams, saying that by the end of the session Adams "told me that I had convinced him that there had been no wrongful manipulation of intelligence. . . . "

By 1984, however, McChristian had added a key sentence as to why he had agreed to the meeting: "I thought it was important to set the record straight and Adams seemed to be sincerely interested in finding out the truth."

In the 1983 statement, McChristian praised Westmoreland, saying his commander was thoroughly immersed in the intelligence situation. "General Westmoreland was traveling throughout South Vietnam visiting U.S., Vietnamese and free world forces daily. There is no one who knew better the influence of terrain, weather and the enemy on these missions. I have no personal knowledge of any conspiracy to suppress or alter intelligence on the enemy in Vietnam."

In April 1984, however, this praise disappeared. He said: "A career military officer must expect criticism. His whole life is devoted to the noble concept of defending the Constitution of the United States. . . . Such criticism is healthy. It keeps public servants honest. One hopes it will be constructive criticism. If misused it can do great harm."

In both affidavits, McChristian swore that when presented with a cable that drastically increased the number of irregulars carried in the order of battle, Westmoreland had reacted by saying, "If I send this cable to Washington it will create a political bombshell." But there was a sharp contrast in how McChristian viewed his commander's decision not to send the cable back to Washington.

In 1983, McChristian simply stated, "Although this was the first time that he had ever questioned my intelligence, he certainly had every right to do so, especially since he had not been briefed in detail on our intelligence holdings. . . ."

In 1984, McChristian had a more critical view. "I was disturbed by General Westmoreland's expressed concern over political considerations," he said. "At no point during our meeting did he ever question the methodology or the evidence on which these estimates were based."

In 1983, McChristian sharply criticized Crile's editing, particularly the sequence in which the former intelligence chief pointed at his ring and uttered the word "dishonorable." McChristian recalled he had told Crile in a phone conversation several days after the broadcast that he was upset with the "improper" judgment call.

But in April 1984, McChristian backpedaled, amplifying his earlier remarks and ending up with praise for the documentary producer. " . . . By using the term 'improper,' I did not mean to convey that I felt George Crile had purposefully misrepresented my position or acted unethically.

"I have at all times found Crile to be professional in his conduct and sincere and honest in his desire to find out the truth."

Which version McChristian would favor in court seemed to be anyone's guess.

Like all the other witnesses, McChristian devoted his first moments on the witness stand to a laundry list of his accomplishments. And, like many of the other ego-driven men involved in the trial, the tan, fit, burly general with a shock of silver hair praised himself with gusto. According to this testimony, McChristian had made the key intelligence decision of the 1962 Cuban missile crisis. He explained how he had set up a special task force for the Department of the Army to collect intelligence on the situation in Cuba.

He had decided to focus on a part of Cuba that he felt had been ignored by U.S. photo-reconnaissance planes, and " . . . that was the flight that discovered the missiles in Cuba."

It was this desire to look at every scrap of information that had led McChristian to set up CICV—the Combined Intelligence Center, Vietnam—when he signed on as Westmoreland's "J-2" in July 1965. In McChristian's view, CICV, a joint effort with South Vietnam, was "the data base for the command not only on Order of Battle information, both ground forces and political, but it was the data base on area analysis, on all mapping, on all photography of the country, on all studies of terrain, all studies put out to assist units in their planning for activities, it was the research and analysis center, where you could get all this information."

This explanation of CICV contrasted sharply with those of Westmoreland's witnesses, who dismissed the operation as a training exercise for the South Vietnamese. McChristian viewed CICV as "one of the finest supports of combat intelligence that was ever developed in support of our forces in wartime and absolutely an essential part of what we were doing."

Colonel Gains Hawkins had been CICV's OB chief, and, like the organization itself, he was superior, McChristian testified. "I found that he was extremely conscientious, paid great attention to detail, worked well with his people. I had full confidence in him and I thought he did an outstanding job."

With the importance of CICV established, Boies focused McChristian on the irregular forces. McChristian told the court unequivocally "it was my strong conviction from the beginning" that the order of battle should include these units.

The self-defense and secret self-defense forces had constituted a military threat, he said, because "Their overall object[ive] in the war was, number one, to extend their control over the South Vietnamese people, number two to reduce the control of the government of Vietnam over these people, number three to bolster the will of the South Vietnamese people to support their cause and number four to undermine the will of the American people to continue such a war."

McChristian conceded these irregular forces had not had any offensive military capabilities. But "that wasn't their job," he insisted. "Their job was to carry out these roles, these missions down within the hamlets and the villages, and they were also looked upon as a training base and mobilization base to upgrade the local and main Vietcong forces."

After this exchange, Boies reprised the bit of theater that had already worked so well. He handed McChristian a crude, hand-made grenade, which the general accepted gingerly, identifying it as a "beer can"-type grenade typical of the weapons manufactured in villages and hamlets.

McChristian said the grenade had been given him by Company B of the 503rd regiment of the 173rd Airborne in March 1967. He told Boies that the self-defense forces could "easily" manufacture such a grenade, further establishing the threat these forces had posed to American troops.

Next, Boies asked McChristian to recall that fateful day between

May 10 and May 15, 1967, when he took the cable containing higher enemy-strength estimates to Westmoreland.

As this showdown between the two West Pointers began, Westmoreland did not shift in his seat at the left of his defense team's table. Nor did his expression change perceptibly.

"What did General Westmoreland say to you after he read that cable?" Boies asked.

"I took that cable in to General Westmoreland, and I stood in front of his desk and I handed it to him," McChristian recalled. "I gave him a little bit of background on what it was. He read it. He looked up at me and he said, 'If I send that cable to Washington, it will create a political bombshell.' "

Because Westmoreland, a West Pointer sworn always to tell the truth, had already testified that he had not used these words, Boies repeated the question.

"Sir, I want to ask you, are you absolutely positive General Westmoreland used the term 'political bombshell' during that meeting?"

McChristian answered with conviction and passion.

"Yes I am. I am as sure of it as I am seeing people in front of me right now. I was so surprised by it that there were enough words said there that burned themselves right into my memory. . . . "

McChristian went on to refute even more of Westmoreland's testimony in a fast-paced exchange that left little doubt that the two officers had distinctly different versions of what had happened that day.

"Did General Westmoreland ask you about the components of the category known as irregulars at that meeting?"

"I don't recall," McChristian answered. "But if he had, I would have certainly pointed out what happened at the Honolulu conference. . . . I think it would have stuck in my mind. I don't recall any discussion on that."

"General Westmoreland has also testified . . . he said to you, 'Joe, with respect to the self-defense and secret self-defense, we are not fighting those people. They are basically civilians. They don't belong in any representation, numerical representation of the enemy.' Did General Westmoreland say that to you?"

"No, sir," McChristian said.

"General Westmoreland also testified . . . that he asked you for a briefing. Did General Westmoreland ask you for a briefing at that meeting?"

"No, sir, he did not. If he had asked me for a briefing, I would have immediately . . . had to go back and set up requirements for a briefing. . . . That was not asked of me."

"Did General Westmoreland decline to send the cable that you gave him?" Boies asked.

McChristian described the exchange. "General Westmoreland said to me—first of all, when he told me it would create a political bombshell, I said 'General, I don't see why it should. Send me back and I'll explain to anyone who wants to know what we've been doing to collect this information.' And he said, 'No. Leave it with me.'"

Boies paused for a moment to let the meaning of this information sink in, then gave McChristian even more room to attack Westmoreland.

"At any prior time in your military service had you ever had a superior officer discuss with you the political implications of an enemy strength estimate?" Boies asked.

"No, sir," McChristian said.

"Did you believe it was improper for General Westmoreland to hold your cable?"

"I think that for a military man to withhold a report based upon political considerations would be improper," the witness answered.

After a brief recess, Boies pressed McChristian further about the cable, particularly the implications of Westmoreland's pocket veto.

Boies finished his examination with one last key question for McChristian, asking him if before the May 1967 meeting "had General Westmoreland or anyone else at MACV ever suggested to you that the self-defense forces should not be included in the order of battle calculations?"

"General Westmoreland had never suggested to me that they not be included," McChristian answered.

"Had anyone at MACV ever suggested that they not be included?"

"No, sir," he said, almost meekly.

That was the last time McChristian seemed meek, or even patient. After the lunch break, it was as though a different man took the stand. He did not like being cross-examined.

From David Dorsen's first question, McChristian had his verbal dukes up, tossing off non-answers laced with sarcasm. McChristian had treated Boies as an equal, but his approach with Dorsen was that of a commander to a very dim-witted private.

"Was it your responsibility as J-2 to interpret the facts and issue reports based on facts?" Dorsen wanted to know.

The general responded, "We are getting to the point now, Mr. Dorsen, that I think the context of what you're talking about becomes very important. So I think if you have something specific now, because there are many types of reports I was involved in, I think that I should be shown the context of what you're talking about."

Dorsen was not flustered. "General McChristian, I was asking a general question about your responsibilities as J-2."

"I think it would be very misleading for me to give a general [response] to that question," the witness persisted. "I had under me maybe as many as 5,000 Army intelligence troops under my operational control. I handled those differently than other people. . . ."

Dorsen, demonstrating remarkable self-control, managed to thread his way through this verbal barbed wire, casting some doubt on McChristian's memory of the conversation with Westmoreland about the enemy-strength cable.

He asked if McChristian knew Westmoreland had never received a detailed briefing on the enemy-strength increase reported in the cable. McChristian conceded that point, but asserted, "But it doesn't mean that he wasn't aware of what was going on and that higher figures were expected. . . ."

"You briefed the chief of staff, but you didn't brief General Westmoreland personally, did you?" Dorsen asked.

McChristian replied, " . . . If General Westmoreland wanted a briefing on these things, he would ask for it."

"Didn't General Westmoreland tell you in words virtually identical to the ones I am using, 'I can't understand this and I want to be briefed. Do not send it out'?"

"No, sir."

"Did he say anything like—"

"He said 'leave it with me. I want to go over it.' "

"He said that?"

"Yes."

"Did he also say 'I can't understand this'?"

"No, sir."

"Did you ever tell Mr. Adams—Samuel Adams—prior to the date of the broadcast, that General Westmoreland told you 'I can't understand this'?"

"I don't recall saying that, I'd have to see whatever context you have, Mr. Dorsen."

Dorsen leaned over calmly, dug out a leaf from Adams' voluminous notes, and showed McChristian the page where Adams had recorded McChristian saying exactly that.

McChristian looked uncomfortable, and said he could not remember using those words with Adams. "I always made an effort, before this trial came about when I was under oath, not to quote General Westmoreland," McChristian said.

Dorsen moved to enter Adams' notes into evidence. This forced Boies to object and call notes produced by his own witness "hearsay." As the opponents strode up to the left-hand side of the judge's platform for a private conference, it was clear that this would be a tricky maneuver for Boies. The CBS attorney was in the awkward position of having to argue against his own client. "While I don't have any reason to believe this is not authentic," he said, "it is also the case that there hadn't been any foundation laid. . . . "

Leval had a suggestion for resolving the problem quickly. Why not simply have Boies ask Adams if he had made the notes? Then Boies could relay his answer to the court. "Why is it not admissible as Adams' statement that General McChristian said that to him?"

Boies countered that the section Dorsen referred to was an incomplete paragraph. He also questioned the "propriety" of using notes from a defense witness to cross-examine an unrelated witness. Boies lost the argument, though, and Leval gave Dorsen the green light.

Westmoreland's lawyer, seeking to soften McChristian's testimony, finally was able to return to asking McChristian about the circumstances surrounding Westmoreland's refusal to send the cable. "Haven't you stated under oath that General Westmoreland had every right to go over the material, especially since he had not been briefed in detail on intelligence holdings?"

McChristian refused to give ground. "This is correct," he answered. "But he didn't at that meeting ask any questions about it. . . . There was only one reason given to me, and that was the political one."

Dorsen thought he had another way to impeach McChristian's testimony. But this was also secondhand. Notes obtained from Don Kowet showed that McChristian had told a different story about the fateful cable to the author of *A Matter of Honor* than he did on the witness stand.

Kowet had asked McChristian, "Did you have the feeling at any time that you were being asked to suppress information?" According to Kowet's notes, McChristian had answered, "No, absolutely not."

McChristian explained this discrepancy the way he explained away his purported conversation with Adams about the cable. "In speaking to Mr. Kowet, there were several things I was very guarded about," he said. "One, I didn't want to give quotes on General Westmoreland. I wanted to state things the way I understood them and I wanted to give him an overall general picture of what was going on. . . . "

He agreed he had made the statement to Kowet, but said talking to a journalist was different than talking under oath.

Trying to further impeach McChristian's testimony, Dorsen turned to an outtake from the documentary. Although McChristian had testified earlier that day that the words "political bombshell" had been "burned" into his memory, excerpts from his interview with Crile found the intelligence chief far less emphatic on what Westmoreland had told him after receiving the cable:

"I had the definite impression that he felt if he sent those figures back to Washington at that time, it would create a political bombshell. . . . "

Again, McChristian tried to explain this inconsistency away by supplying the same answer he had used for the Adams and Kowet interviews: " . . . I was trying to avoid quoting him and I was trying to give an impression of what happened."

Dorsen tightened the noose, asking, "You wouldn't have lied to Mr. Crile though, would you have?"

"I would not lie to anybody," McChristian said.

"You remember Mr. Crile asking you 'Do you remember any of his words?' . . . and whether you said 'I can't recall his exact words at this time, but that is my strong impression of exactly what happened'?"

After Dorsen showed McChristian the page of the videotape transcript, the general replied, "Yes. At this particular time I was aware of what General Westmoreland had stated, and I was not telling him the exact words. . . . I was giving him the gist of the facts that did happen."

Dorsen also got McChristian to admit that, even under oath during the deposition process, he had had a hard time recalling the exact words General Westmoreland had used in the conversation. Satisfied he had done fairly serious damage, Dorsen moved on to another subject important to his case—the key May 19 briefing attended by Admiral Sharp. Evidence from this meeting had been dramatically introduced earlier in the trial.

"Now isn't it a fact, General McChristian, that there was a briefing conducted by MACV intelligence on May 19, 1967, attended by General Westmoreland, Admiral Sharp and yourself?"

"I have absolutely no recollection of attending any meeting like that," the witness answered.

After arguing back and forth with Dorsen about this briefing, McChristian conceded that because he left Vietnam soon after that date, "my replacement who was in-country at that time would have more than likely been involved."

McChristian also could not remember a briefing on the size and strength of enemy regulars conducted by Colonel Hawkins for the high-level Mission Council staff on May 28, 1967. Nor could he say whether this briefing had been ordered by General Westmoreland—a key point, because if Westmoreland was ordering briefings on the subject, he could hardly be trying to suppress the figures.

In his final series of questions, Dorsen tried to get McChristian to attack the propriety of portions of the CBS documentary as he had done in his affidavit. But no sooner had he begun than Boies objected. After listening to the two lawyers argue about this line of questioning at the sidebar, Judge Leval decided, "I don't think asking him whether he thinks something is improper or not is a correct line of inquiry. I think it's appropriate to ask him . . . was it a correct representation of what he understood himself to have said in the interview?"

Leval said Dorsen's emphasis on the word "improper" was an effort to get McChristian to pass judgment on the editing process, an area best left to expert witnesses.

Dorsen didn't like Leval's limitations and decided to end his cross. As he walked back to his table, it appeared to observers in the courtroom that the Westmoreland defense team had done a reasonably successful job of blunting the impact of an important witness. McChristian's attribution of the phrase "political bombshell" seemed less certain than it had before the cross-examination.

But then Boies dropped a bombshell of his own.

Westmoreland, it turned out, had been using his West Point ties to pressure McChristian against co-operating with CBS. Throughout the hullabaloo surrounding the broadcast and the trial, McChristian had kept quiet about this, but the CBS lawyer decided it was time to play his trump card.

"I didn't want to quote General Westmoreland," McChristian explained to Boies on redirect examination. "I had a strong reluctance to bring out anything about him other than my own impressions. . . . I just didn't want to have any dirty laundry taken care of in public."

But under oath McChristian had little choice.

"Did there come a time . . . when General Westmoreland called you on the telephone and told you in words or substance that he thought that conversation that he had with you in May of 1967 was a private conversation between West Pointers?" Boies demanded.

The silver-haired general faced the silent courtroom and answered simply, "Yes, sir."

Boies then started to hand McChristian his own notes of a phone call Westmoreland had made to him around January 21, 1982—just before the broadcast aired. Westmoreland, according to those notes, said "he thought our conversation was private and official between West Pointers. I replied that I spoke the truth. . . . He said that he has stood up for and took the brunt of Vietnam for all of us. He as much as accused me of being the one mainly responsible for his integrity being impugned [by CBS]."

This memo was so potentially devastating to Westmoreland's case that Dorsen quickly objected. Leval beckoned the two sides to the bench.

" . . . Why do you think you should be allowed to offer it?" the judge asked Boies.

After listening to the arguments from both men, Leval made a decision that gave neither side exactly what it wanted, but allowed Boies to question McChristian about the conversation. In his ruling, Leval indicated he was well aware of the damage these notes did to Westmoreland's case:

" . . . The problem is that the particular piece of evidence has a more prejudicial effect than just supporting the witness' credibility . . . because it puts down in writing a statement attributable to General Westmoreland which General Westmoreland denies, but which if the jury believes to be true carries an implication of dishonesty on General Westmoreland's part, which is quite a different thing than the basis for your offering it, which is to explain why he, McChristian, gave a weaselly answer or a false one to Kowet."

Leval refused to let the actual notes be admitted as evidence.

Boies now needed to drive home his point with words. He walked over to the witness stand, taking a position close to the jury box, and asked his question again, for emphasis.

"I may have asked you this but I want to be certain. Did there come a time when General Westmoreland called you and told you that he believed that your conversation with him in May of 1967 had been a private and confidential discussion between West Pointers?"

McChristian's answer, once again, was emphatic.

"Yes, sir."

Boies established that McChristian had taken notes of this conversation, then asked, "In or about January 1982 did General Westmoreland in a telephone conversation tell you in words or in substance that he had stood up and taken the brunt of Vietnam, in his words, 'for all of us'?"

Again, McChristian said, "Yes, sir."

Next, Boies tried to ask McChristian if Westmoreland, in the course of the conversation, had told him Lieutenant General Daniel Graham "was very upset with the CBS broadcast," but Dorsen objected and Leval agreed with him.

Boies, however, had more ammunition. "Did there come a time . . . in 1982 . . . subsequent to the CBS broadcast, when General Westmoreland wrote you a note in which he stated in words or in substance that he had demurred in increasing the OB without further analysis?" Boies asked.

"Your honor, object[ion] unless the entire passage is read," Dorsen insisted.

After getting McChristian to establish he had received the letter between March 1 and April 2, 1982, Boies read the passage into the record:

"Joe, here is the letter I mentioned on the telephone. CBS has, maliciously or through ignorance, confused my demurring in increasing the OB, without further analysis with your constant theme that the enemy had the capability to pursue a war of attrition to which I fully agreed."

With this one-sentence extract from a letter written by Westmoreland himself, Boies managed to knock down much of the general's carefully crafted defense. Now it would be hard for the jury to fully believe that Westmoreland, as he had testified, wanted more studies, more briefings, more information on the enemy. Westmoreland's letter also made the charges in the documentary more credible.

(In a post-trial interview, Westmoreland said Boies had cast both the phone call and the letter incorrectly. The general explained he had called McChristian "as an old friend and former colleague and expressed my surprise that he would go on national TV without the courtesy of informing me. I told him in essence that it was an unusual performance and alluded to the confidence that had traditionally prevailed between West Point graduates. I added that I was disappointed to have him add to the burden I already carried for those of us who fought an unpopular war.")

Boies wasn't finished. He had one more question that he figured would help seal his case.

"Did you receive a telephone call from General Westmoreland in or about June 1984 in which . . . [he] told you in words or in substance that you were both expendable?" Boies asked.

"Yes, sir, I did," the witness said.

(After the trial, Westmoreland said Boies had taken this remark out of context. "I called him when I learned he was personally involved with CBS and had not retained a lawyer for himself, but was relying on the CBS lawyers. I cautioned him that, in his own interest, he should realize that in the hands of clever lawyers, we were both expendable." And looking back on the trial, Westmoreland ruefully admitted, "I must say that Boies was clever.")

After Boies said he had no more questions, McChristian asked, "May I explain something . . . "

"No," Leval said. "No speeches. Only answers to questions."

"Let me just ask one more question," Boies said. "I think I know what the witness has in mind and I probably should clarify that, with the court's permission."

"All right," the judge agreed.

"I have used a number of notes and letters from your files," Boies said. "Is it the case that these were produced pursuant to a subpoena in this case?"

"Yes, sir," McChristian answered.

"Was that subpoena served on you by the plaintiff's counsel, if you recall?"

Dorsen popped up to say, "Object[tion]." Leval sustained him.

McChristian still managed to make his point: he had finally come forth with damning evidence against Westmoreland due to legal maneuvers by the general's own lawyers, not because he was in league with CBS.

Boies said later that he had obtained the notes "very late in the game," only after Capital Legal had served a subpoena and McChristian "turned over everything he had." McChristian had refused to tell the CBS legal team about the phone conversation and he had ignored their efforts to pry loose his notes. "Most of the time, McChristian was trying to protect Westmoreland," Boies said, adding that there didn't seem to be any animosity between the two men. But he noted that McChristian, who had his forty-fifth West Point reunion during the trial, was under a lot of pressure from his colleagues not to testify. "I think he received a lot of calls. And I think he resented that pressure."

19.

The End of the Line

T H E next CBS witness, retired Colonel Gains B. Hawkins, was
a sharp contrast to the military men who had preceded him on
the stand. "The Hawk," as he was known in Vietnam, once described
himself as "an aged, overweight retired Army Colonel who never even
became a member of the regular Army [and] who never attended the
Army's Command and General Staff College. . . . "

Which is not to say Hawkins was not a product of West Point.
He was. But it was West Point, Mississippi. Rural born and raised,
Hawkins liked to play the country-boy role to the hilt. In a 1983 speech
to a Civil Air Patrol banquet at Maxwell Air Force Base in Alabama,
he offered a homespun parable to explain how an unlikely fellow such
as himself could end up among the nation's military elite.

Hawkins told the group about John, his next-door neighbor back
home, whose hound dog, Fred, was without a doubt the ugliest animal
in Mississippi. Fred was brindle in color, swaybacked, and had one
leg that was shorter than the others. He had lost half a tail in a lawn-
mower and had a constant sniffle and a drippy nose. Nevertheless,
John entered Fred in every dog show in Mississippi and all the surrounding states, pitting the hapless creature against beautiful dalma-
tions, elegant poodles, and graceful greyhounds. After observing this
ritual for a year or so, Hawkins asked John, "Why do you insist on
showing old Fred at these high-class dog shows? You know he'll never
win a prize." As Hawkins told it, John answered, "I know that, Gains.
Old Fred will never win a prize—but at these high-class dog shows he
does get to meet a lot of fine-looking dogs."

Hawkins never did win that most coveted of military prizes, a
general's star, but he rubbed shoulders with a lot of people who did.
And while the colonel's "aw shucks" manner might not have helped

him in the military, CBS David Boies was betting on it to charm the jury.

Behind the good-old-boy façade lay a sharp mind. A World War II veteran, Hawkins had left the Army at the end of hostilities and re-entered during the Korean War, deciding to make a career of his intelligence specialty. The Army honed his flair for languages with courses at military schools and Stanford University.

When he was posted to General McChristian's J-2 staff in February 1966, Hawkins was no stranger to Vietnam or wars of national liberation. He had landed at the Pentagon in the late 1950s as the Army's chief intelligence officer for Indonesia. In that job, he made a quick tour through Southeast Asia, including stops in Vietnam and Malaya, where he took a firsthand look at communist guerrillas while accompanying British troops to the field.

In 1962, Hawkins left the Pentagon for United States Army Pacific headquarters in Hawaii, where he first served as an OB officer under General McChristian. He returned briefly to the mainland, serving in a "boring" job as a personnel officer at Fort Holabird, Maryland. Seeking a challenge, he wrote to McChristian in Saigon and asked for a job.

Throughout all these assignments, Hawkins refined his knowledge of guerrilla warfare. He could quote from Mao Tse-tung's *Primer* or General Vo Nguyen Giap's *People's War, People's Army* as well as any jungle cadre. Long before he arrived in Vietnam to become chief of McChristian's OB section in MACV J-2, Hawkins had memorized Giap's description of North Vietnam's guerrilla war against the French: "Each inhabitant was a soldier, each village was a fortress; each party cell, each village administrator a staff."

McChristian gave Hawkins the opportunity to refine his knowledge of guerrillas in the fall of 1966, commissioning two exhaustive studies of the various guerrilla "fish" that swam in the sea of battle in South Vietnam. These studies—RITZ, which concentrated on the self-defense forces, and CORRAL, which examined the political cadres—paralleled work done in Langley, Virginia, by CIA analyst Sam Adams. By the spring of 1967, with the studies completed, Hawkins reached the same conclusion as Adams: the MACV order of battle under-counted by about 200,000 the enemy that U.S. troops faced in Vietnam. In a guerrilla war, Hawkins believed it essential that these irregulars make it into the record books.

On May 28, 1967, Hawkins briefed General Westmoreland on the results of the RITZ and CORRAL studies. And, as Mike Wallace related on the CBS documentary, Westmoreland reacted strongly to

Hawkins' work. At this point, Hawkins told the CBS cameras, the U.S. commander said, "What am I going to tell the press? What am I going to tell the Congress? What am I going to tell the President?"

In the documentary, Hawkins recalled meeting Adams and telling him " . . . I thought our figures were lower than they actually should be." But he was a good soldier. "I am a staff officer and I defended the command position. . . . If it was immoral or illegal or reprehensible, the fault is here," Hawkins told CBS.

If David Boies could get Hawkins to repeat these damning phrases on the witness stand, quickly following the devastating testimony of General McChristian, he believed he could attain his original goal in this libel suit: proving the absolute truth of the broadcast.

Newspaper reports of Hawkins' two days on the stand depicted Boies and this crucial witness as demolishing Westmoreland's case. The *Washington Post*'s headline screamed, "CBS Witness Says He Cut Estimate: Ex-Colonel Testifies Westmoreland Balked at Higher Troop Figure." The *Post* also reported that "On the stand, Hawkins seemed to say that his two direct superior officers at that time, Brig. Gen. Phillip Davidson and Col. Charles Morris, both of whom testified against CBS, reportedly tried to get him to cut numbers for enemy estimates in the summer of 1967."

Unfortunately for Boies, although Hawkins excelled at "seeming to say," when it came to testifying to exactly what happened the colonel couldn't remember much. As it became clear that "The Hawk" might not deliver the needed goods, Boies tried to compensate by falling back on his considerable repertoire of courtroom tricks. Judge Leval eventually found Hawkins' testimony so lacking in substance that he harshly criticized the CBS lawyer. Initially, Hawkins seemed an ideal witness, knowledgeable and easy-going. The colonel bore an uncanny resemblance to Yoda, the Zen-like hero of the movie *Return of the Jedi*, and his measured responses rang almost as wise and true as those of the fictional Jedi master. Since it looked as if the one-two McChristian-Hawkins punch would be a sure thing, Boies moved quickly and confidently to the core of the case, asking Hawkins, "Did there come a time when you personally concluded, sir, that the estimates for the enemy's self-defense force included in the MACV order of battle were too low?"

"For the self-defense force?"

"Yes."

"Absolutely, sir. They were ridiculously low."

Next, Boies asked Hawkins about the May 1967 briefing he had given Westmoreland on higher enemy-strength estimates. The easy smile on the CBS attorney's face said this was going to be a piece of cake as Hawkins condemned Westmoreland in court with almost exactly the same words he had used in the documentary:

"I will tell you in substance because I cannot remember the precise words," Hawkins drawled. " . . . The substance of General Westmoreland's statement was that these high figures were politically unacceptable. The sum and substance of his statement included statements like: 'What will I tell the President? What will I tell the Congress? What will be the reaction of the press to these higher figures?' "

But Boies' roll ended almost before it began. Dorsen broke the flow of the questioning with a series of objections that chipped away Hawkins' credibility. As it turned out, Hawkins could remember the words that were used on the CBS documentary, but not much else. He was even forced to admit, "I have no recollection of who all was sitting around the table at that briefing."

He did, however, testify that as he was preparing to go to the August 1967 National Intelligence Estimates conference at the CIA's Langley, Virginia, headquarters, McChristian's successor, General Phillip Davidson, had continued to invoke the "command position." Asked what Davidson had told him about higher enemy-strength figures, Hawkins replied, "General Davidson reiterated to me that these figures were unacceptable."

Davidson's reasons for holding enemy-troop-strength estimates at 300,000 were the same as Westmoreland's, "political," Hawkins testified. "I never heard any criticism of our methodology."

Boies also needed Hawkins to explain one indisputable error Crile made in the documentary, when the colonel was inaccurately depicted as referring to the figures he brought to Langley as "crap." Hawkins actually was referring to the original figures MACV had received from the South Vietnamese. Boies, wanting to clear up this "crap" which weakened his case, asked Hawkins if he had ever used "crap" to describe the Langley figures to Crile. Hawkins said he had talked to Crile on many occasions off-camera, including an all-night session after the filmed interviews. Crile had arranged for Hawkins and his wife to see a Broadway play that night, but since he was tired he had declined, inviting Crile over to his hotel to talk instead.

Hawkins, in the kind of aside he could not resist, recalled that the play for which he had had tickets, "ironically, was 'Ain't Misbehavin'.' "

As the courtroom exploded with laughter, Judge Leval admonished Hawkins, "I think perhaps now you are going a little too far."

After the laughter subsided, Boies got the answer he wanted. Hawkins said, "I told Mr. Crile in effect they were crap, the figures we brought to Langley were crap, that they did not represent what I thought to be—considered to be the true estimate of enemy strength."

Dorsen continued to object, and finally an exasperated Leval called the lawyers to a sidebar conference, saying to Boies, " . . . In my view, you have not laid an adequate foundation for his testimony that there was a command position."

Boies tried to explain, but Leval interrupted, saying, "Well it's of marginal relevance."

"And great prejudice," Dorsen chimed in.

Boies did manage to convince the judge that Hawkins' testimony about Davidson was quite relevant to the "command position" argument, but Leval warned Boies to be more precise in his questioning.

The CBS lawyer strode back to the lectern and began to ask Hawkins about what he had told Crile and Adams before the broadcast, trying to establish that CBS had performed its journalistic job adequately. Hawkins had no trouble with his memory on this subject. He said Crile and Adams had first contacted him by phone in January or February 1981 and he had told Crile then that while "a great many of the precise details that had occurred during the summer of 1967 probably would be very difficult for me to recall, . . . I supported Adams' thesis that there had been an intelligence fraud which had occurred during the summer of 1967. . . . "

Hawkins said he had also told Crile that MACV had "skewed and screwed" the strength estimates during the summer of 1967 in a "terrible misrepresentation of intelligence."

But Boies still needed to prove CBS had had a basis for its attack on Westmoreland. So he asked Hawkins, "Did you discuss with Mr. Crile in 1981 who was responsible for the dishonesty of MACV's enemy strength figures?"

Hawkins shot back, "I told him it went back to General Westmoreland himself."

Boies asked how Hawkins knew this.

"Because General Westmoreland had established a ceiling. . . . No competent intelligence analyst can function under a ceiling," the witness declared.

Boies turned to the two briefings Hawkins had given Westmoreland. Briefly rehashing the May meeting, Boies focused on the June encounter, not knowing that the next day Dorsen would try to use Hawkins' answers as a lever against the CBS attorney.

In the June session, Hawkins said, he had "skimmed a few off the top . . . and I wrote a lengthy preface to explain that this was not a dramatic sudden increase in enemy strength." Hawkins said he had explained that the higher numbers were "a book increase—that there had been enemy there all along but we had not had . . . intelligence information to process and document this increase." He again told Boies, "I skimmed some off the top, a few thousand, sir, because I was not able to believe—"

"No, no," Leval interrupted sharply, cutting Hawkins off before he could stray beyond the question.

The "skimming" had not satisfied Westmoreland, Hawkins testified. Boies wanted to ask what had happened after the June 14 briefing, but Leval would not let him.

Instead, the judge chewed Boies out. "I must say, my perception is that you have approached the examination of this witness backwards . . . in several instances you have done it backwards," Leval said in a sidebar conference. The judge then gave Boies specific suggestions on how he would like to see Hawkins questioned, lecturing the experienced courtroom lawyer in much the same way he had tutored the inexperienced Dan Burt.

The logical way to examine Hawkins, Leval said, was to underscore the information that had come to him from above, from his superiors—Colonel Morris, General Davidson, and General Westmoreland. "But if you do it the other way and you don't fill in the top adequately, there are serious problems," he said.

When Leval finished, Dorsen jumped in with his complaints. Dorsen said he was particularly irritated about questions relating to the June 14 briefing. He told Leval why. Hawkins had been deposed on that subject just the day before, at which time he "repeatedly testified that the only thing he recalls anyone saying at the June 14 meeting was something not by General Westmoreland but by Robert Komer, who said 'This is Byzantine.' And I think that is totally inadequate. . . . "

Boies lamely explained to Leval that he had conducted his examination of Hawkins in this manner because "it is clearer to enable the jury to understand what the facts were." His argument collapsed with the explanation, "Obviously, I am not entitled to do that without a foundation, but I think that if there is a permissible foundation, even though it may not be as strong as it might be if I had laid minimal foundation, I am entitled to do that and then pick it up."

Leval wasn't buying this. "I don't care if you laid even a minimal foundation for the proposition that he was under orders . . . ," the jurist said. "He hasn't said a word—he never mentioned 300,000 except in that answer. There's absolutely nothing in it and I mean, you know, I thought at first that it wasn't a serious problem because I assumed that there must be a vast amount of basis for it. Maybe there isn't."

No more Mr. Rogers persona. Leval continued to shred Boies' performance. "I would suggest that if the analogy is to [Byzantium], that you don't build a cupola before laying the foundation stones, but you do it the other way around."

Boies seemed unruffled by this onslaught, but his thoughts were racing. "I am often relaxed, but I am never indifferent," he later said. "I'm not tense, but that has more to do with the physical state than anything else. Physically I'm not tense, but mentally, emotionally, I'm very engaged."

Even the king of legal cool was showing some signs of strain from the cumulative pressures of the trial. As a rule, Boies liked to relax outside the courtroom and forget about work, but this was getting to be impossible. "There was probably not sixty minutes that went by during the trial when I was away from it, when I did not think about the trial at least once," he said. "Even if you're doing something . . . playing touch football with your children or something like that, in the middle of doing that, all of a sudden you'll find yourself running through a line of questioning. . . . It's never far from you."

When Boies started questioning Hawkins again, he appeared to follow Leval's directions. But the specifics remained somewhat sketchy, with the foundation still lacking mortar. The CBS lawyer asked the witness how he had arrived at the figures the MACV delegation took to the Langley conference.

Hawkins said he had had a number of conversations with General Davidson. One of those involved a key issue of the war: body counts. Davidson, Hawkins related, had wanted him to develop "a formula which would attrite the guerrilla forces by use of the body count that was reported from the field commands."

Hawkins testified this was a difficult task. "There was no way to tell whether these people were guerrillas, or self-defense, or just farmers out there with a buffalo, or the 256th Regiment, or whatever the hell they were, and so I made a note."

After all, Hawkins explained, " . . . A young colonel just doesn't tell a brigadier general, 'sir, you're full of stew.' "

In this instance, however, Hawkins said he had stood up to Davidson, going back several days later to tell him, "Sir, this study is not feasible."

But the pressure to cut the number of enemy had continued from both Davidson and Colonel Morris, and Hawkins eventually had given in.

"Finally, I told General Davidson and Colonel Morris . . . 'Now if you don't like these figures, you just make up your own rules and

I'll carry out the orders. I'll carry out your instructions. You give me the damned figures and I'll crank them into the order of battle and I'll support them.' "

It was after this conversation that Colonel Morris had started delivering his official figures, which "did not add up," Hawkins said, but rather "subtracted down to the original" figure of 300,000 enemy troops.

Hawkins said the actual enemy count in the early summer of 1967 had been "approximately 500,000, a little more than that, the best I can recall. I don't recall figures too well. That's one of the few figures I recall—300,000, 500,000, and moving back down to 300,000."

Boies wondered if Hawkins' superiors had given him any explanation for the rollback.

"Only . . . that it was politically damaging, unacceptable, whatever, what I just testified to before," Hawkins said. But before heading to Langley he had had a conversation with General Godding during which the command position on enemy-strength figures was laid out and, though "he could not recall details," that figure "would not exceed 300,000."

Time was running out before court adjourned for the day, and Boies wanted to end with the jury firmly focused on Hawkins' honor. Boies also was not above playing to the press, and knew that the last bit of testimony often figured prominently in the news coverage.

So he zipped through a series of questions designed to enhance Hawkins' credibility while further damaging Westmoreland's. The questions flew by so quickly that Dorsen's attempts to protest were missed in the rapid-fire exchange:

"Colonel Hawkins, you have made some serious charges today about yourself and about others?"

"Yes, sir."

"I want to ask you whether you are absolutely certain that those charges are true?"

Dorsen tried to object, but Leval overruled him.

"Do you have any animus or ill will toward General Westmoreland?" Boies continued.

"No, sir, none whatsoever."

"Do you have any animus or ill will to the United States Army?"

"No, sir. I carried out these orders as a loyal officer in the United States Army, sir."

Dorsen tried again, insisting, "Your honor, I move to strike the answer as not responsive."

"Sustained," Leval said.

Though Leval technically ruled this answer out, the damage had been done.

When Dorsen showed up at the courthouse the next morning, he was a man on a mission. He was furious. In his hand was a copy of *The New York Times*, which quoted Hawkins' last response from the previous afternoon. The quote was correct, but there was no mention in the story that the remark had been disallowed. If Hawkins' comment had made a bigger impression on the *Times* than did the judge's ruling, there was a good chance it had also impressed the jury, Dorsen figured.

The lawyer requested a meeting with Boies and Leval in the judge's robing room before court convened. He complained, loudly, that Boies' examination from the previous day had been confusing and prejudicial. The CBS lawyer had shifted back and forth between state-of-mind evidence and evidence on the truth-and-falsity issue, Dorsen said, "eliciting conclusions before the basis was established. . . . "

Dorsen concentrated most of his anger on Hawkins' parting shot —the colonel's testimony that he had just "carried out orders." The word "orders" was totally uncalled for, Dorsen said.

This time it was Leval whose memory was fuzzy. "Fill me in. What was that? Remind me," he said.

Dorsen obliged, reading the last exchange from Thursday, including his objections. Then he told Leval about the *Times* story.

Hearing this, Leval said, "I am sorry."

But Dorsen wasn't finished. He continued to harp on the press coverage, particularly the use of the word "orders . . . without any indication that the answer was stricken. I think that is potentially prejudicial, your Honor."

Dorsen asked Leval to tell the jury specifically that Boies' questions were not evidence, stricken answers were not evidence, and that the word "orders" was not supported by the record.

Leval asked if Dorsen meant he should instruct the jury as to which objections had been sustained, but this was the last thing Dorsen wanted. Repeating the exchange between Boies and Hawkins might further imprint it on the jury's consciousness.

"No," he said. "Just say to the jury that the examination terminated with a question and answer, that the answer was stricken and the jury should not consider that answer."

If Leval wanted to say something to the jury about Hawkins' testimony, however, Dorsen had plenty of suggestions. Essentially, he felt the testimony should be disregarded.

"And it's not as though this witness' position and familiarity with the evidence is unknown to counsel," Dorsen said pointedly. Hawkins had been "prepared to an incredible extent" by the CBS legal team, he revealed. Sam Adams or CBS attorneys had visited Hawkins in Mississippi ten times since the lawsuit was filed in September 1983. And each of these visits had lasted two days or longer.

"I do not believe there is a foundation for Colonel Hawkins testifying as to a command position . . . ," Dorsen argued. "One of the problems, your honor, is that the record is very confusing as to what he is basing it on."

Using a transcript of the previous day's testimony, Dorsen went over each instance he found objectionable. Admitting he was in a no-win situation because striking the comments would make them more memorable, Dorsen said, " . . . I think I am entitled to an instruction that this testimony is not admissible on the truth or falsity as to whether there was such a command position—"

Finally, Dorsen ran out of complaints. Boies' answer was cool and logical. " . . . I think the procedure of waiting until a direct examination is closed and then making these kinds of objections and motion to strike is inappropriate.

" . . . The time to make objections is when the testimony is being given and I think that it is disputive and prejudicial to go back over a transcript later, striking out bits and pieces or giving instructions of this kind."

This argument, of course, ignored the fact that Boies had sped so quickly through Hawkins' examination that it would have been hard for Dorsen to stop him. But Boies had another argument. He contended Dorsen was just trying to "confuse" the jury about a witness who was very harmful to Westmoreland's case.

Boies said both sides had been confronted with testimony that they didn't like. "The court will recall Mr. Carver bursting out with 'It's a lie,' which I might note was also totally reported in *The New York Times*, even though it was stricken. There have been a number of other outbursts, including outbursts by the plaintiff, that were stricken and duly reported in *The New York Times*."

At some point, perhaps the jury should be reminded of all the testimony that had been stricken from the record, but to single out quotes from Hawkins would be "unfair and inappropriate," Boies said. He offered to examine Hawkins again if necessary.

Leval thought a moment, then said he found merit in both lawyers' arguments. Pondering Dorsen's charges, he repeated his criticism of Boies from the day before, saying, "I did not understand for the life of me the manner in which the examination, the direct examination of Hawkins, was conducted."

These were harsh words, but, as it turned out, just the beginning of Leval's rebuke. And his criticism didn't stop with Boies. He would join forces with Dorsen in questioning Hawkins' suitability as a witness.

"I was wondering after court," Leval said, "why on earth you proceeded in that fashion, Mr. Boies. I was wondering whether you were concerned about his ability to remember. I haven't read these depositions. You say to me that in his deposition he has gone through five and six and ten times and is capable of testifying again and again to all the foundation stones that are necessary for the conclusions that he expressed. I heard you say that a few minutes ago.

"I didn't know that yesterday, and I was wondering whether you proceeded in that fashion because you were worried that his memory might be so spotty or might go in and out, so that you wouldn't get the answers that you needed.

"I did find it a confusing examination. I found it confusing possibly to the plaintiff's prejudice."

And as for the briefings on higher enemy-strength estimates, Leval said, "I don't think that Hawkins . . . is qualified to say whether in his mind General Westmoreland or General Davidson or anybody else who might have been present at that briefing reacted in agreement or in disagreement with the figures that had been briefed. He can testify to what was said to him. He can also testify to looks, to gestures, to a lot of other things, but not to acceptance."

The instructions Dorsen requested were proper, he said. Dorsen's protests over Boies' tactics were also proper. "But I think that Mr. Boies' answer that it's unfairly prejudicial to him to have such limiting instructions and striking occur after the end of the direct examination is also appropriate."

The way to handle the problem, Leval concluded, might be to wait for Dorsen's cross-examination and Boies' redirect examination and make any necessary rulings at that time. Otherwise—if Dorsen wanted the jury to be instructed now about what part of Hawkins' testimony to ignore, Leval would do so.

But the judge warned, "If that's what you want, I think your choice is either to request these instructions, in which case I will give them, and let Mr. Boies reopen his direct, or withdraw your request and say that for record purposes you are satisfied with the state of the record."

"Can I have a minute to think about it, your honor?" Dorsen asked. "I just want to speak to Mr. Burt."

After conferring with the lead lawyer, Dorsen told Leval, "I will proceed on the cross-examination, your honor." The Westmoreland defense team did not want to risk letting Boies reopen his direct examination.

Hawkins played the clown during Dorsen's cross-examination, lacing his answers with expressions that would have been more at home in a sleepy Southern Elks Club than a New York City courtroom. He drew long laughter from the public, jury, lawyers, and even Judge Leval.

Hawkins made a good sit-down comic, but Dorsen's cross-examination undermined the credibility of this important CBS witness. Dorsen snared the Mississippi colonel with his own words. (After the trial, Boies admitted that if someone just read the trial transcripts, Hawkins didn't fare well in the cross-examination. But, he said, that ignores the reality that a trial is part theater and part presentation of facts. Hawkins' presence and manner made him a strong witness for CBS, Boies said, with the jury finding him quite believable.)

On March 21, 1967, Hawkins had written his wife a brief, chatty letter from Saigon. Now, a decade and a half later, the note cast doubt on one of the main points of the CBS documentary: that General McChristian had been transferred unwillingly out of Vietnam because he would not play ball the way Westmoreland wanted on the enemy-strength figures.

In this letter dated two months before the fateful McChristian-Westmoreland May meeting, Hawkins told his wife, "Did I tell you Gen. McC's leaving in June? He gets the 2nd Armored Div at Ft. Hood, Texas, I think. Glad he got his command. He wants the third star— and the fourth."

This did not square with the tales told by either McChristian or Hawkins to CBS. And CBS had had possession of the letter before the broadcast, although Hawkins, in his deposition, had testified he gave it and other letters to Sam Adams after the broadcast. Dorsen had Hawkins read a section of that deposition into the record, raising questions about the accuracy of his memory:

" . . . I made a mistake. I just didn't remember when. I thought that I didn't send them until after the broadcast and I was 99, almost 100 percent certain that I didn't send those letters to him until after, and he didn't ask for them until after the broadcast. I made an error there in recalling the date."

In the discovery process, the Westmoreland defense team had also uncovered a draft of an article Hawkins had written that contradicted the former OB chief's lavish praise of McChristian from the witness stand. In the draft, Hawkins described his former boss as "relentlessly ambitious." Getting the colonel to admit he had used those words, however, was not easy.

Not only did Hawkins dodge Dorsen's questions, but the CIA and NSA attorneys who sat silently observing the trial also decided to interfere at this point, sending a note to Leval cautioning that part of Hawkins' manuscript might impinge on national-security issues.

After Leval guaranteed that Hawkins would not threaten the "national security," Dorsen continued with his questions. Hawkins knew full well Dorsen had the manuscript, but he decided to play coy.

"Would you describe General McChristian as relentlessly ambitious?" Dorsen asked.

"General McChristian was a hard driving man," Hawkins offered. "He drove himself, he drove others. He worked me like a mule and I did not resent it."

"Colonel Hawkins, would you describe General McChristian as a relentlessly ambitious man?"

"I'm not sure that I have ever described him as that—a relentlessly ambitious man—before, but if I did, I would like to modify that statement. . . . "

Dorsen produced the draft manuscript. He asked Hawkins if he was the author.

"Yes, may I expand upon it, sir?"

Hawkins and Dorsen then got into a peripheral discussion about what documents CBS had shown the colonel between the time of the broadcast and the trial.

"I read affidavits, I read depositions, I read cables, I read some memoranda," Hawkins droned.

Dorsen tried to interrupt, but Hawkins brought down the house by drawling, "Is this evil, sir?"

Finally, Dorsen managed to get Hawkins to read the section describing his impressions of McChristian when he first met him in World War II. It said, in part:

"I knew little about him then (lieutenants on division staffs don't fraternize much with colonels who were staff chiefs), but I vaguely disliked him out of what paucity of knowledge I had concerning him. He was a cold man. (And these are my impressions and presumptions.) He was a relentlessly ambitious man. He had a passion to excel. He drove his staff subordinates unmercifully. He drove himself with no more mercy. He was not a likeable man."

Hawkins decided to use humor to soften this harsh description. After reading the extract, he paused briefly and remarked, "I think General McChristian might be proud of this statement." Again, Hawkins spiked the courtroom laugh meter.

Dorsen asked Hawkins to read another section of the manuscript aloud. Again, Hawkins played it for laughs.

"God, this is getting better all the time," he said. "I'm not a bad writer, even on the first draft." After the laughter abated, Hawkins read an excerpt that bolstered the original assessment of McChristian as an ambition-bound man. McChristian would find a way, "come hell or high water," to use his position of J-2 at U.S. Army Pacific as "a stepping stone to his first bright general's star," Hawkins had written.

The manuscript also raised serious questions about how the order of battle had been put together. Hawkins had written that an enemy sighting categorized as "possible" was equivalent to a guess. But when asked to elaborate, Hawkins' memory again failed him.

"I don't remember having ever made that statement. It's possible that I could have used somewhat loosely the term, yes. It would depend on the circumstances," Hawkins answered Dorsen.

Dorsen once again had Hawkins look at the manuscript. While writing about the criteria set up to enter enemy units into the OB, Hawkins had made a handwritten note which said, in part, "If it's labeled . . . 'probable' we are almost certain and if 'possible' we're just guessing." Faced with his own handwriting, Hawkins finally 'fessed up.

Next, Dorsen asked a series of relatively routine questions about the Honolulu conference and the classification of guerrillas. Hawkins' answer gave a marvelous insight into why the U.S. Army in Vietnam had engaged in obscure twists of the English language. The word in question was "infrastructure," used to describe the VC political apparatus.

"Infrastructure is not normally a word which is used on the sidewalk or the family dinner table," he said. "It was a term used in intelligence and I think everybody knew what it meant there, but I—I think it would have been more understandable if we had simply called it the Communist government of South Vietnam.

"But you see what political ramifications that would have, sir. That would say—that would imply that we were recognizing the legitimacy of a government, an enemy government of South Vietnam, which we never did. We referred to it as the infrastructure, as a shadow government."

Dorsen returned to the colonel's letters. While working on studies that showed a huge increase in enemy-strength estimates, Hawkins had been writing home to his wife that the enemy seemed to be losing its effectiveness! Boies strenuously objected to the introduction of this piece of evidence, which Adams and Crile had had in their possession before the documentary aired. Boies argued that Hawkins did not discuss how the war was going, just the ceiling placed on enemy strength.

Dorsen prevailed. Leval allowed him to read to the jury a portion of Hawkins' May 4, 1967, letter home, in which the colonel wrote, "Can't see that the VC and NVN can take many more big losses."

Dorsen asked Hawkins if he had read the letter correctly.

Hawkins, his clowning all but gone, answered, "Yes, sir, you read the letter accurately, but it stands open for some interpretation on my part."

As Dorsen's cross continued, it appeared that Hawkins remembered very little of what had happened in 1967 in Vietnam except what he had told the CBS cameras. For his next jab at Hawkins, Dorsen used a document from a CBS deposition witness, Colonel Barrie Williams. Attached to the Defense Intelligence Agency in the Pentagon in 1967, Williams had made a trip to Vietnam from March 13 to April 3, 1967. He had detailed the mission in a "Trip Report" memo dated April 10, 1967, stating that among the people he contacted was Hawkins.

Hawkins remembered meeting Williams "briefly" during that Saigon trip, but he did not remember anything about a part of the visit described in the memo. Williams said MACV had given him information on both an increase in enemy irregular strength and an increase in enemy political order of battle, which was contained in appendixes "C" and "D" of his report.

Hawkins said he could not recall the discussion. "I may or may not have been involved in these conversations. This information was information that they obtained from going out to the Combined Intelligence Center and I do not recall that I would have been actually involved in the discussions that went on with the different analysts out at the Combined Intelligence Center."

Dorsen had saved his best shots for last. He turned to the cable on increased enemy strength that McChristian said Westmoreland had refused to send. Dorsen asked Hawkins if he had helped prepare that cable.

"I do not recall the instance of the cable, sir," Hawkins said.

Dorsen pressed him. "You have no recollection?"

Hawkins answered, "I have no recollection of that cable, sir. There were so many cables that I was involved in preparing during the 18 months over there, I can't pick out from my mind and say that I have a recollection of this particular cable."

Dorsen then asked Hawkins if he knew whether or not a letter had been sent from MACV J-2 (McChristian) to CINCPAC (Admiral Sharp) on the subject of enemy strength. Hawkins couldn't recall this either, not even after Dorsen showed him a cable from CINCPAC on June 10 referring to the May 19 letter.

Dorsen then asked him, "Under the procedures that were in existence then, would you have participated in the drafting of such a letter . . . ?"

"In most instances, anything that went out of MACV pertaining to the order of battle, enemy order of battle, that General McChristian would have handled, I would have had some input to it, something to do with it, because it was his policy that I . . . would have been involved."

Dorsen asked if he recalled the May 28 briefing he had given Westmoreland. Hawkins, who had already testified repeatedly about that briefing, answered "yes." Then Dorsen inquired if Hawkins remembered a briefing given for Admiral Sharp about ten days earlier.

"I do not recall such—participating in such a briefing, sir."

"Under the procedures in effect at MACV intelligence, wouldn't you have participated in such a briefing had it occurred?"

"Ordinarily, I would have, sir," Hawkins said, but added, "I am not sure who would have participated because, sir, I remember nothing about a briefing for Admiral Sharp that has been mentioned in documents that I have seen prior to my testimony here today."

Dorsen trapped Hawkins on this answer the same way he had during much of the cross—with the letters home. The lawyer asked if the colonel had learned prior to May 19, 1967, that Sharp was going to visit MACV.

"I may have known about such a visit," Hawkins said. Knowing full well what was ahead, he added, "I think perhaps it's reflected in a letter that I wrote to my wife about a visit from Admiral Sharp."

"By coincidence, it's exhibit 213F, Colonel Hawkins," Dorsen said flatly.

Hawkins tried humor again. "Yes, sir. We are both familiar with my letters, Mr. Dorsen. My wife probably doesn't remember as much." Hawkins looked over the May 17, 1967, letter with exaggerated concentration, then said, "This is very interesting, sir. I don't remember reading this right recently, but it clears up some of your questions, sir, you have been asking me."

Hawkins, predictably, got another laugh.

Dorsen ignored it and shot back, "We did give you your letters back, didn't we, Colonel Hawkins?"

Unable to resist another laugh, Hawkins answered, "Yes, sir. I have the entire packet. If you had not sent them back you would have heard from my wife," adding, "They weren't gems."

After the laughter in the courtroom faded, Dorsen asked Hawkins if the letter had refreshed his memory. Did he now remember giving Sharp a briefing?

"It does not refresh my recollection as to having to—having participated. It simply refreshed my memory that Admiral Sharp was due in Saigon."

The answer, however, ignored the content of the letter, which Dorsen decided to make Hawkins read aloud. It said: "Admiral Sharp is due in next week. General McC doesn't have to brief him. Think General McC is stacking arms today [military jargon for getting ready to go home]. I'm ready to do a little stacking myself, except that I'm still four months off."

Despite the letter, Hawkins said he could not recall any briefing. He could not recall even hearing of any briefing of Admiral Sharp on May 19. So Dorsen had Hawkins look at what had become known in the trial as the "Finkelstein memo," the document discovered in the Army's historical records in Carlisle, Pennsylvania. The memo showed there had been a briefing on enemy strength at a high-level MACV staff meeting on May 19, 1967.

Among other things, the memo said: "A, the advisability of releasing the information presented in a VC Irregular Forces strength in South Vietnam briefing without further refinement was questioned."

" . . . Does this refresh your recollection as to whether you heard on or about May 19, 1967 that there was a briefing . . . ?"

"The only briefing I know about," Hawkins stubbornly insisted, "is the briefing or briefings that I gave to General Westmoreland on the 28th of May, as corroborated in letters to my wife, and on the 14th of June, as corroborated in letters to my wife. And the reason I recall these was because it was a sort of traumatic experience. I gave many other briefings, but I had no reason, I guess, to remember those."

Dorsen continued to press Hawkins to remember, but the witness could not. Court recessed for lunch and the cross-examination of Hawkins was adjourned until Monday so Boies could conduct the direct examination of another witness who had scheduling problems.

When Hawkins stepped down from the stand that Friday, February 13, with just a few days remaining for the attorneys to make their case, he left many questions unanswered. Why was his memory so selective? Why could he recite conversations with Westmoreland for the CBS cameras—and for Boies—almost verbatim, but could not recall things he had written to his wife?

Why couldn't Hawkins recall the briefing for Admiral Sharp? Who had briefed Sharp that day?

David Dorsen thought these were excellent points to explore when he continued his cross-examination of one of CBS's stellar witnesses.

He never had the chance. During the weekend, Dan Burt would decide to settle with CBS. The next time all the participants walked into court, it would be for a perfunctory session as the judge dismissed the jury.

20.

Advance to the Rear

IT was by now a familiar scene—a hotel meeting room crammed
with reporters and television cameras waiting to chronicle the
latest twist in the long-running legal joust. But this was part of the
Final Development, and the crowd was larger than usual, seemingly
straining the walls of the overheated room at the Harley Hotel on this
Monday afternoon, February 18. Some 250 people were wedged into
the modest chamber, many of them sitting on the carpet amid a
jumble of camera and microphone wires, sweating uncomfortably
under the TV lights. Some read wilted copies of the morning papers,
whose front-page headlines announced the astonishing news: "Westmoreland to Drop Libel Suit" and "General Seeks Suit's Dismissal."
The *New York Post* put it most bluntly: "Westy Raises the White
Flag." It was over. That was certain. But the timing was a total shock,
and so were the apparent terms of the settlement. The news conference was late starting, and as the clock ticked, the reporters traded
theories and rumors, trying to ignore the jungle heat.

Finally, General Westmoreland and his entourage appeared at
the doorway. Gingerly, they made their way to the podium, with Dave
Henderson leading the patrol around the people seated on the floor.
Kitsy, her smile set a little too firmly, paused several times to embrace
favorite reporters. Westmoreland was dignified, unruffled. The fatigue
that had seemed to hang over him during the last weeks was even
more pronounced, but his jaw was firm and his bearing erect. Oblivi-
ous to the heat and sporting a red necktie, he was trying hard to look
like a winner. With Kitsy at his elbow, the general stared boldly over
the bristle of microphones and into the multiple camera lenses.
Clutched in his hand was a two-page joint statement which he had
signed less than twenty-four hours before and which had been filed

with the court that morning along with a one-paragraph stipulation dismissing the suit. Kitsy gripped a handkerchief.

In a weary but strong voice, Westmoreland calmly read the one sentence in the carefully phrased document which he felt returned to him what he had been seeking all along: his honor.

"CBS respects General Westmoreland's long and faithful service to his country and never intended to assert, and does not believe, that General Westmoreland was unpatriotic or disloyal in performing his duties as he saw them."

The general paused a moment as if weighing the scant handful of words—eight sentences in all—against the protracted battle he had waged, then drew himself up taller and plunged into his prepared remarks:

"If that statement had been made after the CBS program was aired, it would have satisfied me. After my press conference in Washington three days after the broadcast, it would have satisfied me. After the publication of the *TV Guide* article, it would have satisfied me. If made after the publication of the book *A Matter of Honor*, it would have satisfied me. If made during the first days in federal court, it would have ended the episode.

"The court action has certainly exposed some of the problems and complexities of producing intelligence on an elusive enemy. The court action has certainly exposed some of the problems and complexities of producing a television documentary. Indeed, the court has emphasized:

"1. The enemy's Tet Offensive was a severe defeat.

"2. The scope of the enemy's offensive did exceed expectations.

"3. The size of the enemy troops committed was in line with the estimates of my intelligence chief, General Davidson.

"4. Our American troops did an impressive job in fighting the enemy forces in South Vietnam, and did not lose a battle of significance."

Looking out over the assembled crowd, he said, "I hope and trust that the conclusion of my action against CBS will be a benchmark in putting our Vietnam experience behind us and allow historians and scholars to assess the facts of that war in accurate and non-sensational terms.

"I brought this suit against CBS to defend my honor and to affirm constitutional principles which include the rights provided by the First Amendment. Thank you."

Reporters examining the actual statement were puzzled. The proclamation seemed somewhat vague and overly brief. Aside from the passage about loyalty, which the general and Burt read aloud three times, the paper said only that:

" . . . The matters treated in that broadcast—and the broadcast itself—have been extensively examined over the past two-and-a-half years both in discovery and then through documents and witnesses presented by both sides in federal court.

"Historians will long consider this and other matters related to the war in Vietnam. Both parties trust their actions have broadened the public record on this matter.

"Now both General Westmoreland and CBS believe that their respective positions have been effectively placed before the public for its consideration and that countinuing the legal process at this stage would serve no further purpose. . . .

"General Westmoreland respects the long and distinguished journalistic tradition of CBS and the rights of journalists to examine the complex issues of Vietnam and to present perspectives contrary to his own."

There would be no monetary award, no jury verdict, and no retraction. There would not even be free TV air time to rebut the CBS show, as the network had offered before the suit was filed. On the surface, the settlement looked like much less than the general could have commanded before the trial. Nevertheless, he was claiming victory.

"I got all I wanted," Westmoreland said, adding that the joint statement amounted to an apology from the network. Later that day, he told a reporter from *The New York Times*, "I figured it was the best I could get. . . . It was in essence an apology. One does not have to use the word. One apologizes in other ways. If CBS had apologized in the first place, none of this would have happened." He also told the *Times* he had feared that CBS might "strike back" or become his "perpetual tormentor."

At the news conference, however, he said only that he now planned to go back to South Carolina and "try to fade away," para-phrasing a famous line from another general he admired, Douglas MacArthur.

"We think this is a good settlement," insisted Dan Burt, looking subdued and almost as exhausted as his seventy-year-old client. This was not the same man who had promised only months before to "dismantle" CBS, topple George Crile, and whittle Mike Wallace down to size. The legendary point man for "60 Minutes" had never even made it to the witness stand; he had been scheduled to testify the next day.

The attorney told the reporters that Westmoreland's only goal in filing the suit had been "to clear his name," saying, "That, in my heart, is what I believe has been done. Many said the dispute didn't belong in court, but there was no alternative. And now this case has ended, as it began, in an unexpected fashion."

Burt confirmed that he had been negotiating a possible settlement since the suit was filed in September 1983. "All I can tell you is that what I never could get, I got. It was the equivalent of an apology. That's how I see it. Others may see it differently."

He denied the deal had been struck due to dwindling funds, a belief there was no chance of winning the suit, or a loss of confidence by Westmoreland. The general, for his part, said he continued to have absolute faith in Burt. "I have no regrets and I believe if I had it to do again, I probably would," he said.

The throng was unconvinced. They demanded to know if the agreement did not in fact mean that the old soldier had "given in to CBS." They clamored to know more about the negotiations that had resulted in the settlement, firing off volley after volley of questions. What did the terms really mean? Westy calmly referred them back to the statement. The reporters rephrased their questions, but Westmoreland stubbornly stood his ground. This was clearly the general's show, and the word "surrender" was not, as Westmoreland himself might put it, in his lexicon.

A half-hour later, it was over, and the mob scooped up notebooks and electronic gear and began migrating several blocks uptown to another news conference.

At the Dorset Hotel, CBS officials were likewise announcing they had got what they wanted, but with less reserve and grace than Westmoreland. Strutting confidently before a bank of thirteen television cameras and looking much less battle-worn than their adversaries, within moments they had all but abrogated the joint statement and declared the surprise ending a CBS victory.

"Our purpose here is not to calibrate who won and who lost," said Van Gordon Sauter, wearing his trademark bow tie and flanked by Mike Wallace, George Crile, David Boies, and network attorney George Vradenburg. But Sauter, calling the suit "perhaps the most significant in the history of television," quickly emphasized that Westmoreland had withdrawn without money or a retraction. And the documentary, after being "subjected to perhaps the most intensive scrutiny ever brought to bear on a journalistic effort," had been fully vindicated, he said. The network conceded no major factual errors in the show.

"Nothing has surfaced in the discovery and trial process now concluded that in any way diminishes our conviction that the program was fair and accurate," he said, gesturing grandly with his pipe as the makers of the show beamed. He said the network should not be "intimidated by those seeking to constrain free inquiry," adding, "We feel now, as we did three years ago, that this issue should never have been brought to court."

Sam Adams at first seemed to be absent, but there he was, hanging in the background, well out of camera range and far from the microphones. He watched bemusedly as the CBS representatives brushed aside Westmoreland's explanation of the settlement.

"I personally do not view that statement as an apology," Sauter said.

Crile agreed, saying, "I don't know how [Westmoreland] came to interpret it that way. Maybe he was thinking of what [Vermont Republican Senator] George Aiken said [to President Johnson and the Senate] about Vietnam [in October 1966]: 'Declare victory and leave.' Perhaps in that context he could justify it. But it was not in any remote notion of the word an apology of any sort."

David Boies declined to describe the settlement as "a total victory," but insisted the joint statement said nothing new. CBS had never questioned that Westmoreland's motives were good ones, he said. "That's something I've been saying for a long time, and it is undoubtedly true. I said it in my opening statement to the jury, so if that's all Mr. Burt wanted, he had it then."

This was, as Westmoreland's advocates would later point out, not quite the case. Boies' assessment of the general had been substantially less generous in October, when he said, "One can conceive of a situation in which one genuinely believes we ought to be in that war, we ought to continue to escalate and continue to add more troops and the only way to do this is to convince people we are winning, convince people there is light at the end of the tunnel."

But the CBS lawyer made it seem unlikely that Burt had settled just because he had finally negotiated the arrangement he wanted. The deal was struck, Boies said, because Burt during the weekend had dropped his persistent demands for "money or an apology or both."

Asked if he was disappointed not to see the case through to the end, Boies admitted he would have preferred a jury verdict, saying he believed CBS would have won. But, flashing a boyish grin, the lawyer added, "When a plaintiff wants to drop a lawsuit without any money or apology, I think you ought to let him."

Sauter said he doubted the case would have a "chilling effect" on the media. It certainly hadn't happened yet at CBS, he said, charging that the public had "an unnecessary apprehension of the media."

"It's a great day for journalism and CBS in particular," Wallace proclaimed. "Maybe there were not any winners or losers. The public will make up their minds."

Reporters massed in the cavernous ballroom pointed out that

because the suit was dismissed "with prejudice," Westmoreland would be unable to sue if "The Uncounted Enemy" were shown again. They wanted to know when the network, which obviously held the program in high esteem, would repeat the show. Sauter hesitated and folded his arms across his chest, finally saying, "We have no intention at this time of rerunning the broadcast."

The reporters repeated the question. Considering all the publicity the show had received due to the trial, good ratings were virtually guaranteed, they said. Sauter's reply was stern. Reporters at news conferences, he barked, should not try to program CBS. At this point, the journalists, surprisingly, backed off, asking few other confrontational questions. Overall, they seemed to go much easier on CBS than they had on Westmoreland.

It would be back to business as usual, Sauter said. George Crile, who had worked two years at defending himself, would be reinstated at his old job in the network's documentary unit. Mike Wallace, who had cut back his work at "60 Minutes" to attend the trial, would return to full-time reporting. CBS planned no changes in its procedures as a result of the case, although Wallace said it might be "sensible" for him to be more involved in any such documentary in the future. The network that had never lost a libel suit and never settled one by agreeing to pay damages would walk away with its record intact.

Two and half years of litigation, at least a half a million pages of legal documents, and dozens of witnesses later, little had been decided except not to continue. The CBS crowd went off to plan a lavish victory party at the New York nightclub Régine's. The general returned to his hotel room to rest up for an appearance on ABC's "Nightline" and then, presumably, to fade away.

Both sides, however, would have trouble laying down their arms. They continued the fight in the media from the moment the news conference ended. In an interview with Cable News Network, Mike Wallace, like Crile, evoked George Aiken, saying Westmoreland had followed the late Senator's advice, declaring victory and getting out. "I still believe there was a conspiracy," Wallace told other reporters. "I believe it even more after so many people came forward to support CBS in that courtroom."

For his part, Westmoreland scoffed at the CBS witnesses, snorting, "They sat there regurgitating rumors and suppositions and myths and barracks gossip." But he did not deny that McChristian's testimony had upset him. "I never had any indication that he had a vendetta against me," the general said. "This totally perplexes me. I saw him maybe a hundred times in Vietnam and after that in Washington, and he never brought it up. I just don't understand it."

Privately, some of the participants in the CBS case indicated they were truly sorry for the general, saying he had been a pawn in a doomed campaign against the media waged by right-wing ideologues.

But Westmoreland was seeking no sympathy. He insisted his battle had been well-advised and would have a major impact. "Senior officials at CBS and at other networks have approached me and said: you have contributed a service," he told *The New York Times*. "We have been more truthful, more careful because of what you have done."

Crile had no argument with this claim.

"Certainly the documentary left a strong judgment, a harsh judgment," the producer told the *Boston Globe*. "And when that happens, you probably have an obligation to open up your airwaves instantly for a healthy debate. You have to invite General Westmoreland to come on with his best advocate."

* * *

David Dorsen, meanwhile, was steaming. Although he was co-counsel on the case and had shouldered the lion's share of courtroom work during the past few weeks, he first heard of the settlement on Sunday night, after the deed was done. And he didn't even find out from Dan Burt. He learned of the deal when a reporter called at about 9:30 p.m., hoping for a comment. As Burt and Boies were shaking hands over the finished document, Dorsen was toiling away at the offices of Donovan & Leisure, fine-tuning a set of questions he felt would impeach Hawkins' testimony when the cross-examination continued.

"At first, I didn't believe it," he recalled. "Then I was outraged at not having been consulted. After talking to Jim Moody, I became convinced it happened. I was in a state of shock. I was working while Dan was drinking champagne with David Boies."

Dorsen had been nowhere near ready to quit. McChristian had made a powerful impression in the courtroom, that was true. But his testimony, when considered apart from the man, was not really so devastating. "In the end, he was saying, 'I don't know what happened after I met with Westmoreland. For all I know, and I don't know, everyone in the world was told about [the cable that would have been a "political bombshell"].' " Hawkins, on the other hand, had such a poor memory that he would almost surely have stumbled over the numbers when pressed. "The idea that Westmoreland quit because of Gains Hawkins is a disservice to the truth," the lawyer said. "There were no surprises in what he said. . . . Dan did not read the whole Gains Hawkins deposition."

Dorsen said he did not expect the jury to follow all of the interplay discrediting McChristian's and Hawkins' testimony, but insisted it would have made sense at the end. "The summation in a case like this, for our side, was critical. I think we had a respectable shot. . . . " If Burt had not bailed out, he said, "The most likely [verdict] was finding the broadcast false and that CBS didn't act recklessly. . . . "

Quitting with a chance of winning was one thing, but quitting without advising your co-counsel was quite another, Dorsen said. "I expected to be consulted because I was involved in just about every phase of the case. . . . George Leisure had another major role to play because he knew a lot about the case. . . . To make a major decision of that nature without consulting George Leisure and me is inexplicable."

Leisure first learned of the settlement when he opened his morning paper. "I was stunned," he told *Time*. "I was unaware that negotiations were going on."

Dorsen confronted Burt on Monday morning, asking what had happened. "He said things like 'it was a judgment call; I had to strike while the iron was hot; I was afraid of a leak.' I think as far as a judgment call, that presupposes having available all the best information on the subject. Striking while the iron is hot, I don't understand what that means in the context. The offer, as I understand it, had been made a year earlier, it was substantially the same terms. A leak, I find insulting. There were no leaks, certainly none that I had any remote connection with."

Nonetheless, Jay Schulman said, Burt felt certain that Dorsen had talked to reporters during the trial. "It's perfectly possible this is Dan's paranoia," he said, "but the important thing is that Dan believed that. David was very often busy pointing out to the world, to whoever would listen, that Dan was beyond incompetence as a litigator. David was clearly and manifestly looking for his big day. When you're looking for a big day, you talk to the press."

At the same time, Burt was president of Capital Legal, which was funding the case, and his staff lawyers were only a few years out of law school, Schulman said. "You've got four green lawyers. Their judgment is, let's just put it bluntly, naïve. He's got David Dorsen, who he doesn't trust. And he doesn't just mistrust David from the trial. He mistrusts David from before the trial. He mistrusts David's judgment in depositions. He distrusts David's experience about strategy although he is an experienced litigator."

Burt was the boss and the boss made an executive decision, Schulman said, adding, "I don't think the best litigator in the country, and I've known quite a lot of them, would have won this case for Westmoreland on truth."

The settlement may indeed have been the best the general could get by the end of the trial, but in the summer of 1984, before the case went to court, CBS had offered more—a carefully worded statement plus free air time. The network steadfastly refused to pay any damages, but at that time had agreed to contribute to Westmoreland's legal fees, Dorsen said. The general, however, had declined. One source close to Capital Legal said it was because the former commander wanted "several million dollars." Another insider said Westmoreland was holding out for an explicit apology and a retraction. George Vradenburg said that before Crile took the stand, Burt had made an offer to drop the suit in exchange for $5 million in legal fees and a statement that CBS was convinced the general had not misled his superiors. CBS had turned him down, Vradenburg said. Throughout the trial, other settlement offers were floated by both sides, but none was seriously considered until several weeks before the end of the case.

Dorsen's anger over the settlement did not go unheeded.

Connie Bruck, writing in *American Lawyer*, sharply criticized Burt for the way he ended the case. She said, "Burt created Westmoreland v. CBS and rode it to national prominence. Then, when the going got tough, he abandoned the case—and negotiated his client's unconditional surrender." She added, "No one on Burt's team . . . knew that any settlement negotiations were taking place, let alone that final legal papers were being signed."

"That's just bullshit," Burt said. "It's just ridiculous. That's absolutely crazy. There were other people who knew about it. Dave Henderson. But, you know, you don't hold negotiations in a public square. Westy was absolutely informed. Had been for the whole two and a half weeks. I talked to Tony Murry about it . . . I discussed it with Tony at length Sunday afternoon, before the papers came. I'd been discussing it all weekend with Dave Henderson.

"Mr. Leisure was not a part of the litigating team . . . ," he said. "David [Dorsen] I did not consult. I had asked him a number of times what he thought the chances were, and he was not unduly optimistic. You go with your judgment. . . . You have to keep your client in mind. That's my rule. . . . Remember, four-star generals in a suit like this, it's for them to make their own decisions."

"Dan understood that I was his client and that I had the final say," Westmoreland confirmed. "It boiled down to his judgment, to which I agreed. It was based on a long thought process. . . . Dan told me categorically that if I didn't buy the rationale and if I thought differently, it would be all right with him. He was ready, willing, and able to proceed. This business of Dan not leveling with me as a client is not supported by the facts."

But Westmoreland also said, "The foundation had run out of money. That was definitely a factor. If we lost, CBS would have appealed it and appealed it. How in the hell we could have afforded it, I don't know. Dan was worried about that, too. I don't think the foundation would have handled it."

The incident that clinched the decision to pull out was when Burt saw the judge's draft instructions to the jury, both men said.

On Monday, February 11, the two sides met with Judge Leval to discuss the final days of the trial. "Both parties wanted a general verdict," Burt remembered. "Up or down . . . Neither party wanted a judgment on truth or falsity at that time."

There was a good reason Burt and Boies were hoping for a single verdict. That way, if Westmoreland lost, he could still claim "The Uncounted Enemy" was false but blame the result on the well-known difficulty of a public official proving constitutional malice. CBS wanted to avoid the possibility of what had happened to *Time* in the Sharon verdict—a win tarnished by the jury finding that the magazine had indeed published an untruth. But Leval had other ideas. He was going to tell the panel of twelve men and women to ponder the separate issues in the case: truth, injury, state of mind, libel, and defamation. Even this scenario might have been worth the risk if Westmoreland had had a good enough chance of winning, like Sharon, on the crucial truth-falsity issue.

By Wednesday, although he had not yet seen the draft of Leval's jury charge, Burt was starting to get nervous. He called Vradenburg to seriously discuss a truce. He wrote out a longhand version of a possible joint statement and showed it to Westmoreland. Two days later, Burt's worst fears would be realized.

He recalled the meeting between himself, Boies, and Leval at 2:50 p.m. on Friday, February 15, when "I read the first draft. I read what I wanted to read. There was only one thing I was interested in. He handed us the draft charge. He's talking. I flipped it open and I was only looking for one thing: what was the burden [of proof] on falsity?"

Burt's face fell as his gaze settled on the dreaded words: "clear and convincing evidence." He had hoped that the jury would be asked to consider only whether there was a preponderance of evidence that the CBS broadcast was false, a less strenuous burden. Clear and convincing evidence was something else again. It greatly increased the chance that the jury would find the CBS broadcast true, which would be the same as deciding Westmoreland had indeed participated in a conspiracy to hide enemy intelligence from the government and the American people.

"Leval went on, and stopped a minute, saying, 'Of course you haven't had time to read it yet, so I'll wait for your comments.' And I said, 'Well, your honor, I did happen to flip through it and looked at one thing and, frankly, that's a pretty heavy burden here.'

"If he loses on truth, it will kill the old man," Burt told the judge.

On Sunday morning, when the settlement was almost certain, Leval's office called with a message from the judge that the decision on burden of proof was tentative. "The judge is always willing to listen," they told Burt.

Too much of a gamble, Westmoreland's lawyer decided. Westmoreland agreed. On Monday, after the settlement, Burt said, he had talked with Leval and discovered he had made the right choice. "The judge said, 'I understand the arguments, but I think that I have to look to the court that's going to review my opinion, my decisions, and I think this is how they would go.' It's always a guess. It's always a bet what the upper court will do. . . . "

Shaking his head, Burt said softly, "The burden [of proof] was too heavy. We didn't know what the judge was going to do until he gave the charge."

"The odds were no better than the flip of a coin," Westmoreland said. "And that was not good enough."

The general who had fought so hard to bring his case before the public chose to settle in private, leaving almost as many questions unanswered as did the Vietnam War. Public figures could not expect to do well in a libel battle against the press. That was clear. It was also obvious that trying was expensive. The case cost Capital Legal more than $3 million, and estimates of CBS's expenses range from $5 million to $10 million. But the exercise seemed to prove little else.

* * *

The initial reaction of the news media, which ultimately had as much riding on the lawsuit as CBS or Westmoreland, was a combination of relief and confusion. The claims made by both sides were meticulously reported on television and in the newspapers. The coverage of the settlement was almost excruciatingly balanced. On the nation's editorial pages and in analysis pieces, however, it was being called a surrender.

"All the face-saving stipulations, statements, comments and rationales offered by Westmoreland and his lawyer do not, and will not, stand up against the cold reality that the other side wasn't the one that blinked first and asked to have the heavy shelling come to an end," Frank Lombardi wrote in the New York *Daily News*.

Lombardi and several other journalists called the move a strategic "advance to the rear."

Newsday flatly stated, "Common sense indicates that no one drops a 19-week lawsuit at the end of its 18th week unless:

"1. Money or other recompense has been forthcoming in amounts sufficient to constitute redress, or

"2. The case has fallen apart, is, indeed, so far gone on its way to perdition that even the hope of an eccentric or recreant jury must be surrendered.

"The second possibility is, on every shred of available evidence, what happened in the Westmoreland case."

Editorial cartoonists favored the image of the evacuation helicopter, some depicting a hasty escape from the federal courthouse. Mike Shelton, a Marine Vietnam vet and cartoonist for the Orange County, California, *Register*, showed a helicopter departing from atop the CBS Building, with Dan Burt telling Westmoreland: "Let's just say we've achieved a 'settlement with honor.'"

Lyle Denniston of the *Baltimore Sun* said the settlement at least provided some indication that Westmoreland's loss had not been total. "If the case had gone to the jury and the verdict lost, there would have been no hint of vindication."

Reporters were quick to compare the claims made by both sides at the end of the trial to the end of the Vietnam War. "This was to be one of the great trials of the century," *Newsday* said. "It did not end even with a whimper. It just stopped happening."

Denniston, who called the episode "the most threatening legal case ever pursued against the American press," said, "Not only the general's leadership, but the entire war effort, was made to seem even more openly political as thousands of pages of formerly secret documents brought into the trial revealed the close interplay of homefront criticism and battlefront decision-making.

"Although the judge, Pierre N. Leval, had warned the jurors that the libel lawsuit case was not an attempt to reassess the Vietnam War, the bulk of the testimony cast the war effort in a strong negative light. The general's pleas to remember the unsung heroism of his troops went unheeded in the evidence."

The *Sun* editorial page said the case should never have gone to court, insisting it could have been adequately aired in the court of public opinion, "the court of last resort." "He chose to sue instead for libel," the editors wrote. "Now he has lost, no matter what face he chooses to put on it, and he deserved to lose."

The New York Times agreed the case belonged out of court, saying, "No jury should have to plumb the meaning of the Vietnam experience. . . ."

* * *

On Tuesday, at 10:30 a.m., Leval signed the papers that ended the case and dismissed the twelve jurors and four alternates, releasing them from eighteen weeks of mandatory silence. The courtroom for a few moments turned as festive as Mardi Gras—which, in fact, it was. Randy Frost, the twenty-four-year-old college student, strode over to

Westmoreland and asked for his autograph. Lawyers and journalists mingled with the panelists, who readily admitted they were disappointed at not being able to render a verdict. Most of the jurors indicated they had been leaning toward CBS, but even those favoring the network said Westmoreland had presented a compelling case, particularly with such witnesses as Robert McNamara. They agreed deliberations would likely have been long and difficult. But it was clear Westmoreland's chances would have been less than fifty-fifty.

Art instructor Patricia Roth and accountant Philip Chase, talking freely with an ebullient Mike Wallace, said they believed the broadcast was absolutely true. But Michael Sussman, an accountant from Manhattan, said he felt the CBS documentary unit might have tricked Westmoreland into appearing guilty on camera. "If I ever were a soldier, I'd like him to be my general," the *Washington Post* quoted Sussman as saying.

The jury foreman, Richard Benveniste, said he was stunned. "We went so long to come to an end like this. I'd have liked to have gone the whole route. It was right at our fingertips—like a fish at the end of the hook that gets away, taking your whole fishing reel," he told *USA Today.*

Leval tried to console the jurors, who had listened to almost 300 hours of testimony, by pointing out that the ending was most appropriate.

"The jury system in this country is an extraordinary thing," he said. "Juries are composed of men and women drawn at random from lists of citizens who are then given great responsibility and power. We demand of them that they put aside bias, listen to the evidence and judge as fairly as they would wish to be judged. It's a tall order, and you have shown from the first that the job was in good hands.

"The settlement of the action deprives you of the opportunity to render a verdict. I can understand if you feel a sense of letdown, a sense of disappointment. I want to suggest some thoughts on the other side.

"We have been participants in a most interesting and unusual proceeding, a trial seeking the judgment of history. There can be no such thing as the legal power to fix the judgment of history. Such judgments must be left to study, reflection and debate.

"We have watched the creation in this courtroom of an extraordinary, unique and rich record for historians to study. I suggest that the value of this proceeding may have more to do with the record it has created for history than with the verdict it could have produced.

"Judgments of history are too subtle and too complex to be resolved satisfactorily with the simplicity of a jury's verdict, such as 'we find for the plaintiff,' or 'we find for the defendant.' Also, they are too subject to debate and disagreement to be resolved by any legally constituted authority.

"I think it is safe to say that no verdict of judgment that either you or I would have been able to render in this case could have escaped widespread disagreement.

"So I suggest to you that it may be for the best that the verdict will be left to history. . . . "

Next, Boies addressed the jury, apologizing for being boring at times and thanking the panel for its patience and attention. "This was a very good jury."

When his turn came, Burt said, "I certainly at least for the first time in this case can agree with everything that Mr. Boies has said. . . . "

After the commotion in the court died down, Mike Wallace was whisked away by anchorman Dan Rather and Don Hewitt, producer of "60 Minutes," for a private celebration at the "21" Club.

At the same time, the CBS Broadcast Group issued a statement congratulating the jury for its "unstinting attention" and Leval "for the authority and impartiality that characterized his handling of this case." The network also applauded the courage of the military and civilian government officials "who came forward at great personal and professional cost to support the broadcast." Back at "Black Rock," the CBS offices, Ed Joyce, now president of the news division, sent senior producer Burton Benjamin a memo thanking him for his "unblemished integrity" in conducting the network's internal investigation of "The Uncounted Enemy."

* * *

Taking their cue from Leval, the nation's newspapers and magazines flexed their rough-draft-of-history muscles during the following weeks and months, shaping an assortment of verdicts in the case.

Alexander Cockburn, writing in the *Nation*, said CBS had "snatched compromise from the jaws of victory," settling for a "backstairs surrender" because it feared a "second trashing of old Westy by an uppity network would have aroused public indignation."

Several more moderate publications contrasted the case with the earlier decision in Sharon vs. *Time* magazine, noting that CBS had behaved more responsibly than *Time*. They applauded the network for its internal review, the Benjamin Report, and chastised *Time* for refusing to the end to admit to any journalistic sloppiness.

But most journalists had at least some criticism for CBS, suggesting that the network had left many interviews on the cutting-room floor that could have helped Westmoreland's side of the story.

"CBS, in effect, won the suit, but that doesn't mean they did a wonderful reporting job," said Spencer Klaw, editor of the *Columbia Journalism Review*.

Former CBS News president Fred Friendly told *New York* magazine that the Benjamin Report "should have been done before [the show] was broadcast. . . . It's called editing." The magazine's media writer, Edwin Diamond, observed, "The dancing on the grave of Westmoreland's case suggests how little CBS really learned from its three-year-long battle over the documentary. All that pain and no gain."

Stanley Karnow, author of *Vietnam: A History*, told *Newsweek*, "They deserved each other—it was a lousy program and Westmoreland was a lousy general."

In his *Newsday* column, Pulitzer Prize winner Murray Kempton said, "CBS's broadcast was unfair, although not defamatory, because it put all the blame on him alone," noting, "Economies in punishment are the American way."

"His head was still high but his cause lay trailing in the dust," Kempton wrote.

Joe Saltzman, chairman of the Broadcast School of Journalism at the University of Southern California in Los Angeles, took aim at the CBS News guidelines in an article for the educators' magazine *USA Today*. He said the trial should encourage TV journalists to sometimes shoot for slightly less "spontaneous" interviews in the interest of fairness. " . . . One would hope that it would make electronic journalists and their executives rethink their medium and what it does to the inarticulate, reflective, or just plain scared, who simply cannot speak spontaneously about anything but who have much to say if broadcast journalists take the time to listen and to help them express themselves in an alien medium."

"Everyone in the business has looked at his own practices in light of Westmoreland and that is good," George Watson, vice president of ABC News, told *U.S. News and World Report*.

Al Vecchione, president of MacNeil-Lehrer-Gannett Productions, agreed, saying, "It scared the pants off some people, but they were probably the people who needed their pants scared off."

The *New Republic*, which called the trial "the anticlimax of the century," doubted there would be any "chilling effect" on the news business. "The outcome of Westmoreland vs. CBS shows that a news organization with vast resources can usually grind down a libel plaintiff who has less money to spend. And if America's media giants feel chastened by the Westmoreland suit, and redouble their efforts to be accurate and objective as a result, so much the better. . . .

"The most important thing the Westmoreland trial provided was

a reminder—that the conduct of the war, as well as the p
over its conduct, involved many deceptions."

Even the Jesuits—a group at ease with complicated
got into the analysis, writing in *America* that the real
trial was that it "showed the value of free flow of inf(
democratic society. The balance between competing values is no
always easy to maintain and it must be constantly re-examined."

Ernie Schultz, executive vice president of the Radio Television
News Directors Association, said the public would cast the final vote
in deciding what, if anything, CBS and Westmoreland had won or
lost. "And that verdict is not in yet." Numerous newspaper editors
agreed, grimly noting that, whatever the public might ultimately
decide, it had already been given ample reason to doubt that the press
is as careful as it should be.

Another verdict, meanwhile, was taking shape in legal and
congressional circles. The Westmoreland and Sharon trials may not
have resulted in clear-cut praise or condemnation of specific military
conduct, but they underscored a need for reform of current libel law
and for media outlets to protect themselves. Although many libel cases
are dismissed before they go to court and most jury awards are over-
turned on appeal, legal experts pointed out that defense costs have
skyrocketed in the past years. So have the number and size of awards.
In 1982, 54 percent of libel cases that went to court were decided in
favor of plaintiffs. By 1984, the figure had reached 87 percent. Before
1980, only one libel award had ever exceeded $1 million. In 1982,
nine jury awards topped $1 million. Two years later, the number had
grown to eleven and by 1986, Henry Kaufman of New York's Libel
Defense Resource Center said average damage awards had reached
$2 million. A 1986 report by the Gannett Center for Media Studies at
Columbia University showed that since the 1964 *Times* vs. Sullivan
decision, damage awards, after adjustments for inflation, had increased more than 400 percent and the cost of defending a libel suit
had risen by as much as 400 percent. The American Society of Newspaper Editors said it costs an average of $95,000 to defend against a
libel suit, but some insurers estimate the average as high as $150,000.
"About 80 percent of the money spent in libel cases goes to defense
costs, not jury awards," the Gannett study said.

In an article for *Folio* magazine, John Lankenau, a partner in
Lankenau, Kovner & Bickford (Victor Kovner was Crile's lawyer),
urged publishers to secure adequate libel insurance and adopt screening techniques to reduce the risk of lawsuits. Among other things, he
suggested checking the fairness record of writers and editors before
employment, and hiring fact checkers and lawyers to review volatile

articles. He also urged reporters to save their notes for at least a year, saying the notes would provide a good defense.

Other lawyers insisted reporters should always destroy their notes, arguing that the research materials could just as easily be used against them.

Representative Charles Schumer, a Democrat from New York, was so upset by the costs of the Westmoreland suit that in June, he introduced a "libel reform act." This first-ever federal libel law would put substantial limits on what a public figure could gain through a libel action. It would bar all "punitive" damages, require an injured party to sue within a year, and heap all the court costs onto the losers. And even if the press lost a case, it would not have to pay if it could prove it had tried to verify the accuracy of the story or if it printed a retraction within ten days. Schumer himself acknowledged that the bill was probably unconstitutional. But he and other concerned Congressmen said hearings on the proposal would be a first step in trying to reduce the cost of litigation—a problem that "threatens to deter news organizations from aggressive reporting."

That threat was already a reality, many journalists and lawyers said.

Michael Massing, who interviewed 150 journalists and media lawyers for a *Columbia Journalism Review* article on the effects of recent libel cases, said, "I came away convinced that a chill has indeed set in." Massing found that smaller newspapers in particular, with less to spend on defending themselves, were cutting back on investigative pieces. Libel-insurance premiums had jumped 100 percent or more since the Westmoreland case, he found. Many journalists still voiced "business-as-usual views," but "What surprised me . . . was the number of journalists willing to concede that libel is indeed forcing them to back off."

Irvin Lieberman, publisher of the *Main Line Chronicle* and other Pennsylvania weeklies, said, "Now we are concerned only with births, weddings, deaths and stuff like that."

"The effect's not quantifiable," CBS senior producer Phil Scheffler told *CJR*, "but I can't tell you that there isn't some reporter somewhere—maybe even at '60 Minutes'—who's found a good story and decided to let it go because he didn't need the *tsouris*, the worry."

"We won't see as many significant efforts by the press to deal with the most important and powerful people in our country," agreed First Amendment lawyer Floyd Abrams.

Washington libel lawyer and author Bruce Sanford, who called the Westmoreland and Sharon suits "as much public relations as legal battles," stopped short of forecasting a major chill, but said the intensive press coverage of the trial would probably have some impact on future reporting. Few journalists would care to have their work examined in such depth by their peers, he said.

Likewise, public officials considering suing a major news organization in the future would give long, hard thought to how Westmoreland had fared, even though the general made some gains by focusing public interest on his cause, Sanford and others predicted.

"The general leaves this fray worse off than when he began his suit," Abrams told the *Baltimore Sun*. "The trial went far toward wounding General Westmoreland's credibility—even beyond the wounds inflicted by the program itself."

"You'll wait a long time before you'll see another public figure in a libel case," Burt predicted.

Without a verdict, however, impact on actual libel law was negligible. The case put journalistic practices in the spotlight, but the beam was narrow: one TV show, one military argument. And the heart of the controversy, the conspiracy charge, was never resolved. In the end, CBS and the general merely agreed to disagree.

"As the general may have finally recognized, history is no less fickle than journalism," a *New York Times* editorial concluded. "His reputation remains a totem in a wider conflict, both for opponents of the Vietnam War and the defenders who put up the millions that financed his suit. His duty done, there is only one way for him to achieve the dignity he asks: Keep answering the questions of those who may try honestly to understand a painful memory, but otherwise stand aside."

21.

The End of the Tunnel

L E S S than a month after the denouement, Westmoreland
returned to the firing line, traveling to Washington, D.C., to
address the National Press Club. The last time he had confronted the
formidable body was in 1967, as the Vietnam War was grinding into
high gear. This time, the mood was a good deal lighter. It was the
Ides of March, the day associated with Caesar's fall, but it was also
the birthday of First Amendment architect James Madison and one
day before "Freedom of Information Day." The ballroom of the club
was packed. The applause went on several long moments when Westy
was introduced, and the general's smile was wide as an ammunition
clip. He waved a victory wave of the variety that commanders perfect
for delivery from a jeep, standing, while rolling through the main
street of a liberated city. But it went over just fine here.

"I feel somewhat like Daniel as he was about to be thrown into
the lions' den," he joked, surveying the room in mock horror. "Daniel
was asked if he was scared. 'No,' he said, 'only curious.' Then Daniel
asked, 'Are those lions hungry?' 'No,' replied the denkeeper, 'but they
are armed to the teeth.' When I told my wife that I had accepted your
invitation to the den, she replied, 'We must inscribe that act of bravery
on your tombstone.' "

The throng laughed and applauded again.

Westmoreland then briefly rehashed his legal ordeal, saying he
had filed suit against CBS because he had felt he had no other re-
course. Ultimately, however, he had discovered he had chosen the
wrong theater and found that questions on matters of historical importance do not belong in court. "I do not believe that either side won
what it wanted. The time, energy and talent—to say nothing of money
—that went into this affair could have been better used.

"What I learned as a result of my grueling experience is a little late in life. At the age of 71, which I will be later this month, it is hard to admit that one can be naïve enough to be subjected to an event of this kind, even to the extent of cooperating in an interview to make it all possible! But having done so, I feel an obligation to try to find a better solution for the future which will help others avoid falling into a similar trap."

The solution? He suggested setting up a review board of journalists and private citizens, much like the former National News Council, which had died in 1983 due to lack of support from the press, particularly CBS and *The New York Times*.

There was no grudge against CBS, he said. "Neither do I bear any animosity whatsoever toward the media in general. . . . Any action by the government or others to try to restrict the media would be undesirable. But if the media itself does not set up and adhere to proper standards, there will be increasing pressure for outside interference."

He said he, like the assembled reporters, was concerned about the "chilling" effect of libel suits. "On the other hand, a letter to the editor has little effect except perhaps to satisfy the writer who wants to get something off his chest. There is a need for something in between."

If a national review board were set up, he said, those who submitted a case to the panel would agree to abide by its decision. No damages would be awarded.

"This procedure would not deprive anyone of the right to go to court if they so choose," he said. "But the mere existence of such a council would provide a safeguard and a reassurance to the public as to the responsibility of the media."

In Press Club tradition, the president of the organization then selected questions from a heap of notes that had been passed to the front of the room during the speech. Many referred to the widely reported rift in Westmoreland's legal camp. They wanted to know if the general had been well represented by Capital Legal Foundation and Dan Burt.

"I was satisfied," he roared. "Those people did a magnificent job. I've never seen people work harder in my life. . . . I'm very proud of them."

He said he had no second thoughts about the decision to settle the case.

Another questioner wondered if Westmoreland were a member of Fairness in Media, the group headed by conservative Senator Jesse Helms of North Carolina that was trying, unsuccessfully, to take over CBS, and would later try to get network news anchor Dan Rather fired.

When the laughter died down, the general chuckled, "I am not a member of that organization. I have not bought any CBS stock."

Next, he was asked what everyone really wanted to know. Had he done it? Had there, as the documentary indicated, been an effort to conceal enemy troop strength?

Westmoreland wasn't about to give any ground at this point. "There was no conspiracy involved," he said. "Everybody in Washington knew about it."

Turning again to the journalism business, he said, "There should be adventurous reporting. . . . My plea is only that it be fair. . . . It is essential that you clean up your act."

When it was over, the audience, which had interrupted with applause at least eight times during the speech, jumped up in concert, giving the general a hearty ovation. Afterward, several journalists reminded the general that the National News Council had been alive in 1982 when the dispute over "The Uncounted Enemy" began. The existence of the forum clearly had not prevented Westmoreland's lawsuit, they said pointedly.

Still, it was an unusual event. Such an overwhelmingly favorable reception at the Press Club was almost unheard of. True, the audience was not just journalists. Many of the tables were filled with public-relations executives and military guests. But the reporters at the head table and those scattered throughout the room and in the balconies appeared to be charmed by the general.

The same week, at the annual Gridiron dinner, where Washington's media elite and high-level government officials entertain each other by poking fun at themselves, Westmoreland got a bigger hand of applause than Walter Cronkite.

*   *   *

Back home in Charleston, South Carolina, the general reviewed the lessons of the lawsuit in a more somber light, admitting somewhat ruefully, "If I had known then what I know now, I would have certainly explored in depth another way."

Opening the mail that was piling up in his stucco office, he found that 98 percent of it endorsed his decision to settle with CBS. And yes, he was convinced that without the trial his story would never have been adequately presented to the public. Throughout the saga, he had felt that both truth and public opinion were on his side. But had his honor been restored? This he could not say for certain.

"The bottom line seems to be that Westmoreland didn't get all that he hoped for but he has made a contribution to the matter of accuracy and fairness," he said. "I think the way they received my talk at the Press Club tends to support that."

The general's spirits were high and he spoke generously of his opponents, calling George Crile "a very bright fellow, very articulate, a very good witness," and adding, "I must say Boies' was clever." But beneath his acceptance and easy wit lay a certain sadness.

McChristian's testimony will haunt him forever.

"Psychologically, it was the most difficult experience I've ever had," he said. "It's incomprehensible to me. I thought Joe was a friend of mine. I was absolutely bewildered. He didn't have anything to hide; I didn't have anything to hide."

The general speculated that McChristian had been mesmerized by Crile, who perhaps "exacerbated his feelings that he hadn't been given a fair deal." No explanation seemed satisfactory.

"It's a strange thing. I called up Phil Davidson and my chief of staff, Dutch Kerwin, a couple of days ago . . . and I asked them, do you remember anything involving anyone who was unhappy about the order of battle? Anybody who asked that this be reconsidered? Did you ever detect this attitude, were you ever aware of anyone who had a view and wasn't able to express that view? And they said no, never. Did McChristian ever talk to you about this? And then explain? No, he never did to me, either. All of these are very, very puzzling things."

But he stood by his view that the order-of-battle dispute had never been an important issue.

"The whole thing is so silly—a little sliver—to have this one thing slapped out as something important and decisive. We never paid attention to those numbers. I didn't. It was a bookkeeping exercise. . . .

"I'm not mad. I'm just disillusioned."

*   *   *

Burt returned to Washington, his life in near-shambles. His marriage, strained to the breaking point during the last few months, appeared doomed. Workers at Capital Legal said the once cocky lawyer was depressed. He felt betrayed by the press reaction to the settlement, they said, particularly by the scathing story in *American Lawyer* entitled "How Dan Burt Deserted the General" that accused him of orchestrating Westmoreland's "unconditional surrender" and using the case for self-promotion.

Capital Legal, after spending some $3.5 million or more on the trial, needed money desperately, but most of the foundation's mail— as much as 85 percent of it, one worker said—was against Burt. Richard Mellon Scaife, who had already picked up $2 million of the tab, at the end of February 1985 donated $150,000 to the foundation in what looked like a vote of confidence, but the key funder was bitterly disappointed by the results. A major conservative backer of

Capital said Scaife was horrified by the way Burt had handled the
case and was saying privately that "anyone else" could have done a
better job.

A year later, Burt's future looked brighter. His marriage had
survived and he had successfully sworn off swearing. He was slowly
rebuilding his private law practice, but said the Westmoreland case
had left him "badly hurt," costing him $800,000 of his own money.
The Capital Legal Foundation was "ruined" and might not ever recover, although it appeared as feisty as ever, thundering off on new
"free market" crusades.

In an interview three weeks after the settlement, however, Burt
was still badly shaken.

"If I had known when I started what the Westmoreland case
would take, I wouldn't have touched it," he said at that time, slowly
shaking his head. "But I made a promise. He's a very decent old man.
And I kept it. I kept it at tremendous cost.

"There were two losers—CBS and Dan Burt. The general, however, regained what had been lost.

"He's got his name back, he is granted a lot of accolades wherever he goes," Burt said, referring to the recent speeches. "He wanted
an accounting. He got an accounting. That is what the case is all
about. William Westmoreland would have gone to his grave a traitor
had he not drawn them up and 'called.' . . . It is fundamentally unfair
and indecent in a free and civilized society to tie the burden of a national tragedy to the soul of a seventy-one-year-old man who was doing
his duty. That is what the show did. And that's wrong."

But it was never a personal vendetta against George Crile, although "Crile did a very bad show, picking on an old man because
that made his show. It's bad journalism and I think that's very destruc-
tive." Journalism is "an institution in our society that shouldn't get
screwed over," he said.

Dismissing accusations he and Westmoreland were tools of right-
wingers bent on destroying what they believed to be the liberal media,
he said, "If I am, I would expect to get more from it, in every way,
man. That's what's so lonely and hurtful.

"The guys on the right hate me. The guys on the left hate me,"
he joked, leaning back in his chair, hands behind his head, his octagonal glasses sliding down his nose. Maybe Burt wasn't depressed
after all. Maybe he was just relaxed for the first time in two and a half
years. The lawyer's more or less permanent scowl seemed to have
eased.

It had been rough going, he admitted, ever since the change of
venue. If the case had been tried in South Carolina, things would
have gone quite differently. That was the turning point.

"My own guess is that we would not have gotten the Benjamin Report, short of the Supreme Court, out of that judge in South Carolina, because that was a tough decision to make. In terms of public attention, public focus, we were better off in New York. But as for the ultimate outcome—win or lose—probably better off in South Carolina.

"It was always an Indians-versus-chiefs case . . . and a lot of jurors in South Carolina, I thought, would be very sympathetic to Indians."

In retrospect, Burt said, another mistake he had made, was to concentrate so much of his pre-trial effort on proving malice. He had never guessed that the military testimony would prove so powerful in a libel trial, and he handed David Dorsen responsibility for building that part of the case.

"I didn't take any military depositions," he said. "If it were today, that would be reversed."

He also confessed that he had not been prepared for the massive public-relations attack CBS launched against him after the suit was filed. "I'm naïve. I'm a dumb bastard. I thought, 'fair fight,' you know. What happened is I had grievously hurt a major American corporation and they hurt back."

But the torment had been worth it, he said, because now CBS "can't get away from it. It'll follow them forever and reporting is going to change. I think that's good. That's healthy. I [mounted] the only credible attack that has ever been mounted on CBS. And I did it. I cost those suckers [millions]. And as long as I'm around, it could happen again.

"I get revenge. There's no mistake about that. . . . At CBS today, they're asking what in the hell caused all this, how did this come about at the biggest network in the country, the biggest in the world? And it wasn't to screw CBS. It was to give the general back his name. That was all the game was ever about. The dumb bastards. They should have understood it. . . . I didn't have any visions of the media. I knew shit about the media when this thing started."

*   *   *

Burt was right. At least one person at CBS was asking how the case had come about—Mike Wallace, the much heralded witness the network never got a chance to call to the stand. Wallace had been prepared to testify that documentaries are a "collaborative effort," with much of the work devolving on the producer. Now he had a warning for everyone, reporters and producers alike.

"Be damned careful," he said. "Look—I have always been careful, and the people with whom I work here respect that. Having said that, put it through your typewriter once again or put it through the screening process once again to make absolutely certain that it can withstand the kind of scrutiny that we give other people, other events —government, business."

He said the CBS management had not looked at "The Uncounted Enemy" closely enough, and held George Crile to blame for not insisting they look closer. "He should have demanded it."

"George did a superb job of reporting, that is now apparent," Wallace said. "Not just in getting his facts straight, but in cajoling, persuading men still on active duty in the Army or CIA to come forward and say, 'I erred, I cooked the books, I participated in a fraud,' or 'I stood by and failed to blow the whistle in spite of my knowledge of that fraud.' He did a wonderful job of that."

Nevertheless, Wallace said Crile ultimately had let his co-workers down.

"Guidelines? They are superfluous, in my estimation. Accuracy and fairness should be the guidelines, and if we cannot be trusted to be accurate and fair, we shouldn't be working at CBS News. Where George let us down was in busting those guidelines needlessly."

Wallace said there was no reason to interview George Allen twice. There was no excuse for allowing Allen to go into the editing room. And there were "certain phrases that could have been left in, certain answers, that would not have diminished the impact of the documentary" but would have put it above reproach.

"Now it turns out that the substance of the broadcast was dead accurate, as we said all along," Wallace acknowledged. "But we could have avoided all the months and months of scrutiny and the whole painful trial process if George had been more straightforward in the way he put together his final piece.

"This is for history, so it seems to me that we've got to be absolutely straightforward. I've said this to George, he knows that I feel this way and he knows that I feel he in a sense let us down by doing it the way he did. I have respect for him. I have admiration for his reportorial abilities. He was and remains my friend. But because this case was as important as it is, it seems sensible to level here."

Wallace shouldered some of the blame himself.

"I shouldn't have been so greedy," he said. "When you take on a chore like this one, you've got to be able to give a good deal more time than I was able to give to it. I should have understood that. The so-called star system does not work in a broadcast like this. In a tough, long investigative piece, the lead correspondent has to be more involved. The producer cannot do it by himself, and both CBS News management and I should have understood that better."

He recalled that he had tried to withdraw from the show in its early stages of production, but was persuaded by his higher-ups to stay, "ostensibly just to do the so-called major interviews. That was a mistake. A mistake on the part of my betters to persuade me to do it and equally a mistake on my part in going along."

But Wallace had no doubt that the word "conspiracy" was aptly used. That was no mistake. That he would not change.

"What is conspiracy? Conspiracy is two or more individuals acting together to achieve a desired—in this case, wrongful—end. It doesn't mean treason and it doesn't even necessarily mean illegality. . . . There is not the slightest doubt in my mind, there remains not the slightest doubt, that orders went forward from COMUSMACV to see to it that an enemy troop strength ceiling was observed. That's the bottom line."

Wallace said that his role would be larger in future documentaries, but that he could never have total control. "I was almost totally dependent on George Crile's research. And that of Sam Adams and Alex Alben. How do you avoid doing that in the future? Just don't accept the job. I am quite serious when I say that I am the point man for a team of reporters . . . who inhales all the research they put in front of me and do some of my own and then go public with it."

On "60 Minutes," however, Wallace has always had more input. "The producers, the researchers do most of the donkey work, the long, hard, tedious reporting. That still is so. But the five correspondents are involved with that material all the way through. At every turn from conception to final edit, the producer has to clear each tough call with the correspondent. . . . If that had happened on [the Westmoreland show], there would not have been a trial."

He said the American public understands more about news reporting than it is given credit for. "I believe that this vaunted gap between the public and the press, this vaunted credibility gap, is vastly overstated. My pal [Don] Hewitt likes to say that the most popular broadcast on the air every single day is the evening news. If you put all three together, you get 60 percent of all TV sets in America, in use at that time, tuned to the evening news. Does that speak to the fact that 60 percent of the people distrust the networks? And when you add Ted Turner to that . . . It is quite apparent to me that there isn't this great distrust of network television."

But Wallace insisted networks should offer an immediate right of reply after airing a controversial show.

"There should never have been a lawsuit and there wouldn't have been one if all of us at CBS had been more intelligent in handling the reaction to that broadcast. None of us wanted to give. We believed our piece was accurate and we declined to entertain or air caveats from those who disagreed until after Dan Burt had persuaded General Westmoreland that a lawsuit was the way to go.

"It seems to me the time is long past when we should offer some kind of access. . . . We've got to come up with a format for giving access for legitimate, thoughtful dissenters who feel their personal or ideological ox has been gored."

Immediately after the trial, he said, the network was tarnished by the episode, but eventually the public would realize that CBS management had demonstrated ample interest in fairness and accuracy. Publication of the Benjamin Report proved that.

"I think that CBS News [and other networks] will probably emerge stronger in that there will be a fresh look at broadcast standards, the necessity for nitpicking accuracy," he said. "And that's all for the good."

But as for the predicted "chill," in an interview more than a year after the trial, Wallace pronounced the forecast inaccurate.

"There seems to be an undiminished appetite for tough investigative pieces on the networks," he said. "But there is an equal determination to make sure that those pieces can bear close scrutiny."

*   *   *

George Crile agreed, at least in part, with Wallace's criticism and suggestions. "It could have had more voices," he said of the program. "I could have put more voices in."

The real impact of the Westmoreland case would be a move in broadcast journalism to "balance off" reporting, giving people who may have been cast in an unfavorable light "more or less equal time" to reply, he said. "There's a tendency to want to do that right now. My solution would be to do more documentaries. To be fair, but if you have strong conclusions, have a good old-fashioned debate to follow."

He strongly suggested closer network scrutiny of controversial shows in the future. "Nitpicking is fine. I wish it had been done in the case of the broadcast. I turned it in two months before and thought it would be nitpicked to death. I think there is a lot of room for change."

Crile said he was smarting from the press attacks on him. "There's nothing more complicated than having the tables turned and being reported about," he said. "People can be wrong in criticism and right in criticizing.

"A reporter has a kind of godlike power to organize reality and declare who a person is, what a story is. And if you sit on the other end, you see frightening truths about our profession. My experience going through this is reporters are arrogant sons of bitches when they get on to a fashionable story. . . . There's no interest in listening to you if you're the target. Not even honor among thieves."

But the irony is not lost on him. "I see myself in them," he admitted. "The experience has humbled me into realizing that you not only can be a better reporter, but you really should be," he said. "I've come to recognize the impact of writing on people's lives and on the country's life—it's made me respect the responsibility connected to it."

In the end, Crile said, all he won was the right to work. He survived a major bloodbath at the network several months after the trial, and in September 1985 the network renewed his contract for four years, shifting him to work with Mike Wallace on "60 Minutes."

Crile's first story of the 1985 season—"Fairness in Media"— seemed to prove that his new attitude was more than just talk. The report on Bob Harris, the brains behind Jesse Helms' effort to subdue CBS News, "caused a great deal of consternation at CBS," Crile recalled. Harris, a twenty-six-year-old muscular-dystrophy victim, was leading the charge against the network in his job as research director of Helms' National Congressional Club, the political-action committee that spawned Fairness in Media.

To do the report, Crile had to go through Raleigh, North Carolina, lawyer Tom Ellis, the head of the club, who at first feared that the producer and Wallace planned to do a "hatchet job" on Harris but "became convinced that George was a guy who had some character to him." Ellis wanted Crile to sign a letter saying he would treat Harris fairly, but Crile refused, saying "[you'll] just have to trust my judgment as a reporter." As Ellis told it: "I ripped the letter up; he did the story. It was very fair to Bob, overly fair to us. He played it straight."

After the segment aired, Ellis sent Crile a wood plaque bearing the inscription: "George Crile, a man of his word!" He said if Helms ever takes over the network, "George is going to have a job. . . . I think he'd make a damn good president of CBS News."

* * *

Ira Klein, meanwhile, was paying a bigger price for his part in "The Uncounted Enemy," according to author Don Kowet, who had since gone to work for the *Washington Times*. The film editor was not working and it was not from choice, Kowet said. "He simply can't get a job. There's no question that the notoriety from the trial has hurt his career. He got a lot of publicity."

Klein declined to discuss the details of his employment situation, saying only that he is doing what he wants to do and that he has had several offers from the networks. In another twist, Klein's reputation would be truly vindicated in July 1985. He was nominated for an Emmy for his film-editing work on an episode of Bill Moyers' "Walk Through the 20th Century."

* * *

Perhaps the only clear winner in the Westmoreland case was Sam Adams.

"Sam really emerged in a very clear-cut way as having properly identified something that was being suppressed way back when . . . ," Crile said. "The trial really overwhelmingly demonstrated that large numbers of significant people agreed with him and they respected his work and that it was significant."

Even Westmoreland came away admiring the eccentric analyst. "I must say he's a likable fellow," the general said. "He is. He's an absolute enigma to me. I don't think I've ever seen a man quite like him before. He is an interesting fellow. And the irony of this whole thing is that Sam Adams, who influenced so many people in the hierarchy of the organization . . . associated with the conduct of the war, he was at the level of a second lieutenant. He was posing as a field marshal! And he [thought he] knew more about how to fight the war than I did. I mean, that's the irony of this whole thing," the general laughed. "It's absolutely ironical. But he is a likable man. I don't believe he's crazy."

Westmoreland had not kept his promise to fade away. He turned up in the nation's newspapers even more frequently than he had before "The Uncounted Enemy." He marched with Vietnam veterans in Texas. He spoke out on liberty in a cover story for *Parade* magazine.

It was Adams who returned to the background, disappearing into the Virginia hills near the headquarters of his beloved CIA. After the settlement, he spent three weeks in Costa Rica, "looking at butterflies." Then he remarried and embarked on fatherhood for the second time with a newborn son, Abraham.

Adams' anonymity began at the CBS news conference. There was a good reason the consultant was not up front with the self-proclaimed victors. He hadn't been invited. "I would have said what I thought—that Westy had himself a draw—and that wasn't what they wanted to hear at the time," he explained.

No longer bound by the restraints of the lawsuit, he was more of a liability to the network than an asset. He was appalled that CBS had settled the case, saying, "They chickened out. They should have sat tight. We would have had no problem with the jury."

Adams also was "not a big admirer" of the CBS legal staff. "And I don't think Boies is all that terrific. Burt was better than Boies," he said, referring to Capital Legal's pre-trial work. "Of course, once he got in front of the jury, it all fell apart." The CBS case was much too conservative, he complained. It could have been stronger. "Boies and CBS were playing it too much as if they were going to lose. They wanted to have a good record for appeal."

What happened instead, he said, was that Westmoreland walked away "looking okay—not good, but okay."

"In one sense, you can even say Westy won. He's looked on now as a grand old man. I think that's what his image is. If CBS had not let him off the hook, *Parade* magazine would not be doing an article on him."

Adams does not begrudge the general this acclaim, saying, "I liked him better than anyone else in the trial. We're both government bureaucrats."

But was Westmoreland, in truth, a conspirator?

"Absolutely not. He's a patriot. The guy doesn't think in those terms," Adams said, criticizing Crile for his overuse of the red-flag word "conspiracy" in his preparatory work for the broadcast. That was "Mickey Mouse Watergate stuff," he said.

"George and I had many, many arguments—no, conversations— about that. I flipped. I said, 'George, what the hell are you doing?'"

The use of "conspiracy" in the actual show, in Mike Wallace's opening referring to the military hierarchy, was all right, however. "That was accurate," he said.

"Who knew about the manipulation? I have always been at odds with the documentary on this. It wasn't right to pin the whole thing on Westy. I think that was, by and large, bullshit. There were a lot of people who were aware of the political problems. Rostow was clearly aware. Earle Wheeler . . . As far as cutting the local forces, not many people knew. That was a Danny [Graham] operation approved by General Davidson. . . . "

Despite any lingering disagreement with the subtleties of the documentary, the lawsuit was worth it, he said. The debate will now show up in history books as a major issue. "It may not be resolved as a major issue, but as the evidence perks up, it will show there was dirty work at the crossroads at MACV headquarters.

"Of course, I may be talking as the totally converted," he admitted. This is, after all, an obsessed man talking, he seems to say.

Adams doesn't talk to George Crile much anymore. He got a telegram from Mike Wallace when Abraham was born, but hasn't heard from him since. Once a week, he calls Mississippi to check in on Gains Hawkins, who had a cancerous lung removed in early 1986. Mostly, Adams spends his days at his rented house on a Christmas-tree farm near Purcellville, revising the autobiography he started a decade ago. He promises himself to have it finished by September 1986, but his work station is a minefield of distractions for the analyzing mind.

Out the window, three miles away, lie the sprawling foothills of the Blue Ridge Mountains. Somewhere out there is the road that leads to the farm where he buried secret documents all those years ago. And just beyond the horizon lie Langley and the CIA. He has a front-row seat at Sam Adams' personal history.

When the book is published, Adams said, he'll get a job teaching, or in a think tank, or go on the lecture circuit. Preferably, it will be a think tank that closely resembles the CIA. Hell, he said. Might as well admit it. He still wants to go back to work for the Agency.

"I'll put in an application. I have no expectations whatsoever they'll accept. I'm just rather curious to see what they'll do."

But if they say yes?

"I'll join," he said eagerly.

Appendix A

When, not if, the Supreme Court and the various federal district and appellate courts finally decide to allow cameras into their courtrooms, Judge Pierre Leval's ruling on Cable News Network's petition to cover the Westmoreland-CBS case will serve as a beacon of understanding to light the way.

Although the rules of the federal court system required him to turn down CNN's request, Leval's September 19, 1984, opinion consists mostly of carefully thought out arguments for ending the federal ban on cameras in the court. Cameras serve both the public's right to know and the purposes of history, Leval said, then added his almost fervent opinion that the cameras might also serve the image of judges well. This self-serving argument might be the one that finally turns the federal judiciary around.

Cable News Network (CNN) petitions for permission to record and distribute live comprehensive televised coverage of this trial. The petition recognizes that the introduction of cameras and recording equipment into a federal court proceeding is contrary to Canon 3A (7) of the Code of Judicial Conduct for the United States Courts and local General Rule 7 of this Court. The petition requests an experimental exception for the purposes (1) of demonstrating to the federal courts that such use of cameras will not impair or diminish the integrity and effectiveness of a judicial proceeding and (2) of distributing (on a pooled basis) comprehensive coverage of a trial that raises profoundly important questions concerning this country's conduct of the war in

Vietnam and the privileges, ethical responsibilities and liabilities of the press. All parties to the case support the application.

My training in the long tradition that banished the camera from the federal courtroom produced an instinctive negative reaction. I have been taught to assume that cameras would turn trials into vaudeville. A more careful reading of the petition, however, reveals a powerful argument.

There was a time when the blanket exclusion of the camera from the courtroom was understandable and appropriate. Equipment was cumbersome and noisy. Film could not function indoors without either the popping of flashbulbs or glaring stage lights. Television was a novelty, geared toward low-brow entertainment. It was easy, and no doubt justified, to conclude that the intrusion of the camera would disrupt and pervert the orderly conduct of the serious business of courts. Today much has changed. Cameras are small, noiseless and equipped with distance lenses. Modern technology has made film that is sensitive to ordinary indoor light. It appears that filming can be done without the slightest obstruction of dignified, orderly court procedure.

Although in 1965 the Supreme Court concluded that television coverage of a criminal proceeding was incompatible with due process, *Estes v. Texas*, 381 U.S. 532, Justice Harlan opined that "the day may come when television will have become so commonplace an affair in the daily life of the average person as to dissipate all reasonable likelihood that its use in courtrooms may disparage the judicial process" 381 U.S. at 595.

History has shown that Justice Harlan wrote these words with characteristic foresight. More and more states gradually adopted rules permitting telecasting of court proceedings. In 1981 the Supreme Court ruled in *Chandler v. Florida*, 449 U.S. 560, that absent a showing of prejudice, the telecasting of a criminal proceeding did not infringe constitutional rights.

Since *Chandler*, the trend toward opening courtrooms to cameras and telecasting has accelerated. It appears from CNN's petition that 41 of the 50 states now permit live filmed coverage of court proceedings, generally under rules designed to insure that fair and orderly administration of justice is not impaired. The Code of Judicial Conduct governing the federal courts, however, has made no concession.

On consideration of this petition, I have come to question the wisdom of the categorical ban imposed by our code.

1. The experience of a multitude of states has shown that under appropriate rules preserving the court's control over the use of cameras, live filming and telecasting need not interfere in any degree with fair and orderly administration of justice. A single, silent, fixed-

location camera is no more intrusive than the familiar phenomena of courtroom artists working on their skeches and notetaking reporters making entrances and hasty exits to phone in their stories on deadline.

2. I need not consider here whether there may be instances in which live telecasting might create pressures capable of prejudicing the outcome of a trial. Assuming for argument that this is a reasonable, if rare, possibility, it is sufficient answer for cases presenting such dangers to be dealt with as they arise. As the Supreme Court noted in *Chandler*, *supra* at 574–75, the possible importance of excluding cameras from some cases is not a reason to exclude them from all cases.

Here all parties wish the proceedings to be telecast. It is certainly not to protect them that cameras are excluded.

3. *Chandler* and the experience of forty-one states has laid to rest the question whether, in the absence of prejudice, telecasting offends the Constitution. I would venture that the question courts will find more troublesome in the future is whether the mandatory exclusion of the camera violates the litigant's (and perhaps the public's) right to a public trial. But see *United States v. Hastings*, 695 F.2d 1278 (11th Cir. 1983). The Supreme Court has recently reaffirmed the importance of the constitutional principles requiring court proceedings to be held in public view, absent the most compelling reasons to the contrary. See *Waller v. Georgia*, 52 U.S.L.W. 4618 (May 21, 1984) (Sixth Amendment right to public trial encompasses suppression hearing); *Press-Enterprise Co. v. Superior Court*, 52 U.S.L.W. 4113 (January 18, 1984) (voir dire examination of potential jurors covered by guarantees of public trial); *Globe Newspaper Co. v. Superior Court*, 102 S.Ct. 2613 (1982) (state statute cannot exclude press and public from testimony of minor victim of sex crimes without case-by-case determination that compelling interests of the state require exclusion). The question then arises whether good reasons must also be found for restricting the means of public access and the types of media coverage—especially where the restriction effectively precludes the public at large from gaining any meaningful acquaintance with the conduct of court business.

I would think it a strong argument on the part of a litigant— especially in the type of case that arouses strong public interest— that he depends on the monitoring presence of the camera to insure that witnesses tell the truth and that the court does not influence the jury by gesture, expression and tone. See *Gannett Co., Inc. v. De-Pasquale*, 443 U.S. 368, 383 (1979) (openness in court proceedings may improve quality of testimony and causes all participants to perform duties more conscientiously).

4. The public's legitimate interest in obtaining the information it

would receive is beyond dispute. Courts play a vital role in American life, in adjudicating civil disputes sometimes affecting the rights of huge classes, trying criminal indictments and interpreting the laws of the land. The people would have the opportunity to see how the courts function.

That opportunity effectively does not exist today. Of course, the doors of the courthouse are open, but people are busy, and judicial proceedings are time consuming. Generally a trial which takes two full weeks to conduct could be fairly condensed into one or two hours of informative film.

Apart from the public interest in familiarity with the general conduct of courts, the subject matter of this trial is of the most serious public importance. Among the questions in dispute will be whether the high U.S. military command in Vietnam engaged in willful distortion of intelligence data to substantiate optimistic reports on the progress of the war and whether one of the nation's most important distributors of news and commentary engaged in willful or reckless slander. It can be expected that the trial will go beyond the particulars of those two inquiries into issues of appropriate standards for both military commanders and press commentators.

The public interest is thus not the mere voyeurism that emerges for a sensational murder trial. It is a response to a rare debate and inqury on issues of highest national importance.

It could even be reasonably argued that the filming of this trial is more important than its decision: historians and commentators on the war and on the press will not accept the verdict of the jury and the rulings of the judge as definitive answers. They will seek lessons and conclusions by analysis of the witnesses' testimony. The verdict may settle liability as between the parties; but it is unlikely to settle anything for anyone else. Most certainly it will not settle the historical and ethical debates exposed by this action.

5. Finally, I believe it is very much in the interest of the federal judiciary to admit the camera into its proceedings. We are told that the public today holds judges in rather low esteem. We are assumed to be lazy, biased and venal. Recognizing that I do not qualify as a neutral observer, I am persuaded that this view of the federal judiciary is seriously mistaken. Perhaps this results from lack of public familiarity with court proceedings.

Since long before I joined their ranks, I have held federal judges in high esteem; all that I have seen of my colleagues since I joined them has confirmed my admiration. What I have seen is federal judges working long, hard hours with diligence and an unfailing conviction to fairness, determined to run their courts in pursuit of justice. Their remuneration is small compared to what they could easily earn in private life. With the rarest of exceptions (that have been prominently reported in the recent press), their integrity is beyond question. In the more than 20 years that I have worked as a lawyer and later a judge in the New York federal courts, I have never heard so much as a rumor affecting the integrity of a single judge of that bench.

I believe in sum that the federal judges are on the whole an admirable bunch who little deserve the low esteem in which they are held by public reputation. I suggest that the gap between the reality and the perception results largely from the fact that the public has little opportunity to see how scrupulously, how painstakingly and how fairly federal judges conduct court business. Repeatedly, we receive letters from jurors expressing their admiration for what they have observed in the course of their jury service. But the general public, which does not see the federal courts in action, harbors a different image.

Would it not be better for us to adopt rules that will occasionally permit the public to see us at our work and to judge for themselves.

6. I think it a safe prediction that the eventual entry of the camera into the federal courtroom is inevitable, whether this year, in five years or in ten. In the meantime, do we wish to adopt a stance of two feet firmly rooted in the past? Do we wish to hold back the clock by order and fiat?

In my view the petition should be granted for reasons explained above, but the rules of the Judicial Conference and of this court are to the contrary.

Believing that I have no discretion in the matter in the face of those rules, I deny the application, in spite of its merit.

DATED: *New York, N.Y.*

    September 19, 1984

SO ORDERED:

    Pierre N. Leval, U.S.D.J.

Appendix B

JUDGE LEVAL'S DRAFT JURY INSTRUCTIONS

Officially, CBS and General Westmoreland decided to end their court battle days before the case went to the jury by calling it a draw. Unofficially, each side called themselves victors.

There's no sure way to know how the jury planned to vote. However, Dan Burt, after reading Judge Leval's proposed instructions to the jury was convinced there was little hope for him or his client.

In a conference with the judge on February 15, 1984, Burt learned that Leval planned to instruct the jury that they would need "clear and convincing evidence" from the Westmoreland defense team that "The Uncounted Enemy" was false. This was a far tougher legal burden of proof to meet than a "preponderance" of evidence. If Burt needed an example of this point, he had only to look at a case that had been fought at the same courthouse just weeks before. On January 24, 1985, under the "clear and convincing" rule of proof, a jury found that while Time *magazine had indeed published a false paragraph about Israeli General Ariel Sharon, it did not do so with with a "reckless disregard" under that same standard of proof.*

Burt said when he heard he had to meet this type of proof, he remarked about Westmoreland, "If he loses on truth, it will kill the old man." That's when Burt decided to pull the plug.

Judge Leval's draft instructions to the jury explain the differences between these two seemingly arcane types of proof and offer an indication of how the jury would vote under these strictures, which do not leave much room for maneuver.

(Second draft to be shown to counsel for comments—2/17/85)

Westmoreland v. CBS 82 Civ. 7913

Members of the Jury:

If you can remember as far back as the start of this trial, you will recall that I spoke to you of the great power that you hold as jurors and of the great importance of your exercising that power with complete fairness.

You must decide the issues of fact solely on the basis of the evidence presented in the trial.

You may not allow yourselves to be influenced by opinions you had at the start of the trial.

You must put aside opinions you may have had concerning the military; the Vietnam War; General Westmoreland; the CIA; the press; CBS; Mike Wallace; and any others.

I told you at the start, if your decision were to be based on your opinions, we didn't need a trial. We could simply select the jury and ask them for the verdict. That is not the way it is done. The trial has been conducted in a most painstaking manner to place evidence before you. Your verdict is to be based on that evidence. You promised on the first day, during jury selection, that you would put any opinions and preferences aside and would decide on the evidence. Now you must fulfill those promises.

THE ELEMENTS

In order to win your verdict, plaintiff must prove each of the following statements:

I. The defendants' broadcast published a defamatory statement or message.

II. The defamatory statement was "of and concerning" the plaintiff—which means it was about the plaintiff personally.

III. The defamatory statement about the plaintiff was false.

IV. The defendants published the false defamatory statement about the plaintiff either knowing it to be false or with reckless disregard whether it was false.

V. Plaintiff's reputation was damaged by the publication of the false defamatory statement.

I remind you when I speak of publishing a statement I mean nothing more than making it public. It is agreed by both sides that the defendants' documentary, and everything in it, was "published" when it was broadcast on January 23, 1982.

In a moment I will explain in detail each of these elements, except the last—damages—which I will leave till later. You will not consider the question of damages at this stage of your deliberations.

PUBLIC OFFICIAL — SPECIAL RULES

Because General Westmoreland held public office and was a public figure, a libel action brought by him goes under different rules from a libel action brought by an ordinary citizen in private life.

The law recognizes conflicting interests, both of which are entitled to protection. On the one side, the law recognizes the legitimate interest of any person to be protected against publication of false defamatory statements about him.

On the other hand, the law recognizes that it is important to all of us in a free democracy that there should be free, open discussion in the press of the actions of our public officials. If the press incurred liability whenever a derogatory report about a public official turned out to be wrong, regardless whether it was published in the good-faith belief that it was true, the press might be afraid to risk critical commentary, and we the public would be less informed.

For public officials, the law strikes a compromise that protects a measure of the public official's interest in a remedy against false slander, but protects also the public's interest in being able to see open good-faith discussion of the performance of public officials in the press.

Under this compromise, the public official retains the right to bring a libel action for false defamatory statements of fact about him, but he must prove more than merely that the statement was false. He must prove also that a defendant acted with what we have referred to as the prohibited state of mind, that the defendant published the false defamatory statement knowing it to be false, or with reckless disregard of whether it was false.

BURDENS OF PROOF

That compromise also imposes on the public-official plaintiff a more demanding burden of proof than is customary in other civil cases.

The phrase "burden of proof" refers to the obligation to persuade the jury.

It is used in two senses: first to identify which party must persuade the jury; secondly, it sets the standard of how firmly convinced the jury must be before it may render a verdict in favor of the party who bears the burden of proof.

As to the first question, the burden of proof is on the plaintiff. That means—if the plaintiff has not convinced you of any issue, you must find for the defendants on that issue. And if plaintiff does not prove every element to you, you must award the verdict to the defendants.

The second question is: How firmly must you be convinced before you may find for the plaintiff on any issue? The answer is not the same for each of the elements. I just listed for you the five elements that plaintiff must prove in order to win your verdict. As to the first two and the last, there is one standard; as to the third and fourth, falsity and the defendants' state of mind, there is another.

As to the questions (I) whether the statements made by the broadcast had a defamatory meaning, (II) whether those statements were about General Westmoreland, and (V) whether his reputation was harmed or damaged by those statements, plaintiff must prove those elements to you—"*by a fair preponderance of the evidence.*"

What do we mean by "a fair preponderance of the evidence"? A fact has been demonstrated by a fair preponderance of the evidence if, after considering all the relevant evidence, you find it more probable than not that the fact is true. You judge this by the quality and persuasiveness of the evidence.

If the evidence persuades you that a questioned fact was more likely true than not then the party who has the burden of proving that fact has met his burden of proof as to that fact. If, however, the evidence is evenly balanced between the parties so that you cannot decide whether the fact is true or not, then the party who has the burden of proof has failed to meet his burden and you must find that fact against him.

As to the third and fourth elements—whether the broadcast's statement was false and whether the defendants published with the prohibited state of mind—plaintiff must prove these elements to you by "clear and convincing evidence."

Clear and convincing evidence is a more exacting standard than proof *by a preponderance of the evidence*. Clear and convincing proof leaves no substantial doubt in your mind. It is proof that establishes in your mind not only that the existence of a fact is probable but that it is highly probable. Clear and convincing proof must be strong and compelling proof, not merely proof that the existence of a fact is more likely than not. On the other hand, it is not as high a standard as the prosecutor must meet in a criminal case, where a criminal defendant may not be convicted unless the jury finds him guilty beyond a reasonable doubt. You should understand these words as carrying their everyday meaning. You may find for plaintiff only if his proof is *clear and convincing.*

ELEMENTS I AND II:

DEFAMATORY, OF AND CONCERNING

The first two elements concern the message communicated by the CBS broadcast and should be considered together. I will first state them in a single sentence. *Plaintiff must prove that the broadcast contained a statement or message of defamatory meaning—about plaintiff personally.* The first element is that the message must have had a *defamatory meaning*; the second is that it must have been *about General Westmoreland personally.*

Plaintiff must prove these two elements by a preponderance of the evidence.

A. I will first discuss what is meant by "defamatory."

1. Not every critical or uncomplimentary statement is considered defamatory under law. To be defamatory, the statement must convey a message that exposes a person to contempt, hatred or ridicule; that harms a person's reputation, or lowers him in the estimation of a substantial part of the community.

An assertion that is merely unpleasant, offensive or embarrassing or merely hurts someone's feelings is not defamatory.

2. Second, in order to be defamatory, the statement must communicate some fact about the person. It is not sufficient if it asserts a low opinion of the person. For example, if a newspaper or program said of me that I was a lazy or stupid judge or that my decisions were foolish or irresponsible, that would not be a defamation; I could not base a lawsuit on it. If on the other hand it said that I had taken a bribe, or had decided cases based on whether the lawyers were my friends, that would be accusing me of bad acts. It would be a defamatory statement and could be the basis of a lawsuit for defamation.

B. *Of and Concerning.* As the second element, plaintiff must prove, also by a preponderance of the evidence, that the defamatory statement of the broadcast was, in the words of the law, *of and concerning* him. This means that the defamatory message must have been a message about General Westmoreland personally.

It would not be sufficient if the statement accused a group of which the plaintiff was a member. For example, it would not be sufficient if the broadcast accused the military, the Army, MACV or military intelligence. Nor would a statement be defamatory of the plaintiff merely because it accused officers for whom he was responsible as their commander. The defamatory statement must be made about the plaintiff personally for him to prevail on this issue.

C. *What Plaintiff Claims Were the Defamatory Statements About Him.* In bringing this lawsuit, plaintiff has identified what he contends were the defamatory messages about him. You must decide whether the broadcast made any of these assertions about plantiff.

Plaintiff contends the assertions made about him are the following: I will refer to them as the Alleged Libels.

1. In the year leading up to the Tet Offensive, General Westmoreland engaged in a conscious effort to suppress, alter and conceal from his military and civilian superiors critical intelligence on the size of the enemy.

2. In the period from spring to fall of 1967, General Westmoreland willfully and improperly blocked intelligence and evidence on the size of the enemy from being communicated to his superiors.

3. General Westmoreland suppressed and concealed from his superiors that, in addition to the infiltrators his command had reported, he believed an additional 100,000 to 150,000 North Vietnamese soldiers had infiltrated into South Vietnam in the months of September 1967 through January 1968.

4. During the months following the Tet Offensive, General Westmoreland engaged in a conscious effort to conceal from his military and civilian superiors critical intelligence on the size of the enemy force.

You must limit your inquiry to the Alleged Libels. As to each of these, you are to answer the question whether the broadcast made this assertion and whether it made the assertion about the plaintiff personally.

Statements in the broadcast accusing General Westmoreland of deceiving the Congress, the press and the American public cannot be the basis of your finding that the broadcast was defamatory because they are not among the Alleged Libels. They are not what the lawsuit is about. Plaintiff has alleged only accusations that he tried to deceive the President and his military commanders. You may find defamatory content only if you find this message in the broadcast.

D. *How to Decide.* To determine whether the broadcast conveyed any of the messages plaintiff alleges and whether they were defamatory, you are to consider how the average television viewer would have understood the broadcast.

You are to decide this in the context of the broadcast as a whole, including the words, the inflection with which they were spoken, the expressions of the speakers, the pictures, the sound—in short, everything about the broadcast. You may also consider the advertising and prior publicity by CBS about the broadcast in deciding how the average viewer would have understood it.

You should of course consider the literal meaning of the words used in the documentary. But plaintiff is not required to prove that the words in their literal meaning defamed him. Nor is he required to point to any specified sentence or paragraph that states the allegedly defamatory accusation. You must consider the entire broadcast, and you should consider whether it makes these accusations *by inference* as well as by explicit statement. Plaintiff is not required to convince you that every single viewer would have so understood the broadcast to make the accusation. Plaintiff prevails on this issue if you find that the average viewer, watching and listening to the program as a whole, would have understood it to convey the defamatory message about him that he has alleged.

E. If a statement or message about the plaintiff has a defamatory meaning, it may be the basis of a libel suit even though the broadcaster was merely quoting, repeating or broadcasting what someone else had said. The accurate repetition of someone else's defamatory statement is a libel if plaintiff proves all the elements of libel, including that the defendants broadcast it believing it to be false or with reckless disregard whether it was false.

On your verdict form, you have a list of plaintiff's Alleged Libels. As to each Alleged Libel, you will answer whether you find that the documentary made that statement about plaintiff and whether it was defamatory. Your consideration of the other elements of truth/falsity, the defendants' state of mind, and damages will deal only with those alleged defamatory statements that you find were made by the broadcast about plaintiff.

ELEMENT III:
TRUTH OR FALSITY OF THE BROADCAST

A. As the third element, plaintiff must prove that at least one Alleged Libel made by the broadcast about him was false.

B. As I have explained to you, plaintiff must prove the falsity of defamatory statements by clear and convincing evidence. It is not sufficient, as with the first two elements, for him to prove falsity by a preponderance of the evidence—which means only that you find plaintiff's position more likely than not. You must find that plaintiff has demonstrated falsity by clear and convincing evidence.

Although we sometimes discuss this as the issue of *truth-or-*falsity, you must remember that there is no burden on defendants to convince you of the truth of the broadcast. The defendants are free to offer proof of the truth of their broadcast, but by doing so they do not assume the burden of convincing you. The burden remains on plaintiff to convince you it is false.

C. The issue of truth/falsity arises for each specified defamatory statement about plaintiff that you find was made by the broadcast. Plaintiff cannot prevail by proving falsity in other aspects of the broadcast. He is entitled to prevail on the issue of falsity if he proves that one specified defamatory statement made about him in the broadcast was false.

D. To prove falsity, plaintiff must prove that a defamatory statement was false in a significant way. If the statement is substantially true, the plaintiff has failed to prove its falsity, even though he may have proved it false in insignificant details.

How do you tell whether falsity is significant or insignificant? To help you make this distinction, you should think about the gist or the sting of the particular defamatory statement. What is it about the statement that makes it defamatory? What aspect of the statement brings contempt, scorn, hatred or ridicule on plaintiff or lowers his estimation in the eyes of his community? That aspect of the statement can be described as its gist or sting. The statement must be false as to this aspect of the statement for plaintiff to have proved substantial falsity.

Let me give you a crude illustration. Suppose a newspaper writes of me that in 1983 together with Jones and Smith, and armed with a .45 revolver, I robbed a branch of the Chemical Bank on Broadway. I bring a libel suit. The jury finds that I did indeed rob a bank, but the other facts in the story were inaccurate: It was in 1982, not 1983; my colleagues were Harris and Thomas, not Jones and Smith; I was armed with a .38 and not a .45; it was the Chase and not the Chemical; it was on 3rd Avenue, not on Broadway. I suggest the jury might properly find that although I had proved falsity in many insignificant details, I had not proven significant falsity. As to the aspect of the newspaper story that was defamatory, the gist or sting of the libel— the accusation that I robbed a bank—*that part was true.* The defamatory statement was therefore substantially true. The details found to be untrue were insignificant. They did not contribute in any important way to the defamatory nature of the statement. They were not the gist or sting of the libel.

In this case, I suggest to you that the gist of the defamatory statements alleged by plaintiff centers on the charge of General Westmoreland's dishonesty or bad faith in orders given and positions taken by him concerning the reporting of enemy strength in any effort to deceive the President and the plaintiff's superiors in the chain of command. If you find that plaintiff was the subject of defamatory statements as he alleged, in order to prove substantial falsity of those statements plaintiff would have to prove to you that his positions were taken honestly and in good faith and that he made no effort to misrepresent the strength or capability of the enemy to the President or his superiors.

E.1. The issue of truth/falsity relates to plaintiff's own honesty, not to the honesty or dishonesty of other persons. To prove falsity, plaintiff would have to convince you that his actions were honest. It would not be sufficient for him to prove that the broadcast was wrong in charging that other persons had engaged in dishonest acts.

E.2. The question of honesty or dishonesty is central. The question of the accuracy or inaccuracy of the positions taken and reported by MACV also plays a role in your consideration of the truth and falsity of the broadcast, but it is a somewhat tricky issue.

If the plaintiff has proved to you that his reports and positions were correct, then you would undoubtedly conclude also that he had acted honestly and in good faith in making those correct reports and you would find for the plaintiff on the issue of the falsity of the broadcast.

If, however, you find that the MACV positions were wrong, the significance of that conclusion is more complicated.

Plaintiff can nevertheless prevail on the falsity issue. If he proves to you by clear and convincing evidence that, although inaccurate, his positions represented an honest, good-faith effort to interpret the available evidence as accurately as possible, then you would find accusations of dishonesty to be false.

But inaccuracy in General Westmoreland's positions can also support the conclusion that he did not honestly believe in those positions. It would be relevant how extreme you found the inaccuracy of his positions to be and how clearly the intelligence information available at the time showed this inaccuracy. If the inaccuracy was clear and extreme, this could lead you to conclude that General Westmoreland did not believe in his reported figures and acted dishonestly. If the information was cloudy and subject to differing interpretations and if the differences were slight, you might find that these were honest differences of opinion.

Thus you may consider the accuracy or inaccuracy of plaintiff's reports and positions as evidence, but the issue you must decide is whether plaintiff was acting honestly or dishonestly.

General Westmoreland has the burden of convincing you of his honesty.

F. Next I want to discuss the relevance to the issue of truth/falsity of acts done by General Westmoreland's subordinates. The CBS broadcast spoke of widespread acts of falsification at lower levels in military intelligence functions relating to the Vietnamese Communist force strength. You have heard evidence from CBS witnesses stating that such falsification occurred. From plaintiff's witnesses you have heard denials that any such thing took place. It is for you to decide what the facts are. But your decision on this question is not necessarily determinative on the overall issue of the truth or falsity of the broadcast.

For the central issue, I say once again, relates to the honesty or dishonesty of General Westmoreland's acts and statements, not to those of his subordinates. The honesty or dishonesty of the acts of his subordinates may have significant bearing on your findings as to plaintiff's own honesty but not necessarily.

If you find that the broadcast was wrong and that no such acts of falsification occurred at lower levels, that would of course tend to support plaintiff's position, but it does not conclude the question. The question remains for you to decide whether the statements made, reports issued and positions taken by the plaintiff were honest or dishonest. If General Westmoreland has failed to convince you of his honesty and his good-faith belief in the positions he took, then you would find for the defendants on the issue of truth, even though you might find that the broadcast was wrong as to specific acts of falsification done at lower levels.

If you find that acts of falsification did occur at lower levels as the CBS documentary stated, that would of course tend to support defendants' position, but it does not conclude the question. Two questions would be significant: Whether General Westmoreland was aware of and tolerated those acts of falsification and whether those acts were done to support dishonest positions taken by General Westmoreland. Even if dishonest acts were done at lower levels, and even if they were done to carry out General Westmoreland's command position, General Westmoreland could nonetheless prevail on the falsity issue if he has proved to you (1) that he was unaware of such dishonest acts and (2) that his command positions honestly represented his best beliefs.

But he must prove both of these: (1) if he was aware of false actions or of orders to block or falsify reports at lower levels and tolerated them, he cannot prove to you that he acted honestly with respect to intelligence. You would want to consider how likely it was that such actions could have occurred without General Westmoreland being aware of them. Your findings on this might be influenced by your conclusions as to how frequently such actions occurred, why they did occur, how extreme was their effect, and at how high a level did they occur.

(2) If you find that such false actions occurred at lower levels, General Westmoreland must prove more than that he was not aware of them, to prevail on the truth issue. He must prove also that dis-

honest actions at lower levels were not in response to dishonest positions established by him. In other words, if General Westmoreland established positions that were not honest and did not represent his good-faith beliefs, he cannot prove falsity of the broadcast just because he did not see what was done at lower levels to support his dishonest position.

G. The broadcast did not charge General Westmoreland with having personally participated in lower level details of falsification, such as cutting the reported strength of individual units, blocking lower level reports of infiltration or altering the computer data base after Tet. Accordingly, it is not an issue in the case whether General Westmoreland personally involved himself with such lower level falsifications and you could not find falsity based on your conclusion that General Westmoreland did not personally do these things. The issue is, in the things he did do—the orders he gave, and the positions he took—was he acting honestly or dishonestly?

H. I have gone on at considerable length about the issue of truth/falsity because it includes some rather tricky questions on which I felt you could use some guidance. But the gist of the issue can be summed up in a nutshell. The question is whether General Westmoreland acted honestly or dishonestly with respect to the enemy strength in informing the President and his superiors.

I. You may consider on the issue of the truth or falsity of the broadcast only the evidence that was received on that element. You may not consider evidence that was received solely on the defendants' state of mind, or on the issue of damage to General Westmoreland's reputation.

ELEMENT IV: DEFENDANTS' STATE OF MIND

A. The fourth element that plaintiff must prove is the one we have referred to as the Defendants' State of Mind. Plaintiff must prove it by clear and convincing evidence. It deals with the defendants' beliefs about their broadcast. As to any defamatory statement made about him by the defendants' broadcast, it is not sufficient for the plaintiff to prove that it was false; he must prove in addition that a defendant either knew it was false or published it with reckless disregard as to whether it was false.

Now what does this mean?

1. The first branch—knowing falsity—is easy enough to understand. It means more or less the same thing as telling a lie. This standard would be satisfied if a defendant either knew or believed the statement to be false when he published it.

2. The second branch—recklessness—is more complicated. It

does not mean exactly what you might mean when you use the word recklessness in everyday speech. It refers to a special situation.

The reckless state of mind is shown if a defendant recognized that the statement was probably false but went ahead and published it ignoring or disregarding the probability of falsehood.

Whenever I have spoken throughout the trial or speak in these instructions, of the "recklessness" component, this is what I mean. I generally use a shorthand to refer to it, because it is too long to say in full every time. But each time I refer to it, whether I say "reckless falsity," "reckless disregard," "recognition of probable falsity," or some other identifier, I am referring to this standard.

I will repeat it for you.

[Repeat]

The test of recklessness, like the test of knowing falsity, concentrates on the defendants' beliefs about the truth or falsity of their broadcast.

Recklessness is not made out by showing that defendants acted carelessly, negligently or sloppily in making the documentary. It is not made out by showing that defendants did not do a perfect job; or by your finding that factual errors occurred; it is not made out by showing that a more prudent or more reasonable reporter would have exercised greater care to avoid errors or by showing that defendants were unfair to General Westmoreland. Even if defendants did not act as reasonably prudent reporters or editors should, that is not sufficient to establish reckless disregard or prohibited state of mind.

The test is essentially subjective. The question is not what others might have thought about defendants' acts, or what you think. It does not look to whether the defendants acted reasonably in making the documentary. It does not look to whether other reporters or producers would have believed the defamatory statements or whether you the jurors would have believed them.

It looks at the defendants' beliefs. As to each defendant, it asks whether he recognized a probability that the defamatory statements about the plaintiff were false but went ahead disregarding it.

B.1. As to the first three elements that dealt with the meaning of the broadcast and its truthfulness or falsity, whatever answer you reached was the same for each defendant. The issue of the defendants' state of mind is different. It examines the state of mind of each defendant, and you must answer the question separately for each defendant. For each defendant and as to each false defamatory statement you find, you must answer whether that defendant had the prohibited state of mind.

How do you answer that question for the defendant CBS, which is a corporation and does not have a state of mind? To determine this as to CBS, you look at the beliefs of the persons CBS charged with responsibility for the content of the broadcast. If you find that any of them had the prohibited state of mind, then you will find that CBS did also. If none of them did, then CBS did not, even though other CBS employees (who were not responsible for the content of the broadcast) might have believed the broadcast was false. Defendant CBS is answerable for the state of mind of an particular person to whom CBS gave responsibility for the content of the broadcast.

The persons who had responsibility for the content of the broadcast are George Crile, the producer; Mike Wallace, the correspondent; Sam Adams, the consultant; Joe Zigman, the associate producer; Howard Stringer, the executive producer; Andrew Lack, the senior producer; and Roger Colloff, then vice president and director of public affairs.

CBS may be found liable only if you find that one of those persons proceeded with the prohibited state of mind.

If that state of mind has not been established as to one of those persons, it cannot be attributed to CBS.

As to each individual defendant, Mr. Wallace, Mr. Adams and Mr. Crile, you must consider his state of mind separately. In order to find any one of them liable you must find that he personally had the forbidden state of mind. You may not find any one of them liable by reason of the state of mind of another person. You may not find any of them liable because you found CBS to be liable.

2. I want to emphasize that the element of the defendants' state of mind refers to their beliefs *at the time of the broadcast (1/23/82)*, not earlier or later. If you found that a defendant doubted the truth of the broadcast's message at an early stage of its production, that would not be a basis for holding the defendant liable—if by the time it was aired he had become convinced it was true. Nor would it matter that a defendant or a responsible CBS employee developed doubts after the broadcast. If you have heard evidence of disbelief or doubt by any of them at an earlier or later stage, you may consider it only to help you decide whether they disbelieved or substantially doubted the truth of the broadcast at the time of its airing.

3. In deciding whether any defendant disbelieved or recognized a probability of falsity of the broadcast you should consider all the evidence that has been received on the defendant's state of mind.

This includes what was told to Mr. Adams, Mr. Crile and Mr. Wallace by the persons they interviewed—both on camera and off camera. [It includes statements of persons who agreed with the broadcast thesis and those who did not.] It includes the documents the defendants read dating from the 1967–68 period and includes also books and reports they read dating from a later time commenting on military intelligence in that period.

You may consider whether all of this did or did not support what the defendants put in the broadcast, remembering however that the question is not whether you would have relied on and believed it, but whether the defendants did.

If the defendants genuinely believed what they put in the broadcast, it makes no difference whether you would have drawn the same conclusions from the materials defendants found from their research.

On the other hand, if a defendant had the prohibited state of mind of knowing or reckless falsity, you must find for plaintiff on this issue even though the defendants' research may have included documents or interviews that supported the broadcast.

I told you earlier that the defendant could commit a libel merely by repeating accurately a defamatory statement made by someone else. If you find that the defendants' broadcast repeated a false defamatory statement about plaintiff made by someone else, you must evaluate the state of mind with which defendants include the accusation.

It is of course proper for reporters to interview others in researching their stories. That is an important way for them to get information. If the reporter or editor or broadcasting company publishes such a defamatory statement and it is found by you to be false, you must decide whether it was published by the defendants with the knowledge that it was false or whether the defendants recognized that it was probably false, and published it anyway disregarding that probability. If plaintiff has proved that, then plaintiff has proved this element.

If on the other hand the defendants believed the truth of the source's statement in broadcasting it, the defendants have not committed any offense even though the source may have deceived the defendants by deliberately lying.

4. I emphasize again that it is not the defendants' reasonableness that is at issue but rather their beliefs.

C. *Problem Issues.* I want to discuss with you certain categories of evidence—not because they are more important or less important than any other category—but because they could lead you to confusion. I discuss them only to avoid such confusion because these categories of evidence may be considered in certain ways but not in others. These types of evidence have relevance, but they are not determinative.

1. *Thoroughness of Research.* First, the thoroughness of the de-

fendants' research. You may of course consider thoroughness. Defendants argue that they did a very thorough job interviewing some 80 witnesses and consulting thousands of documents over months of preparation. Plaintiff argues that defendants decided what they wanted to say at the outset and were thorough in interviewing witnesses who would support their thesis but didn't speak to significant witnesses who would have contradicted it.

You may consider both of these arguments but only insofar as they bear on the issue of knowing or reckless falsity.

You are not to put yourself in the position of the television editor or critic deciding whether the research was or was not sufficiently thorough. There is no obligation in libel law to acquire the strongest evidence through the most careful research. The legal obligation is that a defendant may not broadcast with knowing or reckless falsity, as I have explained to you.

If you find that CBS failed to interview a witness who would have been important, this could affect your finding *on defendants' state of mind* if you find that a defendant disbelieved or recognized probable falsity of the broadcast and deliberately avoided the witness so as not to receive information that would show it to be wrong.

But if the plaintiff has failed to show disbelief, or recognition of probable falsity on the defendants' part, you may not find for the plaintiff merely because you think in fairness or in the interests of better journalism they should have sought out such witnesses.

If you find that defendants had sources they believed to be reliable and truthful and relied on these sources in publishing, then they did not act with the forbidden state of mind, even if you think that a more thorough investigation might have prevented error in the broadcast or that you yourself would not have believed the defendants' sources.

2. *Reliability of Sources.* You may consider whether the sources the defendants claim to have relied on in making their broadcast were reliable or not, but only to help you decide whether you find that defendants in fact believed and relied on those sources. If you find those sources to be of such little value that you do not believe the defendants' claims that they relied on those sources, you might then find that the defendants disbelieved their broadcast or recognized a probability that it was false. If, on the other hand, you believed the defendants' claim that they believed and relied on those sources, it is of no significance that you might think they shouldn't have relied on them.

3. *Bias, Ill Will, Toward Plaintiff.* Plaintiff contends the defendants were biased against him. If you find this is true, it is relevant evidence but only for limited purposes. If you find the defendants had a bias, or harbored ill will toward the plaintiff, you may consider

whether such ill will led the defendants to publish defamatory statements that they knew were false or as to which they recognized a probability that they were false. If defendants did so, plaintiff has proved the prohibited state of mind.

But if plaintiff has failed to prove that defendants published false statements knowingly or with reckless disregard, then it would make no difference that a defendant was biased against the plaintiff.

4. *Previously Formed Belief.* Plaintiff contends also that the defendants started on their investigation with an already fixed premise and conducted their investigation with a closed mind seeking only such evidence as would confirm their premise. If you find this to be true, you may consider it in determining whether defendants made the broadcast with the prohibited state of mind. If you find that defendants' commitment to a previously adopted premise led them to broadcast things they had learned were not true or led them to proceed recklessly, disregarding the recognized probable falsity of their broadcast, plaintiff has proved that defendants had the prohibited state of mind.

On the other hand, you may not find for the plaintiff on this issue only because you find that defendants' mind was made up already at the start of the investigation. It is normal that reporters investigate where their suspicions or beliefs lie. If the defendants believed in the truth of their documentary at the time it was broadcast, the law of libel is not violated by the fact that they formed the belief long before.

5. *Fairness of the Broadcast.* Plaintiff contends the broadcast was unfair in several respects. You may consider this contention insofar as it helps you decide the issues of defendants' state of mind. If you find unfairness in defendants' conduct in making the broadcast or in the finished product, it may be evidence of bias which in turn you may consider in deciding whether the defendants were motivated by such bias to publish with knowing or reckless falsity. Also you may consider whether any unfairness involved the publication of material known to be false or the reckless publication of material recognized as probably false. If so, plaintiff has proved the element.

But you must recognize that unfairness or one-sidedness does not in itself establish the prohibited state of mind.

Under the libel law, there is no obligation to be fair or to present both sides of the story.

When a newspaper, book or broadcast comments on the actions of a public official, as long as it acts honestly in good faith by not publishing false matter knowingly or in reckless disregard of a recognized probable falsity, it has no obligation under the libel law to act fairly, present both sides, seek out witnesses on the other side or even publish their statements. There is no legal obligation even to interview the subject of its criticism. How a broadcast chooses to act in these respects is a matter of its editorial policy; in these matters it is free to act in whatever manner it thinks best.

Recognizing the importance of free and open discussion in the press of the actions of public officials, the law of libel imposes no obligations of fairness or evenhandedness on the press. The publication of commentary that flatly accuses public officials of bad and dishonest acts, without including their denials or the evidence to the contrary, is a daily event. Each of us is entitled to our own opinion whether this is a good or bad thing. But your opinion on that subject may not enter into your deliberations as jurors.

You may not act in the role of super editor or TV critic and base your decision on whether you think the broadcast would have been better or fairer if it had been investigated or presented in a different manner.

The libel law concerns itself with truth and honesty, not with fairness. The obligation under the libel law is not to publish false defamatory matter knowingly or in reckless disregard of probable falsity. You may consider factors of unfairness only to the extent that they support a finding of knowing or reckless falsity. The issue you are to decide is whether the plaintiff has shown such knowing or reckless falsity.

6. *Tone of Questioning.* Plaintiff contends the defendants used a friendly and encouraging tone in questioning witnesses who supported the thesis of the broadcast but used a harsh accusatory tone with General Westmoreland and the witnesses who supported him.

You may properly consider this contention on the issue of defendants' state of mind. If you find that the tone and manner of the questioning were used by defendants to prevent adverse witnesses from bringing out the truth, this would be evidence supporting a finding of the prohibited state of mind. If you find the tone of questioning showed bias on the part of the defendants, you may consider that in the manner I explained earlier.

You must recognize on the other hand that using a harsh tone in questioning is not prohibited by the libel law. The use of a harsh questioning tone is a proper journalistic technique, [just as it is a proper technique for a lawyer conducting a cross-examination. (?)] It may be useful to bring out the truth. It can also be used to create confusion or conceal the truth.

You may consider the tone of questioning in deciding whether the defendants broadcast false matter knowingly or in a reckless disregard of its probable falsity. But a hostile tone of questioning is not a sufficient basis for finding the prohibited state of mind.

7. *Editing.* Plaintiff contends that in defendants' editing of the interviews, the writing of the narrative portions and the construction of the broadcast, defendants created misleading distortions. You may properly consider such contentions and such evidence, insofar as they support proof of the prohibited state of mind.

Editing is a proper and necessary part of news or commentary. When a witness has been interviewed at length, editing is necessary if a quotation is to be presented without broadcasting the entire interview. A broadcaster has considerable latitude to edit such material in whatever manner he thinks best, and cannot be found to have acted with improper state of mind merely because the jury disagrees with the manner in which the editing selection was made. If the editing produces a fair account of the views the witness expressed, there would be no prohibited state of mind even though the editing might have changed substantially a particular sentence spoken by the witness.

On the other hand, if a broadcaster in the course of editing so distorts the material as to present a false account of the witness' views and gives false support to the broadcast's accusation, this could amount to publication of knowingly false defamatory material. The question once again is not whether you like or dislike the editing process generally or the editing done on this documentary. The question is whether defendants broadcast defamatory material they knew to be false or broadcast it recklessly despite recognition of probable falsity.

I have discussed these arguments with you not to increase or to lessen their importance. How much importance you attach to those kinds of proof is for you alone to decide. I have discussed them only to avoid confusion—to be sure that you consider them only for their proper purposes under the libel law.

DELIBERATIONS, EXHIBITS AND QUESTIONNAIRE

A. *Order of Deliberations.* You will deal with the elements I have explained one by one, reaching a verdict on each element before proceeding to deliberate on the next. You will deal with them in the same order that I have followed in explaining them. I have prepared a questionnaire which sets forth in order the questions you must answer. In a few moments I will go over the questionnaire in detail.

B. *Exhibits.* It is most important that, in considering each element, you use only the evidence that has been admitted on that element. When you consider the question of the truth or falsity of the broadcast, you will use only the evidence received on that issue and will not consider evidence received on the issue of the defendants' state of mind, or on the damage to the plaintiff's reputation. And when you move on to consider the defendants' state of mind, again you will use only the evidence received on that issue and will not consider evidence admitted on truth, or other questions.

We have arranged several devices to help you follow this instruction.

First, you will be given a master list of the exhibits which tells you next to each identifying number what the exhibit is and, in the right-hand column, what is the element on which the exhibit is received. This master list has been divided into separate lists which will be given to you. One is labeled Truth/Falsity; it includes the exhibits on that issue. A second is labeled Defendants' State of Mind which lists all the exhibits received on that issue.

Also, the exhibits will be divided into separate boxes. One box will be labeled Truth/Falsity. When you deliberate on that issue you will use only the exhibits in that box. When you have answered that question and move on to the issue of defendants' state of mind, you will put the *truth* exhibits back in their box and use only the exhibits contained in the box labeled Defendants' State of Mind.

Furthermore, each exhibit will be stamped on its face (at the upper left-hand corner) to indicate the element to which it relates.

C. *Questionnaire.* Now please follow with me the questionnaire.

I & II. The first section of the questionnaire is numbered I & II because it covers both the first and second elements. You will see listed here the four Alleged Libels that plaintiff contends were conveyed by the broadcast. As to each of the four, you will answer three questions:

1. Whether the broadcast conveyed this statement or message;
2. Whether you find the message to be of defamatory meaning;
3. Whether that defamatory message was *of and concerning* General Westmoreland.

When you have completed this part of the questionnaire, if you answered YES to all three questions for any one of the four Alleged Libels, you will then check the box showing you have found for plaintiff on that Alleged Libel. If you do not have three YES answers, you check the box indicating that you find for defendants on that Alleged Libel. If you find for plaintiff on any of the four Alleged Libels, you will send me a note through the marshal advising me simply that you have completed the questions for Elements I & II, and you will move on to consider Element III—truth or falsity.

If you do not find for plaintiff on any of the Alleged Libels, you should send a note advising of that fact and I will then give you further instructions.

III. You will then turn to the question whether plaintiff has proven the substantial falsity of defamatory statements made about him by the broadcast.

You will answer only as to Alleged Libels on which you found for plaintiff in Elements I and II. If you found for defendants on any of the Alleged Libels for Elements I and II, you need not answer any further questions on that Alleged Libel.

For any Alleged Libel, if plaintiff has proved to you that it was substantially false, you will check the line indicating that you find for the plaintiff. If plaintiff has failed to prove the substantial falsity, you will check the line showing that you find for the defendants.

When you have answered the questions on the form as to truth/falsity of the broadcast, you will send me a note through the marshal advising me simply that you have completed the questionnaire for the element of truth/falsity. You will not reveal in this note what decision you have reached.*

IV. *Defendants' State of Mind.* After completing the questionnaire on truth/falsity, you will proceed to decide the issue whether the defendants broadcast their documentary with the prohibited state of mind.

On this issue you must answer separately as to each defendant. The form so provides. It lists the three individual defendants in alphabetical order and then lists CBS. You may consider the defendants in whichever order you choose, but remember that you may find against CBS only if you find the prohibited state of mind on the part of one of the persons to whom CBS gave responsibility for the content of the broadcast, and you may find against an individual defendant only if you find that he personally acted with the prohibited state of mind.

Under the name of each defendant, the questionnaire states "On the question whether plaintiff has proved that the defendant acted with the prohibited state of mind, we find for plaintiff ___ (or) for the defendant ___."

---

* The record will reflect that it was the joint request of the parties that the verdicts on truth and state of mind be announced simultaneously rather than separately when reached. The court would have preferred separate announcements as done in *Sharon v. Time Inc.*, but yields to the joint request of the parties.

For each Alleged Libel, you will check whether you find for plaintiff, or for the particular defendant.

When you have completed these questions, you will advise me by sending a note through the marshal that you have made your findings on the state of mind element.

At that point, I will call you into the courtroom to receive your findings on the first four elements.

Index

Sydney Shaw covers telecommunications and the media for United Press International from its headquarters in Washington, D.C. Born in Midland, Texas, she coedited several alternative publications at Texas Tech University in Lubbock, Texas, during the late 1960s. She has also worked as a free-lance artist and writer.

Bob Brewin covers electronic media for the *Village Voice* in New York. Born in Boston, Brewin served with the United States Marine Corps in Vietnam in 1965 and 1966, and started his journalism career with Reuters in New York in 1970.

Brewin and Shaw are married to each other and live in Washington, where they take long bike rides when writing assignments don't interfere.